THE BLACK BOX

CONTEMPORARY ASIA IN THE WORLD

CONTEMPORARY ASIA IN THE WORLD
David C. Kang and Victor D. Cha, Editors

This series aims to address a gap in the public-policy and scholarly discussion of Asia. It seeks to promote books and studies that are on the cutting edge of their disciplines or promote multidisciplinary or interdisciplinary research but are also accessible to a wider readership. The editors seek to showcase the best scholarly and public-policy arguments on Asia from any field, including politics, history, economics, and cultural studies.

South Korea's Grand Strategy: Making Its Own Destiny, Ramon Pacheco Pardo, 2023

War and Peace in the Taiwan Strait, Scott L. Kastner, 2022

Power and Restraint in China's Rise, Chin-Hao Huang, 2022

Line of Advantage: Japan's Grand Strategy in the Era of Abe Shinzō, Michael J. Green, 2022

Japan's Aging Peace: Pacifism and Militarism in the Twenty-First Century, Tom Phuong Le, 2021

Japan's New Regional Reality: Geoeconomic Strategy in the Asia-Pacific, Saori N. Katada, 2020

Dying for Rights: Putting North Korea's Human Rights Abuses on the Record, Sandra Fahy, 2019

GMO China: How Global Debates Transformed China's Agricultural Biotechnology Policies, Cong Cao, 2018

Nuclear North Korea: A Debate on Engagement Strategies, revised and updated edition, Victor D. Cha and David C. Kang, 2018

Japan, South Korea, and the United States Nuclear Umbrella: Deterrence After the Cold War, Terrence Roehrig, 2017

Japan's Security Renaissance: New Policies and Politics for the Twenty-First Century, Andrew L. Oros, 2017

The China Boom: Why China Will Not Rule the World, Ho-fung Hung, 2015

Nation at Play: A History of Sport in India, Ronojoy Sen, 2015

The Japan–South Korea Identity Clash: East Asian Security and the United States, Brad Glosserman and Scott A. Snyder, 2015

For a complete list of books in the series, please see the Columbia University Press website.

VICTOR D. CHA

THE BLACK BOX

Demystifying the Study of Korean
Unification and North Korea

COLUMBIA UNIVERSITY PRESS

NEW YORK

Columbia University Press
Publishers Since 1893
New York   Chichester, West Sussex
cup.columbia.edu
Copyright © 2024 Victor D. Cha
All rights reserved

Library of Congress Cataloging-in-Publication Data
Names: Cha, Victor D., 1961– author.
Title: The black box : demystifying the study of Korean
unification and North Korea / Victor D. Cha.
Other titles: Demystifying the study of Korean
unification and North Korea
Description: New York : Columbia University Press, [2024] |
Series: Contemporary Asia in the world |
Includes bibliographical references and index.
Identifiers: LCCN 2024000872 (print) | LCCN 2024000873 (ebook) |
ISBN 9780231211086 (hardback) | ISBN 9780231211093 (trade paperback) |
ISBN 9780231558730 (ebook)
Subjects: LCSH: Korean reunification question (1945–) | Open source
intelligence—Korea (North) | Korea (North)—Relations. |
Korea (South)—Relations.
Classification: LCC DS917.444 .C238 2024 (print) | LCC DS917.444 (ebook)
| DDC 951.904/3—dc23/eng/20240315
LC record available at https://lccn.loc.gov/2024000872
LC ebook record available at https://lccn.loc.gov/2024000873

Cover image: © Universal History Archive/UIG/Bridgeman Images

CONTENTS

A Note on the Korean Text   vii

1. THE BLACK BOX   1
WITH SEIYEON JI

2. THE UNITED STATES–REPUBLIC OF KOREA ALLIANCE   18
WITH NA YOUNG LEE AND ANDY LIM

3. TECHNOLOGY AND CYBERSECURITY   39
WITH JULIAN FOX, KATELYN RADACK, JAE SEUNG SHIM, AND REBECCA SPENCER

4. MARKETS AND CIVIL SOCIETY   78
WITH MARIE DUMOND

5. UNIFICATION THEORIES   113

6. UNIFICATION DATA   144
WITH MARIE DUMOND AND ANDY LIM

7. THE HARDEST OF HARD TARGETS 170

Acknowledgments 201

Appendix 1. Codebook for Event Data on U.S.-DPRK Relationship 205

Appendix 2. List of U.S.-ROK Joint Military Exercises, 2005–2015 225

Appendix 3. Microsurveys of DPRK Citizens and Sample Answer Sheets 227

Notes 241

Bibliography 281

List of Contributors 313

Index 315

A NOTE ON THE KOREAN TEXT

ROMANIZATION OF the Korean language has long suffered from a lack of a single, agreed-upon standard for spelling, which is why you will variously see "Kim Jong Il," "Kim Jong-Il," and "Kim Chŏng-il" in the press and academic publications. For names and places that will be familiar to many readers, such as "Kim Il-sung," "Kim Dae-jung," and "Pyongyang," Revised Romanization is used. For names of people and places less familiar to the casual observer, McCune-Reischauer Romanization is used. And for those who aren't acquainted with Korean, Chinese, or Japanese names, it bears pointing out that in nearly all cases (with the exception of a few whose names are widely known and/or used in the reverse order, such as Syngman Rhee), Korean, Chinese, and Japanese names are written in their traditional order, with the surname first and the given name last.

THE BLACK BOX

1

THE BLACK BOX

North Korea, of course, is now and always has been one of the, if not the toughest intelligence target [in the world].

—James Clapper, U.S. director of national intelligence, April 2013

I pledge to solidify the foundation so that we can successfully host the joint 2032 Seoul-Pyongyang Olympics and stand tall in the world as one Korea by achieving peace and reunification by 2045, which will mark the 100th anniversary of liberation.

—Moon Jae-in, president of South Korea, August 15, 2019

THERE IS no country on the face of the earth that has been more consistently described as unknowable than the Democratic People's Republic of Korea (DPRK or North Korea). A small, isolated country tucked into China's continental flank, this state—and its line of mysterious dictators—has become associated with the definition of unpredictability and mysteriousness.

The *New York Times* profile of Kim Il-sung in 1961 started with "the sleepy-eyed, rotund North Korean" and called him a "North Korean enigma."[1] The cover of the *Economist* magazine in June 2000 carried a picture of the then-North Korean leader Kim Jong-il in dark sunglasses, expressionless, with one arm raised in salutation. The caption read, "Greetings, earthlings."[2]

After Kim Jong-un took power, the cover of *Time* magazine in February 2012 featured a picture of him with the title "Lil' Kim," along with the description, "Inside the bizarre world of North Korea's Kim Jong Un, the untested leader of a nuclear nation."[3] In January 2016 the cover image of the *New Yorker* magazine showed a baby Kim Jong-un with his nuclear "toys"—a reference to Kim's recent announcement that the country had tested a hydrogen bomb.[4] A year later the *New York Times* called him "a moody young man with a nuclear arsenal."[5]

The references to North Korea's mysteriousness are rivaled only by the comical treatment of the regime by the West. In September 2013 *Saturday Night Live*'s cold opening featured a skit with a Kim Jong-un impersonator giving a speech at the Supreme People's Assembly with a cameo appearance by former National Basketball Association professional and avant garde personality Dennis Rodman. A February 2017 comic strip in the *Denver Post* showed Kim Jong-un flipping burgers at a family barbeque surrounded by empty lawn chairs, and reading a newspaper headline of Kim's orchestrated murder of his half-brother with the caption, "Hey, where did everybody go?" A December 2011 *New York Times* cartoon depicted the death of Kim Jong-il with the deceased leader face down at his desk, his forehead just missing the big red nuclear button and aides in the background saying, "That was close!" The Sony Pictures Entertainment movie *The Interview* (2014) comically depicts Kim Jong-un as an obsessed fan of Katy Perry who never quite lived up to his father's expectations.

These and countless other phrases used to describe North Korea have both created and perpetuated the view that I euphemistically call the Korean "Black Box," meaning that the world can observe readily the regime's external behavior, but that very little is known about the inner workings of the country. Every discussion of North Korea, even by proverbial "experts," is prefaced with the qualifier that no one really knows what is going on inside the country and that even the experts are stumped, all reduced to making educated guesses about the regime's intentions. If premodern Korea was known as the "Hermit Kingdom," North Korea is not just the modern era successor, but on a scale exponentially more severe.[6] Unknown internal forces generate North Korea's rambunctious actions that even the best analysts cannot diagnose because of the regime's airtight lockdown on all information.

The North Korean regime prefers this level of opacity and volunteers very little information about itself. In part, this is a defensive measure designed to combat perceived enemies all around its borders.

But it also uses its opacity to convey a level of dangerous unknowability—what Thomas Schelling once described as the "threat that leaves something to chance"—that will keep its adversaries acting with caution.

Without access to information, viable entry to the country, or a transparent press, most analysts throw up their hands in despair when it comes to understanding the country. The study of North Korea finds itself in the land of speculation. As U.S. intelligence analyst Patrick McEachern writes, North Korea is a "data-poor country," and this often discourages scholarly inquiry.[7] Explaining, understanding, or predicting North Korea becomes a veritable Rorschach test where anyone's pet theory can be confirmed by ambiguous data. For the West, the most noteworthy aspect of North Korea is its nuclear weapons program, for example. The lack of information about North Korea, however, allows analysts and policymakers who see these weapons as offensively intended to make as credible an argument as those who see the programs as defensively intended and emanating from deep insecurity. Most assume that the true answers to questions about North Korea sit behind a veil of secrecy that ultimately may be known only to those with the highest government security clearances.

The perceived lack of information on North Korea is augmented by language barriers and the "echo chamber effect," in which the lines blur between fact and fiction. One publication describes this reverberation particularly well when it comes to North Korea: "The media . . . brands unverified statements as established facts over time through repeated reporting by other outlets."[8] The echo effect is compounded for Korean language-deficient researchers who rely on unverified translations of North Korean texts.

Governments have the capabilities to circumvent both the echo effect and language barriers, yet the challenges of knowing North Korea are real. Former director of national intelligence (DNI) James Clapper and his predecessors would not refer to the regime as one of the "toughest intelligence targets" in the world for no reason. Given the absence of any opening with the Western world, there is not a great deal of human intelligence that can be collected. The country's insulation from the internet and global connectivity generally renders scant information from collecting signals intelligence. As one scholar explained, "Penetrating the inner workings of Kim Jong Un's mind is an old-school challenge, not a high-tech one. North Korea's nuclear program is a terrifying reminder that technology can only go so far; that human intentions can be unfathomable, even to ourselves; and that divining them is an art, not a science."[9] And while satellite imagery can convey in great detail pictures from the sky, North Korea uses cloaking, deception tactics, and thousands of miles of underground tunnels and facilities to compromise this form of information collection. Despite hundreds of millions of dollars of national technical means thrown at the North Korea target, for example, the world learned that North Korean leader Kim Jong-un and his wife had a baby daughter, Ju-ae, only from former NBA player Dennis Rodman after his trip to Pyongyang.[10] The reveal came during an exclusive interview with the British *Guardian* newspaper after Rodman returned from his second visit to North Korea in September 2013. In the interview, Rodman said, "I held their baby Ju-ae and spoke with Ms. Ri [Sol-Ju, Kim's wife] as well. He's a good dad and has a beautiful family. Kim told me, 'I'll see you in December.'" Former DNI Daniel Coats told Congress in May 2017 that North Korea "is one of the hardest, if not the hardest, collection nation that we have to collect against." Director of the Defense Intelligence Agency Lt. Gen. Robert Ashley, reiterated this in his testimony to Congress in March 2018, calling North Korea "our hardest intelligence collection target."[11] Thus the truth is that governments probably know less about North Korea than the layperson thinks.

KOREAN UNIFICATION

The uncertainty surrounding North Korea, its inner workings, and its future is inextricably intertwined with Korean unification. The fate of the former informs the likelihood, contours, and timing of the latter. In this regard, unification is a future unknown based on an existing unknown. Moreover, the opacity surrounding North Korea pales in comparison to that surrounding the prospect of Korean unification. The period of division into two Koreas—externally imposed in 1945 by competing Cold War superpowers on a people that had been a single nation for thousands of years—now approaches eight decades and spans the course of two centuries. If any self-professed expert tells you that they can predict when the two Koreas will become one, they know not what they say. No one knows when or how unification will take place. And perhaps because there is no fount of information about unification, anybody can be an "expert." Many predictions of its imminent occurrence lay on the trash heap of history. One scenario for unification, a "soft landing," predicts a phased integration process of the two systems after a period of tension reduction. The two political and economic systems would find a way to operate in harmony, driven by resurgent nationalism and ethnic identity. After secret negotiations between the two Koreas led to the North-South joint communiqué in 1972, hopes for unification were dashed when progress did not move beyond signatures on a piece of paper. When the North and South Korean leaders met for the first-ever summit in 2000, the now-famous pictured embrace of Kim Jong-il and Kim Dae-jung raised expectations of the start of a "soft landing" process, but this also proved false, as would subsequent summits between future Korean leaders.

The other scenario for unification, a "hard landing," envisions unification by collapse, with the South taking over and absorbing a beleaguered North. Experts predicted that this type of unification would shortly follow the fall of the Berlin Wall and German reunification. When this did not happen, similar predictions emerged in the wake of the famine in North Korea in the mid-1990s when an estimated 10 percent of the population perished. When this too did not come to pass, many more expectations of unification proliferated after the sudden death of Kim Il-sung in 1994. North Korea's defiance of this prediction did not discourage new predictions of North Korean collapse after the sudden death of Kim Jong-il in 2011 and the power transition to an inexperienced and seemingly unprepared Kim Jong-un. Much of the speculation about unification depends on the resilience of the North Korean state, which has defied every prediction of collapse. Unification also depends on the unknown intentions of the North Korean regime's leadership. In this sense, the two topics of this book are inextricably intertwined.

We also know very little about how the powers surrounding Korea would react to unification, except that they would consider the development vital to their national interests. Occupying a critical position at the heart of Northeast Asia, the Korean peninsula connects maritime and continental Asia in a way that engages the geostrategic interests of all powers, including the United States. Koreans are hypersensitive to this point, given the lack of input the country had in the fateful decision by great powers in 1945 to divide the country. The first joint communiqué between the two Koreas established the principle that unification should be achieved "independently" and "without foreign influence." This principle has been repeated in subsequent inter-Korean summit statements decades later. Yet the reality is that Korean unification is too significant an event to happen in a vacuum. Korea is not just valuable intrinsically in terms of all that a unified nation has to offer, but also strategically in the sense that Russia, China, Japan, and the United States do not want to confront a Korea dominated by the others. Japan historically has seen the peninsula as a "dagger" pointed at the heart of the island nation by threats from continental Asia. China has viewed Korea as the land bridge for Japanese aggression. Russia views the peninsula as the vital piece connecting Eurasian energy and commerce with Northeast Asia. The United States saw Korea during the Cold War as a bulwark against communism and today sees it as a critical ally in the Indo-Pacific on everything from security to democracy to supply chains. Thus it is not by historical accident that Japan, China, the United States, and Russia have fought many wars in and over Korea. The only known element of unification is the goal, as expressed by South Koreans, that a unified Korea that is whole, peaceful, prosperous, and powerful.

The upshot is that Korean unification manifests a cascade of uncertainties in terms of prospects, timing, process, expectations, opportunities, and fears. The South Korean Unification Ministry's website frames unification as guided by principles of "mutual prosperity" and "noninterference by external powers" but offers no guidelines on how to operationalize these principles.[12] A Brookings Institution report, like many other think tank studies, asserts that unification will remove one of the "most dangerous legacies of the post–World War II era" and will fundamentally transform Northeast Asia, yet it cannot predict when and how this would happen.[13] Another study noted that a strategy for Korean unification is stymied by the inability to predict which of three scenarios—collapse, conflict, and peaceful—is most likely.[14] A RAND study cautions that there are not three but nine paths to unification, with each holding vast uncertainties that neither North nor South Korea is prepared for.[15] Korean public views on when unification will happen are all over the map, with roughly 25 percent saying it will never happen, 13 percent saying it will happen within a decade, and even smaller percentages believing it will happen within five years.[16] Former U.S. diplomats have argued that time is running out for North Korea, but the United States, South Korea, and China have done little to prepare for what would follow its eventual demise.[17]

Comparisons to Germany's reunification only underscore the lack of information about Korea's case. The economic, political, and social gaps between the two Koreas will be much wider than those between the two Germanies. A report by the Carnegie Endowment for International Peace notes how these economic differences can create not just economic instability but also unforeseen political instability.[18] In addition, China will pose a much more complicating factor for Korea than the Soviet Union did for Germany.[19] But experts have no good answers to address the fundamental dilemma surrounding China—it could be a major opponent of Korean unification, but it remains unwilling to discuss unification contingencies with South Korea and the United States. Indeed, uncertainties abound as to whether Koreans even want unification, especially among younger generations for whom national division and fratricidal war are merely events in a history textbook rather than anything they identify with. The same study noted that almost 50 percent of South Koreans in their twenties do not identify with unification and perceive North Korea as a "stranger."[20] Another scholar concluded that there is no consensus in Korea about what "kind of country a unified Korea should be."[21] The multitude of uncertainties surrounding Korean unification invites cautious and careful planning for the future, yet the one thing German unification has taught the world is that watershed change can come suddenly and without warning.

All this uncertainty colors the darkness of the Korean black box. That darkness, unfortunately, is not the target of much research or policy. We know so little about unification because it is a hypothetical scenario and bereft of any timetable. This is not a good combination for governments to plan around. Policymakers can ill afford to devote their time and resources to anything but what is immediately in front of them, with little time to look in the rearview mirror or to gaze into a crystal ball about the future. The intelligence community must serve the immediate taskings of policymakers rather than venture into academic exercises about future unification scenarios. And to the extent that the military prepares for future contingencies, these focus on future wars against North Korean or Chinese aggression rather than the complex political, socioeconomic, and geostrategic kaleidoscope of uncertainty presented by Korean unification.

North Korea and Korean unification present a chasm of unknowns that need to be addressed for the benefit of experts and policymakers working on Korea and Asia. Without understanding one, we cannot understand the other. Because Korean unification ultimately will be informed by North Korea's future course, the more we know about one, the more we will learn about the other.

YOU KNOW MORE THAN YOU THINK YOU KNOW

The opacity surrounding Korean unification and North Korea may appear intimidating. If governments, with all their experts and exquisite intelligence capabilities, come up short, then is anything really knowable? The point of this book is that you, the layperson, can know more about the Korean black box than you think. This may seem like a bold statement. How could it be? This short book is dedicated to demonstrating that there is ample open-source information to understand Korean unification and North Korea. More often than not, researchers are discouraged from even trying to study the North Korean regime and its inner workings, intimidated by the lack of data. Taken as a collective, the chapters in this book illustrate that North Korea and unification are not as black a box as is commonly held. Through different research tools, we can unearth data and learn more about these mysteries than we ever imagined.

My colleagues and I attempt to show that the Korean black box is complex but not complicated. It is far from transparent, but there are some core tendencies and behaviors that can be gleaned from study of the country related to four core issues: (1) military provocations, (2) views of the U.S.-ROK alliance, (3) asymmetrical military capabilities, and (4) marketization. Regarding unification, we unearth new data about two topics that are central to any expert conversation about unification: (1) microsurveys of the North Korean people's hopes, aspirations, and desire for unification; and (2) the mix of opportunities and threats generated by unification and the relative prioritization of these by the United States, China, Japan, and Russia. Through the collection and analysis of different forms of data, we can avail ourselves of much more information about the country and its actions and even gain some insights on the process and predictability of unification. Moreover, this data can be acquired through open-source, unclassified collection methods, making it accessible to those outside of the intelligence organs of governments.

THE DANGER OF POLICY WITHOUT DATA

Why is it important to collect more data about these topics? Because policy is empirical. That is, good policy cannot be made without reliable information. If there is no empirical basis for policy, then decisions are determined entirely by personal beliefs, biases, ideology, or politics. Leaders can choose any course of action they wish because the dearth of empirical facts does not lead them to a right or wrong course. Or, as one scholar observed, "Partisans in the debate over whether to engage the North question whether the state has or can uphold any of its international commitments. Both sides can select data to bolster their argument, but this selection does not serve a fruitful analytical purpose."[22] One of the main tasks of intelligence organs in any government is to prevent this type of uninformed policy from being made. Intelligence agencies do not make policy, but they help to avert bad policy. They provide empirical data and analysis to help inform good decisions. Making policy without this kind of support could have major consequences for national security, especially regarding the Korean peninsula, where decisions related to countering a nuclear weapons state could jeopardize U.S. forces in the Indo-Pacific theater, allied forces, or even citizens in the U.S. homeland.

There is, of course, a vast intelligence establishment designed to provide the best possible information, carefully curated and analyzed, to help policymakers. But, as described earlier, the challenges posed by North Korea's opacity are real. This forces analysts to be tempered and highly conditional in their judgments, which gives the policymaker a thin foundation on which to base decisions. For this reason, policy toward North Korea is almost always reactionary and tactical rather than strategic. This is even more pronounced with unification, where the absence of empirical data makes it hard to plan strategy.

We need better data to make better policy. Without it, the chances of bad policy go up and the dangers of miscalculation and escalation grow worse. On the Korean peninsula, the two most likely potential sources for conflict are generated from the two topics of this book: North Korea and unification. Hosting the most militarized border in the world, Korea could see nightmarish contingencies involving a collapse of the North and unification given that the balance of forces is arrayed in such a way that they are on a hair-trigger response mechanism. North Korea's military is trained to respond immediately to any signs of U.S. or South Korean belligerence. North Korea will immediately heighten its level of military readiness and action, setting off triggers to escalate reciprocally on the U.S. and South Korean side. All it takes is one spark to destabilize the fragile standoff on the Korean peninsula, and the escalation ladder will be very difficult to control, especially between two sides that have no military communication with each other. The stakes for peace on the peninsula and in Asia could not be any higher.

THE YEAR OF "FIRE AND FURY": WHAT HAPPENS WITHOUT DATA

Regarding North Korea, some argue that data is not necessary when it comes to predicting the regime's actions. In the absence of data, we can simply assume rationality (or irrationality) of actors because that is the most parsimonious way to think about the problem. For North Korea, that means basing policy on one of two extremes: (1) North Korean leaders are "crazy and unpredictable"; or (2) North Korean leaders are not crazy because "even dictators want to survive." The dangers of basing policy on these assumptions became eminently clear in 2017 when a U.S. president, who did not have much of a penchant for data, crossed swords with North Korea and nearly took the peninsula to war. Over a period of twelve months, tensions ratcheted up to unprecedented levels.

Three weeks after Donald Trump's inauguration in January 2017, North Korea carried out a test of solid-fueled medium-range submarine-launched ballistic missile (SLBM) using new cold launch compressed gas canisters, demonstrating dramatic advances in a survivable nuclear weapons capability. It tested ballistic missiles thereafter in March (twice, including four missiles launched simultaneously into Japan's Exclusive Economic Zone (EEZ) and a failed missile test), in April (thrice), in May (thrice, including the new Hwasong-12 intermediate-range ballistic missile [IRBM]), in June (once), in August (four ballistic missiles), and in September (Hwasong-12 IRBM).[23] Notably, in July and November North Korea carried out three intercontinental ballistic missile (ICBM) launches (Hwasong-14 and 15 or KN-20, KN-22) on lofted trajectories that indicated a range deep into the continental United States.[24] In September it conducted its sixth nuclear test, a claimed hydrogen bomb test with an explosive yield in excess of 100 kilotons of TNT, which was by far its most powerful test.[25] All told, in the final year of Barack Obama's presidency in 2016 and the first year of Trump's, North Korea launched thirty-four ballistic missiles and tested three nuclear weapons, which demonstrated vast improvements in weapons capability, including warhead miniaturization, solid fuel propellant, mobile launch options, higher-yield nuclear bombs, and ICBMs capable of ranging across all the U.S. homeland.

While the Trump administration used these provocations to rally universal international condemnation and enlist tougher sanctions compliance, these measures were overshadowed by President Trump's unusually personal and escalatory rhetoric directed at the North Korean leader, the reciprocation of which raised the specter of inadvertent conflict on the Korean peninsula in a very tense period in the first eighteen months of his presidency.

In response to the August 2017 missile launches, Trump threatened publicly to rain on the adversary "fire and fury like the world has never seen."[26] Not to be outdone, North Korea responded on August 9 by detailing a plan to launch four IRBMs targeted in the waters near U.S. bases in Guam.[27] Trump replied on Twitter (now X) two days later that military measures were "locked and loaded."[28] Kim Jong-un followed three days later with public references to his review of the "Guam strike plans"; release of a picture of him standing next to a thermonuclear weapon small enough to fit atop an ICBM; and then an actual thermonuclear test on September 3.[29] In an address before the United Nations General Assembly on September 19, Trump threatened that the United States would "totally destroy North Korea" and derided the leader as "Rocket Man [who] is on a suicide mission for himself and for his regime."[30] Kim responded two days later calling Trump "mentally deranged" and declaring that the American president would "pay dearly for his [UN] speech."[31] Kim's foreign minister warned that Trump's threats would make a North Korean missile attack against the U.S. mainland "inevitable."[32] The United States sent B-1B strategic bombers to skirt the North Korean coastline two days later as Trump tweeted, "they [North Korea] won't be around much longer!"[33]

This extraordinary public standoff between the leaders departed from the posture of previous administrations, which also took hardline policies toward North Korea but always measured their public statements, stressing the need for diplomacy and a peaceful denuclearization outcome. The rhetoric by Trump and Kim, with casual references to war, was unprecedented and precipitated a dangerous spiral of escalation. This was exacerbated by signals that the Trump administration was considering a spectrum of military options ranging from limited "bloody nose" strikes to more expansive offensive operations.[34]

The "bloody nose" strike, in particular, was based on the assumption that a limited military strike on the regime would not prompt retaliation by North Korea, either conventional or nuclear in nature, because the regime would make the "rational" calculation that its country would be obliterated by the U.S. military if it struck back. Instead, it would awaken to the danger of defying Trump and would return to the denuclearization negotiating table. This thinking was flawed in numerous ways: First, it assumed rational restraint by North Korea after taking a strike by the United States. Second, it assumed such rationality after the decades-long assumption that there was an element of irrationality and unpredictability to North Korea's decision-making. And third, it assumed that North Korea would not respond to U.S. military action with a nuclear attack because it would be rationally deterred from doing so.[35]

There could not have been a better showcase for how ill-informed policy can emerge from a leader who had little empirical knowledge of the problem. Additionally, the president's reported desire to tweet out calls for the evacuation of U.S. dependents from Korea might have easily sparked a conflict given the hair-trigger military signals and warning systems on both sides of the demilitarized zone (DMZ).[36] Such a tweet would have sparked panic among the 200,000–250,000 American nationals in Korea, as well as Korean citizens. The stock markets would have plummeted at the prospect of war. If North Koreans saw Americans leaving the peninsula, this would have automatically set off higher alert and mobilization levels for the North Korean military, which in turn would have set off countermeasures by the U.S. and South Korean forces, potentially spiraling out of control.

Of course, war did not happen. South Korea ramped up diplomacy to avert the disastrous course. This author, along with other experts, also spoke out against the "bloody nose" strike plan (the administration subsequently dropped this author's nomination for ambassador to Korea).[37] Trump shifted from a policy of extreme confrontation to summit-level engagements to befriend the North Korean leader from 2018 to the end of his presidency. Trump's first summit meeting with Kim Jong-un took place in Singapore in June 2018. Although a media spectacle, the summit's four-paragraph joint document rehashed old ground rather than offering new steps on denuclearization. A second summit meeting took place in February 2019 in Hanoi in which the two leaders failed to reach agreement on implementing denuclearization. Despite a third meeting in Panmunjom in June 2019, more theatrics (Trump became the first American president to step across the Military Demarcation Line into North Korea), and numerous private letters between Kim and Trump, there were no tangible denuclearization steps beyond a halt to testing, which the North Koreans gradually rescinded as they could not get Trump to lift economic sanctions. From May 2019 through the remainder of Trump's term, even as Pyongyang engaged in dialogue with Washington, North Korea finished as hard as it had started, duplicating the number of missile tests done in 2017 (more than twenty), though Trump countenanced the latter tests as falling below the threshold of ICBM or nuclear tests. In the end, however, the three years of diplomacy produced no denuclearization steps and could not arrest further development of the weapons programs.

The Joe Biden administration adopted a policy bereft of Trump's wild extremes of personal insults and summit theatrics, and one that remained consistently open to diplomacy with North Korea at any place and at any time. After an initial year of relative silence, most likely due to the Covid-19 pandemic (addressed in chapter 7), North Korea resumed a vigorous cycle of provocations and missile tests in 2022 and 2023 aimed at demonstrating more advanced intercontinental ballistic missile threats to the U.S. homeland, more sophisticated nuclear weapons technology, and potential tactical nuclear weapons capability. In the fall of 2022 the regime enacted legislation guaranteeing automatic nuclear retaliation for any military attack against its country. Knowing this now, Trump's bloody nose strike plan five years earlier could have started a nuclear war on the peninsula.

The dangers of the year of "Fire and Fury" in 2017 are illustrative of how quickly the situation with North Korea can spiral out of control. Indeed, the poor record of negotiations with North Korea over the past three decades should humble policymakers into an appreciation of a better empirical understanding of one of the perennial unsolved security challenges for the United States.

UNPACKING THE BLACK BOX

This book uses different methodologies for collecting data to better understand the Korean black box. It does not claim to be comprehensive nor highly technical in its analytic methods. There are many others who could do more sophisticated work with our data. But the purpose of this book is to inform public policy circles about the value of an empirically based understanding of Korea by offering some distinct and original data that gets inside the black box on four critical areas of study—armed provocations, the U.S.-ROK alliance, asymmetrical threats, and marketization. The data collected in this book also sheds light on the black box in two respects related to North Korean perceptions of unification and unification "blind spots" (i.e., relative priorities of surrounding countries regarding the unification process). We hope that others will find it useful.

Chapter 2, "The United States–Republic of Korea Alliance," uses new data to understand the extent to which the alliance is threatening to North Korea and elicits military belligerence from the regime. Where this discussion has been most apparent in current policy relates to U.S. and South Korean joint military exercises (JMEs). These exercises, conducted at various intervals throughout the calendar year, aim to allow U.S. and ROK troops to exercise together to maintain military readiness and therefore serve as a deterrent to any military adventurism on the peninsula. Yet North Korea has claimed that these exercises are "war games" that are provocative and destabilizing to peace on the Korean peninsula. North Korea responds to them belligerently with armed military provocations but blames its own belligerence on the joint exercises. In this chapter we test the proposition of whether U.S.-ROK joint military exercises are destabilizing to peace on the Korean peninsula by introducing new data about the impact of the exercises on North Korean provocations and U.S. diplomacy.

Chapter 3, "Technology and Cybersecurity," provides an updated study of the status of North Korea's cyber activities. Building on an earlier CSIS report in the aftermath of the cyber hacking of Sony Pictures Entertainment in November 2014, this chapter describes the evolution of North Korea's cyber activities and the relationship between this activity and broader macroeconomic policies of the country. Cyber activities would appear to be the blackest of black boxes, but in this chapter we show that open-source research can provide a vivid picture of the activities and the threats they pose.

Chapter 4, "Markets and Civil Society," looks at how the growth of markets has affected society in North Korea. We do this through a series of first-ever microsurveys that capture original data on how citizens *inside* of North Korea think about the growth of markets, the value of outside information, and the legitimacy of the state. While there is much data available from interviews with defectors from the country, there is a bias in this data since all interviewees have already made the decision to vote with their feet and opt for a new life outside of the country. The interview data presented in this chapter is compared with interviews and polling of the North Korean defector population in South Korea to see if those inside the country carry similar critical views of the state as those outside. The chapter raises the question of whether the growth of markets is spawning a civil society in North Korea.

Chapters 5 and 6 focus centrally on the topic of unification. They constitute the first-ever study that defines quantifiable metrics for how to think about unification. There are many concerns and fears when it comes to unification. For example, the Chinese fear a wave of refugees coming across the border; the Americans worry about "loose nukes" scenarios; the Japanese worry about resurgent nationalism of a united Korea; the South Koreans worry about the economic cost of unification. After an initial overview of different theories of unification, we attempt in chapter 6 to measure the level of concern, the priorities, and the level of knowledge of Americans, Chinese, South Koreans, Japanese, and Russians regarding ten critical issues associated with unification. We also feature microsurvey data on the untrodden ground of how and whether North Koreans desire unification as well as their views on nuclear weapons. Understanding the relative concerns and priorities of all the parties provides important data to measure where interests overlap and where they diverge. This, in turn, could help to prevent misperception and miscalculation when unification happens.

Chapter 7, "The Hardest of Hard Targets," is the conclusion of the book. It summarizes the main findings from the studies. We believe that the chapters go some distance in demystifying the Korean black box. The book tells original stories that are new when compared with the existing literature. It uses new data, not acquired before, to tell these stories. The data is not only original in the open sources but may be useful to governments because it focuses on longer-term yet not insignificant social issues that government officials have neither the time nor the inclination to collect.

In the end, we acknowledge that we still tell only an incomplete story, but we believe that these chapters overturn some conventional wisdoms about Korean unification and North Korea that are based on little or inaccurate data. Most important, these studies de-ideologize the discussion of these topics. Policy discussions around these perennial security challenges are often based on politics, or ideology, or emotion, or on whose voice in the debates are loudest. Instead, the arguments presented here are based on data. This data will support some "hawkish" positions on Korea, but it will also support some "dovish" policies.

Readers may disagree with the data presented in the book. We welcome a discussion based on data rather than one based on ideology and affect. And we welcome others to use our data or to build on it.

2

THE UNITED STATES–REPUBLIC OF KOREA ALLIANCE

FOR DECADES, North Korea has justified its missile tests, conventional military actions, terrorist attacks, and nuclear tests by stating that these have been provoked by the threat posed by the alliance between the United States and the Republic of Korea. As long as the United States, the most powerful military power in human history, stations troops on the Korean peninsula and maintains a "hostile policy" toward Pyongyang, the North Korean government argues that it is justified in its belligerent disposition. In Victor Cha's own meetings with North Korean government interlocutors, they never defined exactly what "hostile policy" meant. That is, they never defined what aspects of the alliance were threatening, nor what actions the United States could take to assuage their concerns. Nevertheless, the argument propagated by this view is that the world fundamentally does not understand the black box of North Korean threat perceptions. As some have suggested, the regime's militarization since 1948 is not offensively and aggressively intended. Instead, a core security dilemma pervades the problem of an insecure regime that arms itself for survival against the alliance rather than for pursuit of revisionist goals.[1] In this chapter we bring new data to analyze the long-held proposition by North Korea that the U.S.-ROK alliance is threatening to the regime by looking at the degree to which a signature element of the alliance—joint military exercises—elicits reactions from North Korea that fundamentally destabilize the security situation around the peninsula. In this regard, this chapter seeks to decipher the black box of North Korea. What do North Korean leaders fear? Are they threatened by the U.S.-ROK alliance? Are the alliance and its activities obstacles to peace on the Korean peninsula?

TRUMP-KIM SINGAPORE SUMMIT, 2018

Emerging from the unprecedented first summit meeting between the leaders of the United States and the DPRK in Singapore in June 2018, Donald Trump held a lengthy press conference in the Capella Hotel boasting of his accomplishments in securing peace on the Korean peninsula with his new friend, Kim Jong-un. Carrying on for more than sixty minutes, without any sleep for twenty-five hours (he admitted), Trump declared that the perennial North Korea nuclear problem was well on its way to being solved; moreover, he announced his commitment to the DPRK leader that the United States would stop joint military exercises with ally South Korea.[2] Neither the South Koreans nor Trump's own Department of Defense had a say in this decision. In addition to complaining about the cost of the exercises, which are designed to maintain allied readiness and deterrence to preserve peace on the Korean peninsula, Trump called the exercises "provocative":

> Yeah, we've done exercises for a long period of time, working with South Korea. And we call them "war games," and I call them "war games." And they're tremendously expensive. The amount of money that we spend on that is incredible. . . . We fly in bombers from Guam. . . . And what I did say [to the DPRK leader] is—and I think it is very provocative. I have to tell you . . . it is a very provocative situation when I see that, and you have a country right next door. So under the circumstances that we are negotiating a very comprehensive, complete deal, I think it's inappropriate to be having war games.

Number one, we save money. A lot. Number two, it is really something they very much appreciated."[3]

Whether intentional or not, Trump's statement reflected a wholesale adoption of North Korea's traditional criticism about a core element of the U.S.-ROK alliance's defense and deterrence function. First, the DPRK refers to these exercises as "war games" that are a rehearsal for an invasion of the North. Second, the exercises validate Pyongyang's claims of U.S. "hostile policy" that justifies the regime's pursuit of nuclear weapons. And third, these exercises provoke a belligerent response from North Korea. Though this might sound like empty rhetoric, these perennial accusations by North Korea have had significant policy effects. The United States and the ROK have felt obligated to consistently mount a public relations campaign explaining that the military exercises are defensive in nature. The United States has on occasion invited North Korea to observe the exercises (the North has never accepted the invitation). The United States has also canceled, postponed, or modified exercises in the past to avoid eliciting a North Korean reaction that might negatively affect ongoing diplomacy. For example, not only did Donald Trump cancel U.S.-ROK joint military exercises after his summit with Kim Jong-un at Singapore in order to facilitate diplomacy, but President George H. W. Bush also canceled annual Team Spirit exercises in 1992 for the same purpose.[4]

Implicit in all these actions is the assumption that what North Korea declares is in fact true. Because Pyongyang has consistently and vocally claimed that U.S.-ROK military exercises are provocative, analysts and policymakers alike interpret this as a clear and true signal emanating from the black box of North Korean threat perceptions. Moreover, Washington and Seoul operate on the assumption that U.S.-ROK military exercises always lead to negative North Korean responses, worsening relationships, and increasing tensions on the peninsula. Is this really the case? Do U.S.-ROK military exercises really provoke North Korea? Do these exercises heighten tensions by compelling North Korea to respond belligerently? Or is North Korean belligerence provocative but harmless? That is, are they face-saving measures for Pyongyang, with the net effect of neither ratcheting up tensions nor providing a blow to diplomacy?

We ask these questions because a cursory review of the history indicates that the evidence is mixed. While there is evidence that North Korea conducts more provocations after U.S.-ROK joint military exercises, there is also evidence that they continue negotiations and carry out denuclearization steps after such military exercises.[5] For instance, in 2007 several U.S.-DPRK high-level negotiations, including minister-level, talks took place only a few weeks after U.S.-ROK exercises. And in 2008 major steps in implementing the Six-Party Talks denuclearization agreement took place even though Washington and Seoul were engaged in a cycle of military training exercises. If such diplomatic steps take place while exercises are being conducted, can we really say that this allied military training is that damaging to stability on the Korean peninsula?

In this chapter, we open the black box of North Korean threat perceptions. We test empirically the validity of the proposition that the U.S.-ROK alliance is threatening to the North by examining whether a mainstay of the alliance—joint military exercises or JMEs—are provocative. Using an originally constructed dataset, we run a time series analysis to test if JMEs had an impact on the overall state of U.S.-DPRK relations from 2005 to 2015. We compile a time series dataset that measures on a weekly basis over this decade the positive and negative state of U.S.-DPRK relations. This allows us to determine whether JMEs—by virtue of eliciting North Korean responses—have a net negative, positive or neutral effect on ongoing diplomacy. If they do, then there would be validity to the proposition that JMEs may be destabilizing to the peninsula because they provoke North Korea into actions that ratchet up tensions and therefore should be halted to promote diplomacy.

Our analysis reaches the counterintuitive conclusion that JMEs do *not* have a significant negative impact on U.S.-DPRK relations. Instead, we find that the state of relations in the previous week (i.e., the pre-JME state of U.S.-DPRK relations) is the best predictor for outcomes in the U.S.-DPRK relationship during the JME. This suggests that while JMEs might lead to more belligerent responses from North Korea, as suggested by some authors and pundits, the net effect on U.S.-DPRK diplomacy is neutral—i.e., JMEs do not heighten U.S.-DPRK hostility or destabilize the peninsula.

PREVIOUS STUDIES

There is a dearth of research that systematically measures the relationship between JMEs and U.S.-DPRK relations. Most of the current research use quantitative methods to test the relationship between U.S.-ROK JMEs and DPRK provocations.[6] Vito D'Orazio conducted a statistical test of the relationship between exercises and North Korean aggression by using event data collected from the Integrated Crisis Early Warning System (ICEWS).[7] Robert Wallace's quantitative analysis examined the correlation between North Korea's internal conditions and diplomatic aggressiveness toward certain issues, including U.S.-ROK joint military exercises.[8] Both analyses concluded that there was no statistically significant correlation between the military exercises and DPRK provocations. Jordan Bernhardt and Lauren Sukin, by contrast, see a relationship between joint military exercises and belligerent North Korean threats and actions. They find that the intensity of the DPRK response depends on the perceived threat of the JME, which in turn is tied to variation in the components of the JME (e.g., field versus command-post exercise).

The literature incorporating large-N data helps us only partially to understand policy debates on U.S.-ROK JMEs and DPRK belligerence. This is because the identification of patterns in North Korean responses to allied joint military exercises does not answer the question of whether such military training heightens tensions or harms overall relations. For example, the U.S. decision to cancel JMEs in 1992 and 2018 was based on the forecast that North Korean provocations in response to these exercises would be harmful to the diplomatic momentum then underway. But the current literature does not fully examine this policy assumption. D'Orazio codes North Korean responses to U.S.-ROK exercises using a uniform metric that does not account for different types and levels of belligerence by the North. An event that causes North Korea to issue a threatening statement certainly does not have the same diplomatic impact as an event that causes it to launch a ballistic missile. Second, although the literature captures a general trend in North Korea's response to military exercises, it does not really answer the policymaker's question about whether U.S.-ROK military exercises are "provocative." For the policymaker, the fact that Pyongyang may or may not respond to military exercises with a belligerent act is not as important as whether that belligerent act translates into a fundamental change in the overall relationship between the two parties. For example, if JMEs result in a DPRK missile test, this test is not deemed as "provocative" to the policymaker if there is no ensuing spiral of tensions, and the overall direction of diplomacy has not been harmed. Bernhardt and Sukin do an excellent job of demonstrating a relationship between JMEs and North Korean belligerence, as well as explaining how the composition of the JME affects the type of DPRK response. Our argument does not seek to contest D'Orazio or Bernhardt and Sukin's findings. We try to understand the relationship between JMEs and *diplomacy*.

We want to test this relationship because a cursory review of history suggests real questions about a definitive link between JMEs and diplomatic destabilization. For one, Pyongyang has never used the execution of a U.S.-ROK JME as a "talks-stopper" in diplomacy. North Korea has never demanded cancellation in advance of a planned JME as a precondition or "talks-starter" for initiating diplomacy. Also, North Korea has never terminated ongoing talks because of JMEs despite its threats to do so. For example, in 2007 and 2008, two annual U.S.-ROK JMEs (spring exercise "Foal Eagle" and fall exercise "Ulchi-Focus Lens") were conducted as scheduled while the Six-Party Talks were in progress. Despite the North Korean delegation's threats to leave the talks if the JMEs took place, it did not. In June 2007 in the aftermath of the Foal Eagle exercise, North Korea executed its part of the agreement inviting IAEA inspectors back into the Yongbyon nuclear facilities; Pyongyang also hosted high-level U.S.-DPRK talks in Pyongyang for the first time in a half-decade. Later that year the DPRK signed a second Six-Party Talks agreement (the October 3rd Joint Statement) despite the Ulchi-Focus Lens military exercise in the prior month.[9] North Korea took even further steps toward denuclearization the following year, including demolition of the Yongbyon cooling tower despite the fact that both Foal Eagle and Ulchi-Focus Lens exercises were conducted as scheduled.

These examples beg the question of what the dependent variable should be in a study of the causal impact of U.S.-ROK military exercises. The existing literature defines this dependent variable or policy outcome as the presence, nonpresence, and degree of North Korean belligerence. We define the dependent variable not as the belligerent response to the JME, but as the overall impact on diplomacy. We look at whether JMEs are truly tension-heightening by assessing the net effect of JMEs on the state of U.S.-DPRK diplomacy. Under what conditions does a North Korean belligerent response to a JME harm diplomatic momentum?

To fill in this gap, we utilize a diplomacy dataset not previously available to the existing literature to undertake an empirical study designed to measure the impact of U.S.-ROK allied JMEs on U.S.-DPRK bilateral relations. Data is collected related to two sets of regular exercises each year, one in the spring and one in the fall. The time period covered is one decade (2005–2015). The dependent variable is measured as the positive or negative state of U.S.-DPRK diplomacy after the exercises.

Understanding the relationship between JMEs and the overall state of U.S.-DPRK relations is important not just because it is understudied in the academic literature but also because North Korea has clearly signaled its displeasure with joint military exercises, calling them provocative, threatening, dangerous, and significant justification for North Korea to enhance its nuclear deterrent and preemptive strike capabilities.[10]

Second, U.S. policymakers seem to have internalized North Korean rhetoric as they accept without question that joint military exercises ratchet up tensions such that the suspension of the exercises is believed to act as a palliative on the overall diplomatic situation. When the Trump administration canceled Exercise Vigilant Ace in December 2018, the Pentagon's stated reason was "to give the diplomatic process every opportunity to continue."[11] Trump was not the first U.S. president to act on the assumption that the joint military exercises are provocative and detrimental to diplomatic efforts. During U.S.-DPRK diplomacy in the 1990s, the Clinton administration treated U.S. joint military exercises as a "carrot" or "stick" in negotiations with DPRK.[12] George H. W. Bush canceled exercises in 1992 during inter-Korean diplomatic negotiations as "part of our efforts for improvement of South-North relations and reduction of tension."[13] Bill Clinton resurrected the exercises in 1993 as a "stick" but canceled them again in 1994 through 1996 to avoid any disruption to ongoing nuclear diplomacy.[14]

Indeed, the wisdom of canceling military exercises on the Korean peninsula has been the subject of a number of policy debates. These debates center on (1) whether canceling the exercises harms military readiness (it does); and (2) whether the potential downgrading of readiness because of less exercising is worth the gains in diplomacy.[15] But as important and knowledgeable as this literature is, no one addresses the core question of whether JMEs actually harm U.S.-DPRK diplomacy. The literature (and the policy) simply assumes this to be true because the North Koreans assert it as such.

RESEARCH DESIGN

In this section, we discuss the research design of our analysis. First, we provide definitions and operationalization criteria for our two main variables: overall state of U.S.-DPRK relations, and U.S.-ROK joint military exercises. Second, we discuss issues related to constructing a time series data of the two variables, including selection of a natural time unit. Third, we describe and justify the two types of statistical tests used for the time series analysis.

DEPENDENT VARIABLE: OVERALL STATE OF U.S.-DPRK RELATIONS

The dependent variable in our study—the overall state of U.S.-DPRK diplomacy—is measured using two simple dimensions: positive and negative. We import two conceptual assumptions in constructing this measure. The first assumption is that positive events create a "positive" state of diplomacy, and that negative events lead to a "negative" state of diplomacy. Positive events are defined as those that improve the relationship by increasing one or both parties' expectation that the other party will cooperate in the future, therefore positively affecting U.S.-DPRK diplomacy. Positive events range from statements such as expressing a willingness to negotiate or announcing a moratorium on the nuclear weapons program, to diplomatic actions such as talks, negotiations, and agreements (Six-Party Talks, February 13 Joint Statement, IAEA inspection, etc.).

Negative events are defined as events that worsen the state of diplomacy by decreasing one or both parties' expectation that the other will cooperate, therefore negatively affecting the relationship. This can range from hostile rhetoric to actual belligerent behavior such as cutting off military hotlines, missile firings, and nuclear tests.

We further divide negative and positive events into two subcategories in terms of scale: major or minor. Minor events have lesser impact than major events in both positive and negative dimensions. For instance, minor negative events include hostile rhetoric or small provocations such as cutting off hotlines and short-range missiles. Major negative events include long-range ballistic missile launches, lethal military aggression at sea or on land, and nuclear tests. A more detailed measurement criteria and codebook can be found in appendix 1. Table 2.1 is a 2 × 2 visualization of the measurement criteria of events used to construct the data.

The second assumption is that diplomacy at any given slice of time has both dimensions present. No relationship is all positive or all negative. Even the most cooperative bilateral relationships experience conflicts by virtue of the fact that interests do not always converge. The United States and Canada, for example, enjoy one of the most amicable bilateral relationships, but the two have filed twenty-eight World Trade Organization trade dispute cases against each other.[16] Therefore both aspects should be considered when measuring the overall state of diplomacy.

Using these criteria, we construct an eleven-year database of events (both positive and negative) in U.S.-DPRK relations between 2005 and 2015. A more detailed description of this database including the sources can be found in the codebook in appendix 1.

Next, we convert the event data into a daily time series dataset of U.S.-DPRK relations. Following the categorizations of events in table 2.1,

TABLE 2.1

		Dimension	
		Positive	Negative
Scale	Major	+2	−2
	Minor	+1	−1

we are able to construct a composite variable that measures the overall state of diplomatic relations and track its change daily. For instance, on any given day, if there is one positive event of minor scale, the overall tone of relationship is 1. If there is one positive event of major scale (+2) and one negative event of minor scale (−1) on a given day, the overall tone of relationship is 1. If there are no events, the baseline is 0. We track and measure the state of diplomacy over eleven years from January 1, 2005, to December 31, 2015.

INDEPENDENT VARIABLE: JMES

In this chapter we use two selection criteria for the JMEs. First, we only include JMEs conducted between the United States and the ROK. Both countries conduct many different types of joint military exercises with other partners, both bilaterally and multilaterally. But historically, the U.S.-ROK exercises described earlier are the ones that elicit the strongest response from North Korea because their sole purpose is to train for contingencies against DPRK including, a second ground invasion, regime collapse, missile and nuclear tests, and cyberattacks. While the United States conducts exercises with other allies, such as NATO, Australia, and India, these are not directed at North Korea.

Using the same logic, we include only the regular biannual U.S.-ROK JMEs and exclude the ad hoc ones. This is because these exercises (1) are the largest in scale and scope; (2) have been staples of alliance readiness for decades; and (3) have been the target of North Korea's narrative of U.S. "hostile policy."[17] Exact names and dates of the exercises between 2005 and 2015 are provided in appendix 2. We code the JMEs as a binary variable that takes the value of 1 if JMEs are in progress on a given day, and 0 if not.

TIME SERIES DATA: NATURAL TIME UNIT

The natural time unit for our analysis is weekly (starting Sunday), as opposed to days or months. Weekly values are constructed by aggregating the daily values over seven days. We choose the week as the natural time unit because decisions in diplomacy tend to have a longer time horizon than one day and generally shorter time horizons than one month. It is unlikely that states will respond to each other's actions on a daily basis because decision-makers must work policies through the interagency bureaucracy and experience institutional lags that slow a policy output. This is true not just in democracies but also in nondemocratic regimes like North Korea since decisions still need to trickle down the chain of command to be executed. Kim Jong-un might be calling all the shots, but he is probably not going to be the one drafting the statements or operating the missile launchers. This is especially true in U.S.-DPRK relations given the different time zones in which the two countries are located. Following the same logic, monthly time horizons are too long of a delay to track the overall state of diplomacy. It is unlikely that North Korea would wait for a month before responding to U.S. actions. For these reasons, we measure the state of U.S.-DPRK diplomacy with weekly values.

STATISTICAL TESTS

We conduct two types of time series analyses on our variables.[18] First, we use the Cochrane-Orcutt Estimation (COE) procedure to test the relationship between JMEs and U.S.-DPRK diplomacy. COE runs a linear regression adjusting for autoregressive errors which are often present in time series data. We test for a meaningful association between JMEs and its effect on the state of U.S.-DPRK diplomacy correcting for serial correlation. We code the intervention (JMEs) as a binary variable, which takes the value of 1 when JMEs are in progress during the given week and 0 otherwise.

Second, we run an autoregressive (AR) model on the weekly time series data. This test analyzes if the state of diplomacy in the previous week can sufficiently predict the state of diplomacy in the present week. We assume in this test that JMEs do not have any impact on the overall state of diplomacy, and we test if the simplest and the most common predictor (state of diplomacy in the previous week) is sufficient to explain the state of diplomacy in the current week.

Additionally, we use the AR model to forecast the future state of diplomacy and test its accuracy. In this test, we assume that the past week's state of diplomacy is the best predictor for that of the present week, and we then analyze if the AR model using past values can sufficiently predict future values as well. By using the first nine years of data as the training set (2005–2013) and the remaining years as the test set (2014–2015), we compare the predicted values and the actual values to assess forecast accuracy.

ANALYSIS

DESCRIPTIVE ANALYSIS

Before conducting the statistical tests, we first plot the weekly values for U.S.-DPRK diplomacy from 2005 to 2015. As figure 2.1 shows, we can infer several descriptive characteristics about the diplomacy over time. First, we observe several upward spikes in 2005–2006 and again in 2006–2007, as well as some notable negative downward spikes in 2009–2010. It appears as though U.S.-DPRK relations have experienced positive diplomacy as well as negative diplomacy over the past decade, where each bout can last for a year and up to several years. From this we can infer that a long-term time series analysis is the right method for analyzing the U.S.-DPRK relationship. Inferences made by looking at a short slice of time might lead to an incorrect or biased conclusion. Second, figure 2.2 decomposes the data in figure 2.1 and plots positive diplomacy and negative diplomacy separately. Positive bouts of diplomacy are represented as solid lines, and negative bouts are represented as dotted lines. The most notable feature here is the significant amounts of overlap between positive and negative periods. This confirms our initial assumption that relationships can have both negative and positive aspects present at the same time.

STATISTICAL TESTS

We conduct two types of time series analyses to assess the impact of JMEs on U.S.-DPRK diplomacy. In the Cochrane-Orcutt Estimation procedure, a regression model is first fitted using ordinary least squares (OLS) method. An estimation of autocorrelation is calculated from the residuals of the OLS regression. This estimate is then used to remove autocorrelation from the data, after which regression

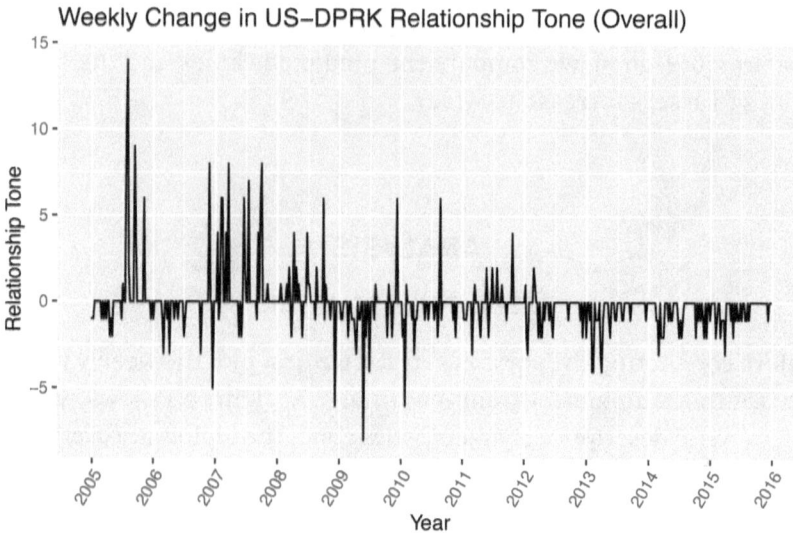

FIGURE 2.1 Weekly change in U.S.-DPRK relationship tone (2005–2015).

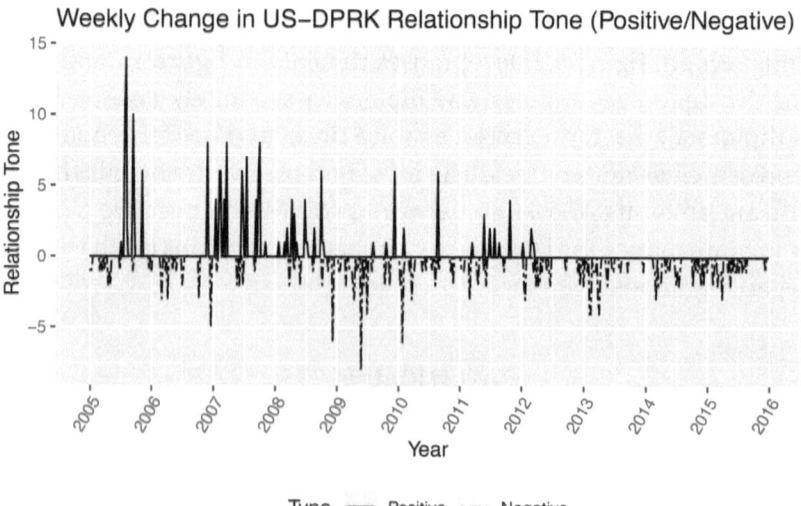

FIGURE 2.2 Weekly change in U.S.-DPRK relationship tone decomposed (2005–2015).

parameters are newly calculated. This process is repeated until the parameters converge, in which case it is assumed that there is no more autocorrelation in the residuals. In our model, the maximum number of iterations is set at 100, and the decimal value to reach for convergence is 8. The COE procedure is especially well suited for time series data, which often have autoregression errors.

As seen in table 2.2, there is no significant correlation between JMEs and U.S.-DPRK diplomacy. Therefore we cannot reject the null hypothesis. While the coefficient for JMEs variable is negative, it is not statistically significant. This means that JMEs do not significantly affect the overall tone of relations between the United States and the DPRK. While JMEs might lead to more provocations from North Korea, as suggested by other authors, this negative reaction does not set off a spiral of tensions that ruin relations. It is most likely that North Korea's provocative responses to JMEs (if they are in fact responses *to* JMEs at all) are motivated by domestic concerns rather than deteriorating diplomacy with the United States.

North Korea's provocations often overlap with significant events in domestic politics. For example, the country undertook a series of provocations, including two antiship cruise missile fires and a satellite launch using ballistic missile technology in late March to mid-April 2012.[19] These actions came as a surprise to Washington, Seoul, and the international community since the missile tests took place shortly after the DPRK agreed to a moratorium on nuclear tests, long-range missiles launch, and IAEA inspections at Yongbyon (Leap Day Agreement).[20] These actions shifted U.S.-DPRK diplomacy from positive to negative, as represented in figure 2.2 by the downward dip in early 2012 that continues until 2015.

TABLE 2.2 Correlation between JMEs and U.S.–DPRK relationship tone

	Dependent variable: U.S.–DPRK relationship tone
JMEs	−0.136
	(0.233)
Constant	−0.071
	(0.095)
Observations	575

Note: $^{*}p$ $^{**}p$ $^{***}p < 0.01$

As puzzling as these provocations may have seemed to the world, they overlapped with several important events at home for the DPRK regime. On April 10, 2012, Kim Jong-un formally succeeded his father by claiming various titles, including "supreme leader," chairman of the Workers' Party of Korea Central Military Commission, and membership in the Politburo and its presidium, completing his formal control over party and military.[21] And on April 15 North Korea celebrated the posthumous hundredth birthday of the North Korean founder Kim Il-sung.[22] Seen in this light, North Korean actions most likely stemmed from domestic legitimacy needs of the new leader and some muscle flexing to accompany his consolidation of power.

If JMEs do not affect the tone of U.S.-DPRK diplomacy, then what variable could create change in the relationship? To answer this question, we run a second simpler test, which is an AR1 model, on the weekly state of U.S.-DPRK relations without factoring in the JMEs. The idea tested in the AR model is that the best predictor of behavior at time t will be behavior at time t-1.[23] Given that JMEs are not significantly correlated with U.S.-DPRK diplomacy (as the COE test suggests), we test to see if the best predictor of "present value" is "past value."

Table 2.3 presents the results of the AR1 model as well as additional models tested for over-fitting. Model (1) represents the results of the AR1 model. And as seen in the table, the value at t-1 (status of relations in the previous week) is a statistically significant predictor of the state of diplomacy in the current week.

We also ran three additional models for comparison. Model (2) is an AR2 model that uses value at time t-2 to predict values at time t. Model (3) and (4) are moving average (MA) models. MA models are like AR models because they assume that the past influences the present, but MA models posit that the impact of the previous value lasts for a limited period (q periods) and dissipates thereafter, unlike AR models, which posits that the impact of the previous value diminishes exponentially. Model (3) is an MA model with 1 period (MA1), and model (4) is an MA model with 2 periods (MA2).

When comparing the fit across the four models, the first model (AR1) fits the best, having the lowest AIC value.[24] Also note that the value of intercept is slightly negative across all models (−0.095), which suggests that the baseline tone of U.S.-DPRK diplomacy between 2005 and 2015 is negative.

Most important, in all four models, the previous week's state of diplomacy (value at t-1) shows statistically significant coefficients of roughly the same value (roughly 0.2). This means that the previous week's state of relations affects the current week's relationship the best, whether we assume an autoregressive process where shocks diminish slowly or a moving average process where shocks last and disappear.

Additionally, we test the forecast accuracy of our model. We use the first nine years (2005–2013) of our time series data as the training set and the remaining years (2014–2015) as the test set. We run an AR1 model on the training set and use the same model to generate predicted values for the next two years of U.S.-DPRK diplomacy. This test determines if a model generated by using the previous week's value to predict the present week can also predict the future state of diplomatic relations as well. We then plot the predicted value with the actual values to check their accuracy.

As seen in figure 2.3, the model predicts quite well. The solid line is a plot of the actual values in U.S.-DPRK diplomacy, and we can see

TABLE 2.3 Correlation between U.S.–DPRK relationship in current and past week

	Dependent variable: U.S.–DPRK relationship tone			
	AR (1)	AR (2)	MA (1)	MA (2)
	(1)	(2)	(3)	(4)
Relationship tone t-1	0.217***	0.206***		
	(0.041)	(0.042)		
Relationship tone t-2		0.051		
		(0.042)		
Relationship tone t-1			0.194***	0.203***
			(0.038)	(0.042)
Relationship tone t-2				0.071*
				(0.040)
Intercept	−0.095	−0.095	−0.095	−0.095
	(0.089)	(0.094)	(0.084)	(0.089)
Observations	575	575	575	575
Log Likelihood	−1,112.118	−1,111.370	−1,113.725	−1,112.117
sigma²	2.802	2.795	2.818	2.802
Akaike Inf. Crit.	2,230.236	2,230.739	2,233.450	2,232.235

Note: *p**p***p < 0.01

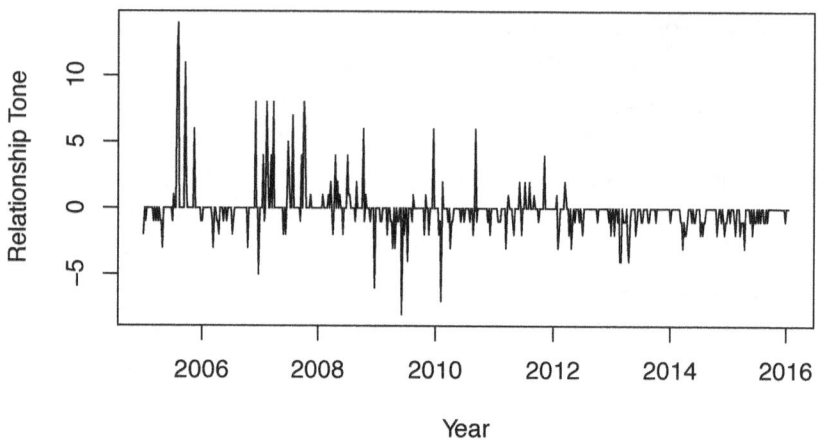

FIGURE 2.3 Forecasting U.S.-DPRK relationship tone.

that the state of diplomacy during 2014–2015 was largely negative. The model generates consistently negative values during these years, as represented by the bold line. In the figure, the line seems very close to 0 as all the predicted values sit between −0.001104 and −0.000877. The important point to note is that all the predicted values are negative values. Also, we can see that all the actual values between 2014 and 2015 sit within the 95 percent confidence interval of the forecast, as represented by the dotted line.

POSSIBLE EXPLANATIONS: DOMESTIC FACTORS AND ALLIANCE DYNAMICS

We have found that JMEs have a null effect—they do not affect the overall state of U.S.-DPRK diplomacy. North Korea may respond to JMEs with small provocations, but that does not seem to lead to a downward spiral of tensions. What, then, could account for this outcome? One can surmise some possible explanations for the null effect of JMEs on diplomacy.

First, domestic factors may be at play. Leaders of nondemocracies face the task of maintaining credibility and reputation in foreign policy like their counterparts in democracies.[25] Because autocratic leaders depend heavily on the support of domestic elite groups to survive politically, the threat of being ousted by a coup is always lingering, which makes them accountable for their words and actions.[26] This "audience cost" dynamic might be at play in North Korea's case. The legitimacy of the North Korean leadership derives from a domestic narrative that justifies draconian control of the population and expropriation of all resources of the state as necessary to defend against external threats. Anti-American rhetoric and self-reliance are two of the core propaganda themes that the regime is built on. Demonstrating the ability to defend the nation vis-à-vis great powers such as the United States is crucial to the regime's domestic legitimacy.

What this suggests is that North Korea has every domestic incentive to respond provocatively to U.S.-ROK JMEs.[27] Since Kim Jong-il officially succeeded Kim Il-sung in 1998, "Strong and Prosperous Nation" (강성대국) has been a key theme mentioned in New Year's statements. His successor Kim Jong-un has also stressed the regime's ability to thrive independently as a socialist nation, especially in terms of its strong military and self-defense capabilities. If North Korea's belligerent responses are motivated largely by domestic politics, then it is less likely that these responses will trigger further escalation. In this sense, the provocations might constitute a bit of political performance art or "kabuki"—a routine response to a routine exercise that ultimately is designed to feed a political narrative rather than a broader altercation with the adversary.

Second, and relatedly, North Korea's belligerent responses to JMEs might be driven by the motivation to "save face." As a small, isolated country, North Korea's intense insecurities compel it to respond to every military action by the adversary in order to demonstrate strength. North Korea's provocative responses to JMEs could therefore be symptomatic of a de facto reputational "face-saving" strategy rather than an actual reflection of a desire to submarine the diplomacy. That is, the regime counters strength with strength, but with no intent to escalate further. Moreover, the United States and the ROK understand Pyongyang's reputational motivations and therefore do not respond in kind.

A third explanation relates to alliance lobbying. This posits that there is no escalation dynamic in U.S.-DPRK relations after JMEs because of South Korea's efforts to mute the deleterious effects of North Korean provocations. This applies to, but is not limited to, progressive South Korean governments that want to maintain a stance of engagement with North Korea. These governments (e.g., Kim Dae-jung, Roh Moo-hyun, and Moon Jae-in) generally prefer to downplay U.S.-ROK JMEs to preserve engagement policies. However, if JMEs go forward and North Korea responds to them belligerently, then Seoul implores Washington to not escalate nor give up on the diplomatic track. For these reasons, Seoul lobbies its ally characterizing North Korean actions as "routine"; watering down the significance of the act (e.g., withholding reporting on whether projectile launches are ballistic missiles or not [the former being more severe]); and characterizing DPRK belligerence as "attention-seeking" signals for diplomacy (e.g., a missile test is really an "olive branch" for talks).

A fourth set of explanations for why JMEs trigger DPRK belligerence but have a null effect on overall relations has to do with restraint on the part of the United States. There are three dynamics at work. First, the United States has historically advocated restraint on the use of force in the face of DPRK provocations. Even when DPRK belligerence has resulted in the death or detention of U.S. military personnel (e.g., 1968 USS *Pueblo* seizure; 1969 EC-121 shoot-down; 1976 Panmunjom axe murder), Washington has adopted a measured response eschewing further escalation. On occasion, Washington has also restrained conservative South Korean governments from escalating in response to DPRK heinous actions (e.g., 2010 ROKS *Cheonan* sinking; 2010 Yeonpyeong island shelling; 1968 Blue House Raid; 1987 KAL 858 bombing). American restraint on the Korean peninsula, despite ROK protestations to the contrary, stems from the wider scope of its global security agenda—whether this relates to the Soviet threat during the Cold War or China's rise today—which can ill afford a distracting conflagration in Korea. Second, the U.S. policy priority with regard to the DPRK is denuclearization. Thus any DPRK belligerence in response to U.S.-ROK JMEs goes unanswered because Washington's focus remains on preserving or promoting denuclearization talks. For example, when

North Korea conducted its first nuclear test in October 2006, the Bush administration forwent a military response for a diplomatic one (through the UN Security Council). Washington also immediately called for bilateral meetings with the DPRK to keep denuclearization talks alive. Third, the United States generally does not suffer from the same insecurities as DPRK. Washington is confident in its deterrent capabilities to prevent a second DPRK invasion and continuously seeks to improve those capabilities through the JMEs. Therefore Washington need not undertake face-saving responses to DPRK belligerence that might escalate tensions. In sum, all these explanations suggest that JMEs do not set off a negative spiral in U.S.-DPRK diplomacy on the peninsula. One episode of DPRK provocation or one exchange of negative interactions does not automatically lock the two states into a downward spiral.

* * *

We tend to think of North Korean threat perceptions as a black box. Pyongyang claims that the United States has a "hostile policy" and that the alliance is so threatening as to justify claims that the United States stands as an obstacle to peace on the peninsula. In this chapter we tested this proposition by using data to examine the North Korean proposition that U.S.-ROK JMEs, a core element of defense and deterrence in the alliance, are destabilizing to the peninsula.

Our time series analysis shows that while JMEs may cause Pyongyang to issue harsh statements and may even incite the regime to carry out belligerent acts, U.S.-ROK JMEs are not "provocative" in that they do not lead to fundamental changes in the overall U.S.-DPRK diplomatic relationship. In short, if relations were bad before the JME, they remained bad after them; if good before the JME, there was no appreciable decline in relations in the subsequent period despite belligerent rhetoric or actions by Pyongyang purportedly in response to the JME. This suggests that there is no causal relationship between U.S.-ROK JMEs and the state of diplomacy. It is important to note that our findings do not dispute others who find a relationship between JMEs and North Korean belligerence. Indeed, we are agnostic about whether JMEs cause North Korean actions. Instead, we argue that they are immaterial to changing the overall state of tensions (or stability) in the diplomatic game. We argue that even if North Korea may respond with verbal threats and minor kinetic responses, these actions seem to be nothing more than face-saving strategy on its part as it is not actually willing to jeopardize or derail ongoing diplomacy. This suggests that it is a misnomer to label the alliance's exercises "provocative"—the North Korean response to the JME may seem escalatory, and may be portrayed in the media as such, but the net effect on overall relations is insignificant.

The policy implication of this study is that it would be fundamentally flawed to negotiate a change in the status of U.S.-ROK JMEs on the assumption that the exercises themselves induce tension, or that cessation of exercises will serve to reverse a diplomatic downturn. While the North Korean response in terms of rhetoric, counterexercises, or missile shots may ratchet up tensions, this iterative interaction between the United States and the DPRK on the whole does not change relations. There may be other variables that cause change, as noted earlier, and all these variables can be tested using the data provided in this chapter to determine whether one or any combination affect the impact of JMEs on the diplomacy. For policymakers to suspend JMEs as a "confidence building measure," according to our empirical analysis, will not lead to a substantive improvement in relations. Indeed, our analysis calls into question the wisdom of canceling military exercises to give diplomacy a chance on the Korean peninsula. JMEs enforce peace on the peninsula by maintaining strong defense and deterrence capabilities. Manipulating them for political purposes could have the counterintuitive effect of undermining peace if the adversary sees them to be weakening allied deterrence and training readiness, thereby potentially encouraging miscalculation and military adventurism on the part of the DPRK.

3

TECHNOLOGY AND CYBERSECURITY

NORTH KOREA'S cyber activities are arguably the blackest of black boxes. There is secrecy and a dearth of information associated with these burgeoning capabilities, arguably more so than with the regime's nuclear weapons and ballistic missile programs. Indeed, the concern about North Korean cyber activities is a relatively recent phenomenon, having hardly registered a blip on the radar screen until the attack on Sony Pictures Entertainment in 2014. The scope and sophistication of the hack surprised the best cybersecurity experts inside and outside of official governments.[1] Unlike the extant threat posed by nuclear weapons or artillery, the cyber threat operates in a realm that is inherently harder to detect, monitor, defend against, and deter. While North Korea makes statements about their nuclear weapons program, there are no such statements about their cyber capabilities, giving us little to work with. Yet the significance of this threat cannot be overestimated, as this is the most potent asymmetrical weapon in the North's arsenal, potentially surveilling, disrupting, and blinding the systems of the U.S. and South Korean military, critical infrastructure, and business.

To the extent we have any information about North Korean cyber capabilities, this largely remains within the official classified intelligence realm, not accessible to others. Governments and law enforcement have no interest in sharing as they do not wish to compromise the sources and methods of their intelligence gathering and surveillance. Private-sector companies also have knowledge about these activities, but they are interested in minimizing disruption to their business operations and are not interested in sharing information with governments, law enforcement, or experts. This leaves North Korean cyber operators free to work in the shadows as they target their next victim.

The purpose of this chapter is to demonstrate that even this black box is not as black as it may seem. Using open-source materials, we show that sound research can provide a great deal of information about North Korea by (1) tracking the evolution of North Korean cyber activities, (2) identifying the goals of the program, (3) hypothesizing about the strategy that drives the goals, and (4) offering some policy recommendations. My colleagues and I maintain that while this work is based only on unclassified, open-source materials, it still has value-added for experts and policymakers.[2]

EVOLUTION OF NORTH KOREA CYBER ACTIVITIES

North Korea's development of cyber capabilities grows from three elements of its broader military strategy. The first is the "quick war, quick end" offensive strategy. This strategy emphasizes the use of surprise attacks and disruption of the adversary at the strategic, operational, or tactical level to avoid a protracted conflict that the DPRK cannot sustain.[3] The "quick war, quick end" doctrine requires an ability to disrupt the enemy's military operations and command and control systems. Second and related to the first factor, a belief in asymmetric warfare generates the investment in cyber weapons as the way to render a superior military vulnerable to attack.[4] North Korea's warfighting doctrine has always incorporated a two-front strategy, fighting on the front lines, but also deploying special operations forces and other means to disrupt the adversary's infrastructure, logistics, and command centers to compensate for going up against a superior military force.[5] The investment in cyber is part of an asymmetric electronic warfare strategy to target the vulnerabilities of highly networked militaries like those of the ROK and the United States. Third, cyber weapons are well suited to North Korea's coercive diplomacy and brinksmanship tactics aimed at disrupting or leveraging the peaceful status quo to achieve concessions from the opponent, who is more invested in the status quo than the DPRK.[6] As one study summed up, "Cyber operations have become a central component of North Korea's asymmetric military strategy, peacetime provocations, and illicit strategy."[7]

North Korea's cyber capabilities in peacetime largely focus on espionage and criminal activities and are conducted primarily by the regime's clandestine intelligence service, the Reconnaissance General Bureau (RGB), which operates under a number of cyber handles and reports directly to the National Defense Commission and to Kim Jong-un.[8] According to an open-source U.S. government study, Bureau 121 is attributed to the RGB and operates as a coordinating body for all cyber activity. It reportedly has over six thousand staff that operate in Belarus, Malaysia, China, India, and Russia targeting biotech, pharmaceutical, and IT companies in the United States, South Korea, and China. Four units operating within this bureau are the Andariel Group (also reported as a subgroup of Lazarus), Bluenoroff Group, an Electronic Warfare Jamming Regiment, and Lazarus Group.[9] The other two units that house cyber capabilities are the General Staff Department (GSD), and the Korean People's Army (KPA). According to a CSIS report, the KPA cyber capabilities are rooted in KPA electronic warfare concepts, while the RGB cyber units are more involved in espionage and financial criminal activities.[10] Another study finds that Office 91 is designated as the lead unit of cyber operations and has four units underneath it tasked with offensive operations, information warfare, espionage, and hacking.[11] As discussed later, some reorganization of these units took place in response to the Covid-19 pandemic.

North Korea's cyber hackers are for the most part home grown. The RGB is staffed by some 7,000 cyber operatives, who are recruited at an early age as talented math and science students and are taught coding.[12] This is larger when compared with the U.S. Cyber Command force of about 6,200. There is assistance from China, Russia, and Iran in that these students will receive some technical training in the university systems and will seek employment there. For example, North Korean information technology workers are reportedly based in cities like Dalian, working in the gaming design industries.[13] China reportedly also has provided routers and servers, and Russia has provided GPS jamming equipment. Russia has also reportedly sent technical experts to train hackers in North Korea, and Iran has cooperated with sharing information technology. China also reportedly has allowed North Korean cyber units to operate in border cities like Shenyang and Dandong.[14] There may be other forms of assistance, but information in the unclassified realm is scarce.

North Korea's cyberattacks started out as relatively simple distributed denial-of-service (DDoS) attacks against South Korean targets. But they have significantly evolved their capabilities from DDoS to the use of advanced malware. When North Korea carried out its attack on Sony Pictures Entertainment, the operation surprised many experts and law enforcement authorities with its level of sophistication. In November 2014 a hacker group that identified itself as "Guardians of Peace" associated with the Lazarus Group penetrated systems at Sony, ostensibly to disrupt the distribution and screening of the movie *The Interview*, which comically depicted an assassination attempt on North Korean leader Kim Jong-un. However, the operation did much more than that. The malware cyberattacks disabled Sony's computer server and resulted in the leakage of internal information, such as salaries, social security numbers, emails, and the scripts of future movie productions. Sony Pictures postponed the release of the film. Many reports at the time, including one by CSIS, assessed that Pyongyang could use cyber as an instrument to steal data, as well as to potentially destroy critical infrastructure such as water supplies, electricity grids, and even nuclear power plants. The CSIS report posited that "North Korea may be emboldened, either from past success or a miscalculation of its capabilities and adversary resolve and elevate the intensity of its cyberattacks. This could lead to crossing of the use of force threshold and an escalation of conflict with the United States and ROK."[15] Many of these early reports were correct in that North Korea has significantly increased its cyber abilities and diversified its targets since successfully hacking Sony Pictures Entertainment in 2014.

However, the types of cyber activities that we have seen since 2014 could be characterized less as cyber terrorism, and more as cybercrime, with a particular emphasis on financial crimes and petty theft.[16] Perhaps as a result of economic dislocation, unfavorable terms of trade with China, mounting pressure from United Nations (UN) sanctions in 2013, 2016, and 2017, and the three-year Covid-19 lockdown (2020–2023), the North Korean regime has employed hackers, designated generally as "Hidden Cobra" by the U.S. government and also the Lazarus Group, which consist of several Advanced Persistent Threat (APT) groups such as the BeagleBoyz and APT38.[17] These groups began hacking banks, cryptocurrency exchanges, and corporate networks to steal cash, Bitcoin, and data to fund the cash-strapped regime.[18] Hidden Cobra has reportedly been in operation since 2009 and has used vulnerabilities in Adobe, Hangul Word Processor, and Microsoft Word to install malware. Noteworthy attacks included the DDoS attacks against South Korean media, financial institutions, and critical infrastructure in 2011, the cyberattack against Sony Pictures Entertainment in 2014, and assorted cryptocurrency thefts in 2017 (the latter are discussed in detail).[19] As of 2019, North Korean hacking groups have stolen more than $2 billion, which is likely an underestimation given the increasing value of cryptocurrencies such as Bitcoin.[20] North Korean groups also began to reach out to larger cybercrime organizations, notably crimeware powerhouse Trickbot under the codename "Anchor Project."[21] Expanding capabilities and collaborations make the North Koreans a formidable force in the asymmetric cyber battlespace.

North Korean hacking campaigns fit broadly into four categories: financial crimes, espionage, disruption of organizations and governments, and ransomware. The four categories are outlined in figure 3.1, and each includes details of significant successful and unsuccessful hacking operations.

FINANCIAL CRIMES—CASH AND DATA

North Korea has hacked banks and other financial institutions to minimize the economic impact of sanctions. In 2016 North Korean hackers initiated thirty-five payment transfer transactions on behalf

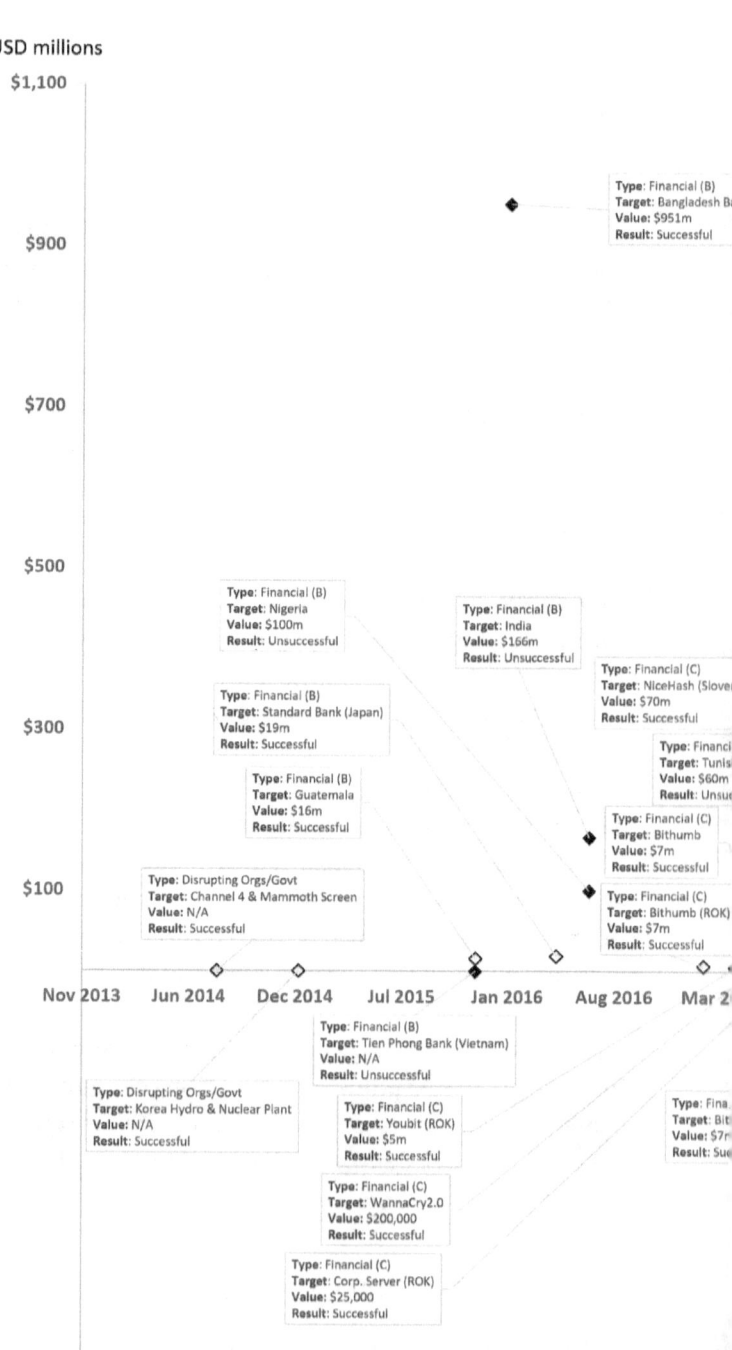

FIGURE 3.1 North Korea hacking operations since 2014.

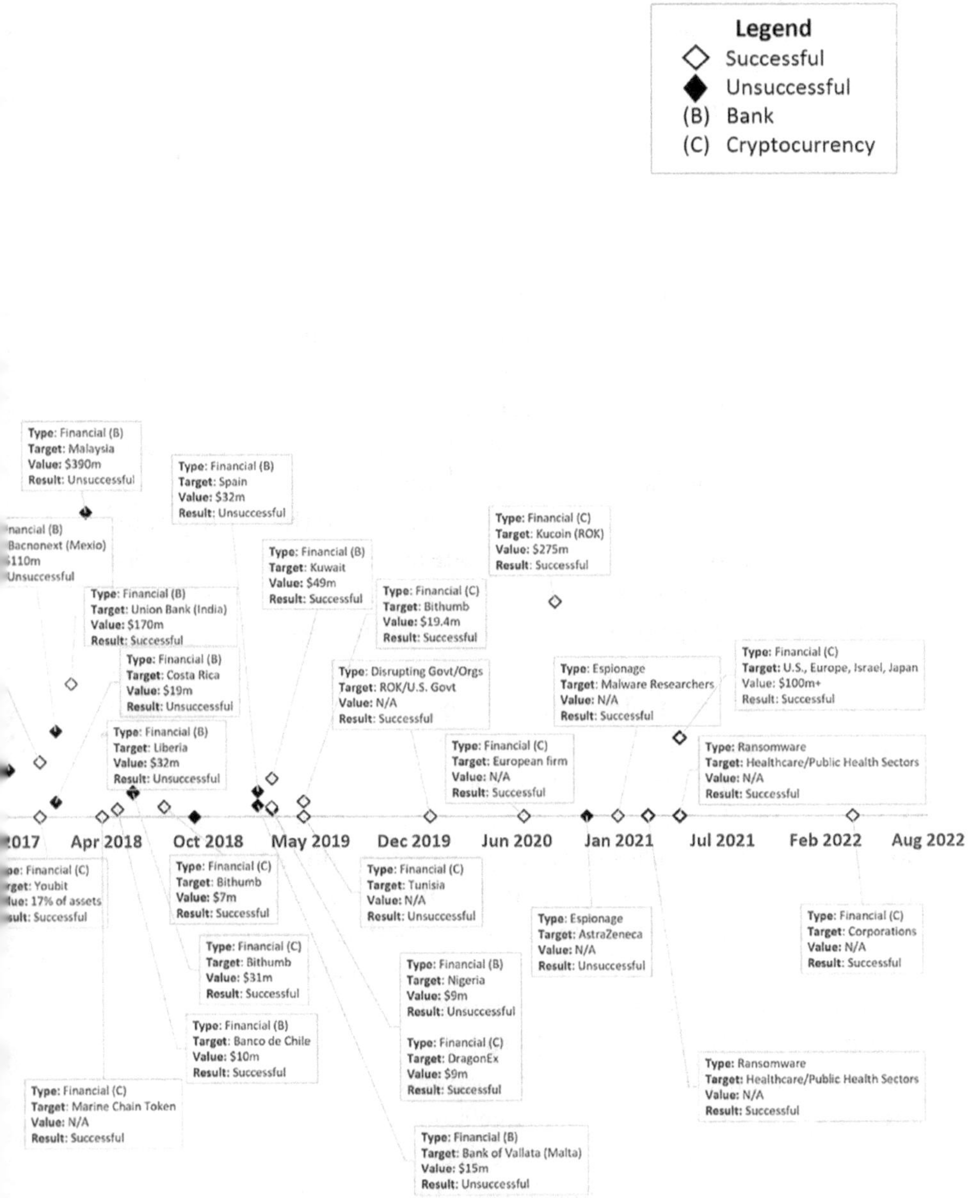
Legend
Successful
Unsuccessful
(B) Bank
(C) Cryptocurrency
Type: Financial (B) Target: Malaysia Value: $390m Result: Unsuccessful
nancial (B) Bacnonext (Mexio) 110m Unsuccessful
Type: Financial (B) Target: Union Bank (India) Value: $170m Result: Successful
Type: Financial (B) Target: Costa Rica Value: $19m Result: Unsuccessful
Type: Financial (B) Target: Liberia Value: $32m Result: Unsuccessful
Type: Financial (B) Target: Spain Value: $32m Result: Unsuccessful
Type: Financial (B) Target: Kuwait Value: $49m Result: Successful
Type: Financial (C) Target: Bithumb Value: $19.4m Result: Successful
Type: Disrupting Govt/Orgs Target: ROK/U.S. Govt Value: N/A Result: Successful
Type: Financial (C) Target: Kucoin (ROK) Value: $275m Result: Successful
Type: Financial (C) Target: European firm Value: N/A Result: Successful
Type: Espionage Target: Malware Researchers Value: N/A Result: Successful
Type: Financial (C) Target: U.S., Europe, Israel, Japan Value: $100m+ Result: Successful
Type: Ransomware Target: Healthcare/Public Health Sectors Value: N/A Result: Successful
2017
Apr 2018
Oct 2018
May 2019
Dec 2019
Jun 2020
Jan 2021
Jul 2021
Feb 2022
Aug 2022
e: Financial (C) get: Youbit lue: 17% of assets sult: Successful
Type: Financial (C) Target: Bithumb Value: $7m Result: Successful
Type: Financial (C) Target: Bithumb Value: $31m Result: Successful
Type: Financial (B) Target: Banco de Chile Value: $10m Result: Successful
Type: Financial (C) Target: Marine Chain Token Value: N/A Result: Successful
Type: Financial (C) Target: Tunisia Value: N/A Result: Unsuccessful
Type: Financial (B) Target: Nigeria Value: $9m Result: Unsuccessful
Type: Financial (C) Target: DragonEx Value: $9m Result: Successful
Type: Financial (B) Target: Bank of Vallata (Malta) Value: $15m Result: Unsuccessful
Type: Espionage Target: AstraZeneca Value: N/A Result: Unsuccessful
Type: Ransomware Target: Healthcare/Public Health Sectors Value: N/A Result: Successful
Type: Financial (C) Target: Corporations Value: N/A Result: Successful

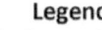

of the Bangladesh Bank, the central bank of Bangladesh to a series of accounts in Sri Lanka and the Philippines, totaling nearly $1 billion. The hackers' cyberattack did not directly target the Society for Worldwide Interbank Financial Telecommunication (SWIFT) network, but rather the machines used within the Bangladesh Bank to access its account.[22] Although a majority of the fraudulent transactions were identified and frozen, the hackers successfully stole $81 million.

The BeagleBoyz, a North Korean hacking group directed by the RGB, also known as APT38, Bluenoroff, Lazarus and Stardust Chollima, employed another cash-based scheme that targeted individual users in a wider-net approach.[23] The group executed several FastCash ATM hacking schemes in which they infiltrated payment-processing networks by placing a Trojan horse program that allowed them to make fraudulent ATM cash withdrawals. In 2016 the North Korean group was responsible for an $18 million heist in Japan where accomplices used credentials stolen from a bank in South Africa to make cash withdrawals. The BeagleBoyz targeted more than thirty countries, primarily in Asia and Africa, in one attack in 2017, and an additional twenty-three countries in a separate attack in 2018. These attacks enabled the hackers to steal tens of millions of dollars, including $13 million from Cosmos bank in India and $6.1 million from BankIslami Pakistan Limited.[24] The hacks left one African bank unable to resume normal ATM services for two months.[25]

APT38 is reported to be the first specialized cyber group tasked to raise funds for the state. It has targeted more than sixteen organizations in thirteen countries since 2014. The stolen funds are most likely used to finance nuclear weapons and ballistic missile development.[26] APT38 stands out among North Korean cyberhackers and relative to such threats from China and Russia for three reasons: First, experts know less about these activities compared with others, which lends to its unpredictability. Second, North Korean attacks tend to be indiscriminate and without malware "guard rails." For example, hacking attempts by the Chinese operate like a doctor's scalpel, trying to do as little collateral damage as possible to targeted networks in no small part to preserve them as viable targets in the future. North Korean hackers operate with blunt force and do inordinate destruction of victim networks as part of APT38's operations, presumably to destroy evidence.[27] Third, most malware is "reversible" in the sense that it will activate only under certain conditions or only for a certain period of time. But North Korean hackers take what some have described as a "scorched earth" or irreversible approach. The malware will have built-in checks such that any efforts at debugging would result in permanent damage to the targeted networks hard drives and related systems.[28]

As early as May 2019, North Korean hackers began inserting malicious code into retail chains' payment software to steal customer credit card data in yet another cash-based scheme. Corporate victims include a U.S. truck parts retailer and Claire's, an international fashion accessory chain. Researchers at Sansec, a cybersecurity firm, believe that the hackers gained access to these corporate networks by conducting spear-phishing attacks on employees to obtain their log-in credentials. To exfiltrate the credit card data obtained from the attacks, the hackers first hijacked a number of other websites, including that of an Italian modeling agency, a music store in Tehran, and a bookstore in New Jersey, and repurposed these sites to receive the stolen data and direct it to North Korea. When attacking Claire's, hackers inserted malware that contained a domain name that closely resembles the real website's name to acquire customer credit card data. Sansec determined that these credit card skimming attacks, known as "Magecart," were likely conducted by the same group because the hacks share several unique characteristics, including a common domain name and Domain Name System (DNS) service as well as the use of a specific sequence of code. According to Sansec, because the credit card skimming attacks used a number of web links that were already associated with previous North Korean hacks, it is likely that North Korean hackers are responsible for these skimming attacks.[29]

CRYPTOCURRENCY

Digital currencies, or cryptocurrencies, and their exchanges have been a particular focus for North Korean hackers because cryptocurrencies are often traded anonymously beyond government control and, therefore, the hacks are harder to trace. Since 2017 North Korean hackers have stolen an estimated $3 billion from crypto-exchanges and in some cases bankrupted their targets.[30] The hackers' first major attack, in February 2017, was on Bithumb, a South Korean cryptocurrency exchange. Hackers stole at least $7 million, in addition to user and trading data. Bithumb was then attacked three more times in the July 2017, June 2018, and March 2019, losing a total of $58 million.[31] Youbit, another South Korean crypto-exchange, was also attacked twice in 2017. In the first attack, it lost $7 million, and in the second attack it lost 17 percent of its assets and was forced to declare bankruptcy.[32] In mid-2017 hackers stole from Coinis, a South Korean crypto company, and three other unnamed crypto-exchanges. In December that year, North Korean hackers stole $70 million from NiceHash, a Slovenian crypto company. In 2018 hackers attempted to steal over $2.6 million in cryptocurrency from Bangladesh. Hackers stole $9 million from DragonEx, a Southeast Asia based crypto-exchange, in March 2019 and in May 2019 targeted UpBit, a South Korean crypto-exchange. In 2020 hackers completed their biggest hack to date, stealing $275 million from Kucoin, a Singaporean cryptocurrency exchange.[33] In 2022 it had its most prolific year yet, stealing an estimated $1.7 billion in cryptocurrency.

While U.S. and UN officials have attributed the attacks to North Korean hackers, the North Korean state is strongly suspected to be involved in many additional large crypto attacks. In January 2018 Japanese crypto-exchange CoinCheck lost more than $530 million in an unattributed cyber-heist. While the mastermind of the attack is unknown, South Korea's National Intelligence Service identified the attack as coordinated by North Korea.[34]

North Korean hacking groups also deployed malware at financial institutions and cryptocurrency exchanges to steal digital currency and user data. From 2018 through 2020, North Korean hackers deployed "AppleJeus," a malware designed to steal cryptocurrency from financial institutions by posing as legitimate cryptocurrency platforms. Associated indicators of compromise include Celas Trade Pro, JMT Trading, Union Crypto, Kupay Wallet, CoinGoTrade, Dorusio, and Ants2Whale. AppleJeus malware allows the perpetrator to infect the victim's computer and gain access to stored information.[35]

The regime's focus on cryptocurrency heists has become more acute since 2020 for several reasons. First, the global sanctions regime against North Korea empowered by a combination of UN Security Council resolutions and the U.S.-led "maximum pressure" campaign during the Obama, Trump, and Biden presidencies have forced the regime's criminal behavior into the crypto space. It has become harder and more costly for North Korea to gain currency through long-practiced activities like counterfeiting, drug-running, and slave labor exports as UN member states are called on to comply with sanctions resolutions. Second, the DPRK's Covid-19 lockdown, including the shutdown of the border with China from January 2020 for three years hence, effectively removed an income source for the regime through its healthy trade with its communist patron. The lockdown dropped bilateral trade with China 80 percent year on year. Third, the relative appreciation of cryptocurrency values during the pandemic and the unregulated nature of the activity make it an attractive target for North Korea's army of some seven thousand hackers and an essential revenue generator for the DPRK regime. Finally, hacking crypto is a low-risk and low-cost alternative yet potentially highly lucrative way to fund the regime.

Not unlike other North Korean practices in illicit trade, the primary method of operation is the use of evasion, deception, and concealment. North Korean hackers with hired third parties act as businesses, employers, or job applicants to get individuals in the target entity to click on a bad link or corrupted pdf file. In the case of Sony Pictures Entertainment, North Korean hackers penetrated the target's systems by getting at least one engineer to click on a job application. Once inside Sony's systems, the hackers gathered data and personnel information for two months before launching an attack that blacked out all computer systems. In the Bangladesh case, hackers succeeded in getting officials in the central bank to open résumé files from job applicants. After penetrating the systems, the hackers remained on the inside for one year before the February 2016 attempt to steal nearly $1 billion.[36] In 2018 Lazarus used a LinkedIn ad for a software developer position to recruit an employee from Redbanc, which is connected with the web of ATM networks in Chile, to download a file

ApplicationPDF.exe for the job application process. The file contained malware that then collected information from Redbanc's systems.[37] In the Axie Infinity case (discussed shortly), hackers also posed as prospective employers through LinkedIn and succeeded in getting a senior engineer at the company, Ronin, to accept a fake job offer with an exorbitant salary. The engineer then downloaded a pdf file with the fraudulent offer letter, allowing spyware to infiltrate the company's systems.[38]

The regime will also deploy different types of attacks to distract the target. It may deploy one type of virus to get the target to deploy antivirus software and focus attention on that back door, while deploying other malware against the unaware victim. It has been reported that the regime also will deploy some simple "false-flag" ransomware attacks against a target in Russian or Chinese to disguise and distract from another, more meaningful malware attack against another targeted network.[39]

A *New York Times* report in 2022 detailed how the regime, after breaching crypto wallets with phishing attacks, will launder the funds through cryptocurrency mixers using multiple streams of digital assets, which makes tracking difficult. The process is slow and deliberate as they move small amounts to avoid attracting attention. The North Koreans then convert the crypto to Chinese renminbi in offshore accounts.[40] Facilitation of this crypto theft is not just coming from unseen Chinese or Russian hackers or unknowing victims of phishing attacks through LinkedIn or Skype; some of the support is even coming from Americans. In April 2022 the Justice Department announced the sentencing of American Virgil Griffith for knowingly conspiring to provide technical advice and services to the DPRK regime on how to use blockchain and cryptocurrency technology to launder funds. Griffith had attended a DPRK cryptocurrency conference in April 2019 (without obtaining an OFAC license) and conspired to get other U.S. citizens to join his efforts.[41] In addition to naming and indicting North Korean individuals (Justice Department action of February 2021 discussed shortly), the United States sought in May 2022 a UN Security Council resolution blacklisting and freezing the assets of the Lazarus Group, which China and Russia vetoed on the grounds that further sanctioning of the regime "will make the

TECHNOLOGY AND CYBERSECURITY   51

situation worse."[42] The U.S. Treasury Department has also sanctioned virtual cryptocurrency mixers Blender.io and Tornado Cash in May 2022 and August 2022, respectively, for laundering North Korean–stolen virtual currency.[43]

While North Korean hacking amounts to cyber theft rather than cyberterrorism, in August 2022 the Biden administration confirmed publicly what many had expected—that these stolen funds are used for financing of weapons of mass destruction (WMD) proliferation, which makes the activity more significant for national security. Deputy National Security Adviser for Cyber and Emerging Technology Anne Neuberger stated that the DPRK "use[s] cyber to gain, we estimate, up to a third of [stolen crypto] funds to fund their missile program."[44] A UN Report in 2022 estimated between 2020 and 2021 the DPRK stole in excess of $50 million in crypto for financing the ballistic missile program. In March 2022 Lazarus Group stole over $600 million in cryptocurrency from blockchain network Ronin used by NFT game Axie Infinity in the largest reported crypto heist to date.[45] A month later, Harmony digital currency platform reported a $100 million theft that is attributed to North Korea.[46] In October 2022 law enforcement and financial regulatory authorities in Japan released a report naming the Lazarus Group and detailing years of DPRK attacks against Japanese blockchain firms and crypto-asset-related firms. These included thefts of $45 million from Zaif Crypto Exchange in 2018 and $24 million from Bitcoin Japan in 2019.[47] A report by Chainalysis estimated that North Korean hacking netted the regime over $840 million in the first half of 2022. The pace of this activity is unlikely to slow down. A former CIA analyst described cryptocurrency hacking as a new "way of life" for the regime.[48] One former FBI agent termed the regime, "a crypto superpower" by any standard.[49]

MONEY LAUNDERING

A UN report in 2019 found that at least one North Korean national was behind Marine Chain, which claimed to facilitate the purchase and sale of ships using an Ethereum-based blockchain cryptocurrency token. Marine Chain was registered in Hong Kong on April 12, 2018, and allowed for partial ownership of maritime vessels to be purchased and traded in exchange for cryptocurrency.⁵⁰ However, the platform actually served as a medium for North Korea to launder money via cryptocurrency. The Marine Chain platform was identified on cryptocurrency social media forums as a direct copy of another marine vessel cryptocurrency platform, shipowner.io. From its registration in April 2018 until it closed on May 28, 2018, Marine Chain was hosted on four different IP addresses. CEO Captain Jonathan Foong Kah Keong was linked to Marine Chain via LinkedIn and quickly identified as a North Korean collaborator who previously supported two companies that facilitated North Korean sanction-evasion activities in Singapore.⁵¹

North Korean hackers have also used social media influencers to launder money on the regime's behalf. Canadian American citizen Ghaleb Alaumary pled guilty for his involvement in money-laundering schemes orchestrated by North Korean hackers. Among Alaumary's coconspirators were Nigerian influencer Ramon Olorunwa Abbas, also known as "Ray Hushpuppi." Abbas is known for showcasing his luxurious lifestyle on social media platforms such as Instagram, where he has over two million followers. The U.S. Department of Justice (DOJ) accused Abbas of conspiring with Alaumary to launder millions of dollars from a North Korean hack of a Maltese bank in 2019.⁵²

OTHER TARGETS OF CYBER ATTACKS

COMMERCIAL ORGANIZATIONS

The WannaCry 2.0 ransomware attack of May 2017 is one of the most notorious cyber incidents of the past decade and falls into both the financial crimes and disruption categories.⁵³ WannaCry 2.0 propagated through two weaknesses discovered by the National Security Agency (NSA), DoublePulsar and EternalBlue, to create a back door and spread in digital systems. Once inside a system, the malware encrypts files, and the perpetrator demands payment in Bitcoin from the user to release the files and unlock the computer.

According to a Health and Human Services Department 2017 report, WannaCry infected as many as 250,000 computers in more than 150 countries around the world and was the largest ransomware attack at the time. The attack exploited a vulnerability in the unpatched Microsoft Windows 7 operating system. The attack targeted high-profile victims, including the National Health Service (NHS) in the U.K., Deutsche Bahn, and Taiwan Semiconductor Manufacturing Corporation (TSMC). The NHS reported not only the loss of patient data, but the cancellation of thousands of appointments and surgeries, relocation of emergency patients, rerouting of ambulances, and limited functioning based on the use of pen and paper rather than computers.[54] TSMC, the world's largest producer of semiconductors, was forced to close production. Even after the malware was disabled and stopped spreading, the fixes did not recover files from infected systems. WannaCry 2.0 was eventually stopped by British cybersecurity researcher Marcus Hutchins, who discovered the malicious program's kill switch. Kaspersky, a cybersecurity firm, estimates the total economic loss from the attack (which it refers to as a cyber "global epidemic") at $4 billion and further warns that many computer systems remain vulnerable. Given the potential spread, especially within key technology and government entities, this cost is relatively small. Furthermore, it is unlikely that the North Koreans made a significant profit from this attack. The ransom message delivered to infected computers demanded payment of $300 in Bitcoin in three days, doubling to $600 in six days; nonpayment resulted in the deletion of the files. However, word spread that payment did not in fact lead to file recovery. The exact paycheck for the owners of the Bitcoin wallets is unknown, but estimates range between $100,000 and $200,000.[55]

Digital forensics matched code lines in WannaCry 2.0 to previous versions of software created by the Lazarus Group.[56] Although North Korean officials initially dismissed the charge that the attack was linked to North Korea, evidence continued to accrue, and in December 2017 the United States formally asserted North Korea hackers were behind WannaCry 2.0. Although no government officials are referenced by name in the report, hacker Park Jin Hyok and the Lazarus Group, as well as their front company Chosun Expo Joint Venture, are named and subject to sanctions.

Some countries agree with the U.S. government that North Korea is responsible for WannaCry 2.0, while also asserting the culpability of the NSA.[57] They assert the NSA should have reported EternalBlue, which allowed the virus to spread, to Microsoft for correction. Instead, the NSA exploited the weakness and reported its existence only once the theft of the information by the Shadow Brokers, a Russian hacking group, became public. Coupled with the Sony hack in 2014, the WannaCry 2.0 ransomware epidemic put North Korea into the top tier of cyber-capable nations alongside Iran, Russia, and China. Moreover, the Lazarus Group emerged as one of the most sophisticated North Korean Advanced Persistent Threat actors, especially in light of its collaborations with the crimeware organization Trickbot.[58]

MATA FRAMEWORK AND DEPLOYMENT OF VHD AND TFLOWER RANSOMWARE

In 2020 Kaspersky discovered that a European firm was targeted with a ransomware called VHD. Kaspersky researchers believe that the VHD ransomware is a more sophisticated version of the WannaCry 2.0 ransomware. The analysis noted that unlike other ransomware attacks in which multiple cyber gangs participate at different points in the hacking process, in the VHD attacks it is likely that the North Korean hackers acted alone. One possible explanation for this change in strategy is that the North Korean hackers did not want to share profits with additional parties, although researchers added that having one group complete the entire hacking process would decrease the attack's efficiency.[59]

Researchers at Sygnia, a cybersecurity company, also found that North Korean hackers are likely behind the latest TFlower ransomware attacks. These attacks employ the MATA framework, which was already attributed to North Korean hackers. The TFlower ransomware was first identified in 2019, but no one at the time was able to determine the creator of the ransomware or the group behind the subsequent attacks. The fact that the TFlower ransomware has now been used in tandem with the MATA framework suggests that North Korean hackers are collaborating with the creators of TFlower, or potentially that North Korean hackers were behind the TFlower ransomware all along.[60]

ESPIONAGE: HEALTHCARE AND VACCINE HACKING

In 2020 Microsoft implicated North Korean groups Zinc (Microsoft's designation for the Lazarus Group) and Cerium (also known as Bureau 325, see subsequent discussion) and a Russian group named Strontium in an attempt to hack at least nine healthcare organizations in Canada, France, India, and the United States.[61] Microsoft accused Zinc of using spear-phishing techniques to gain the credentials of health services employees, and Cerium of engaging in similar tactics and even posing as World Health Organization (WHO) representatives.[62] In December 2020 IBM's X-force, the company's commercial cybersecurity research team, reported that hackers were targeting Covid-19 vaccines' cold chain supply lines via an international spear-phishing campaign.[63]

In November 2020 North Korean hackers targeted British-Swedish pharmaceutical company AstraZeneca, one of the major Covid-19 vaccine developers. The hackers posed as job recruiters to send corrupted job description documents to AstraZeneca staff through platforms such as LinkedIn and WhatsApp. These documents contained malicious code that enabled hackers to gain access to staff computers and potential Covid-19 research. Because the hacking efforts were not targeted, however, they were unsuccessful in procuring substantive research. North Korean hackers also targeted nine healthcare firms, including Johnson & Johnson and Novavax Inc. In February 2021 South Korea's National Intelligence Service accused North Korea of launching a digital espionage attempt on pharmaceutical giant Pfizer, with the intent to steal information on coronavirus vaccines and treatments.[64]

Recent private-sector and U.S. government open-source studies locate the focus of this activity in the RGB's Bureau 325, the existence of which was publicly acknowledged in January 2021. Most likely at the direction of Kim Jong-un, the unit grew out of RGB reorganization of priorities with the onset of the pandemic. This unit drew on existing hackers in different cyber units and newly minted graduates in the computer science and IT fields. It is tasked with targeting major pharmaceutical and biotechnology companies to extract information about

Covid-19 vaccines (and probably newly developed antivirals) and about how the international community was responding to the pandemic. According to a March 2022 Mandiant report, "Bureau 325 houses the DPRK Covid-19 focused unit and corresponds to activities tracked in the open source as 'CERIUM.' We suspect that individuals from several previously tracked clusters—including TEMP.Hermit, and Kimsuky—were also drafted to Bureau 325 to respond to high priority operations from DPRK leadership."[65] Kimsuky, also known as Velvet Chollima, had been known to use malicious malware and spear-phishing attacks since 2012, targeting universities and biomedical engineering expertise. TEMP.Hermit is believed to be an RGB operation that from 2013 targets primarily defense, industry, and financial institutions in South Korea.[66]

TARGETING CYBERSECURITY RESEARCHERS

Starting in 2020, North Korean hackers began targeting cybersecurity researchers using a creative form of social engineering to gain access to the researchers' computer data and networks. According to Google's Threat Analysis Group, the hackers created fake social media profiles on Twitter, LinkedIn, and Discord, among other platforms, and contacted cybersecurity researchers, asking them to work together on projects and write posts on the hackers' blog.[67] Researchers who downloaded the Visual Studio Project files to collaborate on the fake project unwittingly downloaded a malicious program, letting the hackers into their systems. Researchers who clicked on links to the hackers' blog also downloaded corrupting malware. Unlike other North Korean hacking efforts, this attack employed social engineering to fool cybersecurity researchers into believing they were working with like-minded research professionals. In reality, they were giving hackers access to their own computers.[68]

ATTACKS AGAINST MEDIA TARGETS

In 2014 British television company Channel 4 and production firm Mammoth Screen were targets of North Korean cyberattacks.[69] These attacks occurred at roughly the same time as and under similar circumstances to the hack on Sony Pictures Entertainment. Channel 4 and Mammoth Screen announced the production of a new television drama series, *Opposite Number*, in conjunction with Netflix and scripted by Oscar-nominated screenplay writer Matt Charman. The series was set in London, Washington, DC, and North Korea, in which the lead characters, a British nuclear scientist and an American intelligence operative operating undercover as humanitarian aid workers, are taken prisoner by the North Korean regime. The North Korean government strongly protested the new "slanderous" TV series and demanded the British government shut the production down. While the hacks caused limited damage to the British firms, the hackers reportedly had control of data on a scale not unlike that accomplished in the Sony attack. This was enough of a threat to cause the producers to halt production of the show. Producers later claimed publicly that *Opposite Number* did not move forward because of a lack of financing, but the real reason had to do with fears of the damage that North Korea could do to the companies. Although the U.S. government was outspoken about the Sony attack, the U.K. government remained relatively silent in this case.

ATTACKS AGAINST SOUTH KOREAN TARGETS

A major target of North Korea cyber activity has been South Korean firms, governments, and media. North Korean hackers have gone after a diverse set of South Korean public and private institutions, including nuclear power plants and research centers in South Korea since 2014, stealing data through various methods. In December 2014 South Korea's Korea Hydro and Nuclear Power Co. Ltd.—the operator of South Korea's twenty-three nuclear reactors—announced its computer systems had been hacked. Nearly six thousand phishing emails were sent to more than three thousand current and former employees of the company, resulting in the theft of nuclear power plant designs through infected employee computers.[70]

In June 2021 the Korea Atomic Energy Research Institute's internal server was also hacked over twelve days through a vulnerability in the institute's virtual private network (VPN) system. A member of South Korea's National Assembly Intelligence Committee reported that IP addresses connected to the hack were identical to those used by the North Korean hacking group Kimsuky in attacks targeting pharmaceutical companies in 2020.[71] The South Korean government did not confirm what information was stolen, but experts hypothesize that the hackers could have accessed information on manufacturing special equipment based on nuclear power or upgrading graphite moderated reactors. Alongside this attack, Korea Aerospace Industries (KAI) and the Korea Institute of Fusion Energy were also targeted by the North Korea-affiliated hacking scheme. Reports suspect that data on KAI's rocket propulsion technologies developed for the South's first indigenous space launch vehicle were stolen, and other sensitive information on defense technology may have been accessed as well.[72] Although South Korea has one of the most advanced information technology systems, North Korean hackers have successfully attacked and acquired valuable information from a variety of South Korean institutions. North Korean hackers extracted several military secrets from South Korea after infiltrating its intranet in September 2016, according to an announcement by the Ministry of National Defense of South Korea.[73] South Korea stated that the malignant code was similar to the code used by North Korea in the past, and that the hackers' IP addresses were in Shenyang, China, which is near North Korea and has been cited as an operating ground for North Korean hackers in the past.

According to South Korea's National Intelligence Service, in February 2016 North Korean hackers stole the personal information and text messages from the smartphones of scores of key personnel in the South Korean government. In August 2019 hackers targeted a security company that was offering software to South Korean government agencies, such as the presidential residence at the Blue House, National Assembly, Ministry of Foreign Affairs, National Tax Service, and Defense Acquisition Program Administration.[74]

The Ministry of Unification, which also handles North Korean refugee affairs, is another target of North Korean hackers. The ministry reported a doubling of attempted hacks between 2017 and 2018, with more than 630 attempts in the latter year.[75] In December 2019 North Korean hackers stole from a personal computer the names, birthdays, and addresses of 997 North Korean refugees living in South Korea.[76]

The computer was vulnerable to attack due to a failure to follow protocols on storing personally identifying information for refugees on a separate network. North Korea has been known to punish entire families and communities for an individual's infractions, making the identity of refugees sensitive information not only for their own safety, but for that of any family members they left behind.

U.S. TARGETS OF NORTH KOREAN CYBER ACTIVITIES

An unsealed indictment by the U.S. Department of Justice in February 2021 revealed that three North Korean hackers—Jon Chang Hyok, Kim Il, and Park Jin Hyok—were involved in various criminal cyber activities worldwide, including in the United States. The alleged hackers were members of the RGB, stationed in countries outside North Korea, including China and Russia. Park, in particular, was also charged with a criminal complaint unsealed in September 2018. The hackers were accused of engaging in a conspiracy to inflict damage and embezzle data and money from foreign companies and governments for revenge or financial gains. They were also involved in securing strategic and financial interests of the North Korean government and its leader, Kim Jong-un.[77]

According to the indictment, the hackers are alleged to have committed crimes such as the Sony Pictures Entertainment attack in 2014, bank heists around the world from 2015 to 2019 to steal more than $1.2 billion, and cyber ATM cash-out thefts, including $6.1 million from BankIslami's ATMs in October 2018. In addition to penetrating financial firms, the hackers were also involved in cyberattacks targeting cryptocurrencies and other online financial markets, where they were accused of creating and deploying WannaCry 2.0 ransomware and malicious cryptocurrency applications between 2017 and 2020, as well as attacking cryptocurrency companies to steal tens of millions of dollars' worth of cryptocurrency, including a $11.8 million theft from a financial services company in New York in August 2020.

Furthermore, the hackers also used spear-phishing tactics using emails and texts to hack U.S. government offices from 2016 through 2020, where the targets included Department of Defense and Department of State, as well as U.S. government contractors and defense companies.⁷⁸ A report from the United Nations in August 2020 also notes that North Korean hacking groups Lazarus and Kimsuky used spear-phishing techniques to target twenty-eight UN officials, including eleven officials from six members of the Security Council, by sending "security alert" emails with malicious links through the Gmail accounts of the targeted individuals in mid-March 2020.⁷⁹ Moreover, in March and early April 2020, an additional forty UN officials' email and personal WhatsApp accounts became the targets of North Korean cyber operation campaigns.⁸⁰

GOALS AND DOCTRINE OF THE CYBER PROGRAMS

What are the goals of North Korea's cyber program? Were early assessments of their goals correct or incorrect? What is the doctrine, to the extent one can be induced, behind the capability? Is it for defense, deterrence, or offense? These questions are not easy to answer given the opacity that surrounds the program and its purveyors. Unlike the extant weapons programs, these capabilities are more challenging to track through national technical means. In terms of doctrine, there are no reasons for the regime to be transparent about its strategy or goals. Perhaps there are fuller answers to these questions in the official, classified realm. Nevertheless, we can induce some useful propositions, and even answers, from open-source methods.

The first task is to understand, based on the targets of cyber activities, what the goals are and why cyber is the tool of choice to achieve these goals. The three primary objectives of North Korean hacking operations are: (1) acquiring money, (2) disrupting adversaries, and (3) espionage. As can be gleaned from the majority of the attacks since 2014, North Korean hackers have significantly increased their focus on acquiring cash, cryptocurrency, and corporate data as a means to fund the regime, which has been hit with a series of UN sanctions, as well as the self-imposed three-year lockdown starting January 2020 due to the Covid-19 pandemic. In this regard, there is a correlation between the success of economic and financial sanctions and North Korea's increasing use of cyberattacks for petty theft. In 2014 there were only twenty new sanction designations placed on North Korea;

but now this number is well over eighty.[81] Acquiring funds meets several regime needs: keeping the meager domestic economy afloat, bankrolling the lifestyles of the elites, and financing the regime's military programs, including its nuclear weapons development. The hackers' success is at least in part due to the weak regulations and emerging technology supporting the world's new financial technology institutions.[82]

DISRUPTING ADVERSARIES

For North Korea, cyber is the ultimate asymmetric instrument. The regime recognizes the advantage that cyber warfare provides smaller nations that lack traditional military power, and it has invested in developing its hacking capabilities.[83] Kim Jong-un highlighted the utility of cyber war tactics, stating, "Cyber warfare, along with nuclear weapons and missiles is an 'all-purpose sword' that guarantees our military's capability to strike relentlessly."[84] Cyberattacks provide North Korea with the ability to anonymously disrupt the use of high-technology U.S. weaponry by blinding or disabling sensor, guidance, or communications systems. Moreover, North Korea can engage in cyber-warfare with relatively little risk of retaliation because it remains less vulnerable than its primary high-tech adversaries, the United States and South Korea, because it is less wired overall. Less than 1 percent of North Koreans have access to the internet.[85] Because North Korea operates some of its cyber operation cells in other countries (e.g., China), this complicates any U.S. response. Furthermore, because cyberattacks are often diffuse and targets are varied, it is difficult for governments to launch a coordinated response.

According to South Korean intelligence reports, North Korea's RGB employs more than seven thousand personnel, including both full-time cyber operatives and agency support staff, to explore and exploit cyber vulnerabilities within industries and governments around the world.[86] Despite the regime's tight control on information, which effectively prevents the vast majority of North Koreans from accessing the internet, the RGB hacker army is considered to be world-class.

The North Korean regime actively identifies and recruits promising young math and science students to learn coding and join its hacking operations.⁸⁷ The series of high-profile attacks that followed the Sony Pictures Entertainment hack in 2014 have been increasingly sophisticated and appear to be the work of a widening circle of players working in the RGB orbit.⁸⁸ The development of this technologically capable cyber elite is fundamental to the broader aims of the expansion of the cyber program, where North Korean students meet or outpace their American university counterparts in terms of their knowledge of computer science: "Kim Chaek University of Technology and Kim Il-sung University vacuum up the most talented teenagers from the specialized math and computer high schools . . . often outperform[ing] American and Chinese colleges in the International Collegiate Programming Contest."⁸⁹

The North Korean regime also likely receives some forms of assistance from its Russian and Chinese neighbors, both of which have been historical allies. North Korean hackers attend Chinese universities and even work in China, sending funds back to North Korea. According to researcher Ed Caesar's interviews with North Korean defectors, three teams of North Korean "IT workers" were based in the Chinese city of Dalian, making money out of designing mobile video games for the Japanese, South Korean, and Chinese markets. Former U.S. assistant attorney general John Demers also claimed that "North Korea is connected to the world through essentially Russian and Chinese infrastructure. . . . Russia and China are well aware of what's going on and have facilitated some of it."⁹⁰ Analysts also suspect that some North Korean hacks were actually conducted within Chinese borders.⁹¹

ESPIONAGE AND INTELLECTUAL PROPERTY THEFT

The third driver of cyber strategy is espionage. While the first driver is commercial (stealing money) and the second is military (asymmetrical workarounds), the third driver stems from the dilemma faced by the reclusive regime and its ideology. The concept of *juche* or "self-reliance" that undergirds the regime's thinking restricts it from interacting with the world and within the marketplace of ideas in science and technology. Thus the regime relies on its cyber capabilities to spy and to steal knowledge from the outside world in ways that enable the regime to stay cloistered and to remain true to its self-reliance ideology. Nowhere has this been more apparent than in the way North Korea has dealt with the Covid-19 pandemic.

In January 2020 North Korea closed its border with China to prevent transmission of the Covid-19 virus into its country. The regime is deathly afraid of an outbreak for which its decrepit public health system is utterly unprepared.[92] Yet this move also likely added to North Korea's domestic financial pressures and potentially spurred the regime to increase its financial hacking efforts abroad. Covid-19 also presented the North Korean regime with another target: vaccine data. While the exact number of Covid-19 cases in North Korea is unknown—the government claims there have been none—the regime's vaccine hacking efforts indicate that there may be a domestic Covid-19 outbreak or concern about a future spike in cases. The WHO and COVAX estimated that approximately 1.9 million AstraZeneca vaccine doses were allocated to North Korea through the India Serum Institute in the first half of 2021, and an additional 4.7 million doses were allocated in November 2021. The plan was delayed, however, because the North Korean government refused to accept the vaccines, requesting to redistribute them to other countries with urgent needs.[93] Even then, North Korea's public healthcare infrastructure is underequipped for patient delivery, and the economy is struggling as a result of the multiple health and economic stresses.[94]

NORTH KOREA'S CYBER ACTIVITIES IN CONTEXT

North Korea's propensity to carry out cyberattacks does not appear to follow the same pattern as its nuclear and missile provocations. If nuclear tests and ballistic missile launches ebb and flow, cyberattacks are constant. For example, recent studies show that the regime tends to refrain from major ballistic missile launches and nuclear tests in periods when Washington and Pyongyang are engaged in ongoing bilateral diplomatic negotiations, presumably because it does not want to create disruptions to the discussions.[95] But these political considerations have no impact on cyber activities. Since the 2014 Sony hack, the United States and North Korea held three summits in 2018 and 2019. Yet, despite the appearance of cooperation, North Korea continued to ramp up cyberattacks during those two years, targeting banks and other institutions. This discrepancy could be because the regime compartmentalizes its cyber activities—that is, while it may link weapons tests with political pressure on the adversary in periods of nondialogue, it may see cyber as a weapon for financial crimes, intellectual property (IP) theft, and hard-currency generation, untied to broader negotiations with the United States. In other words, cyber is a criminal tool rather than a strategic one.

China's role in the proliferation of North Korean cyber activities is less clear. We know that China has facilitated these activities in the past. As already noted, the Chinese government has allowed North Korean hackers to matriculate and obtain training at its universities, and it has allowed the North to launch attacks from within its borders.[96] It has allowed North Korean IT workers to act as contractors to Chinese tech firms that do business with Western countries. But there is less publicly available data on whether China has been a target of North Korean hacking, whether China has clamped down on such activities, and whether China has offered help to South Korean victims of North Korean hacking. One can presume that the level of cooperation by China over such activities will increase if U.S.-China relations are on a positive track, and that it will decrease as Sino-American relations take a negative turn. Indeed, as U.S.-China competition ramped up during the Trump and Biden administrations, China has been unsubtle in statements that leverage Beijing's cooperation over North Korea as a cost of U.S.-China competition. China's then-foreign minister Wang Yi emphasized "dialogue and peaceful settlement" for denuclearization of North Korea while also claiming that the United States "needs to reconsider its incessant military threats and pressure on the DPRK . . . show its sincerity and make a response."[97] While these statements focus on the denuclearization issue, one can assume that they represent an overall posture by Beijing that would apply to cyber as well, even though it is evident that U.S.-China cooperation to detect and deter further hacking would be beneficial to all.

North Korea's targeting of private-sector and financial entities stems not just from petty theft motives but also from carefully calibrated strategic thinking. While there is no established "escalation ladder" for cyber warfare, states have sent deterrence signals that cyberattacks against critical infrastructure (e.g., water, nuclear power) or government installations would be considered acts against the state worthy of military retaliation. In this regard, North Korea may see financial targets not just as profitable but also as prudent operations in a gray zone of aggression that will not escalate into military conflict. North Koreans also have learned that the private sector will build systems to defend against penetration, but once a hack occurs, the firm generally wants to remedy the problem quickly, even if it means paying off the hacker. This sort of reaction generally weighs against a coordinated response with the government or with other firms. This makes them easier prey for North Korean hackers.

As noted earlier, the proximate cause for cyberhacking of financial institutions may be the economic dislocation caused by North Korea's three-year-long border closing in response to the global pandemic. But the uptick in cyber activities took place long before Covid-19 seized the world and coincided with a secular decline in the health of the economy. Since 2016, North Korea's GDP growth has trended downward.

Such economic uncertainty is a likely driver for hacking for financial gain to fund the government and maintain the loyalty of the North Korean people (see table 3.1).

CYBER DOCTRINE: OFFENSIVE AND DEFENSIVE POSITIONING

Although there is no published doctrine for North Korea's cyber program, one can think about cyber doctrine, strategy, and tactics in

TABLE 3.1 North Korea annual GDP growth

Year	GDP growth (%)
2016	+3.9
2017	−3.5
2018	−4.1
2019	+0.4
2020	−4.5
2021	−0.1

Source: "North Korea GDP Annual Growth Rate," Trading Economics, 2022, https://tradingeconomics.com/north-korea/gdp-annual-growth-rate#.

three categories: (1) peacetime, (2) coercive diplomacy, and (3) wartime. These are not reified categories as North Korean operations will often blur between them, but as a heuristic tool they helps us to decipher and understand better how the regime may think about these capabilities.

As noted earlier, the capabilities are housed in the Reconnaissance General Bureau, General Staff Department, and Korean People's Army. According to a CSIS report, the KPA cyber capabilities are rooted in KPA electronic warfare concepts, while the RGB cyber units are more involved in espionage and financial criminal activities.[98]

The strategy in peacetime is readily inducible from the data. Given economic hardships, the focus has been strongly weighted toward financial crimes, petty theft, and hard currency accumulation, largely under the realm of the RGB. Targeting private-sector entities is particularly useful from a DPRK perspective because they are easy, vulnerable targets, and usually the response is atomized and wanting of more coordination. Targeting governments for cybercriminal actions is also plausible because the gray zone in which cybercrimes operate usually does not escalate into a military conflict. Targeted governments generally will not respond to cyberattacks or espionage attempts with military strikes.

In wartime, North Korea's cyber doctrine appears to center on offensive measures. Portions of it can be gleaned by examining the KPA's existing military doctrine. The KPA comprises North Korea's five military branches: the Ground Force, Naval Force, Air and Anti-Air Force, Strategic Rocket Force, and Special Operation Force.[99] Its operational and tactical doctrine contains three elements: quick/decisive action, mixed tactics, and surprise attacks.[100] The KPA relies on attacks that have "some form of surprise at the strategic, operational, or tactical level" and avoids drawn out conflicts due to concerns about a lack of resources to sustain a fight. The KPA also emphasizes the use of mixed tactics or fighting with both regular and irregular means. The use of irregular means refers to North Korea's strategy of fighting conflicts on two fronts and entails the use of special operations forces to attack or harass key infrastructure facilities, logistic centers, and command centers within its adversary's borders.[101] The DPRK invests in cyber as part of an asymmetric strategy designed to compensate for the inability to rival ROK conventional military capabilities. Other elements of this strategy include WMD, ballistic missiles, and submarine-launched WMD capabilities. The DPRK sees cyber capabilities as a way to disrupt and blind high-tech military networks of adversaries. As a recent study noted, "While the DPRK may not get its own force multiplier from cyber capabilities, it may get a 'force de-multiplier' against the United States and ROK."[102] Relevant cyber operations include targeting weak links to access vulnerable systems, fighting adversaries on multiple fronts by targeting security infrastructures to discover relevant intelligence, and demonstrating power to the international community by targeting adversarial institutions and states. As North Korea's cyber program has expanded, so too has the KPA's reliance on increased offensive cyberspace operations to bolster its multidomain tactical/operational doctrine.

There is some evidence that DPRK views cyber as a strategic weapon. As noted, Kim Jong-un deemed it an "all-purpose sword" in the portfolio of military capabilities.[103] This suggests that in addition to financial criminal activity, North Korea may leverage cyber capabilities as a tool of blackmail or coercion, as it has done with nuclear weapons and ballistic missiles. It also may be part of an offensive military attack strategy. The KPA's doctrine focuses on avoiding a protracted conflict and instead prosecuting quick, decisive strikes frontally and in the rear of the adversary while disrupting their ability to respond. The purpose would be to win early incremental victories before the United States could reinforce its minimal presence on the peninsula. One could see how cyber capabilities that disrupt U.S. and ROK communications and logistics would fit into this strategy.

The Gulf War and the Iraq War in 2003 had a major impact on the way North Korea assessed cyber capabilities. As Joseph Bermudez observes, the KPA carefully monitored U.S. operations, realizing the importance of networked militaries, seamless flow of real time information, and electronic warfare.[104] North Korea learned the importance of employing these capabilities in offensive operations like jamming radars and air defenses, as well as the importance of guarding against vulnerabilities to the adversary's electronic warfare tools. In sum, North Korean cyber capabilities meet the definition of an asymmetric strategy. That is, it pursues the ability not to match the adversary; rather, precisely because it cannot hope to match such modern capabilities, it pursues cyber as an alternative to counter and neutralize the gaps. However, one should fully expect that the KPA has training capabilities aimed at using cyber in a warfighting scenario to disrupt command and control communications of the adversary as part of an offensive blitzkrieg-type attack.

The third element of the doctrine relates to cyber as a tool of coercive diplomacy. This is not unlike a strategic template used by the regime regarding its nuclear capabilities in peacetime. Pyongyang develops its capabilities to alter the balance of power on the peninsula. These new strategic realities give North Korea not only an asymmetric advantage in peacetime, but also a coercive bargaining ability.[105] The strategy leverages the peaceful status quo by disrupting it, thereby compelling the counterpart to pay off the North to return to the peaceful status quo ante. In the longer term, the strategy tries to leverage declining confidence—in the case of nuclear weapons, in the U.S. extended deterrence guarantees—putting more coercive pressure on the South.

One could see how such a strategic logic could be applied to DPRK use of cyber capabilities. In the form of either terrorist attacks or destructive hacking of critical infrastructure, DPRK cyber strategy could be aimed at disrupting the lives of South Koreans in ways that force Seoul to respond. Moreover, the absence of U.S. support in the case of cyberhacks would further weaken Seoul's will. At the same time, U.S. authorities would restrain South Korea from retaliating militarily to cyberhacks to avoid an outbreak of war on the peninsula.

POLICY

Given what we know about the evolution of the cyber threat, its targets, and its goals, what is the policy challenge for the United States? How should Washington deal with this issue given the other issues it faces (e.g., WMD) with North Korea? Are there policies that can be coordinated with allies and partners?

The lack of suitable responses to cyberattacks, including countermeasures and insurance safety nets to cover damages, has harmed the public and private sectors alike. The limited existing defense capabilities demonstrate the need to consider not only how to deter such attacks, but how to react to them—particularly as North Korea strengthens its offensive capabilities and ability to identify and exploit vulnerabilities in technology and policy. Although North Korea's hacking operations have primarily targeted financial institutions, their successes underscore American challenges in U.S. domestic policy regarding critical infrastructure, cybersecurity capabilities, and public-private sector cybersecurity partnerships. Public-private partnerships are horizontal in nature, as neither the government entity nor the private firm controls or manages the other.[106] These complex interorganization entities give rise to many challenges in establishing cohesive and actionable partnership initiatives.

A significant domestic policy challenge for the United States is an alignment of cyberspace defense. The primary goal of cybersecurity in the private sector is protecting and maintaining financial and reputational integrity, while the government's objective is protecting national security.[107] A survey conducted on cybersecurity measures within the private sector showed that innovation centered on saving costs rather than protecting data and information.[108] Given the integrated nature of digital and physical systems, however, protecting data at low cost may be insufficient to protect U.S. national security. Businesses critical to U.S. infrastructure must be incentivized to develop cybersecurity capabilities even if those capabilities might reduce that firm's bottom line.

The U.S. National Infrastructure Advisory Council's (NIAC) domestic cybersecurity policy, analysis, and recommendations also emphasize the importance of upgrading existing infrastructure to protect against cyber threats. Established in 2001, NIAC advises the president on strategies to reduce risk to critical infrastructure sectors, including assessing physical and cyber threats. NIAC is a nonpartisan organization composed of senior executives from the private sector, federal authorities, and state and local government officials, and it operates under the purview of the Department of Homeland Security.[109]

In 2017 NIAC conducted an internal assessment on U.S. cyber readiness and provided recommendations to the White House, two of which are highlighted here due to their relevance to U.S. domestic policy regarding public-private partnerships. First, NIAC recommends that the private and public sector increase the sharing of actionable information regarding cyber threats to firms and government entities.[110] One major problem associated with the current information sharing system is the security clearance process. Security clearance investigations can be lengthy and are a prerequisite requirement to authorizing technical professionals in the private sector to access and operate within secure facilities prior to and following cyber threats and/or attacks.[111] Sharing information relating to cyberattacks requires an authorization process to confirm there is valid reason to grant access to classified information. Efforts to establish a public-private sector relationship pertaining to cybersecurity risk transparency, coordination, and communication will necessitate a standard security clearance framework for private-sector companies involved in critical U.S. infrastructure. The clearance process presents a domestic policy challenge because private-sector employees may not meet the standards required for federal background checks; may choose not to undergo a background check; or, if investigated, add significantly to the current federal security clearance investigation backlog. In January 2021 an estimated 213,000 investigations were in process.[112] Adding private-sector employees to the existing backlog would require years of processing and substantial budget increases.

The second relevant NIAC recommendation is the need to strengthen U.S. cyber capabilities by prioritizing the expansion of cyber workforce programs.[113] In 2021 the Department of Defense (DOD) released the U.S. Defense Industrial Base (DIB) Industrial Capabilities Report, an overview of the defense industry. The assessments indicated that industrial and technology sectors must adapt to the mercurial geopolitical and economic reality of the twenty-first century or leave America in a "permanent national security deficit." The report also presented a significant domestic policy challenge related to developing and protecting critical cybersecurity infrastructure: a diminishing STEM workforce. As of 2019, American students were only 21 and 19 percent of the computer science and electrical engineering student body, respectively, in American universities.[114] The Bureau of Labor and Statistics has forecasted a 12 percent occupation growth in both fields by 2029 within the United States.[115]

Current projections suggest that the United States is preparing to enter a period of unmet demand for technically trained professionals. The upshot is that many industries in the country will become more vulnerable, particularly those in the defense manufacturing supply chain. The DOD's DIB report found that 99 percent of manufacturing establishments within the United States have fewer than five hundred employees and are unprepared to handle a cyberattack. Furthermore, "thirty-five percent of all cyberespionage attacks in the U.S. are targeted at the manufacturing sector."[116] Before the United States can mitigate cyber threats from abroad, it must first solve the domestic policy challenge of developing a technically trained workforce equipped to handle such problems.

In December 2020 NIAC provided a new report to President-elect Biden identifying multiple limitations in existing legislation intended to support critical infrastructure, many of which expanded on previous concerns mentioned in the 2017 report:

- The Cybersecurity State Coordinator Act of 2020, which directs the Cybersecurity and Infrastructure Security Agency (CISA) to develop state and local governments' cybersecurity capabilities, prohibits U.S. intelligence agencies from sharing information or coordinating with the private sector.
- Executive Order 13800 was signed in 2020 to improve access to classified information for owners and technical operators of critical infrastructure to assist with threat response and coordination, but it does not direct private-sector organizations to share cyber threats and does not "specify access to classified information."
- Executive Order 13691 signed in 2015 intended to direct "private companies . . . and agencies to share information related to cybersecurity risks and collaborate in as close to real time as possible," and develop "more efficient means for gathering [relevant] clearances," but not share classified information.[117]

The NIAC reports in 2017 and 2020 demonstrate that senior executives from private industry, government officials, and federal authorities recognize shortcomings in domestic cybersecurity policy, and that not much progress has been made during the three years between the two reports to mitigate the growing cyber risk.

How should the United States deal with this issue given the other issues it faces (e.g., WMD)? North Korea's nuclear threat is easier to manage than its cyber threat in many ways. The international community has already established clear rules and norms surrounding the development and use of nuclear weapons. Furthermore, even if North Korea did decide to launch a nuclear attack, it would invite retaliation that could end the regime. In contrast, there is little legal infrastructure to respond to cyber threats and attacks. Moreover, there is no established mutual understanding on deterrence against cyberattacks between adversaries and allies. In addition, the interconnectedness of the United States, South Korea, Japan, and other allied nations makes them an ideal target for cyberattacks.

North Korea's cyber program is also difficult to separate from its nuclear program, in part because it hacks financial institutions to fund the regime's nuclear and weapons development programs that have been hit by sanctions. Restraining, let alone dismantling, North Korea's nuclear program necessitates cutting off hacking as a means of funding the regime. Therefore, long-term, any plan to curtail either program must tackle the motivations of the North Korean leadership or await regime collapse, both of which become increasingly unlikely as hackers steal billions of dollars.

CURRENT FOREIGN POLICY RESPONSES

In February 2021 the U.S. Department of Justice indicted three North Korean nationals associated with APT38 of hacking and laundering funds to develop the country's illegal nuclear program. These charges demonstrate that despite economic sanctions and the Trump administration's attempts at negotiation, the United States has been unsuccessful in its attempts to halt the growth of the North Korean nuclear weapons program or cyberattacks. In August 2019 the UNSC accused North Korea of stealing nearly $2 billion dollars to siphon into its weapons programs and has already sanctioned firms and individuals associated with North Korean cyberattacks. As noted, the Biden administration tried for a UN Security Council resolution blacklisting and freezing the assets of Lazarus Group in May 2022, but the resolution was vetoed by China and Russia.

Despite the actions of the DOJ and UNSC, the lack of legal framework and regulations surrounding cyberspace is a serious challenge for states who seek to prosecute or punish North Korea for its illicit hacking activities. Challenges to effective cybercrime investigations include unclear reporting avenues, anonymization techniques vis-à-vis evidentiary requirements, timely collection, and the lack of defined cybercrime standards.[118]

SOME RECOMMENDATIONS

North Korea's cyberattacks have focused on stealing cash, cryptocurrency, and data, but the regime's increasingly sophisticated hacking abilities suggest that U.S. government entities and infrastructure, which remain vulnerable, could become future targets. The United States and its allies have imposed sanctions and indicted individuals in response to North Korean hacks. These policies, however, have failed to effectively deter or counter future attacks and strengthen the defensive capabilities of U.S. infrastructure. The U.S. government can pursue a range of strategies to increase American cyber resiliency, as well as respond effectively to, and ideally deter, future hacks.

Increase the quantity and quality of domestic tech talent: While leading American technology companies attract international talent with high salaries, the U.S. government faces a shortage of technology workers and struggles to recruit and retain talent to work in the government and defense sectors. First, the government can increase the quantity and quality of applications by streamlining the security clearance process and by forging partnerships with private firms in order to tap into a larger applicant pool, a move that is reportedly already under consideration.[119] In 2022 President Biden earmarked $11 billion for federal agencies to grow their cyber programs, each of which, including every branch of the armed forces, has developed a cyber division.[120] U.S. policymakers can also implement initial and retraining programs to adapt worker skills to the challenges related to cyber network defense and forensics. Cyber awareness training is already a required annual certification for all federal employees, but steps should be taken to increase routine security protocols, such as dual verification and/or card-enabled log-in on all systems, compartmentalization of sensitive systems, and increased routine scans, both human- and machine-run, for suspicious IPs. Given the prevalence of North Korean hacks on financial institutions, American and global financial firms should also adopt best practices to reduce the likelihood their organizations are hacked.

What are the drawbacks? Increasing the quality and quantity of cyber-proficient technology workers in the United States will be expensive and may require more than the $11 billion allocated by President Biden. Moreover, streamlining the onboarding process for new federal employees in a way that maintains the integrity of the security clearance process will be challenging and will generate additional costs.

Improve domestic and international cyber frameworks and awareness: Cybersecurity is a relatively new domain, and therefore frameworks and tools to enact and regulate laws, particularly on the global level, are in short supply. The United States can build and enforce robust accountability tools working through institutions, starting at home. First, it can follow the recommendations of NIAC and allow intelligence agencies to share hacking-related information with private firms when appropriate. The United States could then expand this model internationally and work with allied nations' cyber-defense institutions to monitor and respond to attacks.

Second, the United States can lead UN members to support the creation of an international body empowered to draft standards of conduct regarding the cyber landscape, particularly regarding acts of theft and sabotage. Codification can then lead to enforcement and create mechanisms governing retaliatory action for nefarious actors and compensation for victims. Although the attribution of cybercrimes will remain a challenge, the existence of a framework will improve coordination among states who seek to identify a perpetrator and offer an avenue for states to discuss these matters openly.

There are no illusions about the challenges of implementing such recommendations. Due to privacy and security concerns, it may be difficult to allow for coordination between cybersecurity firms and the intelligence community. Achieving an international consensus on the rules and norms surrounding cybersecurity will also be challenging. China and Russia both hold significant sway on the world stage and within the UN, actively engage in offensive cyberattacks against the United States and its allies, and have favorable ties with North Korea.

Strengthen cryptocurrency security: Given that most of the cyberattacks take place in blockchain and cryptocurrency, the Federal Trade Commission (FTC) should collaborate with financial institutions to carry out awareness campaigns. Most North Korean hackers breach crypto wallets through phishing attacks and other baits. Due to the anonymous nature of cryptocurrency exchanges, there is a lack of regulation and moderation. This leaves most of the actionable items to prevent hacking on the user's end. While two-factor authentication, seed words, and hardware wallets exist, many applications still allow users to opt out of them. Financial institutions and cryptocurrency exchange applications should invest in further securing crypto wallets and making additional security steps required for users. Moreover, user interaction and exchange should also be moderated in a standardized manner. Passing formal regulations regarding the cryptocurrency market is essential to prevent continued attacks.

Address the vulnerabilities: The most exploited vulnerable technical applications are Microsoft Office and Adobe Flash products.[121] The U.S. government should raise public awareness for institutions using these products to continuously update the products with the latest security patches. Moreover, establishing a communication channel with Microsoft and Adobe can also help fast-track cyberattack meditations. In recent years, North Korea's ransomware attacks have frequently targeted the U.S. healthcare sector. While the joint warning system from the FBI, Treasury Department, and CISA are useful, further steps to better equip vulnerable institutions are necessary. One recommendation is to have an advisor sent from the government to vulnerable institutions. These advisors could train the internal IT specialists on how to encrypt data, conduct regular scans on internet-facing devices, update patches, software, and operating systems, and train employees on phishing and other attacks. Having a formal advisor would incentivize the healthcare sector to make cybersecurity a priority by making the process convenient and effective.

Increase coordination with South Korea: First, the U.S. Department of State and the Ministry of Foreign Affairs of South Korea can affirm their shared values of justice, safety, privacy, and property rights, and to condemn North Korean hacking operations. Second, Washington and Seoul can strengthen communication and information exchange related to cyberattacks among the relevant government agencies, including the Ministry of National Defense, National Intelligence Service, Korean National Police Agency, and their American counterparts. Given that these institutions in the United States and South Korea often have overlapping responsibilities and may compete with one another, both governments should consider establishing a specific channel for discussing and responding to cyber threats to their nations. Such a channel would provide a framework for designating the responsibilities of different agencies as they pertain to North Korea.

Establish multilateral diplomatic dialogue to focus on North Korean cyberattacks: North Korean hackers operate and launder stolen money in numerous countries, including China, Russia, Belarus, and countries in Southeast Asia.[122] The U.S. government should closely track North Korean nationals posing as freelance computer engineers abroad. Moreover, the United States should lead the momentum to pass a comprehensive international convention on criminalizing and prosecuting cybercrimes in collaboration with the UN Office on Drugs and Crime.

Using the Six-Party Talks as a model, where North Korea, Japan, South Korea, China, Russia, and the United States discussed North Korean denuclearization, the United States can take the initiative to reassert strong, multilateral diplomatic engagement as a strategy within the region. U.S. policymakers can attempt to form the rules and norms surrounding hacking by North Korea with the most relevant parties in the region. Countries other than those six nations that are affected by North Korean cyberattacks could be included in any future negotiations with North Korea over its hacking efforts.

Prosecute retaliatory cyberattacks: The United States and its allies can launch retaliatory cyberattacks on North Korean targets to deter future hacks. These hacks could focus on North Korea's nuclear weapons facilities, or on servers with government data of interest to U.S. national security. The counterattacks would demonstrate that the United States and its allies will respond in kind when they, or one of their countries' firms, are targeted by North Korean hackers.

This option is not without challenges. First, it is difficult to trace the origin of a cyberattack, and even if the attack can be attributed to North Korea, it is often difficult to determine the appropriate level of response. Second, North Korean hackers might launch attacks outside North Korean borders, for example in China, thereby complicating a potential response because a counterstrike might necessitate targeting North Korean operations in another country. Finally, and perhaps most important, North Korea's technological backwardness makes it relatively resilient to cyberattacks, as most of the country's networks are not integrated. North Korea therefore enjoys a strategic advantage, because while it remains a hard target, the United States and its allies are integrated and vulnerable. A counterstrike by the United States could lead to a tit-for-tat where North Korean hackers could shift operations to focus on damaging physical power, utility, communication, transportation, or defense infrastructure in the United States or South Korea.

4

MARKETS AND CIVIL SOCIETY

ONE MORNING during a stay in Pyongyang as a U.S. government official many years ago, I was being driven from the guest house to the foreign ministry for some meetings. Along Ryomyong Avenue, the car passed ordinary citizens at a bus stop commuting to work, elders reading the newspaper on a park bench, and uniformed children chasing each other playfully as they walked to school. It was Pyongyang's version of the morning rush hour. I didn't think much of this ordinary scene, other than that it was not unlike 7:30 in the morning in almost any city around the world.

Returning later in the afternoon, my car came upon similarly uniformed students now finished with the school day. Unlike the morning scene, however, these students were now marching in groups down the main thoroughfare with the lead student holding a signboard, which I could make out to be the number of their work unit. Now this, of course, is not like most after-school activities around the world, and as my car passed these students, I looked at their faces and wondered what thoughts must go through the heads of these youngsters. Do they accept these rituals and party obligations without question? Does indoctrination at such young, impressionable ages really work?

The opacity of the North Korean state is so well known that it has become a truism to refer to the country as a "black box." This metaphor extends beyond the government's intentions behind its weapons systems to less ominous elements of the state and society. We know nothing about how the average North Korean citizen thinks. We read a lot about how they are steeped in the writings of Kimilsungism and how the average North Korean has deep and genuine affection for the Kim family.[1]

What we know of the average North Korean largely comes through testimonies of defectors.[2] But these North Koreans are hardly "average," in that they already demonstrate a bias in their thoughts about the country, having made the decision to leave it. Naturally, we should expect their views of North Korea to slant in a particular direction, and to be quite critical of the state. It would not be difficult for any researcher or policymaker to accept the testimony and thoughts of North Korean defectors as genuine, but one would be hard pressed to argue that this particular collection of views can be reliably representative of the population inside of the country who have not chosen to defect or to escape (discussed further later in this chapter).

This chapter describes a method to understand views inside of North Korea using survey data. As far as we know, it is one of the first attempts to do this. An ethnographic study of North Korea is impossible for Americans to do given the adversarial state of official relations between the two countries. Since 2016, however, we have partnered with an organization that has a successful track record of conducting discreet and careful surveys in North Korea. There are obvious methodological issues with surveying the general population in North Korea (to be discussed), but our microsurvey questionnaires were completed in provinces across North Korea. The questionnaires were carried out as natural, in-person conversations between those conducting the interviews and the respondents. The individuals administering the questions were carefully trained to avoid asking leading questions or eliciting specific answers to protect both the integrity of the interview project and safety of the people involved in the conversation. The questionnaire consisted of free-form answers as well as binary choices and controlled comparison questions. Binary choice questions (yes/no; agree/disagree) constituted the majority of the questions given the challenges of doing open surveying in a state where expression is so tightly restricted.

A NOTE ON METHODOLOGY

The sampling method we used was nonprobability, convenience sampling as accessibility to participants was a key concern. This method of microsurveys admittedly falls short of typical survey standards. An ideal public opinion survey would demonstrate three basic traits: First, the respondents would represent a random sampling of the population. Second, there should be no prior relationship between those administering the survey and the respondents. Third, the sample should not just be random, but also somewhat sizable. The purpose of these requirements is (1) to minimize bias in the survey results, (2) to garner honest answers to the questions, and (3) to achieve a representative view of the population.[3]

None of these general survey requirements could be met in the case of North Korea. But one could credibly argue that the nature of surveying in the totalitarian state, with its attendant risks, requires sacrificing some traditional survey standards to obtain ethnographic data on how North Koreans think. For example, random sampling is simply not possible in North Korea. There is no publicly available and readily accessible database of citizens from which to sample on a large scale. Second, interviewers often had a prior relationship with the respondents. This might be anathema in the world of survey practitioners, but it was necessary for surveying in North Korea. One can only imagine that given the draconian state suppression of any freedom of expression, the average North Korean citizen, when questioned about markets or support for the regime by a stranger, would immediately shy away for fear of personal safety. This creates an irony, as Go Myong-Hyun observes, in collecting usable data: "The personal bond between the respondent and the interviewer, which would be anathema to public opinion surveys under more normal circumstances, is ironically the best guarantee of confidentiality and objectivity in the case of North Korea: The respondents can trust that the interviewers will protect the confidentiality of their responses, which in turn allows them to respond truthfully to the survey."[4]

Given the gravity of the consequences—for both questioner and respondent—faced for expressing opinions in North Korea, the methodology of the interview project had to be delimited in order to account for the current conditions in the country and to protect all those involved. Or, as another survey expert noted, "Working in circumstances as difficult as these requires that normal methodological rigor be put aside. The very serious risks assumed by everyone involved demand it."[5]

In the end, the shortcomings of this method are outweighed by the ability to capture the opinions, beliefs, and in some cases anger, expressed in the respondents' results. Conducting the survey itself is a unique and pathbreaking approach to research on the country. These materials provide us with novel insights into the blackest of black boxes—how the average North Korean citizen thinks and feels about the state, their lives, and their future.

North Korea is not a country from which information flows freely. It is not a place conducive to vibrant public discourse. As noted, the vast majority of surveys conducted in recent memory are of North Korean defectors who live in other countries, a fairly well-defined group with similar motivations and beliefs, which therefore does not represent well the average North Korean who has chosen to live in the country. Surveying those only in major cities, or only in the capital city of Pyongyang, would create its own biases; thus the two microsurveys used in this research spanned respondents in eight of nine provinces and covered almost ninety people. We sought a diverse demographic as well. The respondents were somewhat evenly divided by gender and spanned in age from twenty-eight to eighty years old. There is a wide diversity of occupations and education levels among the group as well, ranging from laborers to barbers to doctors.

The questions asked of respondents were standardized to maintain consistency of response. They related to the regime's public distribution system, informal market and bartering activities, outside information, national security (including nuclear weapons), and unification. We also inquired about events that drive respondents' view of the government and of foreign aid.

TABLE 4.1 Microsurvey 2016 demographics

Sample size	36
Age	28 to 80 years old
Gender	20 male; 16 female
Occupations	Laborer, doctor, company president, homemaker, factory worker, barber, cook, sauna worker
Locations of respondents	Kangwon, South Hwanghae, North Pyongan, South Pyongan, Ryanggang, Chongjin City, Pyongyang, South Hamgyong, North Hamgyong, Musan

REFUGEES AND DEFECTORS INTERVIEW DATA

The question that naturally arises is whether two convenience sampling surveys of thirty-six or fifty respondents in North Korea are more useful than the substantive work that has been done on collecting views of the refugee/defector population. The North Korean refugee population in South Korea stands at about 33,856.[6] This group allows for a much larger sample survey size. These refugees have been the subject of interviews by the South Korean government, independent researchers, and the UN Commission of Inquiry on Human Rights in the Democratic People's Republic of Korea (COI). A great deal of useful data has been culled from these interviews.[7] But as one scholar has noted, the refugee population, as large as it is, also has its own biases.[8] For one, much of the population who have left North Korea and resettled in the South since 1998 comes from the two most northeastern and economically decrepit provinces, North Hamgyong and Ryanggang (our study had respondents from all provinces).[9] Since 2003 the number of female refugees far outnumbers males due to Chinese refoulement practices (targeting males) and human trafficking along the border (targeting females). In 2020, for example, women outnumbered men 845 to 202 (our study had a roughly equal balance between men and women).[10] In terms of occupation, almost half of the refugee population in South Korea was unemployed in North Korea or held low-skilled jobs. This contrasts with our convenience sampling, which included this group but also included professional and skilled workers. Arguably, this is the first look at how the more well-heeled in North Korea think about the regime and their lives.

There is no denying that the publication of these microsurvey results is not current, and some critics would even call them old given the number of years since the questioning took place. This is a fair criticism. All that we can say in response is that even though the results are aged, they are not outdated: (1) budgetary, logistics, and safety constraints made it impossible to carry out the surveys on an annual basis; and (2) the Covid-19 lockdown in North Korea from 2020, which remained in place for three years, precluded any access to the population even along the Sino–North Korean and Russian–North Korean borders. The dramatic reduction in numbers of defectors from the North, moreover, under the Kim Jong-un regime (in cooperation with China's Xi Jinping government) has also affected the capacity of defector organizations to access newly departed individuals.

The point of this is not to say that one method is better than the other, but that both are useful for understanding the black box of North Korean society. Indeed, some of the findings of the convenience sampling resonate with the refugee studies. Moreover, our convenience sampling studies were able to elicit average North Korean citizens' thoughts on issues that extended beyond markets to include views on the United States, nuclear weapons, and unification, which is novel and hopefully useful to future researchers. A sample copy of the two microsurveys appears in appendix 3, along with examples of answers from North Korean citizens.

DISSATISFACTION WITH THE PUBLIC DISTRIBUTION SYSTEM

In the command-style economy of North Korea, the public distribution system (PDS) plays a central role in sustenance of the population. It also provides the government with an instrument of political control. As citizens work for the state, they are assured of their livelihood through the PDS. The creation of a second economy through the advent of markets, or *jangmadang*, in North Korea, however, has been an important development over the past twenty-five years.[11] Growing largely out of the failure of the centralized economy to provide food, fuel, and other subsistence needs for the population in the mid-1990s, ultimately leading to the "Arduous March" and famine that killed over two million people, markets started out as a stopgap measure to make ends meet. But as the PDS broke down, "marketization from below" gained traction to become a central element of the national economy, such that in July 2002 the government passed a decree recognizing official markets.[12] This allowed for the monetization of the economy, where supply and demand would determine prices in the market rather than the government coupon or ration system. The government also dispensed with the artificially high value of the won (from 2.2 won to one U.S. dollar to 150 won to the dollar) and decentralized farming collectives, putting local units in charge. Estimates put the number of government-sanctioned markets between three hundred and five hundred.[13] These are supplemented by an unreported but vast number of unofficial or informal (black) markets. They range in size from local, pop-up vendors to some of the biggest markets, like Unification Street Market in Pyongyang, Sunam market in Chongjin, and Okjon market in Pyongsong, with reportedly more than 17,000 vendors in Sunam market, the largest in North Korea.[14]

Our descriptive surveys track attitudes about the markets, the centralized economy, and the state among average citizens. Respondents' discontent with the PDS was evidenced by their very negative responses to the question, "Does the public distribution system provide you with what you want for a good life?"[15] All respondents believed the PDS was dysfunctional. Zero respondents indicated that they currently receive enough through the public distribution system to maintain their livelihoods.[16]

The notion that North Koreans do not rely fully on the public distribution system is not a new finding. However, this survey confirms this finding from North Koreans living *in* the country, rather than from defector testimony. A study by Seoul National University (SNU) of North Korean defectors residing in South Korea spanning from 2008 to 2015 found that a significant number relied on market and barter activities. The percentage of defectors reporting such engagement has been on an upward trend since 2008, when just 56.8 percent of 296 respondents indicated engagement in such activities. In 2015

TABLE 4.2 North Korean engagement in market and bartering activity

Year	Yes (%)	No (%)	No response (%)	Number of respondents*
2011	68.6	27.6	3.8	104
2012	69.3	29.9	0.8	128
2013	74.4	25.6	0	133
2014	69.8	30.2	0	149
2015	76.7	23.3	0	146

*The SNU surveys draw on a pool of North Korean defectors who have arrived in South Korea during the previous year.

Source: North Korean Public Perception on Unification 2015 (북한주민 통일의식 2015), Institute for Peace and Unification Studies, Seoul National University, 2015, 110.

SNU found that the percentage had increased to a high-water mark of 76.7 percent of 146 respondents.

NORTH KOREAN DISPLEASURE WITH ANTIMARKET ACTIVITIES

In addition to broad discontent and lack of confidence in the PDS, North Korean citizens express uniform displeasure over the government's predatory practices toward market activities and individual entrepreneurialism. In answer to a free-response question about what aspects of government activity anger them the most, the public grows most perturbed over antimarket activities imposed by the central government or local officials. The sampling that follows is representative.

Several respondents wrote only the words "currency redenomination" in response to the question. The public harbors deep antipathy whenever the government intervenes in the market. Whether this is done on legal grounds for operating in the black market, through forced tax payments, or through currency redenomination, the government has been known to undertake such activities as a way to siphon disposable income and personal savings out of the system in order to create greater public reliance on the government for subsistence rather than on the market. Survey respondents were likely referring to the currency redenomination in November 2009 that elicited widespread discontent, based on anecdotal accounts. The government

TABLE 4.3 North Korean displeasure with antimarket activities: Free-form responses

Q10. Which event causes you to feel greatest animosity toward the regime?	국가나 사회에 대해 불편, 불만을 하게 된 가장 큰 원인이 무엇입니까?
"Going to prison for the crime of selling things on the black market."	"장사죄로 교화소 가게 됨."
"When the Ministry of People's Safety/Security took the seed money I had saved to do business."	"장사 밑천을 보안서에 빼앗겼을 때."
"Forced labor mobilization, so-called nontax payments, insufficient wages."	"강압적인 노력 동원, 세외(稅)부담, 노임미달."
"Seizure of assets. Being sent to *kyohwaso* (re-education camps)."	"재산 몰수. 교화소 수감."
"Because no one looks after regular citizens in their daily lives."	"일반 서민들의 생활은 누구도 돌보지 않았기 때문입니다."
"Suspension of rations, the burden of nontax payments to the government."	"배급 중단과 세외 부담."
"Inconveniences in daily life. Electrical outages and breaks in running water."	"생활상의 불편 때문. 정전과 수돗물 단절."
"Currency redenomination."	"화폐 개혁."

proclaimed a new currency and required households to exchange the old currency for the new one (100 old Korean won exchanged for 1 new Korean won), but with an upper limit of 150,000 won, thus rendering worthless the remainder of their personal savings (held only in cash). This created mass chaos in markets as citizens were desperate to spend their excess currency, or exchange the currency for Chinese yuan or U.S. dollars before it became worthless.[17] The government's announced rationale for the action was to control inflation, but the real motivation by the government was to counteract the decentralization of power being created by market activity sprouting up all over the country. In short, the government did not like the growing private sector in the markets and increasing prosperity among its citizens. These were seen as threats to the regime's control.

The Korea Institute for National Unification's (KINU) Quality of Life in North Korea survey in 2011 of North Korean defectors living in China in the aftermath of the currency action found a similar sentiment. One of KINU's respondents explained, "What had escalated North Koreans' distrust about the regime even further was the currency reform implemented in November 2009." Another echoed, "There are so many people out there who got bitter about the country because of the [currency] reform. They say that they got robbed by Kim Jong Il overnight." Newspapers reported that there were spontaneous protests (a rare occurrence in the totalitarian state) in cities around the country as well as suicides in protest over the measure.[18] Our microsurveys confirm that similar views are held among the populace living in North Korea, not just among the defector community.

North Korean citizens judge that the state's PDS does not work for them. While the market has pretty much displaced the PDS today, our 2016 survey was the first time we heard from average citizens about the problems associated with it. Particularly for North Koreans who operate in markets (many of the respondents), their vigorous activity in these extra-governmental institutions and their displeasure and downright anger at attempts to interfere with markets suggests that for some, the social contract has broken down between state and society. North Korean citizens do not believe the government provides for the economic livelihood of citizens as they seek to improve their worth through the markets.

CYNICISM ABOUT THE STATE

I took me some Plaxivoid, the Plaxivid, the platypus polish, I took it. The point is that little pill knocked the Clovis right out of my bread basket.
—Stephen Colbert's impression of President Biden after contracting Covid-19, July 2022

Everyone takes work home sometimes. But not Donald Trump. The man barely took work to work. And, also, by the way, it's not "taking work home with you" if you no longer have the job, right? Can we agree on that? You don't have the job, you can't take work home with you. Like if you get fired from your babysitting job, but you still go pick up the kid from school that's just kidnapping.
—Trevor Noah on FBI raid of Donald Trump's home in Mar-a-Lago for alleged security violations with classified materials, August 2022

In the United States and many other democratic societies, criticism and ridicule of the government is standard fare. The White House is the target of daily jokes and standup routines on late-night television and across social media. Political satire at the expense of national leaders and outright criticism of the government are normal parts of both public and private lives in democratic states across the globe.

The North Korean state, however, demands airtight loyalty. Citizens can go to jail for not dusting the portraits of Kim Il-sung and Kim Jong-il that adorn their living room wall, or for inadvertently having the fold of their newspaper crease a picture of the leader. In March 2013 the United Nations Human Rights Council established a Commission of Inquiry on Human Rights in the Democratic People's Republic of Korea to look into the situation of North Korean human rights. The commission found that there is "an almost complete denial of the right to freedom of thought . . . as well as of the rights to freedom of opinion." In its February 2014 report, the commission wrote:

> The Commission finds that there is an almost complete denial of the right to freedom of thought, conscience and religion, as well as of the rights to freedom of opinion, expression, information and association. . . . State surveillance permeates the private lives of all citizens to ensure that virtually no expression critical of the political system or of its leadership goes undetected. Citizens are punished for any "anti-State" activities or expressions of dissent. They are rewarded for reporting on fellow citizens suspected of committing such "crimes."[19]

People who express dissent or criticize the state, even if unintentionally, are subject to harsh punishments and detention, often without trial. Suspects of political crimes may simply disappear, and their relatives may never be notified of the arrest, the charges, or the whereabouts of the alleged criminal. If not executed, citizens accused of major political crimes are sent to a political prison camp, or 관리소 (*kwanliso*).[20] According to defector testimonies recorded in the Korea Institute for National Unification's 2020 White Paper on Human Rights in North Korea, the fear of political prison camps creates a widespread culture of self-censorship of statements to avoid being blamed for being a "language reactionary" (*mal bandong*).²¹ In short, there is no room for "misspeaking" in North Korea.

Undeniably this would be a sensitive topic to broach with the average North Korean, and this is where arguably the relationship between the questioner and the respondent becomes critical. There is no sane North Korean citizen who would willingly answer a question about criticism of the regime in any but one way if they did not know the questioner. And even if they know the questioner, they will still exercise a degree of caution because of the pervasive culture of reporting "disloyals" in North Korean society. The UN commission found that the North Korean state had created a "vast surveillance apparatus" to monitor any expression of sentiments deemed antistate or antirevolutionary through both networks of secret informers as well as state organizations. Formal organizations such as the Neighborhood Watch (인민반 *inminban*) regularly monitor their members, and membership in such a group is required for all North Korean citizens. Neighborhood watches are made up of about twenty to forty households, with a leader appointed to monitor the neighborhood for antistate activities or dissent and to report to the authorities.²² Moreover, should any criticism take place, one must assume this does not happen in the public sphere, given the obvious ramifications. For these reasons, the question in our microsurvey on regime criticism was posed indirectly between questioner and respondent—i.e., not "Do you criticize the regime in private?" but "Do your family, friends, or neighbors complain or make jokes about the government in private?" (이웃, 친구, 가족이 개인적으로 예전보다 국가나 삶에 대해 불평 및 비난을 합니까?). The respondents were not cold-called by the administrators but knew them in some fashion. Questions were discussed in natural and trusted settings with people who were somewhat but not necessarily deeply familiar with each other.

The findings here are quite interesting. Thirty-five of thirty-six respondents answered "yes" to the question of whether they knew of friends, family, or neighbors who complain or make jokes about the North Korean government in private. This is a surprisingly large percentage given the risks associated with such an expression of thought. It suggests that citizens do not just harbor their own opinions about the government but are willing to share these behind closed doors and out of earshot from the local *inminban* or neighborhood watchers. Even in private or among friends, one assumes significant risk when joking or complaining about the government, so this suggests that sentiments are fairly strong and widespread.

A study by Seoul National University of North Korean defectors living in South Korea has consistently found the presence of some level of government criticism. From 2008 to 2020 the percentage of survey respondents who felt the existence of government criticism ranged from a low of 47.7 percent in 2014 to a high of 73.1 percent in 2012. In 2020, 52.3 percent of survey respondents said government criticism existed, compared to 47.7 percent of those who said government criticism did not exist.

One can reasonably assume that defectors would have a more negative or critical disposition toward the government. However, the finding that the overwhelming majority of respondents still living in North Korea also make jokes at the government's expense is novel. It suggests once again that when we look inside the black box of North

TABLE 4.4 Criticism of the regime

When you were living in the DPRK, how prevalent did you think criticism of the government (scribble, leaflet, etc.) was in North Korea?	2008 (%)	2009 (%)	2010 (%)	2011 (%)	2012 (%)	2013 (%)	2014 (%)
A lot	11.1	9.5	N/A	16.7	10	6	8.1
Moderate	49.1	47.6	N/A	51.8	63.1	60.2	39.6
Negligible	29.8	30.8	N/A	19.3	18.5	22.6	28.9
None	10	9.5	N/A	10.5	6.9	11.3	23.5
No answer / error	0	2.7	N/A	1.8	1.6	0	0
# of respondents (1)	296	370	N/A	104	128	133	149

	2015 (%)	2016 (%)	2017 (%)	2018 (%)	2019 (%)	2020 (%)
A lot	6.8	10.1	10.6	9.2	6.0	2.8
Moderate	55.5	48.6	47.7	39.1	41.4	49.5
Negligible	24	25.4	24.2	35.6	30.2	21.1
None	12.3	15.9	17.4	16.1	22.4	26.6
No answer / error	1.4	0.0	0.0	0.0	0.0	0.0
# of respondents (1)	146	138	132	87	116	109

Korean society, there is more freedom of critical thought and judgments about the state than is conventionally accepted and there are more parallels between thinking inside and outside the country evidenced by the defector population data.

DEMAND FOR FOREIGN MEDIA

During my stay at the State Guest House in Pyongyang, I had some time to kill before my next government meeting. My iPod did not work (no Wi-Fi!), my phones had been politely confiscated by my handlers for the duration of my stay (they promised to return them at the end of the trip, which they did), and I was told not to bring any books on the trip. So I turned on the television in my room to find a blank screen with a CNN chyron, but then a message that said, "Channel not available." I surfed through all the channels to find only two. One was playing a recording of a Supreme People's Assembly session (the North Korean version of C-SPAN, I thought). The other was playing a documentary about the heroic efforts of Kim Il-sung to fight against the Japanese imperialists during World War II.

Citizens of free and open democracies are constantly bombarded with media and outside ideas in their everyday lives. For people living in North Korea, the only legally available media and information is provided, approved, and curated by the regime. The control of information in North Korean society is Orwellian, saturated with state propaganda and the ideology of the regime.

Information control is perhaps the most heinous of the North Korean regime's human rights abuses, as it seeks to control the mind, expression, and thoughts of the citizens as a tool of repression. History, current news, and the state of world affairs are all filtered through state controls to align with the ideology of the regime. In North Korea, the act of distributing or consuming outside information and foreign media is criminal. The "Crime of Possessing or Bringing in Corrupt and Decadent Culture" can result in three to fifteen years of detention in labor camps. North Korean escapee testimony has documented cases where death sentences were carried out for individuals possessing especially sensitive content, such as South Korean dramas or the

Christian Bible.[23] In January 2024 the British Broadcasting Company obtained footage of a public sentencing of teenage boys to twelve years in a labor camp for watching South Korean dramas.[24] The UN Commission of Inquiry on Human Rights examined the information environment in North Korea and reported the following: "The authorities engage in gross human rights violations so as to crack down on 'subversive' influences from abroad. These influences are symbolized by films and soap operas from the Republic of Korea and other countries, short-wave radio broadcasts and foreign mobile telephones."[25]

The flow of foreign media and information into North Korea has been well-documented.[26] The demand for this information, however, has been documented anecdotally and largely through defector testimony.[27] From this literature we learn that risks may be great, but North Koreans increasingly access diverse forms of foreign media. They carefully rig radios to gain access to foreign radio and television broadcasts. DVDs and MP3 players are smuggled covertly across borders, and illegal foreign USB drives are traded in informal marketplaces. Through such means, North Koreans access outside information, ranging from weather and news reports to South Korean dramas and Chinese movies. Despite this plethora of insightful literature, we do not have a view into how the average North Korean citizen living in the city or in the countryside actually feels about foreign media.

Our microsurveys, though admittedly of a small sample size, find that nearly all citizens have been exposed to foreign media (thirty-four of thirty-six respondents answered in the affirmative). Respondents answered the following questions:

- Do you ever watch or listen to foreign media, including radio, TV, dramas, movies, USBs, etc.? (라디오, 텔레비전, 드라마, 영화, USB 등을 통해 외부 정보에 접해본 적 있습니까?)
- If yes, how often? (접해본 적이 있다면 얼마나 자주 접했습니까?)
- Do you feel that information about the outside world is useful to you, or not? (정보가 본인에게 유익하다고 생각합니까?)

Ninety-one percent (thirty-three of the thirty-six respondents) watched or listened to foreign media at least once per month, and twenty-one of those thirty-six used foreign media at least once per

TABLE 4.5 How often do you watch or listen to foreign media?

Frequency	Number of respondents
Every day	6
Once a week	12
Once a month	15
Once a year	1
None	2

week. Previous surveys show a trend of between 90 percent in 2012 to 88.4 percent in 2016 of North Korean escapees reporting at least some exposure to South Korean media.[28] Nat Kretchun and Jane Kim's study, moreover, found that once exposed to outside information, many North Korean defectors stated that they continued to pursue this new source of knowledge on a regular basis. One North Korean escapee describes her experience with foreign media: "At first, I watched outside media purely out of curiosity. However, as time went by, I began to believe in the contents. It was an addictive experience. Once you start watching, you simply cannot stop."[29] These findings are the first to confirm from *within* North Korea that exposure to outside information is not limited to escapees from North Korea and appears to be quite uniform across age, regional, and occupational demographics.

One might expect that those living in border regions with potentially more access to outside information would consume more foreign media. Interestingly, all eighteen respondents living in provinces bordering China accessed foreign media only slightly more frequently than those living in other provinces. Twelve of them accessed foreign media at least once per week. In contrast, two of the eighteen respondents living in provinces not bordering China said they had never accessed foreign media; but of those who did, nine respondents accessed it at least once per week. Larger inferences regarding the access rates in provinces of course cannot be drawn from such a microsurvey; however, that quite a number of respondents across provinces were able to regularly access foreign media hints that geography doesn't prohibit the flow of information from the outside world.

Studies done with North Korean escapees living abroad indicate that North Koreans do have a keen sense for when they are being fed propaganda. And so they know when to seek alternative sources of knowledge. Our microsurveys also found that thirty-two of the thirty-six respondents, or 88.9 percent, felt that information from the outside world was useful. Finally, thirty of the thirty-six respondents said they found outside goods and information to be of greater impact on their lives than decisions by the North Korean government. This finding suggests two broader dynamics taking place in North Korean society: First, citizens consider information from external sources not just to be novel, but to be credible, or at least as credible as the propaganda from the government. Second, they seek out foreign media for cultural entertainment, like South Korean dramas or pirated Chinese movies, as has been well-documented. But this media is also sought out for broader political knowledge and understanding, and interestingly, from an entrepreneurial perspective, in terms of markets. One escapee interviewed by Intermedia explains, "People are interested in international politics including U.S.-North Korean relations and inter-Korean relationships, since they influence contraband trading. . . . During tense periods there are certain categories that we avoid purchasing."[30]

VIEWS ON INCOME AND EMPLOYMENT

In North Korea, the government controls the labor market and sets income levels. The government's State Planning Committee is in charge of determining the number of jobs available in each economic sector. The government then decides who gets what jobs and what wages they will be paid. In fact, article 5 of North Korea's Labor Laws actually guarantees all workers will have jobs.[31] This is not unusual for a centrally planned economy, but in North Korea the provision of income by the state is as much a tool of political control as it is a socialist experiment to create a classless society.

What is interesting about the views of North Korean citizens as captured by our microsurveys is that increasingly the determination of income and income levels is happening outside of state control. Our surveys showed that 72 percent of North Koreans currently living inside the country (twenty-six of thirty-six respondents) said they received almost all their household income from markets as opposed

TABLE 4.6 What percentage of your household income is derived from the markets?

Percent of household income	Number of respondents
Almost all	26
More than 75%	9
About 50–70%	1
About 25–50%	0
About 10–25%	0
Less than 10%	0
None	0

to official government-sanctioned jobs. Thirty-five respondents said at least 75 percent of their household income came from markets. Notably, no respondent said that less than half of their income is derived from markets. This finding is anathema to the government's efforts to control the population through the provision of income and shows increasing separation between state and society. It also is a manifestation of the entrepreneurial spirit of North Korean citizens. For many, the reference to market-based income probably reflects additional employment that workers take on to supplement the work they do for the state.

These findings regarding the significance of markets for households' incomes are mirrored by a study done by the Korea Institute for National Unification of North Korean defectors. When asked if they were paid the proper wage or amount by their workplace, only 12 of the 251 people interviewed by KINU said their income was "very appropriate" or "appropriate." (The study was conducted with respondents who had left North Korea between 2010 and 2014).[32] According to an earlier study by KINU of 200 people who had arrived in South Korea between 2010 and 2012, 46.9 percent of them earned their income from vending, daily menial work, contract work, or other unofficial jobs in order to support their families' living expenses.

One of the correlations that becomes clear in the data is that income as well as goods and services derived from the market has a definitive impact on how North Koreans think about the state. Twenty-one of the thirty respondents who said the outside world had a greater influence on their lives than North Korean government decisions also

TABLE 4.7 North Korean citizens' percent of household income from market

Factor with larger impact on life	Nearly all income from markets	More than 75% of income from markets	About 50% to 70% of income from markets	Total number of respondents
North Korean government decisions	5	0	1	6
Influence from the outside world (i.e., goods and information)	21	9	0	30
Total number of respondents	26	9	1	36

said they received almost all their household income from markets (70 percent). Despite the statistical limitations of microsurvey results, these findings suggest that markets are substantively undermining the traditional omnipotent impact of the North Korean government on its citizens' economic lives.

WOMEN AND MARKETS

Gender also influences the balance of market- or government-sourced household income for those respondents in the survey. Our surveys suggest that women's attitudes are most heavily influenced because of their deep integration with market life. In North Korea, women were banned from employment in state-owned enterprises during the 1990s, but women defied the state's gendered expectations to stay at home. They started to engage in informal markets and earning income during the famine. Meanwhile the men were required to remain formally employed in state-owned enterprises (SOEs) that had shuttered their doors. After the market reforms in 2002, women, particularly of middle age or older (in 2008, younger women under forty years of age were banned by the government from working in the markets) became the main players in the markets and the primary income-earners of the family. Today an estimated 15–20 percent of the female population are involved in markets as entrepreneurs, with some becoming *donju* or "money masters" who exercise social and financial power.[33] These women become the hub of information in society about prices in regional markets, currency exchange rates, and the latest government policies over market activity. In a state that emphasizes control, these entrepreneurs are arguably the most mobile citizens traveling between markets within the country and across the border to China. These women enjoy this mobility because the state sees them as unthreatening from a security viewpoint. From society's vantage point, they are also the least likely to engender harsh punishment.[34] The growth of markets in North Korea has effectively reversed traditional gender roles within the family.[35] Or as another analyst put it, "The hierarchy of gender in the workplace provided unexpected opportunities for women to become active in the emerging unofficial *Jangmadang* markets. Male labor by contrast was predominantly maintained on the production line of heavy industry."[36]

Of the sixteen females interviewed, thirteen (or 81 percent) of them said almost all their household income came from markets (65 percent for males). In addition, a higher percentage of female than male respondents said low salaries or currency/market interference caused them to feel the greatest animosity toward the North Korean government. Eleven of the sixteen female respondents gave income/market-related responses when asked, "Which event causes you to feel greatest animosity toward the regime?" (국가나 사회에 대해 불평, 불만을 갖게 된 가장 큰 원인이 무엇입니까?) In contrast, only half of the male respondents cited income/market-related incidents, while the rest pointed toward other factors, such as a lack of freedom, dynastic rule, or defense spending.

TABLE 4.8 Women and markets

Which event causes you to feel greatest animosity toward the regime?	국가나 사회에 대해 불평, 불만을 갖게 된 가장 큰 원인이 무엇입니까?
"Control of market activities."	"장사 통제."
"Control of the markets without providing rations."	"배급제 없이 시장 통제."
"Regulation of the markets."	"장마당 통제."
"No monthly salary given, and we are not compensated enough for our work."	"월급 배급이 없고 일한 만큼 보수가 없다."

It should be noted that while the West may see these entrepreneurial women in markets as agents of social change, this is not necessarily the way North Korean society sees them. Interviews with defectors find that North Korean women do not see their role in markets as a form of gender equality or empowerment; instead, they see their social value as underappreciated—both from the patriarchal family structure and from the government's general denigration of markets as capitalist and ideologically tainted.[37]

GENESIS OF CIVIL SOCIETY?

The results of our microsurveys beg the question of whether there is a nascent and growing civil society in North Korea. If civil society is generally defined as a space where organized social life takes place autonomously from the state, then the activities, information, and way of thinking revealed by our surveys indicate such a space may exist, though on a small scale. The citizens' reliance on markets more than on the state, as well as the belief in foreign media rather than state propaganda, suggest an independence of thinking among North Koreans despite the state's efforts to control thought. The willingness to criticize and ridicule the state suggests further that North Korean people have gained a better understanding of the outside world and their relative deprivation. The reliance on market income over that of the state and the growing predominance of women as breadwinners also suggests upheaval of traditional societal norms and new definitions of social capital. These survey responses indicate that social change is taking place. North Korean people are not merely empty vessels filled with government instructions and propaganda. They have their own minds and opinions, and they are sharing information and interacting outside the dictated boundaries of the state more than ever before. Moreover, new forms of social power and legitimacy are forming outside of the state. As one report noted, this may not constitute civil society in North Korea as defined by the West, but it does reflect the requisite building blocks on which such a society could be built: "The market survival strategies adopted by individuals promote trustbuilding, reciprocity, and information-sharing networks, all of which form the basis for—and help generate—this public sphere."[38]

UNIFICATION

Just as division has been integral to the postwar collective narrative of the Korean peninsula, reunification is part of the Korean collective identity. The development path for South Korea since 1945 has been a very successful one, albeit as a divided nation. Indeed, when and if reunification happens, it will mark the "end of history" in one sense, closing a chapter on Korea dating back to the division of the country in 1945 and starting one anew.

Yet South Koreans don't really think that much about North Korea. Many are fatigued by the constant news stories of North Korean missile tests.[39] When asked how many times they thought about North Korea in a given week, the majority of South Koreans polled (54.5 percent) responded "not at all," or at most once or twice a week (39 percent).[40] Thus it comes as no surprise that South Koreans remain fairly ambivalent about the prospect of managing the difficulties, risks, and costs associated with reunification. A survey in October 2021 by the Institute for Peace and Unification Studies of Seoul National University found that only 44.6 percent of South Koreans felt that unification was necessary. This number represents a downward trend. In April 2021 a survey by KINU of South Koreans found less than 30 percent believed that unification would benefit them individually.[41] There is a strong preference (more than two to one) among South Koreas for peaceful existence between the two Koreas rather than unification.[42] The ambivalence toward unification is particularly high for younger generations. A minority of millennials (12.4 percent) prefer unification over peaceful coexistence, while a vast majority show little or no interest in North Korea (74.1 percent).[43] A September 2020 web survey by independent researchers displayed similar ambivalence. Only 44 percent of respondents agreed or strongly agreed with the statement, "I support unification," and over 62 percent supported peaceful coexistence over unification.[44] A KINU survey of South Koreans in 2017 found that 57.8 percent of respondents said unification was necessary, down from 62.1 percent in 2016 and 69.3 percent in 2014.[45] Another Seoul National University Institute for Peace and Unification Studies survey of South Koreans' unification awareness published in 2019 further explored their views for the main reason why unification was necessary. Some 34.6 percent said shared ethnicity, 32.6 percent said the removal of threats of war between the two Koreas, 18.9 percent said for South Korea to become a more developed country, 10.6 percent to resolve the pain of separated families, and 3.0 percent said for North Koreans to live a better life.[46]

North Korean people's views of inter-Korean unity constitute one of most opaque elements of the Korean black box. We know virtually nothing about how they think about this outside of the official statements by the government. This is because there is no opportunity for them to express such views freely and personally separate from the collective. The state's views of unification have remained fairly consistent: North Korea was the only Korea to truly liberate from the Japanese occupation while the southern half replaced Japanese occupation with that of the United States. Unification will come through a people's revolution that will "liberate" Koreans in the South from foreign military occupation and unite them under the leadership of the "Dear Marshal Kim Jong-un."[47] Whether this outcome comes immediately or slowly through the interim stage of a confederal system (one country, two systems), North Korea will dominate the outcome.[48]

Our study asked North Korean respondents three questions about unification to gain a sense of their beliefs, hopes, and aspirations:

- Will unification happen in your lifetime? / 평생 살아가는 동안 통일이 실현될 수 있다고 생각합니까?
- Do you think unification is necessary? / 통일이 꼭 필요하다고 생각하십니까?
- If yes, what is the main reason that unification should occur? / 질문에 '네'라고 답하셨으면 주된 이유가 무엇입니까?
    - a. Shared ethnicity (North and South are "one race") / 동일한 민족이기 때문에
    - b. Increase economic growth / 경제 성장을 위해서
    - c. Increase international influence / 국제적인 영향력 강화를 위해
    - d. Reduce costs related to division of peninsula / 한반도 분단 상태로 인한 비용 절감을 위해
    - e. Defend against outside threats / 외부의 위협을 막기 위해
    - f. Resolve issue of separated families / 이산가족 문제를 해결하기 위해

The questions were asked as natural in-person conversations between those conducting the interviews and the respondents. The individuals administering the questions were carefully trained to avoid asking leading questions or eliciting specific answers so as to protect both the integrity of the interview project and the safety of the people involved in the conversation. North Koreans apparently deem unification to be quite important and imperative. Nearly 100 percent of North Korean respondents (thirty-four of thirty-six) believed unification is necessary. Moreover, twenty-one, or 58 percent, said unification will happen in their lifetime. This level of enthusiasm for unification stands in stark contrast to their brothers and sisters in the South, who, as noted earlier, consistently poll well below the 50 percent range in enthusiasm for unification.

As table 4.9 shows, the average North Korean citizen defines the unification discourse in ethnic terms, and only a small number define it in terms of national security. The majority of respondents, fifteen (44.1 percent), cited the shared ethnicity between North and South Koreans as the main reason unification should occur; ten (29.4 percent) said an increase in economic growth was the main reason. Five (or 14.7 percent) said unification is important to resolve the issue of separated families. Yet only two of the respondents saw the need for unification in terms of improving Korea's position against external threats, and only one of the respondents saw unification in terms of increasing Korea's external influence. Regarding ethnicity, while the majority of both men and women said the main reason unification should occur was shared ethnicity, a much greater percentage of

TABLE 4.9 North Korean views on unification

What is the main reason that unification should occur?	Number of responses
Shared ethnicity	15
Increase economic growth	10
Increase international influence	1
Reduce costs related to division of peninsula	0
Defend against outside threats	2
Resolve issue of separated families	5
Multiple reasons	1

male respondents selected this reason than female respondents (45 percent of men compared with 18 percent of women). A much greater percentage of men than women also indicated they thought the main reason for unification was to increase economic growth (40 percent of men compared with 6 percent of women). However, a larger percentage of female respondents said the primary reason for unification was to resolve the issue of separated families (12 percent of women compared with 5 percent of men).

These results offer some interesting and novel insights. First, the enthusiasm for unification among North Koreans inside the country tracks with that of defectors in South Korea. A May 2022 study by IPUS aggregating ten years of interview data with North Korean defectors found generally positive perceptions of unification, viewing the outcome as beneficial to the North Korean people as well as considering South Korea as a cooperative partner in the effort.[49] These perceptions remain relatively constant over time. In 2016, of the 138 North Koreans in South Korea surveyed by Seoul National University, 131 people, or 94.9 percent of respondents, said that when they lived in North Korea, they had thought unification was "somewhat" to "very necessary" (a KINU survey in 2017 had similar responses at 95 percent).[50] Second, the North's enthusiasm is not replicated in the South, where concerns about cost and feasibility abound, as already noted. This could reflect a more romanticized view of unification in the North, while for South Koreans, the issue is defined in practical and material terms. Arguably, economic reasons would have ranked more highly (as they did for the defector population) if northerners saw unification solely in practical terms. In the defector community, surveys found the majority of North Korean defectors pointing to increased standards of living and economic development as the main reason they think unification should occur. In 2016 Seoul National University found 46.4 percent of North Korean respondents in South Korea said increased standards of living and economic development were the main reasons they felt unification was necessary.

Another stark contrast in comparative views is with regard to ethnic identity. The percentage of North Korean respondents positively associating a common identity with unification was almost twice that of the South. Our surveys found 41 percent of northerners feeling this

TABLE 4.10 When living in North Korea, what was the main reason you thought unification was necessary?*

Category	2016	2015	2014
Shared ethnicity	42	40	35
Resolve the pain of separated families	12	5	11
Prevent inter-Korean war	17	12	17
Improve North Korean living standards	58	68	69
Economic development of North Korea	6	14	12
Other	3	3	1
No Response	0	4	4
Total	138	146	149

*The SNU surveys draw on a pool of North Korean defectors who have arrived in South Korea during the previous year.

Source: Institute for Peace and Unification Studies, Seoul National University, North Korean Public Perception on Unification 2016/2015/2014/2013–2008 (북한주민 통일의식 2016/2015/2014/2013–2008).

way versus only 23 percent for southerners, according to the 2021 KINU survey cited earlier. Another survey found only 5 percent of South Koreans in their twenties identifying race as an element of unification.[51] This gap could be explained by a younger generation of South Koreans who do not identify the division of Korea as anything other than an event read about in history books, as evident in the fact that nearly 75 percent of millennials in the South have no interest in North Korea.[52]

The North Korean identification of unification in terms of ethnic identity was also matched by a desire to see unification happen sooner rather than later.

On the question about timing of unification, twenty-one of thirty-six North Korean respondents, or 58 percent, said unification will happen in their lifetime. Eight of the thirty-six respondents said they did not think unification would happen in their lifetime, while seven said they didn't know if it would or not. Seventy-one percent of those under age fifty said unification would happen during their lifetime. Of those over fifty, 47 percent said it would happen during their life while 32 percent said it would not. The oldest respondent, age eighty, said he believed unification would indeed take place in his lifetime. These responses could be interpreted as a desire or yearning for unification

TABLE 4.11 Will unification happen in your lifetime?

Response	Number of North Korean respondents
Yes	21
No	8
Don't know	7

by North Korean people that could be fueled by government propaganda; alternately, it could be informed by an understanding of the relative deprivation of the country and a desire to see something better. The belief that unification would happen sooner than later (or never) is unlikely to reflect judgments about the fragility of the North Korean state, as our sample were ordinary citizens without knowledge of official matters. Finally, the belief that unification is a nearer-term event is not shared by South Koreans. By comparison, only 1.3 percent of South Koreans believe unification would happen within five years, while 5.9 percent said unification would happen within ten years, according to the 2022 Seoul National University unification awareness survey.[53]

These microsurvey questions on unification were among the most interesting of the study. They not only provided an unprecedented view of how average citizens in North Korea think about unification but also show differences from the defector population, as well as differences from how South Koreans think about unification.

NUCLEAR WEAPONS

A second microsurvey was conducted in 2017 to focus on two issues—what do ordinary North Koreans think about the state's nuclear weapons programs, and what are their views of the United States? The questionnaire was administered in eight provinces in North Korea, with a sample size of fifty. The questionnaire was carried out as natural in-person conversations between those conducting the interviews and the respondents. The individuals administering the questions were carefully trained to avoid asking leading questions or eliciting specific answers so as to protect both the integrity of the

TABLE 4.12 Survey on attitudes toward nuclear weapons and the United States

Sample size	50
Age	20 to 70 years old
Gender	30 males, 20 females
Terminal education level	Middle school, high school, college, vocational college, and university
Occupational range	Miner, student, collective farm worker, supervisor, soldier, ship repairman, housewife, party official, merchant, teacher

interview project as well as the safety of the people involved in the conversation.

The timing of the survey was particularly significant in that it coincided with the very public and personal confrontation between the United States and North Korea over the latter's nuclear weapons program. Less than seven weeks after Donald Trump's inauguration, North Korea conducted the first of what would be twenty ballistic missile tests in 2017. The North also conducted a hydrogen bomb test in September 2017.[54] The August 2017 missile launches induced Trump's threat to rain "fire and fury [on North Korea] like the world has never seen."[55] Not to be outdone, North Korea responded by detailing a plan to launch four IRBMs targeting U.S. bases in Guam (August 9).[56] Trump tweeted two days later that military measures were "locked and loaded." Three days later Kim Jong-un followed, reiterating his Guam "strike plans"; releasing a picture of a thermonuclear weapon small enough to fit atop an ICBM; and then conducting an actual thermonuclear test on September 3.[57] In an address before the United Nations on September 19, Trump derided the leader as "Rocket Man [who] is on a suicide mission for himself and for his regime."[58] The United States skirted the North Korean coastline with B-1B strategic bombers two days later and relisted North Korea as a state sponsor of terrorism (November).[59] Trump tweeted, "North Korea won't be around much longer."[60]

Amid this extraordinary public standoff between the American and North Korean leaders, and shortly after the November 29 launch of a Hwasong-15 ICBM, North Korean media started reporting that across the country, citizens were joining in national rallies celebrating the "completion" of their nation's nuclear weapons forces. While outside experts have noted the limitations and complicated technical hurdles still facing the North's current weapons systems in achieving a truly global reach, KCNA reported official celebrations by people from all walks of life, including workers, students, local party officials, young people, and members of the Korean People's Army.[61]

Thus, the timing of our surveys, conducted in the summer and the fall of 2017, provided unique insights into how North Korean citizens thought about the state's celebration of nuclear weapons and about the United States. Contrary to the state's glorification of the weapons and demonization of the adversary, the general public's views, at least of those sampled in our survey, did *not* track with the state's views and propaganda.

First, most North Korean respondents did not have a positive attitude toward their country's nuclear weapons program. Forty-three of the fifty respondents expressed "ambivalent" to "highly negative" attitudes toward their country's nuclear weapons program. Only seven expressed a "positive" attitude toward the regime's nuclear weapons program. When asked the question, "Do you think North Korea's nuclear program is the source of national pride?" (귀하는 북한의 핵무기가 국가적 자부심의 근원이라고 생각하십니까?), 70 percent of the answers were negative versus 30 percent positive. Majorities were evident across gender; about three quarters (77 percent) of male respondents felt the program was not a source of pride (twenty-three of thirty) while twelve of twenty (60 percent) female respondents said the same.

North Korea has long propagated the concept of *kangsong taeguk* (강성태국), meaning "rich nation, strong nation" as one of the goals of and justifications for the inordinate proportion of national resources devoted to the weapons programs. The general public, however, did not appear to internalize this narrative. Thirty-six of fifty North Korean respondents (72 percent) did not think nuclear weapons made them a prosperous nation. An overwhelming majority of male respondents (83 percent) felt nuclear weapons did not make them a prosperous nation (twenty-five of thirty). Eleven of twenty (55 percent) female respondents said the same. These are extraordinarily low numbers despite the decades of public indoctrination about the nuclear program.

The negative attitudes are expressed in greater detail with the free-form response question. In the qualitative response section of the

TABLE 4.13 Attitudes toward nuclear weapons

Statement (English)	Statement (Korean)	Respondent identity
"Nuclear weapons are the devil's weapons and will lead to our extinction."	"핵개발은 민족을 멸족시키는 악마의 무기다."	Midcareer soldier from a North Korean province bordering China
"Nuclear weapons are the most dangerous weapons on earth, the power of killing us all, so they should not be developed."	"핵은 모두를 죽게 만드는 최강의 독약이기 때문에 개발을 하면 안된다."	Woman serving as a money lender in one of North Korea's southern provinces bordering the DMZ with South Korea
"I think nuclear weapons development is greatly impeding our economic development because all of the government's money is being wasted on the weapons program."	"핵무기 개발은 경제발전에 막대한 방해가 된다고 생각합니다. 자금을 핵개발에 탕진하기 때문입니다."	Miner from North Hamgyong province
"It's crazy. The people are struggling, but Kim Jong Un only thinks about himself."	"미친 것. 사람들은 힘든데 윗(김정은) 생각만 한다."	Middle-aged woman heading an Inminban neighborhood association

microsurvey, many of the North Korean respondents spoke pointedly about taking a strongly negative position toward North Korea's nuclear weapons. A number of those respondents who expanded on their attitudes cited concerns about the program's consequences for all of humanity. One-third of the respondents cited economic concerns and the negative impact of the program on the lives of ordinary North Korean citizens.

Not all microsurvey respondents spoke negatively of the program. Some took a more nuanced stance. A sixty-year-old railway worker tried to find a balance between the reality of food shortages he observed for the North Korean people and the regime's focus on nuclear weapons development, stating, "The people are busy trying to secure food and yet the government only thinks of this nuclear development, spending millions in the process. But it's done for national power" (백성들은 먹을 것 때문에 바쁜데 핵만 생산한다. 들을라니까 핵개발이 수억이 든다고 한다. 그래도 국력이니까 하는거다). He did think that his country's nuclear weapons program was a source of national pride and agreed with the assertion that weapons do make North Korea a prosperous nation.

A party official said he had a neutral attitude toward the program but admitted he thought "nuclear weapons have prevented other powerful nations from daring to attack us despite our small size"

(핵이 있기 때문에 손바닥 만한 조선을 대국들이 감히 건드리지 못한다). A young teacher from one of the northern provinces felt positively toward the program and thought it was indeed a source of national pride. She explained, "The reason why the big countries like America, Japan, and China have not been able to touch us is because of our nuclear weapons, so developing them is imperative" (미국, 일본, 중국 같은 대국들이 우리 조선을 감히 건드리지 못하는 것은 핵이 있기 때문이다. 따라서 핵개발은 해야 된다). Such positive sentiments toward North Korea's nuclear capabilities were, however, by far in the minority. Moreover, for those who view the weapons positively, there appears to be a clear understanding of the material costs of the state's pursuance of such capabilities. This is echoed in surveys of defectors, some of whom view nuclear weapons as a source of national pride and security for the country but also lament the cost in terms of international sanctions.[62]

The survey responses, albeit from a small sample size, reinforce the notion that the people of North Korea do not simply passively accept as true all the information imparted to them by the government. There are indeed independent, more nuanced opinions that reflect some space—how much is unclear—between the state and society. The ambivalence about nuclear weapons stands in stark contrast to persistent and enthusiastic messages by the state about how these weapons are tied to the strength and competence of the state. The public's tepid response appears to be informed by two interrelated factors: The first is a genuine fear of these weapons and the concern that the state could engage in a nuclear war, or be preempted by a nuclear attack, that would destroy everything. The second is dissatisfaction with what nuclear weapons have cost the country in terms of the disproportionate diversion of national resources to the program, as well as the bevy of sanctions that have stunted the economic development of the country.

VIEWS OF THE UNITED STATES

Our surveys took place at a time when North Korea-U.S. bilateral tensions were high, with many adversarial references by the North Korean state media to the U.S.'s "hostile policy" and the need for the North

Korean people to steel themselves for war. This period of tension is resonant with over a half-century of negative and demonic depictions of America by North Korean propaganda and government statements. North Korean leaders, television announcers, and newspaper editors referred to Donald Trump as an old mad man and a stupid half-wit. They regularly called President Obama and President Bush dehumanizing and derogatory terms. The United States is often referred to as a "pack of robbers" or "rabid dogs." Ever-present propaganda informs North Koreans that Americans are aggressive, hegemonic imperialists. North Korean defectors recount learning from the state that American soldiers, according to one account, "tore off the limbs of innocent Koreans and cut off eyes, noses, and lips and hung them on the trees."[63] An old adage says that North Korean children are even taught basic arithmetic by counting the number of dead American soldiers on two hands.[64]

Given this dominant narrative, our microsurveys revealed some counterintuitive findings. We found that North Korean citizens do not hold uniformly negative impressions of the United States, contrary to the statements of North Korean leaders. Just 32 percent of respondents, or sixteen of fifty, saw the United States as North Korea's enemy. Moreover, 68 percent of North Korean respondents, or thirty-four of fifty, said they did not see the United States as North Korea's enemy. These responses are particularly interesting in that they were given during a year which saw an unprecedented uptick in the pace and severity of North Korean provocations and weapons tests, U.S. and UN sanctions, and President Trump's derogatory statements about the North Korean leader.

Respondents' views regarding the United States as North Korea's enemy did not seem to be divided along gender lines. Of the twenty women in the microsurvey, thirteen, or 65 percent, said they did not see the United States as North Korea's enemy. Similarly, twenty-one of the thirty men in the survey, or 70 percent, said the same.

These findings suggest that North Koreans have sources of information about the United States outside of those provided the government. This could be obtained through foreign media, foreign radio (e.g., RFA, VOA) or through the markets. It could also be due to the history of U.S. humanitarian assistance to the North bilaterally and through the UN World Food Programme. During the famine years, the United States (along with Japan) was one of the top donors to the annual food appeals for the North. While the North Korean government tried to hide from the public the sources of the donations, aid workers reported that it was widely known that the United States was the donor in no small part due to the ubiquitous burlap rice sacks emblazoned with the phrase, "Gift of the American People."

Furthermore, these insights are significant because they stand in contrast with surveys of the defector community arriving in South Korea conducted by Seoul National University. When asked which country they had thought was the biggest threat to peace, these respondents overwhelmingly said the United States. China came in second, with Japan a distant third. Only a handful had thought South Korea was the biggest threat to peace while almost no one pointed to Russia.

The discrepancy in the two sets of responses is not readily explainable, though it is interesting. The timing of the surveys does not really explain the differences as they both took place around 2016. One possible explanation might relate to sample bias. Our survey subjects were fairly diverse in gender, age, education level, location, and profession. Defectors, on the other hand, represent a fairly uniform demographic (i.e., unskilled labor and from the poorer provinces). Perhaps this latter group has less access to diverse sources of information outside of government propaganda, and therefore has a one-dimensional view of the external powers. Another related explanation might have to do with relative exposure to market life in North Korea. Many of our subjects had wide exposure to foreign goods and information in the markets. We do not know if the SNU defector survey subjects had similar levels of exposure. If not, then this might also account for the difference perceptions of the United States.

* * *

North Korea is reputed to be the blackest of black boxes when it comes to society. This is not just because very few Westerners are allowed in the country and no North Koreans are allowed to travel freely, but also

TABLE 4.14 North Korean Defector Survey: While you were living in North Korea, which country did you think was the biggest threat to peace on the Korean peninsula?

Year	United States	Japan	South Korea	China	Russia	N/A
2016	116	5	4	11	2	0
2015	94	18	2	28	1	3
2014	107	14	3	21	0	4
2013	95	9	2	27	0	0

Sources: Institute for Peace and Unification Studies, Seoul National University, North Korean Public Perception on Unification (북한주민 통일의식) 2016–2013. SNU surveys draw on a pool of North Korean defectors who have arrived in South Korea during the previous year.

because the restrictions on speech and freedom of thought are draconian and absolute. For this reason, the assumption is that North Korean citizens are obedient supplicants, and only those who defect from the country are the ones who demonstrate social separation from the state apparatus.

This chapter has used a new methodology—microsurveys of citizens inside North Korea—to try to open this black box and reached five main conclusions. First, North Korean citizens, when asked, do have opinions of the government and its performance that are far from obedient and instead are openly critical. Second, while some of these views track with those of the defector community, there are some opinions by those inside North Korea that differ, therefore demonstrating that the defector community is not entirely a representative sample of North Korean society. Third and perhaps most significantly, North Korean citizens demonstrate a very positive attitude toward market activity and a negative one regarding the state-run economy; moreover, they see their futures tied to the vitality of not just goods, but information generated by the markets. Fourth, contrary to the state-run media's depiction, North Korean people exhibit a highly ambivalent view of the state's pursuit of nuclear weapons. This ambivalence ranges from anger (at the danger posed by the weapons) to distraction (when life is defined by markets more than by national security). Finally, despite a half-century of negative indoctrination regarding the United States, North Korean citizens show a more open attitude toward America and Americans than is commonly believed. While this is not a display of friendship, it is also not the display of unadulterated hatred as dictated by the government.

These microsurveys took place in 2016 and 2017, which makes them somewhat aged but certainly not outdated given the difficulty of accessing the North Korean population. The Covid-19 pandemic forced the country to lockdown only two years after our surveys were conducted, and this lockdown remained in place in 2023. Foreign diplomatic and NGO personnel have still not been allowed back into the country at the time of this writing, thus making any contact with the citizenry very difficult. Defector testimonies also suffer from a lack of substantive updating because of vast declines in the number of escapees due to a combination of the pandemic lockdown and restrictive policies by the DPRK and China.

With regard to unification, our microsurveys offer one of the first looks into how citizens inside North Korea think. Contrary to a decided lack of enthusiasm for unification and overall disinterest in the North as part of their daily lives particularly among younger South Koreans, North Korean citizens generally think of unification in normatively positive terms. They believe it is necessary. They believe it should happen in their lifetimes. And they identify with unification in ethnic nationalist terms primarily and in economic or national security terms secondarily. This reflects more idealistic views of unification than their southern brothers and sisters, who see unification (to the extent they think about it at all) largely in material and economic terms. These views track somewhat but not wholly with views on unification expressed by the defector population. This suggests gaps in thinking among these three segments of the population on the peninsula that would have to be reconciled if and when the fateful day comes.

5

UNIFICATION THEORIES

SURVEYS BY the Korea Institute for National Unification in 2021 showed that only 58.7 percent of South Koreans think unification is necessary.[1] Some observers of the Korean peninsula might find this puzzling. For a country that claims thousands of years of history, why the ambivalent reaction? Do Koreans not want unification despite the fact that national division was not chosen by Koreans but imposed by external powers in 1945? Does the disinterest stem from practical matters like the high cost of unification? Or is it simply the fear of the unknown? More broadly, how do the outside powers Japan, Russia, China, and the United States think about Korean unification? The only war that the United States and China ever fought was over an attempt by North Korea to unify the peninsula by force. Could there be another one over unification in the future? There are many unanswered questions when it comes to unification. The black box metaphor is apt. Or unification is akin to a dark tunnel. We cannot see light at the end of the tunnel, but we presume there is an exit, without any clear sense of what perils or opportunities lie along the way.

Scholars will record the post-1950 period in the Republic of Korea's history as one of the peninsula's most prosperous and eventful. Between 1960 and 2020 the gross domestic product (GDP) of the economy grew from $3.96 billion to $1.64 trillion.[2] Gross national income (GNI) per capita as of 2021 stood at $35,373, compared with a paltry $66 at the end of the Korean War in 1953.[3] South Korea is now at the cutting edge of emerging technology, completely falsifying expert U.S. estimates in the 1950s that the economy would never advance beyond agriculture and light-manufactured goods. South Korea is the only OECD country today that has gone from being a net donor recipient to a net donor provider.[4] Today, South Korea is one of the most wired countries in the world in terms of internet and cell phone usage per household, and its high-end consumer electronics dominate the world market.[5]

South Korea's accomplishments are not only economic; they are also political. The country underwent one of the most peaceful democratic transitions in world history in 1987 and today thrives as Asia's most vibrant democracy.[6] It has also given back to the international community in various ways that demonstrate a commitment to global citizenry. ROK soldiers and nongovernmental experts have been peacekeepers in seventy-one UN missions around the world, including, Afghanistan, Côte d'Ivoire, Haiti, India, Lebanon, Liberia, Pakistan, Palestine, South Sudan, and Western Sahara.[7] Korea's Peace Corps volunteer network, World Friends Korea, is in more than sixty countries around the world, spanning Africa, Central America, the Middle East, Southeast Asia, and South America. It is second only to the United States (amazing when one considers the country's population of only 51 million versus 329 million in the United States). South Korea is a leader in the G20 (it was the first Asian and non-G8 country to host the G20 summit) and in green growth.[8] In almost any context, these astounding accomplishments will be remembered as historically significant, given a span of only seven decades from which Korea started with an unsophisticated economy no larger than that of Cuba in 1950.

As memorable as South Korea's postwar development has been and will continue to be, this particularly inspiring piece of history will always be recorded with an asterisk denoting that the many successes occurred during an aberrant period of *national division*. For thirteen centuries Korea was a unified country. From when the country was organized into three warring kingdoms (Baekje, Silla, Goguryeo) through its colonial occupation by imperial Japan from 1910 to 1945, Korea and Koreans remained a single, unified entity. Japan's unconditional surrender at the end of World War II and the onset of the Cold War drove the United States and the Soviet Union to see value in the Korean peninsula. This value was not intrinsic, meaning a love for the people, a profitable interest in the economy or its resources. Instead, Korea was valued *strategically* in that neither the Soviets nor the Americans wanted the other to have possession of the peninsula as the two superpowers sought geopolitical positions in Cold War Asia. Thus, with Soviet forces already advancing down the peninsula at the end of the Pacific War in 1945, the United States made the decision to propose a temporary division of Korea into northern and southern occupation zones. The recollection of Secretary of State Dean Rusk, then a colonel on General George C. Marshall's staff, along with fellow Colonel Charles "Tic" Bonesteel, of this extraordinarily significant moment in history underscores the expediency of a decision that would unalterably affect the fate of twenty-five million Korean people:[9]

> During a meeting on August 14, 1945, the same day of the Japanese surrender, Colonel Charles Bonesteel and I retired to an adjacent room late at night and studied intently a map of the Korean peninsula. Working in haste and under great pressure, we had a formidable task: to pick a zone for the American occupation. Neither Tic [Charles Bonesteel] nor I was a Korea expert, but it seemed to us that Seoul, the capital, should be in the American sector. We also knew that the U.S. Army opposed an extensive area of occupation. Using a National Geographic map, we looked just north of Seoul for a convenient dividing line but could not find a natural geographic line. We saw instead the thirty-eighth parallel and decided to recommend that.[10]

Prior to the outbreak of the Korean War in 1950, the Soviet Union's brutal occupation of Korea's land north of the 38th parallel;[11] its leadership purge and installation of Kim Il-sung; its opposition to UN administering of elections in northern Korea in 1948; and its distrust of an eventual political union of the country under UN trusteeship meant that Korea's liberation from decades of foreign colonial occupation would now be followed by the new experience of national division. On August 15, 1948, the Republic of Korea was established. And on September 9, 1948, the Democratic People's Republic of Korea was established.

Seven decades ensued in which the two Koreas, constituted of the same people (and in one million cases, divided families), would be pitted against each other as mortal enemies, engaged in what Samuel Kim of Columbia University once described as the politics of competitive delegitimation.[12] The barrier between East and West Germany was porous compared with that of Korea. There was no contact between the two governments or between peoples across the Demilitarized Zone—the most heavily militarized border in the world. South Koreans lived in their half and the North Koreans in theirs, as if two people of the same ethnicity had nothing in common, other than the commitment to be sworn enemies. Natural mineral resource endowments, steady support from Communist China and the Soviet Union, and massive military spending kept North Korea ahead of its poor, agrarian, and politically unstable southern cousin until the mid-1970s, when South Korea's economic growth takeoff turned the tide. By the time South Korea hosted the Olympics in 1988 as a prosperous market democracy, the gaps were insurmountable, and they carry forth to today, when the South Korean economy stands at about fifty-eight times the size of that of North Korea.[13] At various points along this path, the two Koreas made attempts at national reconciliation and peace in 1972, 1990, 2000, 2007, and 2018 that were hampered by mutual mistrust and the threats posed by North Korea's nuclear weapons programs. The story of national division remains remarkably consistent: each Korea seeks security at the expense of the other's insecurity,[14] and living in two separate worlds, acknowledging their own successes, while denying the other's.

Only against the backdrop of national division can we appreciate how much the past eighty years have been an aberration in Korea's history. Unification is part of Korean identity. It is difficult to think of being Korean and not believing that those on both sides of the border are of the same stock, language, and family (literally, in the case of divided ones). Indeed, both Koreas claim to own the new era of unification in their national narratives. For South Korea, this will mean the liberation of the northern people from decades of repressive rule, poverty, and isolation under the cult of personality of the Kim family regime. The Republic of Korea constitution has a provision that grants citizenship to those in the Democratic People's Republic of Korea. For North Korea, unification would mean removing the yoke of foreign occupation (i.e., the U.S. troops on Korean soil), and the promise of nirvana under the rule of the Kim family, who represents the "true Koreans" unsoiled by the evils of external exploitation. Eventual unification of the two halves of Korea, in this sense, will mark the "end of history" and the start of a new era.

THE MYSTERY OF UNIFICATION

Our knowledge of Korean unification, however, is terribly sparse. There are two dimensions to the dearth of information. The first relates to basic data. We just do not possess a lot of empirical facts and figures about unification, aside from some general comparisons to German unification, and economic estimates of the cost of unification.[15] For an event that many see as inevitable, this lack of data is alarming but also unsurprising because governments don't have the time or resources to prepare for a hypothetical outcome.[16]

The second observation about unification relates to perceptions. Korea sits at the intersection of the great powers in Asia: Japan, China, Russia, and the United States. The Japanese see Korea as a "dagger" pointed at the heart of the maritime nation from the Eurasian continent. The Chinese see Korea as the invasion bridge to the Asian continent by hostile maritime powers (e.g., imperial Japan, United States). In international relations, the single most important variable for change is the death and birth of nation-states and the changing of territorial boundaries. In this sense, Korean unification would be a seminal event in Asia's geostrategy that directly engages the interests of all the regional powers, yet we know very little empirically about how these nations' strategists, scholars, experts, and policymakers think about Korean unification. What opportunities do they see? More important, what dangers do they fear? I know of no study today that systematically assesses the perceptions of the surrounding powers and racks and stacks their policy priorities against each other. Instead, this dearth of data has been replaced by a plethora of casual observations repeated over time in scholarly and policy circles that have taken on the character of truisms. Here is a sampling:

- "Unification can come through a 'hard landing' (i.e., collapse of North Korea or war)."
- "Unification can occur through a 'soft landing' (i.e., phased, consensus-based integration of the two Koreas)."
- "Unification will be expensive."
- "Unification will be dangerous and difficult."
- "China fears millions of North Korean refugees flooding across the border with unification."
- "Japan opposes unification because of resurgent Korean nationalism."
- "The United States cares primarily about securing the nuclear weapons in a unification scenario."

Without arguing the merits of these statements, few experts would disagree that these sorts of observations more or less remain in vogue, untouched by serious empirical analysis or scholarly investigation.

There are three reasons for the absence of data. First, as noted earlier, unification is a hypothetical outcome for which governments have neither the time nor resources to conduct deep-dive studies. Second, scholars have acknowledged the importance of unification as a topic of study, but they have filled this space with histories about the unification policies of each Korea rather than deep empirical studies. Third, to the extent governments have done planning for Korea scenarios, these have been focused on operational military planning to deal with contingencies of war or of instability inside of North Korea, rather than unification.

The result is that Korean unification remains a dark, opaque, and unexplored issue. It's not that scholars and experts do not acknowledge unification as an important topic of study, or that policymakers do not believe unification is important to their national interests. The problem is that these people don't know *how* to think about unification. Or, to put it bluntly, if Korea's unification were to happen tomorrow, the United States and surrounding powers would have little sense empirically of *what* matters to each of them, *how* they rank priorities, and *why* surrounding powers have differing perceptions of the situation. Yet all would acknowledge the turn of events as long overdue, significant, and inevitable.

HOW MUCH DO WE KNOW ABOUT UNIFICATION?

This chapter and the next one address the mystery of unification with new and original data that will help scholars and practitioners as they think about unification. Chapter 4 accomplished some of this task by featuring original data on how North Koreans think about unification. While we have polling data on how South Koreans and how North Korean defectors view unification, chapter 4 provided new microsurvey data on how average North Korean citizens consider the topic.

The next two chapters feature the first systematic data on how South Korea and the United States think about priorities and dangers as they relate to unification. Skeptics might look at this study as the indulgence of academics who are trying to measure immeasurable variables for a hypothetical event that is far removed from policy realities. Nothing could be farther from the truth. The scholarly literature has produced descriptive histories of policies on both sides of the DMZ. The think-tank literature has produced some empirical studies about the potential issues associated with unification (e.g., family reunions, transitional justice, military demobilization). And government work has focused largely on military contingency planning in the event of war or collapse. But there is a dearth of analytic work that gives analysts and scholars the tools to think about and plan for unification.

Creating a dataset of each country's assessments of unification that tries to quantify how much experts and officials know about the topic is the first critical step to building good policy and policy coordination among the players in the region. While it has become commonplace to say that there are many "unknowns" and "dangers" associated with Korean unification, these variables have never been measured;

they remain cloaked in opacity. How much do the United States, South Korea, China, and other regional powers actually know about the long-term issues associated with Korean unification? How do countries in the region perceive such issues to be important to their own national interests?

To begin answering these questions, my colleagues and I deployed a set of breakthrough pilot surveys of hundreds of government officials, scholars, and experts from South Korea and the United States. The results of the study are baseline numbers and quantitative markers that will serve as guideposts for future study and planning for Korean unification. While there are many potential scenarios for unification that range anywhere on the spectrum between a "hard landing" (i.e., collapse of the North or war) to a "soft landing" (i.e., phased, consensus-based integration), this study examines the practical issues and opportunities that will arise irrespective of the specific scenario under which the peninsula will be unified.

This data collection is important because misperceptions of national interests and a lack of empirical knowledge on Korean unification impedes smart planning and could instead lead to costly strategic blunders that could, in the worst case, result in armed conflict and lost lives. Planning among all the parties is required, but planning begins with dialogue. And such dialogue cannot move forward productively without some reliable data that captures the level of understanding and the level of concern associated with the multitude of issues that would come with unification. We do not argue that the data presented here is definitive; however, it is a first step to trying to develop metrics for how we think about unification that advances us beyond the truisms of pundits and, we hope, facilitates dialogue and planning among all involved parties.

A NOTE ON METHODOLOGY

A survey of over 300 American and South Korean officials, experts, and scholars was conducted (233 American and 108 Korean participants) to identify "blind spots" with Korean unification. My colleagues

TABLE 5.1 Unification issues

Unification issue	Definition
Conventional weapons	Decommissioning of weapons systems, military personnel, as well as potential integration of some forces and units of the DPRK into a reunified Korean armed force
Cost	Financing the cost of unification
Domestic stabilization	Addressing the domestic disposition of the northern part of the peninsula, including law and order, civil-military relations, political rights, enfranchisement, and political authority after unification
Economic rehabilitation	Economically developing the northern part of the peninsula after unification
Environment	Cleanup of environmental damage and promoting sustainability after unification
Health	Improving health care standards, eradicating disease, and providing accessibility to medicines and medical infrastructure after unification
Human rights	Addressing human rights abuses, accountability, and humanitarian needs after unification
Infrastructure	Repair and reconstruction of associated roads, railways, ports, telecommunications, and supply chains on the peninsula after unification
Nuclear weapons	Location, control, disposition, and disposal of DPRK nuclear weapons and associated programs after unification
Refugees	Management of refugees and internally displaced persons after unification

and I selected ten issues intrinsic to long-term unification planning rather than the short-term specifics of any particular unification scenario. While the way in which unification occurs (e.g., violently or peacefully; through short-term collapse or long-term integration; through a hard or soft landing) will have a natural bearing on the process of unification, the ten policy challenges listed in table 5.1 are likely to emerge in any scenario. Of course, the type of unification scenario may affect the relevance of an issue on the list, but respondents were asked to consider all of them to be equally salient in a unification scenario.

The purpose of the survey is to identify blind spots in unification. Blind spot scores are based on a composite measure of two variables from the pilot survey of U.S. and Korean experts: (1) level of concern and (2) level of knowledge. The first variable assesses the relative level of concern for a unification-related topic to the national interests of the United States, Japan, South Korea, China, and Russia. The highest levels of concern were scored a 4 (vital to national security interest), while the lowest levels of concern were scored a 1 (no bearing at all on national interest). The second variable is the amount of knowledge available to the respondent on the issue, which is defined as intelligence, empirical evidence, analysis, and scholarly literature each country can bring to bear on the issue and on which to base their policy decisions. Here, the lowest level of knowledge was scored a 4 (no information available) and the highest levels of knowledge were scored a 1 (abundant empirical evidence). The results from these two variables were averaged and then combined to produce a composite measure of blind spots for each country. The unification issues with the largest blind spots are those at the nexus of a complete lack of empirical evidence (4) and vital to national interests (4)—a recipe for potential disaster. On the other end of the spectrum, the smallest blind spots result from issues with no bearing on national interests (1), and with abundant empirical evidence (1).

Respondents were also asked not only to assess their own country's unification concerns, but also to estimate those of the other regional players (Japan, Russia, and China). The purpose of these questions/scores was to gain a sense of perceptions that the United States and South Korea have of the interests and priorities of the other countries in a unification scenario. It is hoped that these initial findings will help set a research agenda to build greater knowledge and increase available empirical evidence in each of these critical issues.

This chapter begins with an explanation of the theories and scenarios for unification as espoused in academic literature and in government policies over the past decades. The importance of any of the ten issues listed earlier will be affected by the process of unification and how it is managed. In the next chapter, we present the data based on the U.S. and South Korean surveys for each country's views on the ten issues associated with unification. Observations are made across cases as well—that is, how Americans believe South Koreans think about unification; whether there is overlap in South Korean and U.S. views on unification; and whether there is overlap in how the allies view Chinese, Japanese, and Russian interests and concerns on unification.

THEORIES OF UNIFICATION

The division of North and South Korea following World War II was a defining moment not just for the Korean peninsula but for all Northeast Asia. The strategic environment of the region and the history of the Korean people were drastically altered by this event and the Korean War that followed. Since 1945 the governments of both North and South Korea have prioritized the reunification of the Korean peninsula as a national goal. But unification has been nearly impossible to achieve because of two distinct yet interrelated sets of problems. The first set involves the development of two completely different political, economic, and social systems in North Korea and South Korea over the course of seventy-plus years. Given the enormous gap that now exists, it is widely argued that permanent integration and eventual unification between the two Koreas will be an extremely challenging and costly process. The second set of obstacles and challenges relates to the strategic environment in Northeast Asia. Just as division caused a change in regional dynamics, unification will also forever change the future strategic calculus of all countries in the region. There are many who are concerned with how a unified Korea will align itself strategically. Will it pursue an alliance with the United States or China? Or will it instead pursue a strategy of neutrality and/or autonomy in relation to the regional powers?

With so many important issues at play, it is no wonder that the literature on Korean unification is highly complex and extremely wide-ranging. It covers everything from the history of the national division to the future economic costs associated with the unification process.[17] With a focus on Northeast Asia's strategic dynamics, the literature also often seeks to explain the actions and the motives of actors on three different levels: domestic, regional, and international. A brief analysis, however, shows that there have been at least five "theories" or trends in unification studies that have driven the formulation of policy and scholarship since the end of the Korean War. All theories have been motivated by a combination of ideology and real-world events. But each one is distinct and important to remember because without one, the others could never have emerged.

What is also apparent is that none of these theories has been accompanied by a substantive research agenda. The theories embodied objectives touted at the highest national levels on both sides of the thirty-eighth parallel but were essentially rhetorical vessels, empty of substance, or empirics. This accumulated ignorance contributes to the black box that is unification today. The lack of facts about unification allows governments to accept untested assumptions, to propagate unconfirmed beliefs, and to harbor unverified suspicions as factual. These truisms have contributed to the black box associated with the unification problem today.

UNIFICATION THEORY 1: WINNER TAKE ALL

The first theory of unification emerged after the division of the Korean peninsula and was prevalent throughout the Cold War. During this time, the two Koreas were locked in a bitter battle over legitimacy. The deadly Korean War was fought by the North Koreans and South Koreans in part to have their respective ideological systems and governments recognized as the "one true Korean nation." Even after the Korean War ended, this struggle for legitimacy continued with the notion of "unification by force," or the idea that the only real definition of unification was the crushing victory of one Korea over the other (*pukch'in t'ongil* [북친 통일] or *sŏngong t'ongil* [성공 통일]).[18] This was a classic, offensive realist, and zero-sum view of the problem. Unification was about relative power. The two Koreas were locked in a struggle to the death over territory, ideology, and a way of life and were engaged in a race to see who could topple the other first. Through support from China and the Soviet Union, North Korea fared well in the early Cold War years, registering higher per capita income levels and growth rates than South Korea until the late 1960s.[19] It was during this period, as the South Korean economy started to grow faster than that of North Korea, that we also saw the highest levels of inter-Korean violence.[20] Republic of Korea presidents Syngman Rhee and Park Chung Hee both subscribed to this "winner-take-all" view in the South. The same view was also held by Kim Il-sung in the North. It was a concept that dominated both the policymaking process and the associated academic literature.

The discourse of inter-Korean dialogue during this period was dominated by competitive delegitimation—that is, capitalizing on any opportunity to demonstrate that one's system was superior to the other's.[21] For example, the North Korean military installed a taller flagpole on their side of the border in the 1970s, when they noticed the greater height of the South Korean one. When the South Korean government in the 1980s accepted North Korean flood relief supplies during monsoon season, they publicized the inferior quality of the blankets and rice provided. As petty as these episodes sound today, they epitomized the zero-sum nature of the "unification by force" mentality.

This hardcore stance on each side was solidified by larger international Cold War security dynamics as well as internal economic and political challenges. In the immediate aftermath of World War II, governments in North Korea and South Korea fought each other but also struggled to gain control over domestic enemies that challenged their respective regimes. It was the ultimate zero-sum game played on three different levels: (1) the Cold War stalemate between democracy and communism; (2) the battle for recognition and legitimacy between the democratic South Korea and socialist North Korea; and (3) the domestic struggle between the liberal left (with alleged socialist/communist sympathies) and conservative right (with alleged ties to the Japanese colonial legacy) in South Korea and the internal fight for power and leadership control between communist factions inside North Korea. The two Koreas' rigid ideological beliefs dictated that any small concessions made to the other side would not only be seen as a "loss of face" but were tantamount to an acknowledgment of the superiority of the other's system of governance.[22] In the aftermath of the Korean War, the manic and self-possessed drive for economic success on the part of both North Koreans and South Koreans was not just about attaining material well-being, but the plethora of ambitious economic development plans were designed to demonstrate at a national level that only one Korea was the more powerful and prosperous of the two.[23]

Due to this zero-sum mentality, contact between the two sides was virtually nonexistent for almost twenty years following the armistice agreement that ended the Korean War. Then, starting in the early 1970s, there appeared to be a slight thaw in the Cold War deadlock.

North and South Korean Red Cross officials began negotiations on the reunification of separated families, and additional high-level talks between intelligence directors in the two Koreas eventually resulted in a surprise North-South joint communiqué in 1972. In the communiqué, "Seoul and Pyongyang agreed that unification should be sought through: (1) independent efforts of the two Koreas, and without interference from external powers; (2) peaceful means, not by use of force; and (3) the fostering of a 'grand national unity.' "[24] This communiqué offered a new vision for unification, one that relied at least rhetorically on the principle of peaceful unification between the two Koreas. The document had also provided for "the establishment of the North-South Coordinating Committee (NSCC) which was to serve as the primary governmental channel for direct dialogue on unification issues."[25] Despite this seeming breakthrough in inter-Korean relations, dialogue quickly broke down after recriminating actions on both sides halted the rapprochement.[26]

In the 1980s there were again some brief inter-Korean exchanges, including attempts at sports exchanges, interparliamentary meetings, and talks on family reunions. However, these were dampened by several deadly North Korean provocations, including the assassination attempt on ROK president Chun Doo-hwan in Rangoon in 1983 and the terrorist bombing of KAL Flight 858 in 1987.[27] The Cold War mentality continued to dominate inter-Korean relations and the formulation of unification policy even as the global strategic environment began to change in the late 1980s. Any compromise or concession made to the other side signaled defeat. The policies, a long-lasting remnant from the Cold War stalemate between the democratic free world and the socialist/communist bloc, made it virtually impossible to make any progress in inter-Korean relations. This "winner takes all" or "zero-sum" theory of unification dominated the policymaking process and academic studies on unification up until the early 1990s.

The irony of this period—which dominated in temporal terms the thinking about unification on both sides of the peninsula—is that while each side strove for unification in its national objectives and nationalist rhetoric, neither really *studied* unification. There was no empirical understanding of what unification entailed, and what the policy challenges would be. The closest approximation to any empirical inquiry was Kim Dae-jung's thesis on the three stages of unification.[28] But this was a political document more than an empirical study. In sum, unification was a national slogan for both Koreas, full of fiery rhetoric, but without substance.

UNIFICATION THEORY 2: TOO DIFFICULT, TOO DANGEROUS

The second theory of unification emerged after the end of the Cold War and contemporaneous with the unification of East and West Germany. It was in this period that we saw the first true empirical studies of unification that went beyond (but did not exclude) political rhetoric and ideology. Koreans watched German unification with deep envy, but the realities of how difficult unification would be also started to set in. As cathartic as witnessing the German unification process might have been, South Koreans saw the rampant inflation created by union of the two currencies, and the social dislocation as East Germans tried to assimilate into a new, more fast-paced German lifestyle.

The newly evolving post–Cold War environment had catalyzed a change in perceptions about unification, especially in South Korea. While unification was previously seen as something desirable, it suddenly became something to be avoided because of the staggering costs and the terrible uncertainties. Prior to German unification, little attention had been paid to the process or mechanics of Korean unification. But watching the Germans contend with social, political, and economic integration caused some Koreans to believe that South Korea could "absorb" its northern counterpart. This was largely a far-right, conservative, hard-line view based on a belief that the economy was strong enough and large enough to swallow up the North.[29] But the majority of Koreans saw more clearly the challenges of unification. The theory that unification was "too difficult and too dangerous" emerged and took a prominent place in policymaking and scholarship. Additionally, the changes in perception were caused by growing fears about the economic inequalities between North and South Korea and the increasing instability of the Kim Il-sung (later Kim Jong-il) regime. Korean unification was no longer perceived as a simple "winner takes all" scenario, but as a complex process that would be messy and highly unpredictable.

During this period, there was an intense debate between two different schools of thought on the Korean unification process—the hard landing versus soft landing—largely sparked by international concerns about the stability of North Korea's political system and economy.[30] The work produced in this vein provided a service in pushing further the understanding of unification, largely by creating a paradigm to think about the problem. The two different schools of thought were related to four different scenarios for unification: (1) DPRK regime collapse, (2) military conflict, (3) gradual change in North Korea leading to peaceful integration, and (4) maintenance of the status quo or "muddling through."[31] Scenarios 1 and 2 were associated with the hard-landing school of thought. A hard landing would entail a process whereby "the inability of the regime in power to maintain effective political, economic, social and military control, ultimately lead[s] to the dissolution of the regime and, in the extreme case, the state."[32] A soft landing, on the other hand—most often associated with scenarios 3 and 4—was defined as "a process whereby gradual and controlled implementation of selective economic reforms enables a command economy to assume some characteristics of a market economy, although no regime change occurs."[33] Although different variations of these schools of thought existed in both policy and academic circles, the hard-landing theory of unification predominated in Korean thinking from the end of the Cold War in Europe until the Asian financial crisis in 1997.[34]

There are several reasons why the hard landing theory prevailed at this time. A sequence of unprecedented events befell North Korea. In 1990 the Soviet Union normalized political relations with South Korea, and with this decision, Moscow no longer provided patron aid and trade to Pyongyang. Within one year, North Korean imports of oil from the Soviet Union dropped by more than 50 percent.[35] In 1992 China followed suit and normalized relations with South Korea.[36] Then, in July 1994, Kim Il-sung suffered a massive and fatal stroke, throwing the entire country into turmoil as a young, untested son took the reins of power. Shortly thereafter, massive flooding destroyed annual harvests, leading to a widespread famine in the country that killed 10 percent of the population (over two million people).[37] These events led many officials and experts to predict an imminent collapse of the North Korea regime.[38]

In the late 1980s and early 1990s, the South Korean government itself was transitioning from a militaristic, right-wing authoritarian regime to a democratic one. The ROK economy also emerged from the ranks of poor, underdeveloped countries to becoming one of the "Asian Tigers" with double-digit annual economic growth rates that left the stagnating North Korean economy permanently in the rearview mirror.[39] South Korea showcased its development and democracy to the world when it hosted the Summer Olympics in Seoul in 1988.[40] It was during this period that we began to see the first serious empirical study of unification, largely related to the estimated cost of the enterprise. The ROK Unification Ministry as well as think tanks like Korea Development Institute (KDI) and Korea Institute for National Unification (KINU) and private-sector institutions like Goldman Sachs all calculated the cost of unification, and the numbers were large and frightening to most South Koreans.[41] The primary policy implication of this new knowledge about unification had to do with concerns about a hard landing's damage to the ROK's continued growth prospects, which in turn dampened support for unification along the lines of the German model. Having become a democracy, hosted the Olympics, and gained a seat in the United Nations, all between 1987 and 1991, South Koreans became increasingly proud of their newfound standing in the international community but also feared that a costly and complicated unification process would relegate the ROK back to the ranks of an underdeveloped country. In this sense, unification looked like it would take the country a step backward precisely at a time when it had its sights set on the glide path forward toward reaching the 10,000 USD per capita income mark and eventual OECD status.[42]

Additionally, there was a perceived change in North Korean unification rhetoric during this time. The retreat of communism globally precipitated an existential crisis for North Korea as its main sources of economic aid and ideological legitimacy started to dry up. Faced with a growing external threat, a failing economy, and a conventional military with increasingly deteriorating capabilities, North Korea seemingly shifted its strategy from "achieve unification at all costs" to "maintain regime survival at all costs."[43]

Given these developments, there was little domestic political will to push ahead with North-South dialogue and reconciliation efforts.

Aside from a short, promising period of dialogue between 1988 and 1992, no lasting progress was made on inter-Korean relations throughout the 1990s. At that time, Roh Tae-woo, the president of the ROK, attempted to engage with North Korea under the banner of *Nordpolitik* or Northern Diplomacy, which aimed at pragmatic and nonideological diplomatic outreach.[44] The short period of engagement resulted in the signing of two accords: "The Basic Agreement on Reconciliation, Non-aggression, and Exchanges and Cooperation" (1991) and the "Joint Declaration on Denuclearization of the Korean Peninsula" (1992).[45] While initially these accords seemed to signal progress on both sides by ending decades of mutual nonrecognition, identifying areas of cooperation, and laying out an institutional roadmap for unification, there was again the problem of rhetoric without substance. Korean unification was dominated by political discourse and even agreements, but without any serious study of its meaning. The Basic Agreement in 1991, for example, was not accompanied by joint empirical study of unification by the two Koreas. The subcommittees set up as a result of this agreement were focused again on the politics, largely for domestic consumption.[46]

Unsurprisingly, the agreements ultimately failed to resolve the deep conflicts between the two Koreas. South Korea's normalization of diplomatic relations with the Soviet Union (1990) and China (1992) during President Roh Tae-woo's presidential term also dealt a harsh blow to North Korea.[47] After 1992 North Korea cut off contact with South Korea and refused all opportunities to further engage in inter-Korean dialogue. The subsequent ROK president, Kim Young-sam, also later attempted rapprochement with the DPRK, but revelations about North Korea's suspected nuclear weapons program, and its announced withdrawal from the Non-Proliferation Treaty (NPT) in 1993, only added to the deepening distrust between North and South Korea. Although North Korea later signed the 1994 Agreed Framework with the United States and suspended its withdrawal from the NPT, the DPRK's attempts to freeze South Korea out of the agreement's negotiations left many ROK officials with little inclination or cause to work with the North.[48]

Broader international factors and events did not lend themselves well to Korean unification at this time. Despite the end of the Cold

War and German unification, overall the international security environment was not particularly conducive to making progress on this issue in the late 1980s and early 1990s. While the United States did spend considerable resources trying to resolve the North Korean nuclear crisis during the 1993–1994 period, the U.S. government was also heavily preoccupied with Saddam Hussein and the Gulf War (Desert Storm), as well as the conflicts in Bosnia and Rwanda. While concerned about the DPRK's nuclear weapons program, the United States had little time or resources to devote entirely to North Korean policy or unification policy.[49] China, dealing with its own set of internal problems, including the events in Tiananmen Square in 1989, also had little incentive to change the security status quo in Northeast Asia or tackle the problem of Korean unification. China was busy addressing domestic economic reforms, implementing its plan for a "peaceful rise," and squashing sources of potential domestic unrest.

The result was that the end of this period saw important political agreements among the two Koreas and their neighbors, but these agreements neither individually nor collectively generated scholarship and policy discussions that lent greater transparency to the unification process than the earlier "winner takes all" or *pukch'in t'ong-il* period. What this period did show, however, was that new data did affect policy perceptions of the attractiveness of unification among the government and society. The first real attempt to collect data through the study of German unification and its potential application to the Korean situation set new parameters that emphasized cost, caution, and prudence on how the Koreans and the world thought about unification. These parameters, once set, would act as empirical blinders for the next decade.

UNIFICATION THEORY 3: SUNSHINE POLICY

In 1998 the ROK's new democratic president, Kim Dae-jung, put forward the idea of the "Sunshine Policy."[50] Based on one of Aesop's fables, the policy's inspiration was the story of the Sun and Wind competing to see which successfully could remove the coat of a weary traveler. The Wind went first and blew a cold, fierce wind to remove the coat from the man, but this only caused the traveler to button up and grip the coat even tighter around his neck to manage the elements. After the Wind failed, the Sun then cast rays of sunlight and warmth on the traveler, which caused him to take off the coat.[51]

The Sunshine Policy was in many ways the antithesis of the "winner-take-all" model of unification. It was a non-zero-sum strategy of unconditional engagement designed to open North Korea to the forces of reform. The core assumption underlying the policy was that North Korean belligerence, pursuit of WMD, and otherwise deviant behavior stemmed from basic security deficits experienced by the state. Under this theory, the promise of mutual respect and conciliation to North Korea would lessen the regime's insecurities and reduce the threats posed by its military and weapons of mass destruction. The promise of economic cooperation, moreover, would promote North Korea's internal reforms and opening to the outside world. This process of peaceful political reconciliation and economic cooperation would foster a prolonged period of mutual coexistence, followed by a "one country, two systems" format, which would then be followed by gradual integration of the two systems, and eventually enable reunification through a process of mutual consultation and consensus.[52] The policy was tied to Kim Dae-jung's more liberal political ideology and was subsequently carried forth by his successor, President Roh Moo-hyun (2003–2008), and under President Moon Jae-in (2017–2022).

The emergence of this alternative school of thought was not just due to ideology, however. The Sunshine Policy, which could be called a theory informed by the desire for an "extended soft landing" when it comes to unification, was motivated by hard economic realities. South Korea experienced a massive economic downturn in 1997–1998 when a liquidity crisis required emergency assistance from the International Monetary Fund to prevent the economy from collapsing.[53] This crisis effectively made discussions of unification economically impossible, so engaging with the North Korean regime over the long term, and paving the way for a gradual transition or a soft landing, seemed to be the best policy choice. At the time, the inter-Korean summits of 2000, 2007, and 2018 also gave some hope for long-term reconciliation and peaceful unification.[54] The "sunshine summits" produced two iconic symbols of inter-Korean cooperation, a joint industrial complex situated midway at the waist of the Korean peninsula near North Korea's second-largest city, Kaesong; and a tourism complex

(Diamond Mountain or Kumgang Mountain), also on the northern side of the DMZ. The former project spoke to the economic potential of inter-Korean cooperation, marrying up South Korean capital and technology with North Korean labor to produce light manufactured consumer products. The latter project appealed to the South Korean public who fancied the novelty of a trip across the border to the mythical birthplace of the Korean race, or who hailed from families still divided by the Korean War.[55]

Upon reflection, however, what was so distinct about the Sunshine Policy was two conceptualizations about unification it imparted on policy and scholarship. First, it propagated the view that unification should be pushed to generations into the distant future. In effect, sunshine policies, informed by the empirics of German unification and the Asian financial crisis, were meant to kick the "unification can" down the road. Second and relatedly, the policies socialized an entire generation of Koreans and the world into viewing unification as a "bad thing"—too expensive, too impractical, and too inconvenient—and so it should not be a concern or goal of the current generation or even its children or grandchildren.

The difference between this view and its predecessors was that it assigned a negative normative value to unification, perhaps in reaction to the decades of dominant conservative political ideology that strove for unification as a positive national goal. The prior two theories of unification—Pukch'in t'ongil (March North) and "Too Dangerous, Too Difficult"—never denied that unification would be a formidable challenge for the Korean people, but the costs and pains associated with it would never diminish the positive identification of the goal with Korean identity. Sunshine Policy essentially taught that unification was not necessarily a normatively positive aspirational goal because it implied competition rather than reconciliation with the North, and that competition could drive the country into war, chaos, or bankruptcy. The disavowal of the pursuit of competition and the adversarial framing of North Korea was informed at its core by *minjung* ideology, which stressed the racial homogeneity of the Korean people and its exploitation by external powers. Thus it viewed the northern neighbor as brethren rather than as a sovereign enemy, and any exercise of power aimed at unification or "winning" over the other was a client-state mentality ingrained by external competing powers (the United States and the Soviet Union) that was ultimately self-destructive.[56] A decade of Sunshine Policy essentially taught a generation of Koreans that a legitimate narrative existed in Korean identity that saw unification as something that should be avoided at all costs into the foreseeable future.

At certain times, the Sunshine Policy created friction between U.S. and South Korean allies, as Seoul argued for a conciliatory effort at engaging the North Korean threat rather than greater containment of that threat.[57] As it related to unification policy, there were many critics of the soft-landing theories who argued these theories were flawed because they were basing policy on a set of fragile and unproven assumptions. For example, Sunshine Policy presumed that the only path to a soft landing (presumably preferable to a hard landing) was through engagement and reconciliation. Advocates assumed that there was a linear causal relationship between diplomatic incentives and positive opening and reform in North Korea's political system and economy. Sunshine Policy also assumed that there would be no military conflict associated with a soft landing, while there would be an abundance of it in a hard landing. Finally, the theory assumed that neighboring powers would all naturally support the policy over tougher, containment-oriented approaches.[58]

All three periods of Sunshine Policy produced no new empirical studies of unification. Of course, these periods saw studies of the potential for economic cooperation between the two Koreas and, during Moon's tenure, an added emphasis on transport and energy infrastructure development. But studies explicitly on unification were seen as politically incorrect because they raised the specter of absorption of the North by the South. Again, this was evident in Moon Jae-in's explicit deferral of unification as a national policy, replaced by a policy of coexistence and coprosperity.[59] The opacity surrounding unification instead was treated as an accepted reality that then informed a politically and ideologically motivated imperative to (1) engage North Korea and (2) delay unification indefinitely. The reification of this opacity during the sunshine era not only set the policy but also constrained it in the sense that it set blinders on new policy-related and scholarly thinking. For one decade between 1997 and 2007, truisms became accepted as factual and without further study. And without any new facts unearthed, the discourse on unification could only be thought of in one way.

UNIFICATION THEORY 4: PRAGMATISM

The initial decade of the sunshine era ended with the election of conservative South Korean president Lee Myung-bak in December 2007. Lee was a businessman, not an ideologue. He saw both North Korean policy and unification policy in pragmatic terms. What emerged during this period was a pushing back against a decade of views on unification, not with new information per se, but with political will.

The new theory of unification—the fourth theory—was a pragmatic one tied to Lee's own personal convictions—that is, unification may be expensive, it may be difficult, and it may be dangerous. But Koreans cannot blindly stick their heads in the sand and hope the problems will go away. Instead, as traumatic as unification may be, it could very well come tomorrow, next month, or next year, so it was essential to prepare for the process.

This policy shift was likely informed not only by President Lee's own pragmatic leadership style but also by events unfolding in North Korea that indicated a high degree of both threat and instability to the region. Despite negotiated agreements in 2005 and 2007, North Korea continued to pursue the development of nuclear weapons and ballistic missiles, conducting two nuclear bomb tests and eighteen missile provocations between 2008 and 2013.[60] The massive stroke suffered by Kim Jong-il in 2008, and his eventual death in 2011, led many to predict, once again, that the North Korean regime was on the verge of collapse.[61] In 2010 South Korean attitudes considerably hardened after a North Korean submersible torpedoed and sank the *Cheonan*, killing forty-six sailors in the largest loss of military lives since the Korean War.[62] Later that year, North Korea's shelling of Yeonpyeong Island in broad daylight, captured on citizens' cell phone cameras, raised concerns that North Korea's unstable domestic situation was manifesting itself in external provocations threatening to the entire region.[63] Many officials and experts began to call for contingency planning to deal with the possibility of a North Korean regime collapse due to the threat posed by North Korea's nuclear weapons program and the growing instability of the Kim family regime.[64]

What distinguished this "pragmatic" theory of unification from its predecessors was its call for prudence and preparation. This theory did not make heroic claims to defeat the enemy to the north like the "winner-take-all" view, nor did it make self-professed enlightened claims about cutting through Cold War barriers to engage distant brethren; instead, it argued that the time had come for Koreans and the other countries in Northeast Asia, given the uncertainties in the North, to start preparing for the unification process now.

As one expert close to President Lee explained to me, if there were a bumper sticker for this theory, it would have read: "Prepare today, be lucky tomorrow." What this meant is that the various difficulties associated with unification require that the Koreans benefit from a little bit of luck to manage all the challenges. But luck only comes to those who are prepared. Those who are not prepared are never in a position to be lucky. Thus the concept was not about the overthrow of the North, but about prepositioning oneself to be ready should the fateful day arrive. This view, it was argued, was eminently more practical and sensible than sunshine era's strategy of simply wishing it would go away forever. Moreover, the pragmatist view made no normative assessment of unification—it was a view that could be espoused by hard-liners or soft-liners alike. Though the conservative Lee presidency ended a decade of progressive rule in Korea, this view on unification did not fit easily on the ideological spectrum between the Sunshine Policy on the left and "winner-take-all" on the right. If anything, it advocated that Koreans do their "due diligence" and prepare for the unexpected. In sum, conservatives may want to take North Korea by force, progressives may want to engage the North, but pragmatists worried that North Korea may just fall into South Korean laps one day. And if South Koreans do not take the lead in preparing, it is hard to imagine that other countries would do the same.

This view differed from the Sunshine Policy in one important respect. Preparation for unification did not entail engagement with North Korea. Promises of President Lee Myung-bak's "Vision 3000: Denuclearization and Openness" proposal to bring North Korean income per capita to three thousand dollars were political statements of interest in engagement, but these were highly conditional on DPRK security concessions to render them impracticable.⁶⁵ Instead, the focus was on preparing the South Korean people, not North Koreans.

This theory of unification was informed by limited but new research on realistic scenarios for regime collapse as well as the study of long-term pathways to peaceful unification. But most of the information about unification remained at the political level, this time focused on educating the domestic public about unification. The unification ministry took resources once used for inter-Korean economic cooperation by the previous administrations and focused them on large gatherings attended by foreign policy luminaries to talk more openly about unification as a part of Korea's destiny. I attended a number of these conferences and found an interesting sociological dynamic. Held in the ballrooms of some of the ritziest hotels in Seoul, the conferences hosted the usual requisite VIPs and opinion leaders, but they also invited many high school and college students in the audience. These young people would listen to luminaries like Colin Powell and Richard Haass talking about how unification is part of Korea's destiny.⁶⁶ As cliché as these soundbites may ring, the gatherings played an important role in educating a generation that had been weaned off of talk about unification during the decade of the Sunshine Policy. In the reception hall outside the ballroom, a mega-sized whiteboard invited students to post their thoughts on multicolored sticky notes about unification. Reading these was absolutely fascinating. Students wrote messages like,

> "Before coming to this conference, I did not really think about unification. Now I will."
> "We Koreans need to be ready for unification if it comes to us."
> "I may not want unification, but it can come our way."
> "If our generation doesn't think about unification, who will?"

Taken as a whole, the whiteboard became a rainbow of multicolored sticky notes that manifested an awakening to unification for a younger, affluent, and educated generation who did not suffer through the Korean War, who understand national division only as a historical event in textbooks, and who don't identify themselves with anything north of the 38th parallel. The political objective of these pragmatic efforts was to reverse one decade of "nonthinking" about unification. One of the few substantive research projects on the practical issues related to the unification process, including humanitarian aid, securing nuclear weapons and materials, and treatment for disease outbreaks, was done by a three-year CSIS-USC joint study.[67] But once again, the discourse on unification remained political more than positivist.

UNIFICATION THEORY 5: JACKPOT

The fifth theory of unification, advanced under President Park Geun-hye, evolved from the earlier pragmatic theory proposed under Lee. Like its predecessor, it also called for proactive preparation for unification, but it supplemented this with a positive, normative framing of unification. The bumper sticker for this view, as laid out initially in Park's first presidential press conference in January 2014, was of unification as a "bonanza" or "jackpot" for Korea and her neighbors: "Reunification is *daebak* [a jackpot]. Some Koreans oppose reunification for fear the costs would be too high. I believe reunification would be a chance for the economy to make a huge leap."[68]

According to this theory, unification should be reimagined or envisioned as a process that could offer opportunities for growth, investment, and peace to both Koreas and to all Korean people. This fifth theory of unification does not see the process as the winner-take-all, or something to be feared and delayed indefinitely (sunshine), or even something that we must reluctantly prepare for (pragmatic). Instead, it conceptualizes unification as an opportunity for all Korean people and their neighbors:

> I believe that the Republic of Korea will similarly reach ever greater heights after unification. The northern half of the Korean Peninsula will also experience rapid development. A unified Korea that is free from the fear of war and nuclear weapons will be well positioned to make larger contributions to dealing with a wide range of global issues like international peace-keeping, nuclear non-proliferation, environment and energy, and development. Furthermore, as a new

distribution hub linking the Pacific and Eurasia, it is bound to benefit the economies of East Asia and the rest of the world.[69]

The jackpot theory of unification carried elements of its predecessors. Though at the opposite end of the ideological spectrum from progressive *minjung* thinking, the jackpot theory did share the normative framing of unification as a positive outcome—something that would help to rid Korea of its ills. For Park, this theme resonated with an overarching (albeit unsuccessful) domestic political message of a kinder and gentler brand of conservatism to bring more happiness to Korean society.

The jackpot theory was similar to the pragmatic view on unification in that it left space for engagement with North Korea to achieve a vision of unification, but in a highly conditioned way that effectively rendered it impracticable. Park's unification policy was based on a philosophy of diplomacy called "trustpolitik." This concept sees trust as existing in two interrelated forms. One form of trust is related to confidence-building measures—small steps taken over time that reassure each side that their actions are guided by specific rules and norms, and they can expect the other party to abide by the same rules in the future. This type of trust is built up primarily through cooperation in areas covering nontraditional security or shared public goods like humanitarian assistance or environmental protection. The other side of trust is likened to "credible deterrence"—for instance, if you break the rules, you can trust that you will be punished. Rather than being something dark and negative, trustpolitik and jackpot narratives aimed to paint unification as something bright and hopeful. Confidence-building measures, cooperation, and transparency can pave the way for better inter-Korean relations and peaceful unification in the future.[70] For the North, however, these messages from the ROK president and daughter of former military dictator Park Chung-hee did not elicit any trust or belief that it was serious.

The jackpot theory shares similarities with its immediate predecessor in its efforts to socially re-engineer the previously negative discourse on unification that had taken root over the previous fifteen years. The government operationalized this concept in two ways. First, it produced reports quantifying the "jackpot"—for example, a National Assembly Budget Office report in 2014 found that unification will cost 4.65 quadrillion South Korean won by 2060 but estimated the benefits to be three times greater, at 14.5 quadrillion South Korean won.[71] Second, it spent the annual inter-Korean economic cooperation budgets not on economic projects with the North, but on conferences and public relations campaigns in the South to help younger Koreans in their twenties and thirties think about unification in positive terms. Even the colloquial term *daebak* was carefully chosen as a slang term to identify with younger Koreans.[72] Of note was the effort to reach out not just to college-age students, but to the very young. Pamphlets depicting cartoon figures following the rainbow to a jackpot (i.e., unification) at the end made obvious the desire to connect Koreans at all ages with a positive identification of unification. In 2014 14.3 billion won from the inter-Korean economic cooperation budget was spent toward the construction of the Center for the Future Unified Korean Peninsula to educate the younger generation of South Koreans on the importance of unification. Other unification education activities undertaken by the government included organizing a cohort of teen reporters composed of fifth- and sixth-grade students to participate in hands-on activities like posting articles about unification and publishing off-line newsletters. The government also invested in producing and distributing music videos and animations to ensure that young people can more easily access and understand unification issues.[73] What did we learn about unification during this period? The administration set up a committee of experts and former government officials called the Presidential Commission for Unification Preparation that was nominally headed by President Park. The commission was tasked with deeper analysis of the challenges and opportunities of unification, and making "proposals to the President of the Republic of Korea regarding policy development and implementation for a democratic and peaceful inter-Korean unification."[74]

Despite her eventual impeachment and imprisonment, Park deserves credit for creating a paradigm for thinking about unification that was positive and forward looking. But little has been done to shed any light on the unification tunnel. And that which has been done remains entirely focused on Korea's interests, without any broader implications for U.S. interests.

WHERE ARE WE TODAY?

Moon Jae-in's "peace diplomacy" is essentially a continuation of unification conceptualized in the tradition of the Sunshine Policy and *minjung* ideology. The Moon government felt especially motivated to pursue engagement with North Korea for three expedient reasons: (1) Lee Myung-bak's and Park Geun-hye's successive terms in office led to neglect (in Moon's eyes) of inter-Korean relations for nearly a decade; thus there was much lost ground to make up; (2) Barack Obama's policy of "strategic patience" or nonengagement with North Korea exacerbated the damage done by South Korean conservative governments to the sunshine project; and (3) Donald Trump's threats to take the peninsula to war in 2017 had to be reversed.

The progressive Moon government saw inter-Korean reconciliation and peace as a coordination game, not a conflict game. In their minds, Koreans did not ask to be divided. They were collateral damage from Cold War politics and thus are wrapped in a fundamental security dilemma that needs to be unwound. Their goals were to create institutions of communication, economic cooperation, and greater transparency and predictability across the DMZ.

The Moon Jae-in presidency's policies largely fall within the framework of the Sunshine Policy, though they gave it a more general name, "A Peaceful and Prosperous Korean Peninsula."[75] It made similar assumptions about the problem and viewed inter-Korean reconciliation and peace as the best path to a soft landing. Like its predecessor, the strategy explicitly framed unification in normatively negative terms, instead focusing on reconciliation between the two Korean peoples, while leaving formation of a unified state to the distant future. Moon laid this out clearly in a speech in Berlin, where he said:

> We do not wish for North Korea's collapse, and will not work toward any kind of unification through absorption. Neither will we pursue

an artificial unification. Unification is a process where both sides seek coexistence, co-prosperity and a restored sense of national community. When peace is established, unification will be realized naturally someday through an agreement between the South and the North. What my Administration and I would like to realize is only peace."[76]

Also like his predecessors, Moon's privileging of inter-Korean peace has created some tension with the United States as gaps emerge between his desire and pace of promoting inter-Korean economic cooperation and U.S. sanctions efforts aimed at achieving denuclearization.

Of note in Moon's version of Sunshine Policy is the emphasis on race as the unifying element. This comports with traditional *minjung* ideology and was evident particularly in the summit meeting between Moon and Kim Jong-un in Pyongyang in 2018. For three days, all the ceremonies and substance played heavily to racial unity as an element to transcend all political differences. And in Moon's speech at the May Day Stadium to tens of thousands of North Koreans, he reemphasized that "our people are outstanding. Our people are resilient. Our people love peace. And our people must live together. We had lived together for five thousand years but apart for just 70 years. Here, at this place today, I propose we move forward toward the big picture of peace in which the past 70-year-long hostility can be eradicated and we can become one again."[77]

President Yoon Suk Yeol's "Audacious Initiative" for inter-Korean relations, announced in 2022, shares similarities with its ideological precursors, particularly during Lee Myung-bak's tenure.[78] The initiative specifically conditions South Korean support to the North on denuclearization and promises large-scale food distribution, assistance for power generation, modernization of transportation infrastructure, and promotion of investment flows. Unlike Park's "jackpot" theory of unification, Yoon's plan does not explicitly assign a normative value to unification but suggests its mutually beneficial nature through explicit exchanges that could take place through inter-Korean cooperation. For example, the audacious initiative calls for the exchange of North Korean mineral reserves for South Korean food, projects on climate and ecological preservation of the peninsula, and the provision of medical assistance to reduce pandemic uncertainties.

If Moon's strategy prioritized the achievement of inter-Korean peace, Yoon's proposals are informed by the conviction that such a peace must rest on denuclearization of the Korean peninsula. Otherwise, the declaration of peace might be politically expedient but substantively parlous, and ultimately accepting North Korea as a de facto nuclear weapons state. Thus Yoon's initiatives tie substantial South Korean economic support to concrete, if incremental, steps on denuclearization, unlike other previous administrations. However, the familiarity of these proposals with their predecessors suggests unification policy is tantamount to old wine in new bottles, and advancement in our knowledge remains limited.

* * *

The hard realities of reunification, and the problems associated with North Korea's growing instability and security threat to the region, have caused a definite shift in thinking about the reunification process. Officials and scholars are slowly realizing that short-term "Band-Aid" solutions have done little to resolve the North Korean problem and also have failed to positively shape the long-term strategic environment for Korean unification. There is an increasing realization that serious study of unification is necessary to prepare for the future, and to help broaden the aperture on policy today. In the latter regard, the only facts that we have on unification despite decades of different theories are stylized facts without any real analysis—e.g., unification will be costly; a hard landing is dangerous; millions of refugees will flood China. These stylized facts have narrowed the way we think about policy today to a small bandwidth of policy stasis. Unearthing and disseminating new facts about unification can change the way we think about the future, but it can also widen the aperture on policy today, allowing us to think in ways we could not without new data. The unification surveys in the next chapter aim to take a modest step toward filling this void.

6

UNIFICATION DATA

UNITED STATES VIEWS ON UNIFICATION

A lack of empirical knowledge about Korean unification can impede smart planning and could lead to costly strategic blunders if and when unification comes to pass. To begin quantifying these variables, my colleagues and I conducted a breakthrough pilot survey study of 233 of the top Asia/Korea experts, government officials, scholars, and opinion leaders in the United States, with a response rate of 47 percent.[1] The results of the study are baseline numbers and quantitative markers that will serve as guideposts for future study and planning for Korean unification.

Respondents were asked to assess ten unification issues with two scores. First, how important is the issue to your country's national interests? U.S. respondents were asked to score the issue on a four-point scale as follows:

- HIGH/Score of 4: Vital to the U.S. national interests
- MEDIUM/Score of 3: Of importance, but not vital to U.S. national interests
- LOW/Score of 2: Of low importance to U.S. national interests
- NONE/Score of 1: No bearing on U.S. national interests

Second, respondents were asked to assess the availability of knowledge—defined as intelligence, analysis, scholarly literature, and other empirical evidence—on the given issue to make informed policy decisions. Respondents were asked to score the issue on a four-point scale:

- NONE/Score of 4: No information
- LOW/Score of 3: Insufficient amount of information
- MEDIUM/Score of 2: Sufficient amount of information
- HIGH/Score of 1: Abundant amount of information

The ten issues listed in table 5.1 reflect the gamut of practical issues and opportunities that are to arise with unification regardless of the scenario under which unification occurs. Respondents were instructed to score issues as most significant for national interests with a maximum score of 4, and those issues assessed to have the least knowledge available a maximum score of 4. These split scores were then combined and averaged to create a composite score. The highest average composite score is considered the most acute blind spots for unification according to U.S. experts because they are considered critical to national security, but without much knowledge on the issue. These experts were also asked to score the same ten issues from the perspectives of other countries in the region. The purpose of that exercise is to gain a sense of what U.S. perceptions are of the other countries' blind spots and priorities in unification. Scores for the United States are summarized in figure 6.1.

What most concerns American experts about Korean unification? The findings are novel and in some respects surprising. First, as one might expect, nuclear weapons rank as the top issue for U.S. national interests given all the policy attention they received prior to unification. But this was not considered to be the biggest blind spot by U.S. experts. Instead, as can be seen in the bubble chart in figure 6.1, U.S. experts perceive the biggest blind spot to be domestic stabilization of the northern portion of the peninsula after unification. Domestic stabilization is a bigger blind spot than nuclear weapons because there is very little information to make policy. Indeed, only 31 percent of American experts believed there was "sufficient or abundant"

FIGURE 6.1 U.S. views of unification blind spots.

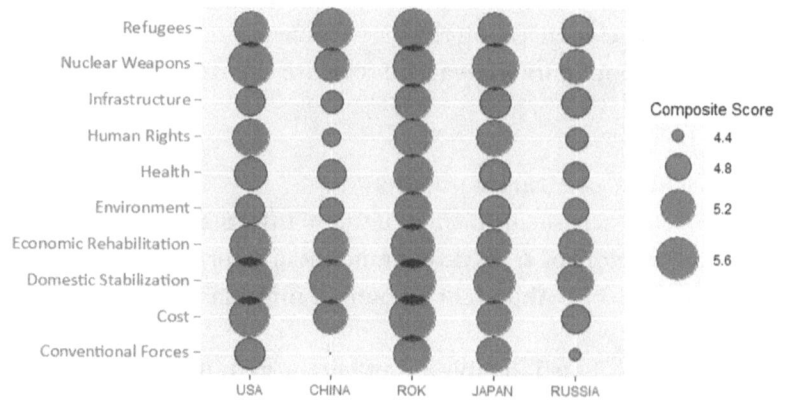

Unification Transparency Index: U.S. experts' perceptions

	United States	China	ROK	Japan	Russia
Domestic stabilization	5.88	5.70	5.87	5.53	5.22
Nuclear weapons	5.79	5.16	5.57	5.87	5.12
Economic rehabilitation	5.55	5.20	5.68	5.14	5.14
Cost	5.47	5.11	5.85	5.21	4.91
Refugees	5.18	5.55	5.54	5.15	5.00
Health	5.09	4.91	5.40	4.98	4.78
Human rights	5.33	4.54	5.35	5.22	4.66
Infrastructure	4.95	4.66	5.27	4.99	4.95
Environment	4.95	4.73	5.28	5.00	4.75
Conventional forces	4.98	4.30	5.30	5.19	4.40

information (score of 1–2) with regard to domestic stabilization, compared with 83 percent for the information metric regarding nuclear weapons. Americans still think that nuclear weapons are a bigger concern for U.S. interests than domestic stabilization (100 percent ranked this as "important or vital" to national interests with a score of 3–4), but the absence of information in the latter case is acute, thereby increasing the composite score.[2] One can surmise that American concerns about domestic stabilization stem from not just a lack of knowledge on the issue, but the generally difficult experiences the United States has had with state-building in other contexts. Lack of control over the process, presumably because the South Korean government would be in control of maintaining social order and establishing political authority, might be another factor. The notion that U.S. military forces would be involved on the ground in maintaining political order would harken back to days of the U.S. military occupation after World War II, which would most likely not fit well with the new Korean government's narrative and might elicit nationalist backlash. All these factors complicate and reduce control over a domestic stabilization process.

Following domestic stabilization in terms of unification blind spots, the next highest score is nuclear weapons, economic development, and cost. The relative priority of the denuclearization issue among the ten unification issues is to be expected given the national security concerns for the United States with the securing, decommissioning, and disposal of these weapons prior to unification. Naturally, we would expect concerns about economic development and cost of Korean unification to register for U.S. experts as having a bearing on U.S. national interests given that positive outcomes on these issues (i.e., postunification growth with minimal cost) would be desirable for U.S. policy objectives in Northeast Asia. Sixty-seven percent of Americans consider economic rehabilitation of a united Korea to be "important/vital" to U.S. interests (score of 3–4), but 70 percent believe there is "insufficient or no" information available (score of 3–4) to inform policy. Fifty-four percent of Americans consider the cost of financing unification to be "important or vital" to U.S. interests (score of 3–4); moreover, of all ten issues, they believe unification cost to be the most lacking in terms of available information (only 25 percent responded that enough information was available).

Surprisingly, U.S. experts do not score human rights as a significant blind spot for unification. Only 74 percent consider it "important or vital" to U.S. interests (score of 3–4). This is somewhat unexpected given the groundswell of opinion on this issue, including the UN Commission of Inquiry Report on Human Rights in the DPRK.[3] In addition, the United States has been the only country off the peninsula that consistently has raised concerns about human rights abuses inside the DPRK to the international community, passing domestic legislation both to appoint a U.S. special envoy and to create a

TABLE 6.1 U.S. levels of concern and levels of knowledge on unification issues

Level of concern	Vital	4		Level of Knowledge	Abundant empirical evidence	1
	Of importance but not vital	3			Sufficient amount	2
	Low importance	2			Insufficient amount	3
	No bearing at all	1			No empirical evidence	4

	Issue	% who answered important/vital (score of 3–4 per issue)	Average level of concern score/issue		Issue	% who answered abundant/ sufficient knowledge (score of 1–2 per issue)	Average level of knowledge score/ issue
Level of concern	Nuclear weapons	100%	3.93	Level of knowledge	Conventional forces	86%	1.68
	Conventional forces	93%	3.30		Nuclear weapons	83%	1.86
	Domestic stabilization	77%	3.11		Human rights/ transitional justice	59%	2.36
	Human rights/ transitional justice	74%	2.96		Refugees	52%	2.42
	Economic rehabilitation	67%	2.78		Infrastructure	40%	2.68
	Refugees	63%	2.76		Domestic stabilization	31%	2.77
	Cost	54%	2.65		Economic rehabilitation	30%	2.76
	Health	37%	2.32		Health	29%	2.77
	Infrastructure	36%	2.27		Environment	27%	2.81
	Environment	28%	2.14		Cost	25%	2.83

refugee resettlement program. The United States has also raised the issue bilaterally with North Korea in the context of denuclearization negotiations.[4] The lower scores on this issue may have to do with American assessments that addressing of abuses and accountability is an issue for South Korea and that any effort at intervention or third-party mediation by an international tribunal should be handled by the United Nations and South Korea.

Ninety-three percent of U.S. experts believe the disposition of the DPRK's conventional forces is "important or vital" to U.S. interests (score of 3–4), ranking it second only to nuclear weapons. But this did not register as an acute blind spot for unification because American experts believe they have the most information of all ten unification issues to make informed policy decisions (86 percent of experts with score of 1–2). Interestingly, environmental cleanup does not register as an acute blind spot for unification in the eyes of American experts, as they do not see a direct bearing on U.S. national interests (only 28 percent, lowest rating of all ten issues with a score of 3–4); but most Americans also feel they have little information about the issue (second only to cost).

There are additional findings with regard to U.S. perceptions of other countries' interests and concerns about unification (see table 6.2). For example, 100 percent of U.S. experts believe that nuclear weapons are "important/vital" to Japan's national interests (score of 3–4). The only other country that American experts assigned a similar level of concern was the United States. Even though nuclear weapons do not rank in the top three blind spots for the ROK, according to U.S. experts, 98 percent of these respondents still assigned "important/vital" to South Korean national interests (score of 3–4), suggesting the potential for trilateral coordination among Washington, Seoul, and Tokyo. Respondents do not see nuclear weapons as prioritized among the top three blind spots for China (ranked fourth). This finding reflects a view among some in the U.S. community who believe that Beijing does not share similar threat perceptions regarding the DPRK's nuclear program because Beijing does not see the program as threatening to Chinese national security.

U.S. experts assess that China and the ROK both would rank domestic stabilization as a top blind spot, higher than the disposition of

TABLE 6.2 U.S. perceptions of other actors' level of concern/level of knowledge

U.S. views of South Korea

	Issue	% who answered important/vital (score of 3–4 per issue)	Average level of concern score/issue		Issue	% who answered abundant/sufficient knowledge (score of 1–2 per issue)	Average level of knowledge score/issue
Level of concern	Domestic stabilization	96%	3.78		Conventional forces	96%	1.39
	Nuclear weapons	98%	3.79		Nuclear weapons	86%	1.78
	Refugees	92%	3.49		Infrastructure	79%	2.07
	Economic rehabilitation	97%	3.64		Refugees	73%	2.05
	Conventional forces	99%	3.91	Level of knowledge	Domestic stabilization	76%	2.09
	Infrastructure	86%	3.2		Economic rehabilitation	78%	2.05
	Cost	95%	3.76		Cost	66%	2.09
	Health	79%	3.02		Environment	55%	2.40
	Environment	70%	2.88		Health	59%	2.38
	Human rights/ transitional justice	82%	3.2		Human rights/ transitional justice	68%	2.15

U.S. views of China

	Issue	% who answered important/vital (score of 3–4 per issue)	Average level of concern score/issue		Issue	% who answered abundant/sufficient knowledge (score of 1–2 per issue)	Average level of knowledge score/issue
Level of concern	Domestic stabilization	94%	3.65		Conventional forces	95%	1.46
	Nuclear weapons	93%	3.46		Nuclear weapons	89%	1.70
	Refugees	86%	3.45		Infrastructure	81%	2.04
	Economic rehabilitation	83%	3.08		Refugees	75%	2.05
	Conventional forces	61%	2.84	Level of knowledge	Domestic stabilization	73%	2.05
	Infrastructure	55%	2.63		Economic rehabilitation	73%	2.12
	Cost	51%	2.55		Cost	41%	2.56
	Health	28%	2.12		Environment	30%	2.77
	Environment	18%	1.95		Health	28%	2.79
	Human rights/ transitional justice	5%	1.60		Human rights/ transitional justice	23%	2.94

(*continued*)

TABLE 6.2 (continued)

U.S. views of Japan

	Issue	% who answered important/vital (score of 3–4 per issue)	Average level of concern score/issue		Issue	% who answered abundant/sufficient knowledge (score of 1–2 per issue)	Average level of knowledge score/issue
Level of concern	Nuclear weapons	100%	3.90	Level of knowledge	Nuclear weapons	77%	1.97
	Conventional forces	82%	3.15		Conventional forces	76%	2.04
	Domestic stabilization	73%	2.91		Domestic stabilization	40%	2.62
	Economic rehabilitation	56%	2.61		Economic rehabilitation	45%	2.53
	Human rights/ Transitional justice	56%	2.67		Infrastructure	38%	2.65
	Cost	56%	2.58		Human rights/ transitional justice	46%	2.55
	Refugees	48%	2.52		Refugees	41%	2.63
	Infrastructure	35%	2.34		Health	28%	2.76
	Environment	30%	2.24		Environment	32%	2.76
	Health	28%	2.22		Cost	36%	2.63

U.S. views of Russia

	Issue	% who answered important/vital (score of 3-4 per issue)	Average level of concern score/issue		Issue	% who answered abundant/sufficient knowledge (score of 1-2 per issue)	Average level of knowledge score/issue
Level of concern	Nuclear weapons	84%	3.22		Conventional forces	88%	1.82
	Domestic stabilization	55%	2.63		Nuclear weapons	78%	1.90
	Conventional forces	53%	2.58		Domestic stabilization	42%	2.59
	Economic rehabilitation	41%	2.43		Infrastructure	38%	2.65
	Infrastructure	36%	2.31		Economic rehabilitation	34%	2.71
	Refugees	26%	2.09	Level of knowledge	Cost	24%	2.86
	Cost	25%	2.05		Refugees	22%	2.91
	Health	7%	1.78		Environment	15%	2.99
	Environment	7%	1.76		Human rights/ transitional justice	15%	3.09
	Human rights/ transitional justice	4%	1.57		Health	14%	3.00

nuclear weapons. They rank it as the highest concern for Chinese national interest of the ten issues (average score of 3.65). This is significant because it suggests the potential for some cooperation over the issue given the symmetry in concerns. U.S. experts predictably rank human flight (refugees) as a top blind spot for China (ranked third), given widely cited concerns by Chinese about this negative externality of unification. But there are also contradictions in China's position, as defined by U.S. experts, in that China highly ranks human flight as a blind spot but does not rank health issues highly, which ranked eight out of ten on a list of those issues most concerning to Chinese national interests (none of the U.S. respondents assigned this as a "vital" interest for China). This is a contradiction because improved health conditions inside of North Korea would presumably be a factor stemming the tide of refugees seeking to enter China as a destination. Of all ten unification issues, only 5 percent of U.S. experts assign human rights as "important/vital" for Chinese interests (score of 3-4) but also believe that China has very little information about the issue relative to the other issues.

Finally, according to U.S. views, Americans believe that Russians have relatively less concern about North Korean nuclear weapons. Only 84 percent assigned it as "important or vital" (score of 3-4) to Russian national interests, the lowest of all countries. At the same time, 78 percent of American respondents believe Russia has a good deal of information about the programs (which is as high a knowledge score as that of Japan at 77 percent). Neither Russia nor Japan ranks economic rehabilitation and infrastructure as top blind spots for unification. Only 56 and 41 percent of U.S. respondents assigned economic rehabilitation as "important or vital" (score of 3-4) to national interests for each country (respectively), and for infrastructure, only 35 and 36 percent of respondents saw this as important or vital to Japanese and Russian national interests. This suggests a possible underappreciation of the role these two countries can play. Japan made significant investments in the industrial development of South Korea after normalization in 1965 and presumably could see similar opportunities with unification. Russia has had a long-standing interest in infrastructure development, particularly in energy and rail infrastructure, and could play a potentially constructive role in unification as well.

SOUTH KOREAN VIEWS OF UNIFICATION

The survey for South Korea included 108 responses from government officials, experts, scholars, and opinion leaders. The response rate was 46 percent.[5]

South Korea's top five blind spots for unification are: (1) domestic stabilization, (2) cost of unification, (3) refugees and internally displaced persons (IDP), (4) nuclear weapons, and (5) human rights. Domestic stabilization is the largest potential unification blind spot for South Korean officials and experts, registering a 5.62, the highest composite score for the ROK. This means civil-military relations, law

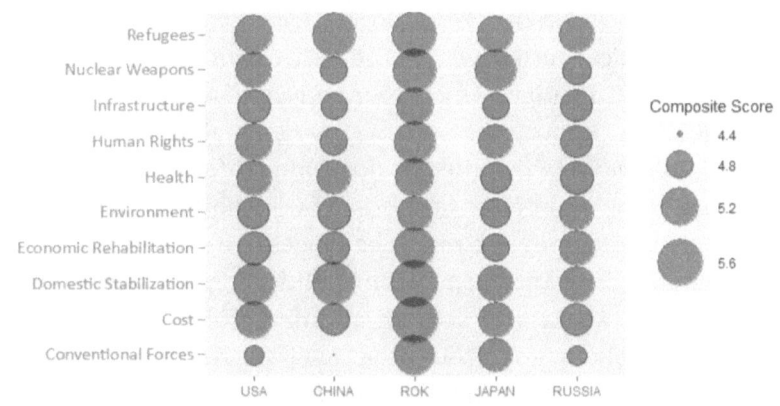

FIGURE 6.2 South Korean views of unification blind spots.

Unification Transparency Index: ROK experts' perceptions

	United States	China	ROK	Japan	Russia
Domestic stabilization	5.39	5.41	5.62	5.14	5.06
Nuclear weapons	5.14	4.81	5.47	5.39	4.84
Economic rehabilitation	4.99	4.96	5.31	4.80	5.06
Cost	5.19	4.96	5.60	5.06	4.96
Refugees	5.24	5.46	5.51	5.14	5.09
Health	5.06	5.04	5.22	4.93	5.01
Human rights	5.15	4.81	5.35	5.02	4.95
Infrastructure	4.98	4.78	5.17	4.78	4.97
Environment	4.94	5.00	5.08	4.88	5.04
Conventional forces	4.60	4.38	5.30	5.02	4.61

and order, and stability in the North represent the issues for which Koreans see great consequences for national interests (94 percent of Korean respondents believed this issue to be "important/vital" to Korean national interests [score of 3 or 4]). Costs related to unification rank a close second for South Koreans at 5.60 (94 percent of respondents scored 3-4), followed by 5.51 for refugees (82 percent scored 3-4), and 5.35 for human rights (80 percent scored 3-4).[6] Ninety-nine percent of Koreans believe that nuclear weapons are "important" or "vital" to national interests (score of 3 or 4), registering the highest concern of all unification issues, but more Koreans believe they have "sufficient" to "abundant" information (87 percent) about the programs than any other issue (second only to conventional forces), which lowered the overall composite score.

Like the United States, South Korean officials and experts feel least confident about the unknowns associated with state-building, law and order, and political authority with the post–North Korean entity that emerges with unification. Ninety-four percent of respondents scored this issue to be "important" or "vital" to national security interests (score of 3-4) but for which there is little or no information available. Chaos and a lack of order or separatism of the northern portion of a united Korea would pose extreme challenges to a smooth transition. Questions about enfranchisement and political representation would abound. South Korea also sees an alignment of priorities among Washington, Beijing, and Seoul because all regard domestic stabilization as a prominent unification blind spot. This could provide a good platform for trilateral coordination.

Second to domestic stabilization, there should be no surprise that unification costs are a top blind spot for South Koreans. Ninety-four percent of respondents score this as an "important" or "critical" national security issue (score of 3-4), but only 76 percent believe that there is "sufficient" or "abundant" information (score of 1-2) available to make informed policy decisions. These uncertainties confirm that while there have been many studies done to estimate the cost of unification, this is ultimately a rather significant unknown that would affect the stability and prosperity of a united Korea.

Regarding the next three blind spots, it is noteworthy that South Koreans rank refugees and IDPs (5.51) on par with nuclear weapons

TABLE 6.3 South Korean levels of concern and levels of knowledge on unification issues

Level of concern	Vital	4
	Of importance but not vital	3
	Low importance	2
	No bearing at all	1
Level of knowledge	Abundant empirical evidence	1
	Sufficient amount	2
	Insufficient amount	3
	No empirical evidence	4

South Korean levels of concern and levels of knowledge on unification issues

	Issue	% who answered important/vital (score of 3–4 per issue)	Average level of concern score/issue		Issue	% who answered abundant/sufficient knowledge (score of 1–2 per issue)	Average level of knowledge score/issue
Level of concern	Nuclear weapons	99%	3.85	Level of knowledge	Conventional forces	93%	1.56
	Conventional forces	98%	3.74		Nuclear weapons	87%	1.62
	Domestic stabilization	94%	3.64		Economic rehabilitation	81%	1.92
	Cost	94%	3.68		Domestic stabilization	76%	1.98
	Economic rehabilitation	87%	3.39		Cost	76%	1.93
	Refugees	82%	3.26		Infrastructure	64%	2.22
	Human rights/ transitional justice	80%	3.10		Human rights/ transitional justice	64%	2.25
	Infrastructure	69%	2.94		Refugees	62%	2.25
	Health	60%	2.76		Health	52%	2.46
	Environment	50%	2.52		Environment	48%	2.56

(5.47). Some might argue that this reaffirms the conventional view that some in the South do not perceive the nuclear threat from North Korea as a direct military threat given extant conventional threats (e.g., artillery) arrayed along the DMZ. However, this survey unearths a different explanation—while 99 percent of respondents considered nuclear weapons important or vital to national security (score of 3–4), which was the highest score of all ten issues, 87 percent believed that information on this issue was "sufficient" or "abundant" (score of 1–2), thus reducing the overall composite score. For refugees, 82 percent of respondents considered refugees important or vital to national interests (score of 3–4), but a far smaller percentage (only 62 percent) believed that information was sufficient or abundant (score of 1–2). So it is not that South Koreans don't care about the nuclear threat, but that they feel they have more information about this blind spot than they do about refugees and IDPs.

The survey revealed some interesting findings regarding Korean attitudes toward disaster risk reduction (DRR) issues. DRR issues such as infrastructure, health, and the environment were perceived to be of lower importance to ROK national interests relative to the rest of the issues. The percentage of respondents indicating these issues were vital (score of 3–4) to South Korean national interests was 69 percent, 60 percent, and 50 percent, respectively. Moreover, the level of knowledge on these issues was also assessed to be low by respondents. For infrastructure, health and environment, for example, only 64 percent, 52 percent, and 48 percent of respondents, respectively, said South Korea had "sufficient or abundant" levels of knowledge on these issues (score of 1–2). But this highlights a potential contradiction between South Korean views of domestic stabilization and the issues of health, environment, and infrastructure. The outbreak of pandemic diseases, large-scale natural or man-made disasters, and collapse of infrastructure in a unification scenario would make it extremely difficult to establish domestic order. And yet the issues of health, environment, and infrastructure received the lowest South Korean composite score rankings in the index, while domestic stabilization received the highest. If the lack of knowledge and concern for health, environment, and infrastructure issues results in reduced policy discussion and disaster preparedness, it could have dire consequences for domestic stabilization. South Koreans may not be entirely aware of the significance that these issues could carry for domestic stability. This points to a need for further discussion on the issues of health, environment, and infrastructure, and the formulation of disaster risk reduction plans.

South Korea also estimates that for China, the largest blind spot with unification is refugees, followed by domestic stabilization, placing both more than one standard deviation above its average blind-spot score. Health and environment ranked a distant third and fourth. These issues would all likely have the most direct impact on China in a unification scenario. Ironically, South Korea assigns more consistency to Chinese views than their own in that all four of China's top priorities are arguably interrelated DRR issues, the handling of which could affect the severity of the refugee problem.

South Koreans estimate Japan's biggest blind spot with unification to be nuclear weapons, followed by refugees and domestic stabilization. Ninety-seven percent of Korean respondents estimated nuclear weapons to be "important" or "vital" to Japan's national interests (score of 3–4). A smaller percentage responded similarly on refugee issues (55 percent) and domestic stabilization (70 percent), but Koreans estimated that Japan knows far more about the nuclear situation (92 percent "sufficient" or "abundant" knowledge [score of 3–4]) than it does about refugees (48 percent "sufficient" or "abundant" knowledge [score of 3–4]) and domestic stabilization (63 percent "sufficient" or "abundant" knowledge [score of 3–4]). Interestingly, Koreans do not assign much Japanese interest to economic rehabilitation or infrastructure (only 49 and 32 percent respectively) in a unification scenario. This runs contrary to the history of Japan's involvement in the economic development of the Korean peninsula and may reflect subjective desires to deny a future role for Japan on the unified peninsula.

The ROK ranks the top four blind spots for Russia as (1) refugees, (2) economic rehabilitation, (3) domestic stabilization, and (4) the environment. Management of each of these DRR issues would directly affect refugee flows and stability on Russia's border with a unified Korea. Eleven percent of South Korean respondents believe human rights and the environment are "important" or "vital" to Russian national interests; 12 percent believe that health issues rank similarly

TABLE 6.4 South Korean perception of other actors' levels of concern and levels of knowledge on unification issues

South Korean views of the United States

		% who answered important/vital (score of 3–4 per issue)	Average level of concern score/issue		% who answered abundant/sufficient knowledge (score of 1–2 per issue)	Average level of knowledge score/issue
	Nuclear weapons	98%	4.00	Nuclear weapons	94%	2.62
	Human rights/ transitional justice	78%	2.38	Conventional forces	92%	1.31
	Conventional forces	77%	3.82	Human rights/ transitional justice	72%	2.60
Level of concern	Domestic stabilization	76%	3.02	Economic rehabilitation	57%	2.39
	Refugees	60%	3.08	Level of knowledge Domestic stabilization	55%	1.58
	Economic rehabilitation	58%	3.00	Refugees	49%	2.06
	Cost	54%	2.21	Infrastructure	44%	2.38
	Health	45%	2.81	Cost	40%	2.73
	Infrastructure	44%	2.61	Health	39%	2.44
	Environment	33%	2.44	Environment	33%	2.62

South Korean views of China

	Issue	% who answered important/vital (score of 3–4 per issue)	Average level of concern score/issue		Issue	% who answered abundant/sufficient knowledge (score of 1–2 per issue)	Average level of knowledge score/issue
Level of concern	Nuclear weapons	85%	3.33		Nuclear weapons	92%	1.48
	Domestic stabilization	85%	3.46		Conventional forces	88%	1.67
	Refugees	84%	3.32		Domestic stabilization	77%	1.94
	Economic rehabilitation	65%	2.86		Refugees	69%	2.14
	Conventional forces	57%	2.71		Economic rehabilitation	69%	2.10
	Infrastructure	41%	2.44	**Level of knowledge**	Infrastructure	55%	2.33
	Cost	30%	2.24		Cost	38%	2.72
	Health	19%	2.11		Health	22%	2.93
	Environment	18%	2.02		Human rights/ transitional justice	21%	2.97
	Human rights/ transitional justice	12%	1.84		Environment	18%	2.98

(*continued*)

TABLE 6.4 (*continued*)

South Korean views of Japan

	Issue	% who answered important/vital (score of 3–4 per issue)	Average level of concern score/issue		Issue	% who answered abundant/sufficient knowledge (score of 1–2 per issue)	Average level of knowledge score/issue
	Nuclear weapons	97%	3.84		Nuclear weapons	92%	1.55
	Conventional forces	82%	3.23		Conventional forces	86%	1.79
	Domestic stabilization	70%	2.85		Economic rehabilitation	67%	2.21
	Refugees	55%	2.69		Domestic stabilization	63%	2.29
	Human rights/ transitional justice	54%	2.55	Level of knowledge	Infrastructure	50%	2.49
Level of concern	Economic rehabilitation	49%	2.58		Human rights/ transitional justice	49%	2.47
	Cost	44%	2.44		Refugees	48%	2.44
	Infrastructure	32%	2.29		Cost	41%	2.62
	Health	25%	2.15		Environment	32%	2.78
	Environment	25%	2.10		Health	31%	2.78

South Korean views of Russia

	Issue	% who answered important/vital (score of 3-4 per issue)	Average level of concern score/issue		Issue	% who answered abundant/sufficient knowledge (score of 1-2 per issue)	Average level of knowledge score/issue
Level of concern	Nuclear weapons	84%	3.21	Level of knowledge	Nuclear weapons	86%	1.63
	Conventional forces	58%	2.73		Conventional forces	74%	1.88
	Domestic stabilization	43%	2.44		Domestic stabilization	41%	2.61
	Economic rehabilitation	38%	2.34		Economic rehabilitation	35%	2.72
	Refugees	28%	2.15		Infrastructure	30%	2.82
	Infrastructure	27%	2.15		Refugees	20%	2.94
	Cost	19%	1.91		Cost	16%	3.06
	Health	12%	1.84		Human rights/ transitional justice	12%	3.19
	Human rights/ transitional justice	11%	1.76		Health	9%	3.17
	Environment	11%	1.81		Environment	8%	3.23

for Russia. But South Koreans also believe that Russians have little information on these issues. Ninety-one percent of respondents believe Russia has "insufficient" to "no" knowledge about health issues, and 92 percent believe similarly about environmental issues. Eighty-eight percent believe Russia also lacks information about human rights. South Koreans also do not believe that Russia has significant national interests in the infrastructure or economic development of a united Korea (only 38 percent and 27 percent assessed these as "important" or "vital" to Russia [score of 3–4]). This is surprising and may be an underestimation as Russia has long-standing interests in railway, road, and energy grids connecting the Korean peninsula to Russian energy reserves for distribution in Northeast Asia.

COMPARING ALLIED PERCEPTIONS OF UNIFICATION BLIND SPOTS

Looking across the two sets of surveys, we can gather additional information about how well aligned the United States and South Korea are regarding blind spots, as well as with regard to perceptions of other actors' interests and concerns with Korean unification.[7] In general, Americans feel they know less about unification issues than Koreans. On responses to the knowledge question across all ten unification issues, 53 percent of U.S. expert responses indicate the United States has insufficient or no knowledge across unification-related topics (score of 3–4), whereas only 30 percent of ROK expert responses indicate South Korea has no or insufficient knowledge across issues (score of 3–4). Forty-seven percent of U.S. expert responses say the United States has "sufficient" or "abundant" knowledge (score of 1–2) across issues, as opposed to 70 percent of ROK expert responses that say the same of South Korea.

Understandably, Korean respondents believe unification impinges more directly on their national interest than Americans do. While 81 percent of South Koreans see unification as "important" or "vital" to national interests, Americans respond at a rate of 63 percent. While 25 percent of U.S. expert responses said the United States has the highest level of concern [score of 4] across the ten unification issues,

Unification Transparency Index: Experts Perception on U.S. by Issues

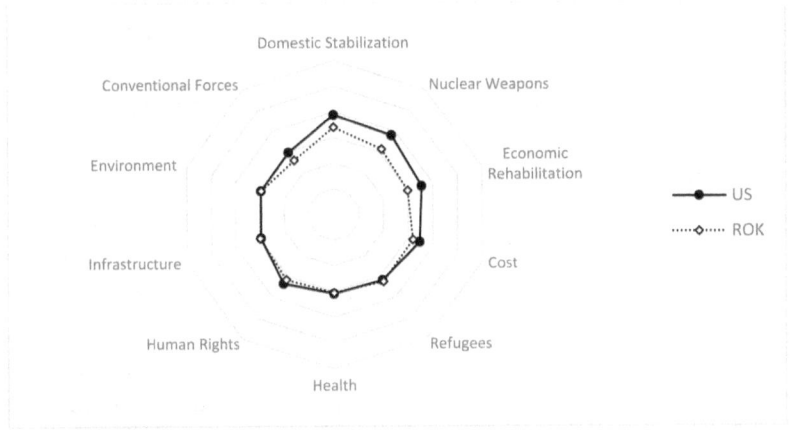

Unification Transparency Index: Experts Perception on ROK by Issues

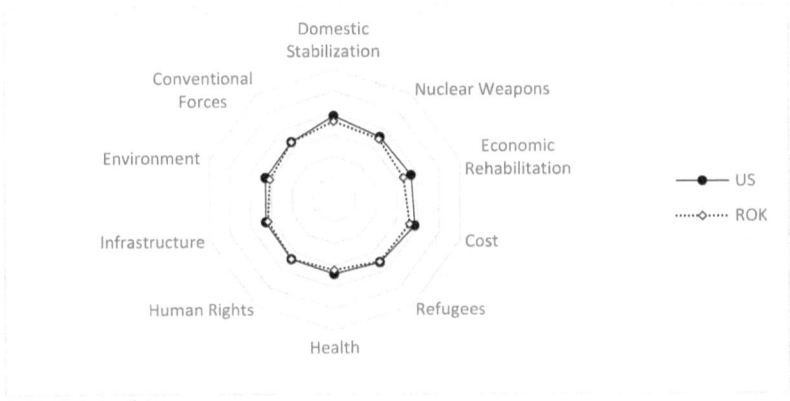

FIGURE 6.3 Unification Transparency Index: experts' perceptions of United States by issues (*top*); experts' perceptions of ROK by issues (*bottom*).

nearly double that percentage from ROK expert responses say the same of South Korea (49%).

Nevertheless, surveys of U.S. and South Korean officials and experts reveal a general complementarity in views on unification, as seen in the spider graphs in figure 6.3.

The overlap in views speaks well to the potential for alliance coordination in planning for a unification scenario. Both allies rank domestic stabilization as their most prominent blind spot with unification. Seventy-seven percent of U.S. respondents scored this issue as "important" or "vital" to national interest (score of 3–4), while 94 percent of South Korean respondents did the same. Koreans, however, feel that they better understand this issue than Americans. Seventy-six percent of Koreans believe they have "sufficient" or "abundant" information versus only 31 percent for Americans. The survey results suggest that the two allies should do more to share information, coordinate policies, and mutually assign management of this potential vulnerability a top priority in unification planning. Korean and American officials could jointly assess the basis for their respective levels of understanding on the issue in the context of bilateral alliance meetings. Experts from both countries could do the same in track-two dialogues or other academic exchanges.

However, there are differences in relative priorities, as there is not a perfect overlap in the two countries' blind spots. Most notably, while American experts consider the disposition of nuclear weapons as their second most prominent blind spot, Korean experts rank it as their fourth, behind cost and refugees. By contrast, the Americans ranked cost and refugees further down their own list at fourth and sixth, respectively. These relative priorities may provide the grounds for discussing a division of labor between the allies with unification tasks, with Americans focused on denuclearization while Koreans focus on refugees and costs.

PERCEPTIONS OF EACH OTHER'S BLIND SPOTS

How the two allies view each other's priorities in unification is as important as how each views its own needs. The former is critical for policy coordination and mutual transparency with regard to concerns and objectives. The survey responses suggest evidence of a basic alignment in U.S. and South Korean blind spots and policy priorities from the U.S. viewpoint. Respondents from the United States ranked the top four issues for South Korea to be (1) domestic stabilization, (2) unification cost, (3) economic rehabilitation, and (4) nuclear weapons. These rankings generally align with South Korean's ranking of themselves: (1) domestic stabilization, (2) unification cost, (3) refugees, and

(4) nuclear weapons. The one caveat here is on economic rehabilitation, where the United States assigns a larger blind spot to South Korea, but South Koreans see it as relatively small for themselves.

However, South Korean estimation of blind spots for the United States in unification does not fully align with U.S. assessments of themselves. South Korea ranks the top four blind spots for the United States in a unification scenario to be (1) domestic stabilization, (2) refugees, (3) unification cost, and (4) human rights. The United States, however, ranks its priorities as (1) domestic stabilization, (2) nuclear weapons, (3) economic rehabilitation, and (4) cost. The absence of nuclear weapons from the South Korean perception of U.S. blind spots might be explained by the higher level of knowledge Seoul assigns as available to the United States on the nuclear issue; 73 percent of South Korean experts said the United States had an abundant amount of knowledge on the issue (higher level of knowledge lowers the overall blind spot score). The inclusion of human rights in the South Korean top ranking of U.S. blind spot scores may reflect the increased policy attention that the U.S. executive branch and Congress have given to this issue since 2012.

While these scores do suggest general complementarity of views between the allies, they also underscore the need for more policy coordination to better hone mutual understanding of policy overlaps and gaps.

U.S. AND ROK VIEWS OF OTHER ACTORS' INTERESTS AND CONCERNS WITH UNIFICATION

The surveys also seek to gauge how the two allies perceive the interests and concerns of the other major actors in the region. Here, there is fairly good overlap or alignment in U.S. and South Korean views.

China is an important actor in any unification scenario. Both Washington and Seoul see the top two blind spots for China to be domestic stabilization and refugees, and both see the disposition of conventional forces to be the least intense blind spot for China (i.e., the compressed side of the spider graph). While this alignment of views does not guarantee that cooperation with regard to China's role in unification is easy, it does tell us that the starting point for the

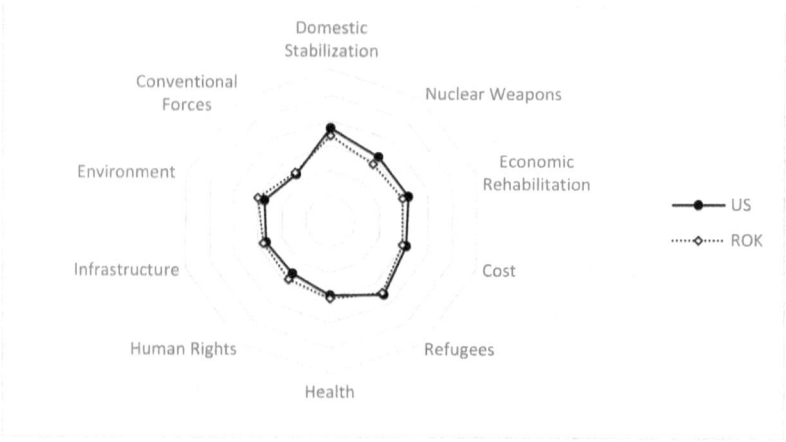

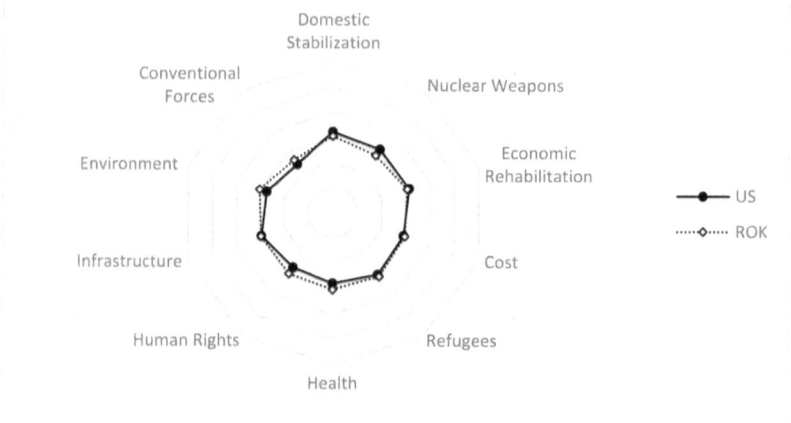

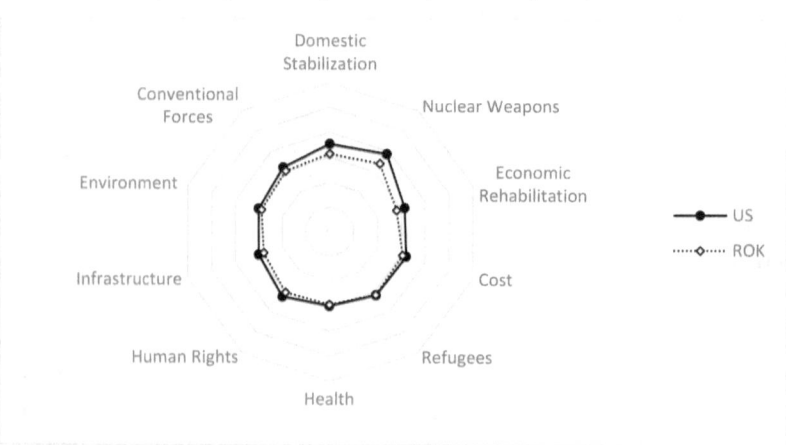

FIGURE 6.4 Unification Transparency Index: experts' perceptions of China by issues (*top*); experts perceptions' of Russia by issues (*middle*); experts' perceptions of Japan by issues (*bottom*).

discussion is a general alignment of U.S. and ROK experts about what China cares most about with unification.

The United States and the ROK have slightly different views when it comes to Japan. American experts identify four blind spots for the ally (in decreasing intensity): nuclear weapons, domestic stabilization, refugees, and cost; South Korean experts identify two for Japan: nuclear weapons and refugees. The absence of domestic stabilization and cost in the ROK assessment could reflect parochial views that Japan should not play a role in Korean unification. These inconsistencies and the sources of them would be a good place to start trilateral policy discussions and research among the three allies on unification.

* * *

This chapter attempted to shine a light through the black box of Korean unification by using surveys to gain a sense of the objectives, needs, and insecurities of the major actors. It is far from a comprehensive set of data for unification. It is a rudimentary and initial survey. However primitive these methods are, they do provide a first effort at bringing some systematic data to a hypothetical outcome that is both inevitable and significant. Understanding how Americans and Koreans think about blind spots in unification, issue-areas of intense concern, and issue-areas lacking in knowledge gives government officials, scholars, experts, and opinion leaders a place to begin a discussion about coordinating and preparing for unification.

These survey results create the first-ever database of expert assessments that tries to quantify how much we know about unification. While it has become commonplace to say that there are many "unknowns" and "dangers" associated with Korean unification, these variables have never been measured and remain cloaked in opacity. The blind spots identified in this chapter tell us something about how much the United States, South Korea, China, and other regional powers know about the long-term issues associated with Korean unification, and how strongly these actors perceive such issues to be important to their own national interests. By beginning to quantify these variables, this survey may help guide future study and planning for Korean unification by identifying gaps in knowledge, agreements on priorities, and areas of symmetry to better inform policymakers.

7

THE HARDEST OF HARD TARGETS

WHEN ONE thinks of North Korea, two images come to mind. One is of a mercurial leadership, with interesting haircuts, a penchant for wardrobes of dark Mao suits, and a burning desire for nuclear weapons. The other is of a state in deep solitary isolation, situated in the center of the most vibrant and economically prosperous part of the world. The famous *National Geographic* luminosity satellite image of East Asia at night captures the North Korea that we have come to know—a country shrouded in darkness while the world surrounding it is awash in light.

Every discussion about North Korea starts with a disclaimer about the regime's unknowability. One expert's description is typical: "the regime's opaqueness, self-imposed isolation, robust counterintelligence practices, and culture of fear and paranoia provide at best fragmentary information, impeding the agency's ability to inform, predict, and warn with a high level of confidence."[1] The "agency" in this sentence refers to the CIA, whose experts have all described North Korea as "the hardest of hard targets." The result is that potential researchers of North Korea are forewarned that the absence of hard data makes it difficult, almost impossible to understand how the regime perceives its interests, its intentions, and ultimately its behavior.[2] Those who are undeterred by such warnings often get drawn to rote conclusions that North Korea is unpredictable and irrational. Studying North Korea is talked about as art more than a science, where "kernels of what might have been truth are often buried under layers of regime mythmaking, rendering it indecipherable."[3]

Far from there being only stray kernels of evidence, this book argues that there is much unmined data on North Korea for researchers to work with using different methodologies. The chapters in this volume have focused on longitudinal data collection, surveys, defector community research, and ethnography, but study of the country is not limited to these methods. Moreover, all the research takes place in the unclassified realm, so it is readily accessible to all. While the findings of these chapters do not profess to explain everything about North Korea, they do teach us about patterns of behavior that give us some leverage on thinking about future actions by the state as well as future developments regarding its society. Some have described the study of North Korea as akin to working on a jigsaw puzzle where you have the individual pieces but do not have the cover of the box with the final picture. The chapters in this book provide additional context to evaluate each piece of the puzzle.

PAST PATTERNS, FUTURE BEHAVIOR?

Studying past patterns can help us to understand future behavior. With regard to North Korean threat perceptions and the U.S.-ROK alliance, we find that future complaints by Pyongyang about elements of the alliance's operation should be taken seriously, but they should not inhibit Washington and Seoul from maintaining deterrence and readiness. Looking back at the data of North Korean provocations over time, our study found that U.S.-ROK joint military exercises—a core element of the alliance—do not heighten tensions, even though Pyongyang claims as much. While North Korea responds to U.S. exercises with belligerent acts, these provocations do not have a substantive impact on the overall direction of U.S.-DPRK relations. They neither plunge diplomatic relations into a negative spiral nor create openings for improvements in relations. Recognizing this "null effect" of the exercises has important policy implications for the United

States and the ROK in terms of how they should think about future exercising, what to expect from North Korea, and what to anticipate to be the diplomatic externalities of those exercises.

Another implication for future policymaking is that the offer of a cessation of joint military exercises to North Korea as a bargaining chip—as was done with the cancellation of Team Spirit exercises in 1992, and more recently with Trump's cessation of exercises after the Singapore Summit in 2018—could have the counterintuitive effect of heightening the chances for conflict on the peninsula rather than reducing them. Joint military exercises are critical to maintaining the combat readiness of the ROK and U.S. forces, which in turn bolsters deterrence and peace on the Korean peninsula. The performance of Russia's poorly trained military in Ukraine only amplifies the point. Scaling down or stopping exercises may be destabilizing to that peace not because they are provocative, but because the inactivity signals a weakening of the deterrent, which in turn could lead to North Korean misperception or miscalculation. Wars start more often than not when the balance of military capabilities is drawn into question, not when it is clear.

Second, this book finds that North Korea will continue to rely on its cyber capabilities as the asymmetric weapon of choice into the future. Kim Jong-un once reportedly described cyber as his "all-purpose sword" to strike the adversary.[4] Other experts have described cyber as an ideal offensive capability for North Korea because it is relatively low cost, capable of inflicting significant damage, and not easily deterrable given the nation's backwardness, which renders it invulnerable to counter cyberattacks.[5] Many experts believed that after the 2014 cyberattack on Sony Pictures Entertainment, North Korean cyber soldiers would be targeting an abundance of soft targets in the United States either to hold them hostage or to destroy them, including critical infrastructure, telecommunications, energy grids, nuclear facilities, and fresh water supplies.

The empirical review in chapter 3 of reported North Korean cyberattacks, however, shows that the nature of these attacks has changed demonstrably. Instead of cyberterrorism, the regime has turned to cybercrimes. While it is hardly comforting to contend with the commercial theft of hundreds of millions, even billions, of dollars and cryptocurrencies, North Korea's focus on using cyber as a tool to gain hard currency is, relatively speaking, better than the alternative of cyberterrorism. Into the future, there is no guarantee that this will continue to be the way the regime employs these capabilities, but this does provide some time to harden our systems against attack and to work with other actors, like China and South Korea, to defend against future attacks. Our findings also suggest that the North's diversion to cybercrime reflects the success of effective financial and trade sanctions placed on the regime by the United States and UN member states. Lifting these sanctions could have the counterintuitive effect of increasing the danger of cyberterrorism, as the regime would no longer need to focus all its energies on hard-currency generation.

Nevertheless, this analysis provides no room for complacency. The success of the Lazarus Group and other North Korean cyber actors, particularly in heists of cryptocurrency, has created a new "cyber-proliferation" risk: the use of stolen digital currency to finance the North's nuclear weapons and ballistic missile programs. Tracking and targeting this criminal behavior needs to become a nonproliferation priority of the Treasury Department and law enforcement.

Third, this book finds that the most important agent for change for the future of North Korea is the growth of markets and the *donju* or merchant class of entrepreneurs. Though the country's political structures remain totalitarian, rigid, and closed, the proliferation of markets, both formal and informal, has opened up the minds of average citizens to new ways to think about the state, their personal livelihoods, and their future. The ethnographic study in chapter 4 reveals how people rely on the markets for their daily sustenance more than they do on the official public distribution system. Because the goods found in the market are more desirable than government handouts, this has, and will continue to have, far-reaching ripple effects on society.

Our microsurveys find that markets are creating a slow but steady "grassroots reform from below," giving citizens something to strive for to make their individual and family lives better. North Koreans trust information that comes out of the market and find it more credible than what the government provides. They have even come to criticize and ridicule the state in private as they realize its inadequacies and injustices. The second or "shadow" economy created by markets has opened up a new space between the state and society. Conversations that take place within and around these markets, be they about the price of rice or the latest TV drama smuggled out of South Korea on a thumb drive, go outside the bounds of that which is dictated by the state. As one study hypothesized, market life entails the use of social capital, trust, and information-sharing that creates a "semi-autonomous public sphere."[6] These forms of interaction constitute a nascent civil society, even in the most repressed country in the world.

The ultimate irony of the markets is that they were created not out of hope, but out of desperation. With the famine in the mid-1990s that killed 10–19 percent of the population, the government's public distribution system broke down, and people were forced to fend for themselves. They resorted to pilfering and salvaging anything they could to sell in makeshift markets. Since that horrible time, official and black markets have flourished. Moreover, the government, even though officially hostile toward capitalism, has become dependent on the markets: (1) as a source of revenue (through taxation of the vendors), (2) as helpful to stabilizing prices, and (3) as part of the *byungjin* strategy under Kim Jong-un (i.e., to pursue economic and security gains at the same time). The government has also created incentives to increase productivity even as it tries to regulate market activity; for example, by allowing families to sell in the markets anything produced beyond fulfillment of government quotas. The government even sought recently to issue public bonds as a way to gain hard currency and give citizens investment opportunities.[7]

The bottom-up reform forces created by market activity can propel change in the state in one of two ways. For one, markets will disrupt the social structure of the state. The rise of the *donju* merchant class increasingly challenges the rigid structure of the *songbun* caste system as North Koreans with capital can earn a powerful and politically connected place for themselves in society outside of that assigned by the state.[8] Markets not only have created power centers outside of the state but also generate potentially influential roles for women in North Korea's patriarchal social order. Women reportedly account for 98 percent of the merchants in the marketplace.[9]

Second, markets could create organized resistance to the state. While the markets have caused ordinary citizens to think more independently and critically of the state, this has not changed the way that ordinary citizens feel about the state's leadership. Survey data shows no hostility toward Kim Jong-un or the legacies of Kim Jong-il or Kim Il-sung. However, citizens express the most anger toward the state whenever it attempts to impose antimarket activities. This could be at the local level where officials try to curtail the hours of operation, or it could be nationally when the government tries to impose a new tax. In 2005 the government tried to ban the sale of grain in the markets to bolster its ration system, and in 2008 it attempted a decree to restrict market hours of operation to three days weekly, each of which was unsuccessful.[10] In 2009 the government's redenomination of the currency (with a cap on the amount of funds to be exchanged) was met with such widespread chaos and anger that the government publicly executed the finance minister as a scapegoat. The numbers affected by such measures, moreover, are quite large and growing. There are reportedly more than one million vendors in the country and on any given day over 100,000 people who circulate through some of the larger markets in the country.[11] Essentially, our survey data shows that any widespread actions by the state targeting the personal savings, disposable income, and "economic rights" that North Koreans feel entitled to through the markets will become a trigger for potential state upheaval.

THE UNIFICATION BLACK BOX

The fourth finding of this book relates to the future unification of the Korean peninsula. While we often associate North Korea's internal workings with black holes, the descriptor also aptly applies to unification. The dilemma is that it remains an aspiration, some dare say an inevitability, of the Korean nation; yet when and how it happens is beyond anyone's imagination. No one knows when Koreans will have to enter the unification tunnel, what the outcome will be, nor what perils (or opportunities) lie along the road. Unification could happen tomorrow with the regime's collapse, and no one would be terribly surprised. Fifty years from now, North Korea may still have staved off unification, and many would not be surprised at that outcome either. This uncertainty, coupled with the wide range of potential outcomes associated with unification, contributes to the lack of information about it. Of unification's many aspects, the one most written about relates to the cost of unification, for which there have been many good studies.[12] Beyond this, however, our understanding of how to think about unification has not moved beyond a handful of stylized facts (e.g., "the Chinese are afraid of refugees; the Japanese, of resurgent Korean nationalism").

Chapters 5 and 6 gathered data about how the countries in the region think about their biggest vulnerabilities or blind spots should unification occur. There is more work that could be done in this vein. The unification questionnaires measured blind spots by asking American and South Korean experts to rank "level of concern" and "level of knowledge" on any given issue. The blind-spot questionnaires could be expanded to include responses from other countries' officials and experts like China, Russia, Japan, and the European Union (we ran out of funding so could not do this). The questionnaires could be refined to go beyond merely priority/knowledge metrics to include, for example, action metrics (e.g., "Would you commit military for this policy priority?"; "Would you commit financial assistance for this policy priority?"). The ten unification topics chosen for the questionnaire could be refined further, breaking down broad categories such as "cost" or "environment" into smaller pieces. Further questioning could tease out some of the inconsistencies in attitudes toward blind spots by the actors—for example, understanding why South Koreans ranked domestic stabilization in the North as the highest concern yet ranked issues critical to sustaining that order, such as health, at a much lower priority. The results could be complemented by gaming scenarios to see, for example, if the stated priorities in the surveys are confirmed by the state's actions. While the unification blind spot questionnaires are rudimentary, they nevertheless constitute a starting point for officials and experts to discuss relative priorities, needs, and fears when it comes to unification.

Our unification data offer some useful prescriptions. For one, sharing knowledge about unification blind spots is a prime area for alliance cooperation and planning. While the United States and the ROK may equally prioritize a certain issue regarding unification (e.g., domestic stabilization), their perceptions of how much they know about that issue can be different. This finding cries out for allied sharing of information. This could be done at the classified level between intelligence officials, military planners, or policymakers. Or if such unification planning is deemed too sensitive politically because of the potential negative reactions from China and North Korea, then it could be done at the expert track 1.5 or track 2 level to inform those in government.

The surveys tell us how Americans and South Koreans assess China, Japan, and Russia's presumed unification blind spots. This permits us to align expectations between the two allies, as well as determine over what blind spots to begin discussions with the other players. In sum, the blind spots from the questionnaires underscore the need for governments to avoid misperception and miscalculation by undertaking empirically based planning on unification and moving away from simplistic stereotyping of each other's concerns.

COVID-19 AND NORTH KOREA

There is much more data about North Korea out there to be mined. Two areas that this book did not cover are communications technology and satellite imagery. In the former case, North Korea has undergone a telecommunications revolution with the proliferation of cellular service, smartphones, and its own form of internet. Phones are now ubiquitous in North Korean society and provide citizens with new ways to access information and organize. At the same time, government efforts to use this technology to control and to conduct surveillance have also grown. There is already very good work published in this area by the likes of Jieun Baek, Jane Kim, Nat Kretchun, and Martyn Williams that demonstrates how much we can learn about this dynamic in the unclassified realm.[13]

Satellite imagery offers a wealth of visual data about the country. Improvements in commercial imagery technology allow for high resolution images with accuracy measured in meters. The advent of high off-nadir (HON) and thermal infrared imagery further augments the ability to see inside North Korea.[14] While understanding how to read and interpret such imagery requires expert training and experience, the proliferation of vendors has lowered the cost, making these services more accessible. Overhead images allow a view into the nuclear facilities, ballistic missile bases, submarine bases, and leadership facilities that are otherwise restricted for any outsider to access. They also allow for longitudinal study of crop patterns, mining activity, and environmental degradation by surveying farms, mountains, and water supplies. The regime carries out deception, diversion, and concealment tactics to counter such activities. Knowing that overhead imagery is being taken, North Korea will also leave certain facilities unconcealed and in plain view as a means of signaling, employing brinksmanship tactics, or simply to flip us the middle finger.

Satellite imagery can provide a wealth of information that opens up the black box, especially when the regime is at its most closed. The Covid-19 pandemic offers a good illustration. A conflagration of factors made North Korea extremely susceptible to the direst consequences of the virus. Decades of malnutrition due to food shortages have left the population with weak immune systems and comorbidities. An already decrepit public health system is strained beyond limits when confronted by a pandemic like Covid-19. And the volume of trade and other interactions with China creates a unique vector for transmission of the virus.

For all these reasons, the regime instituted a comprehensive shutdown of the border, including with China in January 2020 that lasted until July 2023.[15] All travel within the country was banned, and major cities, including Pyongyang, were locked down. Public education campaigns explained the dangers of the virus, and citizens wore masks. According to the WHO, North Korean authorities maintained that they had no cases of Covid-19 inside of the country as a result of these measures; however, only about fifty thousand PCR tests have been administered. The regime reportedly quarantined tens of thousands of possible cases in North Hamgyong, Rason, and other areas, and registered over fifty thousand cases in the military.[16]

The impact of Covid-19 on North Korea has been nothing short of devastating. While North Korea may be the only country in the world to claim no cases, the country has been brought to its knees by the pandemic. North Korea's zero Covid-19 lockdown exacerbated perennial healthcare deficiencies, with supplies of imported medications dwindling to near nothing, basic immunization programs being placed on pause, and sick people prohibited from traveling domestically to access hospitals. The country is also experiencing acute food insecurity, without the importation of food stocks, fertilizer, farming equipment, and humanitarian aid. The United States in July 2021 assessed that 63.1 percent of the total population is food insecure, and some experts estimate that North Korea will suffer sixty-six thousand excess deaths per year as a result of its Covid-19 policies.[17] North Korea's Covid-19 measures have also stifled bottom-up marketization processes, which North Koreans had grown dependent on to support their livelihoods since the late 1990s.

Trade with China, which normally accounts for 95 percent of the country's imports and exports, has plummeted dramatically as a result of the border shutdown, on the order of 80 percent or more (see figure 7.1 and table 7.1). Estimates are that the economy has registered negative growth of between 4.5 and over 10 percent from prepandemic levels (between 2019 and 2020), which is the largest economic contraction since the famine in the mid-1990s. The UN Food and Agriculture Organization reports a dire situation, made worse by flooding in August and September 2020, which destroyed 100,000 acres of crops and left North Korea with an annual food shortfall.[18]

In 2020 the regime applied early and successfully to the global vaccination program COVAX for Covid-19 vaccine distribution but then refused to accept any. It is one of two countries in the world (in addition to Eritrea) that has not begun a Covid-19 vaccination initiative, despite multiple offers from COVAX. In July 2021 it rejected an offer of two million doses of the Astra Zeneca vaccine (out of a six million dose allocation from COVAX).[19] Nevertheless, state media continues to show alarm over the Delta and Omicron variants, and references to bolstering protection against virus transmission.[20]

The international community does not have eyes and ears on the ground. Because of the harsh quarantine requirements, restrictions of movement, and inability to access supplies from abroad, all nongovernmental organizations and foreign diplomatic missions inside

FIGURE 7.1 Impact of Covid-19 on China-DPRK trade, 2019–2021: China-DPRK exports (November 2019–November 2021).
Source: Data downloaded from China General Administration of Customs.

TABLE 7.1 China-DPRK exports by month (November 2019 to November 2021)

Month	Chinese exports to DPRK ($mn)	DPRK exports to China ($mn)
2019		
November	252.4	18.5
December	256.7	22.6
2020		
January	186.8	10.3
February	10.3	0.366
March	17.3	0.617
April	21.8	2.2
May	58.6	4.7
June	87.7	9.1
July	65.9	8
August	19.2	6.5
September	18.9	1.9
October	0.253	1.4
November	0.105	1.1
December	3.4	1.6
2021		
January	0.029	1.5
February	0.003	1.7
March	13	1.3
April	28.7	1.8
May	2.7	0.75
June	12.3	1.8
July	16.8	4.1
August	22.5	6.2
September	55.6	14.2
October	39.8	2
November	34.7	6.6

Source: China General Administration of Customs.

of the country shut down operations, and personnel left the country. The regime banned all foreign tourism. Defectors reportedly are unable to send remittances to relatives in the country because of the comprehensive lockdown. The regime dropped out of the 2020 Tokyo Summer Olympics and 2022 Beijing Winter Olympics for fear of virus transmission. The level of paranoia and self-isolation was extreme, even by North Korean standards. In mid-2021 the government announced the sacking of senior officials over an undefined "grave incident" jeopardizing the country's protection campaign against COVID. When a South Korean official allegedly tried to defect to the North, he was shot, and his body was doused in fuel and burned by North Korea's authorities for fear of virus transmission.[21]

The pandemic has forced North Korea into the blackest of black boxes. Under these circumstances when there is virtually no independent access to the country, satellite imagery can be most useful in providing clues as to understanding North Korea's future actions in dealing with the pandemic. Imagery collection of the Uiju Airbase suggests concrete efforts by the regime to mitigate the harsher effects of the lockdown.[22] Located on the Sino-North Korean border, the airfield formerly housed the 24th air regiment but underwent construction to turn it into a facility for cargo disinfection for trade across the Sinuiju-Dandong crossing. The conversion started in early 2021, including the construction of warehouses, open-air storage spaces, paved roads, and refurbishment of railways, and coincided with the passage of a "Law on Disinfection of Imports" in March 2021. Figures 7.2 and 7.3

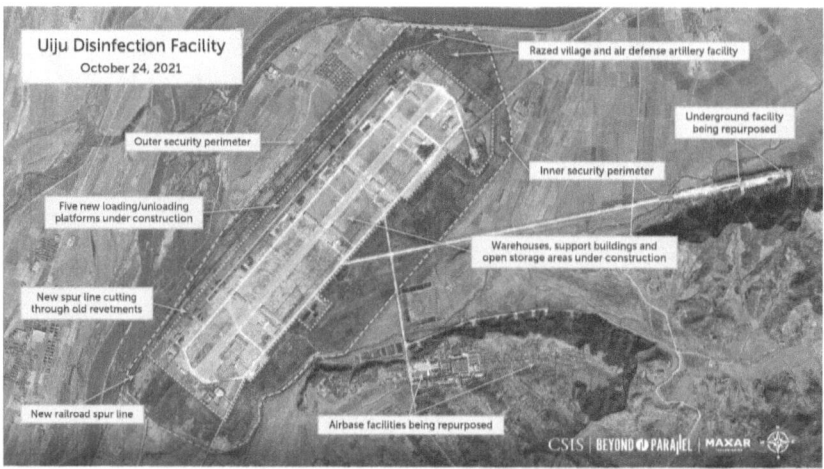

FIGURE 7.2 Uiju Disinfection Facility, October 2021. Source: CSIS, Beyond Parallel, https://beyondparallel.csis.org/north-korea-attempting-to-reverse-covid-19-border-shutdown-with-import-disinfection-facilities/. Copyright 2021 © by Maxar Technologies.

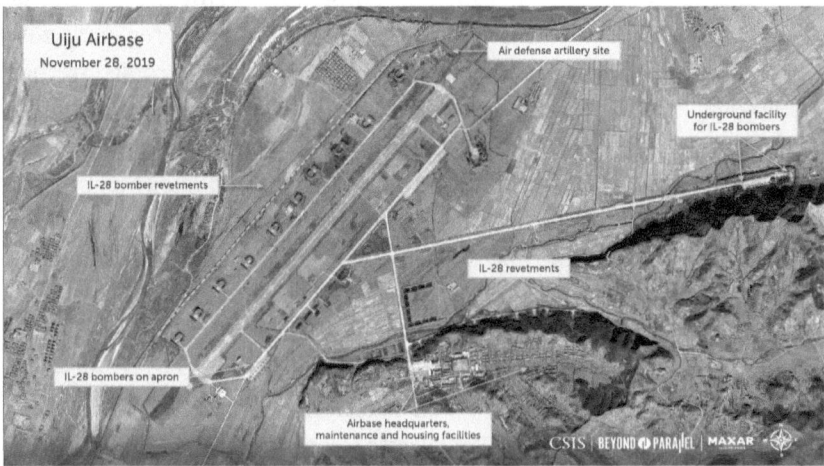

FIGURE 7.3 Uiju Airbase, November 2019. Source: CSIS, Beyond Parallel, https://beyondparallel.csis.org/north-korea-attempting-to-reverse-covid-19-border-shutdown-with-import-disinfection-facilities/. Copyright 2021 © by Maxar Technologies.

are overhead images taken of the facility in 2019 and 2020 showing Uiju's changes. North Korea may also be planning smaller-scale disinfection facilities at airports (Kalma and Sunan), ports (Nampo, Chongjin, Wonsan, and Rason), and the Tumangang-Khasan railroad crossing.[23]

We can induce from these pictures that North Korea constructed these disinfection facilities as part of a strategy that allows for more trade with China but maintains the lockdown until the pandemic subsides, or until it can acquire desired vaccines. In the latter case, the regime probably covets the mRNA vaccine given its rejection of COVAX contributions, its complaints about reported side effects of the proffered vaccines, and its illegal efforts to hack Pfizer's data.

North Korea maintained the lockdown for more than three years, longer than most other countries.[24] The regime has endured periods of extreme hardship in the past, including the great famine of the 1990s that caused up to 2.2 million deaths. By comparison, experts believe the worst-case scenario for North Korea in the event of an unmitigated Covid-19 outbreak would involve around 160,000 deaths.

In addition, the pandemic provided some counterintuitive benefits, at least from the vantage point of the leadership. The regime's zero Covid-19 policies provided the government with tools to strengthen ideological control, dominate markets, and stifle outside information. The regime touted the country's Covid-19 policy as a success that protected the population. One North Korean official reportedly expressed astonishment and indignation about the death toll in countries that "don't follow the rules" and noted that the world could have ended the pandemic if everyone followed what North Koreans did.

Publicly available data provides a window into possible answers as to why North Korea remained locked down for more than three years. If we aggregate North Korea's past reactions to pandemics, the most proximate being the Middle East Acute Respiratory Syndrome (MERS) in South Korea in 2015, and to the Ebola outbreak in West Africa in 2014, its response to Covid-19 is not surprising. A highly contagious coronavirus that was transmitted to South Korea through a single traveler to Bahrain, United Arab Emirate, and Saudi Arabia, MERS generated an alarming two-month public health crisis in the summer of 2015, when South Korea quarantined nearly seventeen thousand people and registered the highest number of cases (186) outside the Middle East.[25]

Comparing North Korea's response to Covid-19 with that of the MERS crisis, the regime carried out essentially the same playbook: (1) it officially claimed that there were no cases of either disease in the country; (2) despite the professed absence of cases, North Korea locked down cities and restricts all internal movements; (3) it utilized the public health situation to request medical assistance from the outside (in the case of Covid-19, it rejected vaccine offers but accepted medical supplies from UNICEF); (4) it canceled participation in international events; (5) it tightened customs and border protection to prevent transmission of the disease. In the case of MERS, South Korea declared its containment of the virus in July 2015, but North Korea did not stop temperature checks at the Kaesong industrial complex—a facility for inter-Korean economic cooperation where virus transmission risks were theoretically high because of direct interaction between workers and managers—until January 2016. This explains the protracted lockdown in North Korea until July 2023.

TABLE 7.2 DPRK responses to Ebola, MERS, and Covid-19

Action	Ebola (March 2014–June 2016)	MERS (May–July 2015)	Covid-19 (January 2020–present)
Claims no case in DPRK	KCNA announces no cases of Ebola in country (10/23/14).	National Institute of Sanitation and Inspection announces no individuals infected with MERS (6/14/15).	Foreign Ministry statement that there are no cases in country (3/19/20). DPRK State Hygienic Control Board says zero cases of Covid-19 in country (4/2/20). DPRK media refers constantly to government's message that Covid-19 is nonexistent (10/16/20).
Restrictions on internal movements	Travel into Pyongyang prohibited (10/28/14). Three-week quarantine for all returning travelers from West Africa (10/22/14).	NGOs report DPRK has suspended internal travel and restricted access to Pyongyang (6/17/15).	All foreigners restricted from movement in Pyongyang (2/4/20). North Koreans not permitted to dine out (2/24/20). Schools suspended for spring (2/27/20).
Public education	Health ministry and Central Hygienic and Anti-epidemic center disseminate information about Ebola outbreak (9/13/14).	Health ministry begins public education campaign about MERS (6/24/15).	KCTV begins airing programs about Covid-19 (1/24/20); shows citizens masking (2/3/20).
Request for assistance	DPRK requests Ebola quarantine equipment from ROK at Kaesong (10/29/14).	DPRK requests thermal imaging cameras and masks from ROK (6/2/15).	DPRK receives assistance from Doctors without Borders on virus prevention (2/20/20). DPRK receives virus diagnosis equipment from Russia (2/26/20); PPE from UNICEF.
Withdrawal from international events	DPRK cancels hosting of World Taekwondo Championships (1/27/15). DPRK cancels Arirang Mass Games (2/14/15).	DPRK withdraws from participation in 2015 Summer Universiade Games in S. Korea due to MERS (6/15/15).	DPRK suspends Pyongyang marathon (2/21/20). DPRK withdraws from 2020 Tokyo Olympics, citing dangers of virus transmission (4/5/21). DPRK does not attend Munich Security Conference (2/6/20).
Border lockdown	Ban on all travel into North Korea indefinitely (10/24/14). DPRK requires temperature checks for all South Koreans in Kaesong Industrial Complex (10/29/14). Quarantine of all cargo at Nampo (11/19/14).	DPRK implements restrictions on border with China, including ban on traders and tourists, disinfection of deliveries (6/17/15).	DPRK suspends air travel with China and all tourism (1/20/20); suspends train service (1/31/20); imposes one-month quarantine on all entering the country (1/28/20). DPRK closes inter-Korean office at Kaesong (1/30/20). Ports closed (3/13/20). DPRK publishes decree to shoot anyone illegally approaching border (8/25/20).
Reopening		DPRK stops temperature scans at Kaesong Industrial complex 6 months after ROK declares pandemic containment (1/6/16).	Conflicted reporting of end to mask mandate, possible incremental reopening (July 2023).

Source: https://www.csis.org/analysis/splendid-isolation-north-korea-and-covid-19; https://www.nknews.org/pro/coronavirus-in-north-korea-tracker/timeline/.

NEW AXIS: RUSSIA-DPRK

The most significant development for North Korea coming out of the pandemic lockdown in mid-2023 has been the growing military cooperation with Russia. Satellite imagery helps shed light on this opaque relationship. Russia's invasion of Ukraine in February 2022 and the precipitous downturn in U.S.-Russian relations even before the war are the permissive conditions for a tightening of relations between Vladimir Putin and Kim Jong-un. Russia's dire need for munitions from North Korea reflects its growing international isolation and the state of its military industrial complex that cannot meet the needs of its own armed forces. Under heavy international sanctions, North Korea also needs food and energy assistance from Russia. Each side also views opportunities in the current context that complicate the security picture for the United States and its allies. The record of quiet but substantive expanding cooperation is clear.

Sergei Shoigu's visit to North Korea in July 2023 was the first by a Russian defense minister since 1991. This was soon followed by the North Korean leader's travel to Vostochny to meet Putin in September 2023, where the possibility of high-end technology transfers was raised, as well as a return visit by Putin to North Korea. Putin vowed to increase political, economic, and security ties with North Korea and said that North Korea's "firm support to the special military operation against Ukraine and its solidarity with Russia on key international issues highlight [their] common interests and determination to counter the policy of the Western group."[26]

Historically, North Korea's interest in the Soviet Union/Russia was largely derivative of its policies toward China, using cooperation with Moscow as leverage in eliciting more assistance from China, or in lieu of Beijing's assistance during certain periods in Chinese history (e.g., Great Leap Forward, Cultural Revolution). During the Sino-Soviet split, for example, North Korea played Moscow off Beijing, as Soviet leaders sought to pull the North's allegiance away from China. North Korea also experiences acute abandonment anxieties when Moscow draws closer to Seoul or when U.S.-Russian or U.S.-China relations are stable. Soviet-South Korean normalization in 1990, for example, realized the ultimate abandonment fear for the late North Korean leader

THE HARDEST OF HARD TARGETS 187

Kim Il-sung as Moscow stopped providing energy to Pyongyang assistance at discounted prices. Russian interest in North Korea is equally transactional, but at the same time relatively consistent over the centuries. Moscow has interest in warm-water ports on the Korean peninsula for its Pacific Fleet and in energy and transport infrastructure projects that connect Northeast Asia to Siberia and the Eurasian land mass through the Korean peninsula.[27]

Commercial satellite imagery provides critical insight into the extent of this opaque, reinvigorated Russian-North Korean cooperation. In January 2023 the White House released imagery of arms transfers from North Korea to the Wagner paramilitary group taking place at the Tumangang–Khasan railroad crossing on November 18 and 19 of the previous year.[28] CSIS Beyond Parallel exclusive satellite imagery analysis observed an increase in the number of iron ore, petroleum, and food railcars at the Tumangang–Khasan railroad crossing between late November and mid-December 2022 (see figure 7.4) shortly after the DPRK arms transfer to the Wagner Group in mid-November (see figures 7.5 and 7.6).[29]

In addition, there has been an unprecedented increase in shipping activity at Najin port in North Korea, which has become the major

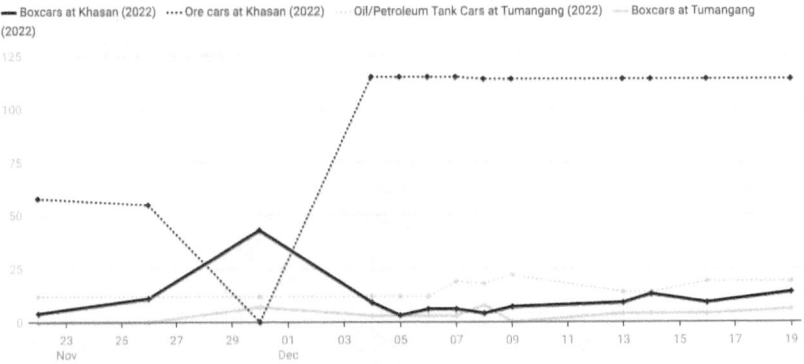

FIGURE 7.4 Approximate count of railcars observed at Khasan and Tumangang in late 2022 after Wagner arms transfer. Ore cars were observed at Khasan, and oil/petroleum tank cars were seen at Tumangang.
Source: CSIS, Beyond Parallel, https://beyondparallel.csis.org/arms-oil-and-coal-the-tumangang-khasan-railroad-crossing/.

FIGURE 7.5 Close-up view of the Khasan rail facility, December 15, 2022. Ore cars and boxcars are seen at the station. Source: CSIS, Beyond Parallel, https://beyondparallel.csis.org/arms-oil-and-coal-the-tumangang-khasan-railroad-crossing/. Copyright © Airbus DS 2023.

FIGURE 7.6 Close-up view of the Tumangang rail facility, December 15, 2022. Oil/petroleum tank cars seen at the station. Source: CSIS, Beyond Parallel, https://beyondparallel.csis.org/arms-oil-and-coal-the-tumangang-khasan-railroad-crossing/ Copyright © Airbus DS 2023.

transfer point for millions of rounds of munitions shipped to Dunai port in Russia.[30]

The implications of the growing military alignment between North Korea and Russia for the United States are clear. The tactical advantage that each foe gains in expanding cooperation complicates U.S. efforts in the war in Ukraine. It also complicates U.S. efforts at shoring up extended deterrence on the Korean peninsula with its South Korean ally as North Korea demonstrates increasingly more capable and potentially survivable ICBMs. In this regard, Putin may be trying to demonstrate that actions taken in Europe by the United States will have consequences detrimental to U.S. interests, not just in that theater but also in the Indo-Pacific.

OTHER BLACK BOXES

Another area of scholarly, data-based research that would be relevant for scholarship and policy is relations between China and DPRK. It is hard to imagine future outcomes of significance on the Korean peninsula that did not engage the core interests of Beijing as North Korea's key economic and security patron. North Korea is the closest thing to a military ally of China, yet we know very little about their shadowy interaction. Neither government reveals anything to the public, for example, about the amount of bilateral assistance provided. When past multilateral agreements have been reached for countries in the region to provide energy assistance to North Korea (e.g., Six Party Talks in 2006–2007), China would not provide information about how much oil and fuel it was already providing to the regime on an annual basis. Part of the reason for this opacity is that policy on North Korea is not made or executed by the Ministry of Foreign Affairs; instead, it is made by the Chinese Communist Party (CCP) and People's Liberation Army (PLA), which are less accountable to public reporting. The other reason, of course, is that neither country wishes the contents of their dialogue to be known to others.

The public narrative of the relationship focuses on the history of fighting together in the Korean War against Western imperialists, as well as the common Confucian heritage and socialist ideology. But the actual relationship is far less sanguine. Tensions run deep, and dissatisfaction is high on both sides. North Korea bristles at the way China treats it as if it were one of China's poorest provinces, excavating natural resources and valuable minerals from the country at dirt cheap prices. China, too, grows frustrated at the North's constant provocations, which prompt global criticism of China to keep its junior partner under control or demands for China to do more sanctioning of North Korea.

Collection of more data through open sources on this relationship is not easy, but not impossible. We can induce lessons about the relationship based on reported trade data, even though this data may be flawed or incomplete. Another way to measure the relationship is to look at the number of high-level meetings between the two governments. One study, for example, counts the number of bilateral meetings by China's president, high-level CCP officials, or high-level PLA and foreign ministry officials with their DPRK counterparts (see table 7.3).[31] The volume of these meetings provides a metric for how close or distant the relationship may be at a cross-section in time. For

TABLE 7.3 China high-level visits to and from North Korea (minister of foreign affairs level or higher), 1949–2022

China	Visits to DPRK (by PRC high-level officials)	Visits from DPRK (hosted by PRC high-level officials)	Total # of summits	DPRK	Visits to China (by high-level DPRK officials)	Visits from China (hosted by DPRK high-level officials)	Total # of summits
Mao Zedong (1949–1976)	6	16	8	Kim Il-sung (1953–1994)	45	34	16
Deng Xiaoping (1978–1989)	17	23	6	Kim Jong-il (1994–2011)	35	38	11
Jiang Zemin (1989–2002)	19	16	5	Kim Jong-un (2011–2023)	11	9	5
Hu Jintao (2002–2012)	32	27	8				
Xi Jinping (2012–2023)	7	9	5				

Source: Andy Lim and Victor Cha, "Dataset: China-North Korea High-Level Visits Since 1953," Beyond Parallel, March 17, 2017, https://beyondparallel.csis.org/china-dprk-high-level-visits-since-1953/.

example, what becomes immediately apparent is that in the first six years of Kim Jong-un's rule and the first five years of Xi Jinping, there was a noticeable absence of any summit meetings compared with previous years. This changed in 2018 when Trump's announcement of his intention to meet Kim Jong-un spurred a series of high-level exchanges between the DPRK and China. This suggests Xi's general disdain for the new North Korean leader (and vice versa) at the outset, but a change of heart, perhaps prompted by concerns about being cut out of a U.S.-DPRK deal. Updating this data and gaining greater granularity on the announced deliverables for these meetings would be a worthy data-gathering exercise.

Another useful data-gathering exercise looks at the locations in which the Chinese host DPRK leaders when they visit China. Again, this is publicly available information that could provide more understanding of the relationship. A study that looks at all Kim Jong-il's visits to China, for example, reveals clearly the Chinese agenda of pushing for economic reform and modernization with the DPRK leader. Table 7.4 lists all types of facilities that the Chinese took the DPRK leader to visit.

It is crystal clear from this list of venues that Beijing's primary agenda is to push economic reform by North Korea in many different sectors (albeit unsuccessfully). More work in this sort of data-gathering of open-source information can shed light on this black box relationship.

POLICY

ON INFORMATION SHARING

Whether you agree or disagree with the data in this book, the chapters make clear that there is much more information to be gathered on North Korea and on unification. The only way to do this is by engaging with the North. More interaction—whether through official exchanges, nongovernmental presence in the country, foreign missions, English-language instruction, or promoting the North's dialogue with other countries, including South Korea—means more information about a country we need to learn more about.

TABLE 7.4 Visits by Kim Jong-il to China, 2000–2011

Date	Place	Venues visited
5/29–31/2000	Beijing	Zhongcuancun IT complex
		Lenovo Computer
1/17–19/2001	Shanghai	Shanghai Bell Telephone Equipment
		Shanghai Hua Hong NEC Electronics
		Shanghai GM Motors
		Paosan Steel Mill
		Human Genome Research Center
		Zhangjiang High Tech Complex
		Shanghai Pudung Software Complex
		Shanghai Sunqiao Modern Agricultural Development Zone
4/19–21/2004	Tianjin	Not available
	Beijing	Zhongguancun IT Complex
		Hancunhe Model Village
1/11/2006	Wuhan, Hubei Province	Chang Hei Optical Fiber and Cable
1/14/2006	Zhuhai, Guangdong Province	Industrial and Commercial Bank of China Software Development Center
		Gree Electric Appliances, Inc.
		Eastcom Peace Smartcard Co.
1/15/2006	Shenzhen, Guangdong Province	Huawei Technologies
		Han's Laser Technology
11/13/2006	Guangzhou, Guangdong Province	VTRON Technologies Ltd.
5/3–7/2010	Tianjin	Tianjin Port
	Dalian, Liaoning Province	Dalian Port Shipyard
	Beijing	Dalian Development Area
	Shenyang, Liaoning Province	Zhongguancun Science Park
		Shenyang Blower Works
		Beijing Park
8/26–30/2010	Changchun, Liaoning Province	Jilin Agriculture University
		Changchun Li Chi Motors
	Jilin, Jilin Province	Changchun Agricultural Fair
	Harbin, Heilongjiang Province	Beishan Park
		Changchun Railway Vehicles
		Jilin Chemical Fiber Group
		Yuwen Middle School
		Harbin Engineering University
		Steam Turbine Factory
		Harbin Huikang Food Company
		Harbin Electric Company

(*continued*)

TABLE 7.4 (*continued*)

Date	Place	Venues visited
5/20/2011	Mudanjiang, Heilongjiang Province	Hailin Farm
5/25/2011	Beijing	Digital China R&D Center
5/20–26/2011	Nanjing, Jiangsu Province Yangzhou, Jiangsu Province	Panda Group (LCD panel plant) China Resources Suguo (supermarket) Jeifang Automotive Company Yangzhou Smart Valley Tech Jingao Solar Panel Hanjiang Economic Development District
5/21/2011	Changchun, Jilin Province	First Automotive Works Group Northeast Changchun Core Area Planning Construction Hall
8/25–27/2011	Tonghua City, Jilin Province Daqing, Heilongjiang Province Qiqihar, Heilongjiang Province	Tonghua Grape Wine Company Daqing Planning Exhibition Hall Apartment Building Construction Site Qiqihar No. 2 Machine Tool Group Mengniu Dairy Manufacturing Company

Source: Andy Lim and Victor Cha, "Visits from Kim Jong-il to China," Beyond Parallel, March 17, 2017, https://beyondparallel.csis.org/china-dprk-high-level-visits-since-1953/.

The open-source information-gathering in this book calls out for more collaboration between governments and scholar/expert/research communities. Properly coordinated, this could promote win-win solutions where data collected outside government channels complements classified work. This is particularly the case with regard to unification studies, where the intelligence and policy communities could benefit from scenario-building and modeling of unification outcomes done by outside experts. In short, the partnership between public and private sectors could allow experts to unearth more data about unification and North Korea, while governments could gain access to data they do not have the time or resources to collect on their own.

The data on unification in this book highlights areas for multilateral cooperation. For example, the unification surveys show that countries in the region have various blind spots regarding domestic stabilization and nuclear weapons. These findings could point governments in the direction of trilateral conversations to share information to address these blind spots. If this is too sensitive to do at the official level, then it could be done in semiofficial (or track 1.5 talks with experts and government officials) or experts-level (track 2) discussions.

ON DENUCLEARIZATION: A THREE-TRACK APPROACH

No book on North Korea and unification would be complete without some discussion of the nuclear issue. The regime's rampant ballistic missile and nuclear testing in 2022–2023 seems unstoppable. The Biden administration has stated six principles for dealing with the threat: (1) the United States remains steadfast in the objective of complete denuclearization of the Korean peninsula; (2) it pursues a combination of pressure and diplomacy to achieve this goal; (3) it will respond to the threat with closer U.S.-Korea-Japan bilateral and trilateral security, military and intelligence cooperation, as well as cooperation on sanctions; (4) it maintains that the United States bears no hostile intent toward the DPRK; (5) the United States remains open to serious and sustained dialogue with the DPRK and is prepared to meet without preconditions; and (6) in the course of negotiations, the United States is prepared to explore practical steps to address regional security and concerns of both sides.[32]

As of early 2024, this policy has been unsuccessful at bringing about a resumption of denuclearization negotiations or a halt to the incessant weapons testing. Nevertheless, the United States and its allies should use the time to prepare a strategy for the eventual resumption of negotiations, whenever that may happen. Such preparation is not about tactics since the type of deal that would emerge is impossible to predict; instead, it should entail a simple set of principles that could guide future diplomacy.

Here is the first rule of denuclearization strategy: don't choose a policy that increases North Korea's nuclear capabilities. But that is exactly what has happened under recent administrations. North Korea now has amassed roughly twenty to fifty nuclear warheads and in the last three decades has carried out more than two hundred ballistic missile tests. Denuclearization is not a near-term possibility, and insisting on it as a precondition for talking (former national security adviser John Bolton's Libya model) is a fool's errand.

Obama's "strategic patience" policy, aimed at waiting the North Koreans out under the pressure of sanctions, did not work. It led to sixty-one missile tests during his two terms. Trump's "fire-and-fury" threats of war in 2017 led to twenty ballistic missile tests. His shift to summit diplomacy and "bromance" with North Korean leader Kim Jong-un did not work either—North Korea conducted thirty ballistic missile tests since the Trump-Kim Hanoi summit in February 2019, paraded two massive new sea- and ground-based long-range ballistic missiles in October 2022, and continues to churn out untold amounts of fissile material. In 2022 Biden saw more missile tests (seventy three as of January 2024) than any previous president. Practically speaking, the first priority is to rein in a runaway program.

Second, no matter how far North Korea goes in weapons development, the United States and its allies are not served well by giving up on the goal of denuclearization, as some have advocated.[33] Accepting North Korea as a nuclear weapons state would be the worst of all worlds: it will elicit intense opposition and abandonment fears from allies like Japan. It will destroy an already fragile nuclear nonproliferation regime and may encourage others, like Iran, to follow suit. Moreover, it would not necessarily buy the United States anything new in negotiations. That is, advocates of accepting North Korea's nuclear weapons status argue that this would be the entry point to more productive arms control negotiations with the regime. But the reality is that any denuclearization negotiation would almost certainly seek agreements such as an operations freeze, test ban, no-transfer-pledge, and restrictions on missile range and payload, among other interim benchmarks that amount to arms control in all but name. Furthermore, the argument that the United States should accept the North's nuclear weapons status because it can be rationally deterred from irresponsible or belligerent behavior is wishful thinking. Russia's threats of nuclear use in Ukraine demonstrate that previously "responsible" nuclear states, when put in the domain of losses, can act very dangerously.

Third, the United States should envision denuclearization negotiations in pragmatic and incremental pieces and should lower any expectations of a "big bang" deal. "Mini-deals" are easier to negotiate and sell domestically because they require lower up-front payments by all sides. This strategy would also gain the support of China, South Korea, Russia, and Japan.

Should denuclearization negotiations commence in the future, the immediate goal should be a verifiable freeze on operations at the Yongbyon nuclear facility, including the uranium enrichment facilities and a test ban, in return for energy assistance and a partial lifting of the 2016–2017 UN Security Council sanctions on general trade. The operations/testing freeze and the sanctions lifting would be reversible by either side if compliance were in question. Many would criticize this deal as "buying the same horse" yet again as in past unsuccessful negotiations, but practically speaking it is in U.S. and allied interests.

The administration might shift the terms of negotiation after the initial freeze to something not tried by past governments. The Six-Party Talks agreement in 2005 during the George W. Bush administration and Trump's Singapore summit each referenced "new relationships" but never sought early results. The reality is that without a fundamental transformation in political relations, nuclear negotiations will remain mired in the tit-for-tat deals of the past that are likely to eventually collapse.

Instead, the two sides should then open a political dialogue channel on a parallel track. The purpose of this track would be to hold discussions on further sanctions-lifting, political normalization, peace regime, conventional forces, cybercrime, and illicit activities. A third track should focus on humanitarian and health assistance and human rights. The three tracks of dialogue are mutually reinforcing but not contingent on one another. Progress on the second track would be somewhat coordinated with progress on the first track. Progress on the third track would not be contingent on denuclearization because of urgent needs of the North Korean people and because such engagement would be a good way to gain more information on the ground.

The rationale for a multitrack approach is that all dialogue with North Korea cannot rest on the first track (denuclearization) because that is the most difficult one. These two additional tracks could lay a path to more normal relations between the two countries. This transformation of political relations could change the distrustful environment into one in which Washington and Pyongyang could together negotiate new denuclearization steps on the first track.

Such an approach would avoid front-loading predictable sticking points in nuclear negotiations while verifiably capping North Korea's WMD programs. The human rights element of the policy would align with U.S. values and be noncontroversial with Congress, and a North Korean concession in this area might constitute a credible signal of its intentions.

After laying out the roadmap for political relations, the negotiations might then shift back to a long-term framework for North Korea's abandonment of all nuclear weapons, focusing on threat reduction or arms control in the interim. The focus would be on containing the weapons program, including minimizing the chances of inadvertent use, nuclear proliferation, and nuclear leakage, as well as a test ban treaty and agreement to limit the range and payload of missiles. This approach would be favored by those who think the United States should focus on practical goals to contain the threat rather than allow unimpeded growth of the weapons program. Biden would have to frame these agreements as interim steps on the path to a verifiable denuclearization to avert criticism that the United States has resigned itself to accepting a nuclear North Korea. While China and South Korea would accept this approach, Japan might be ambivalent if the strategy suggests a de facto acceptance of North Korea as a nuclear weapons state.

The last principle for negotiations is that an engagement strategy is most effective if it is backed by strength. The United States must continue to improve nuclear deterrence and missile defense capabilities, including bringing Korea and Japan into a trilateral nuclear planning group, reinstating the full scope of military exercises, fully integrating early warning data, and expanding intelligence and ballistic missile defense cooperation. The United States should never render vulnerable alliance equities (e.g., troop presence or military readiness exercises) in negotiations without advance consultations with Seoul and Tokyo.

Critics will demand the DPRK's unconditional denuclearization like the Libya model, but this is not realistic given the size of the North

Korean program, nor is it supported by countries in the region (except maybe Japan). Summitry should be left open as a possibility, and the United States should pocket Kim's denuclearization commitment to Trump in Singapore, but more summits make no sense absent the substantive steps outlined earlier. As unpalatable as this strategy may sound, previous ones have not worked. Moreover, the absence of a strategy promises North Korea will perfect its ability to hit the United States with a nuclear missile. Integrating what has worked before with some new elements may be the least worst choice in a land of lousy options.

FINAL THOUGHTS

The late, great scholar Robert Jervis of Columbia University wrote insightfully about the role of misperception in international politics. He wrote about how biases by political leaders and decision-making bodies can impede potential cooperation between nation-states, and about how recognizing these biases can avoid war. In many ways, North Korea and unification are tailor-made for cognitive bias. We know so little about these issues other than what we want to see, and make judgments based on that. We discard pieces of evidence contrary to our preconceived beliefs as aberrant information. If we see North Korea as a country with horns and fangs, then we discount any conciliatory or cooperative behavior as either duplicitous or a sign of weakness.

Regarding North Korea, how we study and talk about the country should change. The media should not ridicule the regime nor dismiss it as unpredictable or irrational. Practitioners should not essentialize it—it is neither a devil with fangs nor a sheep wrapped in a wolf's coat. Our judgments about the country and its people should be based on deep empirical study rather than political or ideological biases. Regarding unification, we should dispense with truisms and seek data-based understanding. While we have no crystal ball as to when unification might happen, practitioners should neither shy away from its inevitability nor let other urgent issues of the day crowd out the important because Korean unification will be the single most significant geopolitical event in world politics since the fall of the Berlin Wall and the unification of Germany.

Readers are welcome to disagree with the data or the findings in this book because debate about empirics is an exercise that validates our conviction that the regime is not a black box. Indeed, it better serves scholars and practitioners to have such arguments. The stakes are too high for the future peace and prosperity of the Korean peninsula for decisions to be made based on anything other than substantive academic and policy research of the country.

The past can never predict the future. Aggregating data about North Korean behavior or unification does not guarantee we can make accurate statements about what is to come. To paraphrase Mark Twain, however, history never repeats itself, but it does often rhyme, particularly in the case of North Korea, given the continuity of the state's leadership over three generations and the consistency of its objectives. Similarly, the history of the Korean peninsula also teaches us that change comes suddenly, not gradually. Whether it is balance-of-power politics in the late-nineteenth century that ended China's sway over the peninsula, the thirty-six-year Japanese occupation, liberation in 1945, national division in 1945, or fratricidal war in 1950, the peninsula's history is one of punctuated equilibria. This more likely than not means that unification will come suddenly rather than gradually as much as Korea would like to prepare for it. While it is not easy to gather data about this topic, this book has demonstrated that researchers should not be intimidated by the task. They should engage proactively, confident that Korean unification is ultimately more knowable than we believe.

ACKNOWLEDGMENTS

O **NE OF** the benefits of being a professor for almost three decades is the chance to work with young, rising experts and scholars. In the case of this book, these rising stars came together from both my academic world at Georgetown University and my think tank world at the Center for Strategic and International Studies (CSIS) in Washington, DC.

The task we had before us was not an easy one—to devise new ways of gathering data about two topics famous for their lack of data. We conducted this research over a period of five years with a grant that enabled us to experiment with many different methods for collecting information about the "black box"—the enigmatic Democratic People's Republic of Korea and the prospects of Korean unification. The research team approached the work with the enthusiasm you would expect of youth, but with the added excitement of knowing that they were blazing new trails about a target, North Korea, famously known as the hardest of intelligence targets by the U.S. government. Every one of them was invigorated by the idea that they might be able to contribute to the intelligence and policymaking worlds by producing novel findings about the way the DPRK and its people think and behave. The researchers were also motivated by the opportunity to create new research about Korean unification, of which the expert community knows very little. Indeed, some of the work from this project was briefed to policy and intelligence communities. All the research and writing for this book was completed at the unclassified level, and the data is publicly available.

Because the research was conducted over seven years from 2016 to 2023, earlier iterations of a portion of the findings appeared in different forms and outlets. Chapter 2, "The United States–Republic of Korea Alliance," is based on research conducted with the hard-working team of Na Young Lee, a doctoral student at University of Southern California, and Andy Lim at CSIS when Na Young was a junior research fellow in the Korea Chair. Chapter 3, "Technology and Cybersecurity," is based on a semester-long practicum conducted with industrious Georgetown graduate students Julian Fox, Katelyn Radack, and Jae Seung Shim in Paul Miller's class in the Master of Science in Foreign Service Program in the spring semester of 2021. After an initial draft was written, the prolific Rebecca Spencer of Stanford University joined the project, adding her expertise on the topic. The initial research and surveys for chapter 4, "Markets and Civil Society," were written with the ingenious Marie DuMond, associate fellow in the Korea Chair at CSIS; earlier and different versions of a portion of the findings were presented on the CSIS Beyond Parallel microsite. The initial research and surveys for chapter 6, "Unification Data" were written with Marie DuMond and Andy Lim, and earlier and different versions of some of the findings were presented on the CSIS Beyond Parallel microsite. Chapter 5, "Unification Theories," has not been previously published in long form; however, an earlier opinion-editorial version that outlined the initial idea appeared as a newspaper column in *Joongang Ilbo*.

I thank the National Security Council for vetting the manuscript. The views presented in this work represent those of the researchers and myself and do not represent the views of the U.S. government.

Numerous scholars and colleagues have offered helpful critiques and comments on the different outputs of this collective research project at various stages. These include Mathew Ha, Sue Terry, Dave Kang, Myong-Hyun Go, Greg Scarlatoiu, Karl Friedhoff, Jieun Baek, and Stephen Haggard. Special thanks go to members of the 2016–2021 CSIS Washington Consortium of Korea scholars who were involved in the project: Bridget Coggins, Sheena Chestnut Greitens, Andrew Yeo, Katherine H. S. Moon, Seong-Ho Sheen, Van Jackson, Michael Green, and John Delury. Though our research was curtailed by the Covid-19 pandemic in 2020 and 2021, each scholar found ways to adapt to the multiple challenges and produce excellent research. While our planned interim research conference in Hawaii on the occasion of the International Studies Association convention was canceled due to Covid-19, all scholars kindly offered feedback on one another's work as well as on this book in the context of our regular Zoom "scrub sessions."

The project benefited from the generosity of CSIS, Georgetown University, and the Academy of Korean Studies. This work was supported by the Laboratory Program for Korean Studies through the Ministry of Education of Republic of Korea and Korean Studies Promotion Service of the Academy of Korean Studies (AKS-2016-LAB-2250001).

On a personal note, researching and writing up the results for this book during the pandemic and while serving a term as vice dean at the university was a unique challenge. Yet the incredible work of my research colleagues at CSIS, Marie DuMond, Andy Lim, Dana Kim, Sang Jun Lee, and Lisa Collins, kept the project moving forward and on schedule. The multitalented Seiyeon Ji managed the project and oversaw its timetable to the very finish, for which I am deeply grateful. Numerous interns devoted hours to help with the manuscript, including Christina Durham, Ahn Hyangseon, Seong Hyeon Choi, Jonghyeok Choi, So Jung Ha, Jaehyun Han, Maika Jones, Soyeon Jung, Suyoung Kim, Hwayoung Lee, Heejae Park, Rebecca Spencer, and Suyoung Kim. To all these hardworking individuals goes the credit of making this a better book, while the shortcomings are mine.

APPENDIX 1

Codebook for Event Data on U.S.-DPRK Relationship

OVERVIEW

This codebook refers to variables in the dataset on events in the U.S.-DPRK overall relationship that are used to assess the tone of the relationship between January 1, 2005, and December 31, 2015.

FILE FORMAT

The dataset is distributed in an Excel (.xlsx) file format, though the analysis (including converting the event data into time series data) is done with an R Programing compatible (.csv) format. The event data is also available online at https://beyondparallel.csis.org/timeline/ as a color-coded timeline format.

Variables in US-DPRK relations 1.0

Column	Variable name	Variable description
1	EventNum	Event number
2	StYear	Start year of event (−9 = missing)
3	StMon	Start month of event
4	StDay	Start day of event
5	EndYear	End year of event (−9 = missing)
6	EndMon	End month of event
7	EndDay	End day of event
8	Duration	Duration of event (in days)
9	Type_event	Type of event 1 minor negative: minor events that worsen relations such as hostile rhetoric, or small provocations (cutting off hotline, short-range missiles) 2 major negative: major events that worsen relations and brings international attention such as long-range missile launch, or nuclear tests −1 minor positive: small gestures or interactions that improves relations, such as expressing willingness to negotiate or announcing a moratorium on its nuclear weapons program −2 major positive: large improvement in relations, such as meetings between delegates, official negotiations, or signing of an agreement
10	EventDetail	Description of the event (key information on who/what/where)
11	EventDetail2	Additional description of the event (additional detail)
12	Indicator	Whether the event took place before or after JMEs of a given year 1. prespring exercise 2. during spring exercise 3. postspring exercise/prefall exercise 4. during fall exercise 5. postfall exercise
13	Source1	Source link for the event (first source)
14	Source2	Source link for the event (second source, different from the first source)

Note: One entry per event.

ADDITIONAL CODING INFORMATION

Here is the list of sources used to construct the event data:

Primary sources
    North Korea's state media statements (Korean Central News Agency)
    North Korea's news media (*Rodong Sinmun*)
    U.S. Department of State statements

U.S. Department of Defense statements
South Korea's Ministry of Unification statements
South Korea's Ministry of National Defense statements

Secondary sources
 New York Times
 Yonhap News
 CNN News
 BBC News
 Korea Times
 Reuters
 Daily NK
 Al Jazeera
 KBS News
 MBC News
 JoongAng Ilbo

Information cross-check: For all events, we used two independent sources to cross-check information such as date, time, and key facts of the event.

Dataset Sample

EventNum	StYear	StMon	StDay	EndYear	EndMon	EndDay	Duration	Type_event
1	2007	1	16	2007	1	17	2	4
3	2007	1	26	2007	1	26	1	1
5	2007	2	8	2007	2	13	6	4

EventDetail	EventDetail2	Type_participant	Indicator	Source1	Source2
Christopher Hill met with Kim Gye-gwan in Berlin to talk about financial sanctions and the SPT	"BERLIN, Jan. 17—Seeking to revive stalled negotiations to end North Korea's nuclear weapons program, the United States held 'substantive' talks with North Korean diplomats here on Tuesday and Wednesday, said the chief American envoy, Christopher R. Hill."	1	1	https://www.nytimes.com/2007/01/18/world/asia/18nkorea.html	https://www.reuters.com/article/uk-korea-north/u-s-ends-3-days-of-talks-with-n-korea-in-berlin-idUKL1892090120070118
The U.S. BIS released a list of luxury items prohibited for export and re-export to the DPRK	"In accordance with recent United Nations (UN) Security Council resolutions and the foreign policy interests of the United States, the United States Government is imposing restrictions on exports and reexports of luxury goods to the Democratic People's Republic of Korea (North Korea), and is continuing to restrict exports and reexports of nuclear or missile-related items and other items included on the Commerce Control List (CCL). To this end, the Bureau of Industry and Security (BIS) is amending the Export Administration Regulations (EAR) to impose license requirements for the export and reexport of virtually all items subject to the EAR to North Korea, except food and medicines not listed on the CCL."	1	1	https://www.federalregister.gov/documents/2007/01/26/E7-1180/north-korea-imposition-of-new-foreign-policy-controls	https://www.dailynk.com/english/us-exports-to-north-korea/
Fifth round of SPT (third phase) in Beijing	"Negotiators on Thursday will resume the long-stalled talks aimed at North Korean nuclear disarmament amid tentative signs of a possible breakthrough in a diplomatic process that seemed shattered four months ago when North Korea tested a nuclear device."	1	1	https://www.nytimes.com/2007/02/08/world/asia/08korea.html	https://www.aljazeera.com/news/2007/2/12/pressure-builds-on-north-korea

(continued)

EventNum	StYear	StMon	StDay	EndYear	EndMon	EndDay	Duration	Type_event
6	2007	2	13	2007	2	13	1	4
10	2007	3	5	2007	3	6	2	4

EventDetail	EventDetail2	Type_participant	Indicator	Source1	Source2
Feb. 13 Joint Agreement—DPRK agreed to shut down its nuclear facilities at Yongbyon, and United States agreed to remove DPRK as a state-sponsor of terrorism and from TWEA	Announcement of 2.13 Agreement (initial action) for implementation of 9.19 Joint Statement—fifth Six-Party Talks Phase 3 Meeting (Beijing)—"North Korea agreed today to close its main nuclear reactor in exchange for a package of food, fuel and other aid from the United States, China, South Korea and Russia.The breakthrough, which was announced by the Chinese government after intense negotiations and welcomed by the White House as a 'very important first step,' comes four months after North Korea tested a nuclear bomb."	1	1	https://www.nytimes.com/2007/02/13/world/asia/13cnd-korea.html	https://www.nbcnews.com/id/wbna17117242
Christopher Hill met with Kim Gye-gwan again to talk about normalization of relations and removing DPRK as a state-sponsor of terrorism	"The United States said today that North Korea must fully disclose its efforts to produce highly enriched uranium as part of negotiations now under way in New York that are aimed at ending North Korea's nuclear weapons program and normalizing relations between the two countries.'They need to come clean on it, explain what they have been doing, why they have been doing it, and ultimately they need to abandon it,' Christopher R. Hill, the chief United States negotiator, said.Mr. Hill was speaking to an audience at the Japan Society in New York prior to a second day of talks with Kim Kye-gwan, his North Korean counterpart."	1	1	https://www.nytimes.com/2007/03/06/world/asia/06cnd-korea.html	https://news.kbs.co.kr/news/view.do?ncd=1311765

(continued)

EventNum	StYear	StMon	StDay	EndYear	EndMon	EndDay	Duration	Type_event
13	2007	3	19	2007	3	22	4	4
32	2007	5	25	2007	5	25	1	2
37	2007	6	7	2007	6	7	1	2
42	2007	6	17	2007	6	17	1	3
43	2007	6	19	2007	6	19	1	3

EventDetail	EventDetail2	Type_participant	Indicator	Source1	Source2
Sixth round of SPT—reached an understanding to transfer back the US$25 million in funds frozen in BDA	The sixth Six-Party Talks Phase 1 Meeting (Beijing)—"Christopher Hill, the assistant secretary of state who is leading the U.S. team at the disarmament talks, said that Chinese officials were working to transfer the money from the Banco Delta Asia in Macao, but that this had been delayed because of 'technical banking issues.'"	1	1	https://www.nytimes.com/2007/03/22/world/asia/22iht-korea.4992016.html	https://news.kbs.co.kr/news/view.do?ncd=1321236
DPRK fired a SRBM off the east coast. Potentially a KN-01	"North Korea fired several short-range missiles into the sea between the Korean Peninsula and Japan on Friday, as talks on ending the Communist state's nuclear weapons programs were stalling over a banking dispute between Pyongyang and Washington."	1	3	https://www.nytimes.com/2007/05/25/world/asia/25iht-korea.1.5864732.html	https://www.joongang.co.kr/article/2740114#home
DPRK fired two SRBMs off the west coast. Potentially KN-01s	"North Korea test-fired short-range missiles off its west coast today, drawing an annoyed reaction from the United States and a dismissive one from South Korea."	1	3	https://www.nytimes.com/2007/06/07/world/asia/07cnd-korea.html	https://news.kbs.co.kr/news/view.do?ncd=1368996
DPRK announced that it will allow IAEA inspectors to enter DPRK	"In an announcement carried by its official press media, North Korea said late Saturday that it had sent the invitation to the International Atomic Energy Agency because a banking dispute with Washington that had been blocking progress toward the North's nuclear disarmament 'has reached its final phase.'"	1	3	https://www.nytimes.com/2007/06/17/world/asia/17cnd-korea.html	https://www.korea.kr/special/policyFocusView.do?newsId=148626322&pkgId=49500257
US$25 million in funds from BDA returned to DPRK	"Christopher R. Hill, assistant secretary of state for East Asian affairs—said that the talks were back on track now that a dispute over $25 million in frozen North Korean assets has been resolved."	1	3	https://www.nytimes.com/2007/06/20/world/asia/20cnd-korea.html	https://jp.reuters.com/article/idUSSEO21460320070621

(continued)

EventNum	StYear	StMon	StDay	EndYear	EndMon	EndDay	Duration	Type_event
45	2007	6	21	2007	6	22	2	4
46	2007	6	26	2007	6	29	4	3
47	2007	6	27	2007	6	27	1	2

EventDetail	EventDetail2	Type_participant	Indicator	Source1	Source2
Christopher Hill visited Pyongyang (first visit by a U.S. ambassador since October 2002) and met with DPRK foreign minister Pak Ui-chan and nuclear envoy Kim Gye-gwan	"The United States' chief nuclear negotiator left North Korea today after a surprise visit with assurances that Pyongyang would slow down its main nuclear reactor, a move that would fulfill a commitment made in February and help speed six-nation talks aimed at dismantling North Korea's nuclear program."	1	3	https://www.nytimes.com/2007/06/22/world/asia/22cnd-korea.html	https://www.nytimes.com/2007/06/21/world/asia/21korea.html
IAEA inspectors visited Yongbyon and the under-construction facility in Taechon	"Meanwhile, an International Atomic Energy Agency team traveled from the North Korean capital to the Yongbyon reactor, about 100 kilometers, or 60 miles, to the northeast. The 5-megawatt reactor, believed capable of churning out enough plutonium for one atomic bomb a year, is at the center of international efforts to halt North Korea's nuclear program. The team was invited by North Korea to discuss details of shutting down the reactor, as it pledged under an international accord in February. It is the first IAEA trip to the facility since Pyongyang expelled its monitors in late 2002."	1	3	https://www.nytimes.com/2007/06/28/world/asia/28iht-korea.1.6381522.html	https://www.dailynk.com/english/iaea-delegation-arrived-in-pyonyan/
DPRK fired three SRBMs off the east coast and into the East Sea (KN-02)	"On the 27th, North Korea launched yet another three short-range missiles. This is the third time missiles have been launched since the beginning of 2007."	1	3	https://www.dailynk.com/english/launching-missiles-merely-routine/	https://www.nytimes.com/2007/06/27/world/asia/27iht-korea.1.6357481.html

(continued)

EventNum	StYear	StMon	StDay	EndYear	EndMon	EndDay	Duration	Type_event
54	2007	7	16	2007	7	16	1	3
55	2007	7	18	2007	7	20	3	4

EventDetail	EventDetail2	Type_participant	Indicator	Source1	Source2
IAEA confirmed the shutdown of Yongbyon facilities	"United Nations inspectors have confirmed that North Korea has shut down its weapons-making nuclear reactor, the UN nuclear monitoring agency said Monday. Pyongyang, meanwhile, warned Washington that the real bargaining over its nuclear disarmament had only begun. The International Atomic Energy Agency's confirmation of the shutdown makes official a hard-won yet fragile diplomatic victory for the administration of President George W. Bush. Washington provided the government it once branded part of the 'axis of evil' with a series of financial and diplomatic concessions to make the much-delayed reactor shutdown possible."	1	3	https://www.nytimes.com/2007/07/16/world/asia/16iht-nuke.4.6680401.html	https://www.npr.org/templates/story/story.php?storyId=12000896
Sixth round of SPT (resumption of first phase halted in March) in Beijing	"Delegates to the six-nation talks aimed at disarming North Korea of its nuclear weapons said they had failed to set a timetable for disarmament during meetings that were scheduled to end on Friday. The chief United States envoy, Assistant Secretary of State Christopher R. Hill, tried to put a positive face on the disappointing result, saying that substantial progress had been made during the talks, but that 'working groups' of experts from the participating countries would need to devise plans for the timing and sequencing of further steps."	1	3	https://www.nytimes.com/2007/07/20/world/asia/20korea.html	https://www.aljazeera.com/news/2007/7/18/six-party-talks-on-north-korea

(continued)

EventNum	StYear	StMon	StDay	EndYear	EndMon	EndDay	Duration	Type_event
56	2007	7	18	2007	7	20	3	4
73	2007	9	6	2007	9	6	1	1

EventDetail	EventDetail2	Type_participant	Indicator	Source1	Source2
Sixth round of SPT concludes with a joint communiqué	"Arms negotiators concluded talks aimed at ending North Korea's nuclear ambitions Friday without setting a firm deadline for the country to disable its nuclear facilities, but top envoys planned to meet again in September. The chief negotiator for China at the talks, Wu Dawei, said working groups would meet before the end of August to discuss technical details for the North's next steps: declaring and disabling its nuclear programs. Earlier this week inspectors from the International Atomic Energy Agency verified that Pyongyang had shut down its nuclear reactor."	1	3	https://www.nytimes.com/2007/07/20/world/asia/20iht-korea.1.6746767.html	https://news.kbs.co.kr/news/view.do?ncd=1394393
Israeli air strike on Syrian facility discovered a nearly completed nuclear reactor modeled on DPRK Yongbyon reactor	"One Bush administration official said Israel had recently carried out reconnaissance flights over Syria, taking pictures of possible nuclear installations that Israeli officials believed might have been supplied with material from North Korea. The administration official said Israeli officials believed that North Korea might be unloading some of its nuclear material on Syria."	1	5	https://www.nytimes.com/2007/09/12/world/middleeast/12syria.html	

(continued)

EventNum	StYear	StMon	StDay	EndYear	EndMon	EndDay	Duration	Type_event
74	2007	9	11	2007	9	14	4	3
77	2007	9	27	2007	10	3	7	4

EventDetail	EventDetail2	Type_participant	Indicator	Source1	Source2
U.S. Russia, China experts visited DPRK to examine Yongbyon facilities	"A U.S. diplomat expressed satisfaction Thursday after a visit by a three-country team of experts to North Korea's main nuclear facilities to determine how to disable the complex so it cannot produce material for bombs. Sung Kim, chief Korea expert for the U.S. State Department, said that the group of American, Chinese and Russian officials had seen the main facilities at the home of North Korea's nuclear weapons program in Yongbyon, 100 kilometers, or 60 miles, north of the capital, Pyongyang."	1	5	https://www.nytimes.com/2007/09/13/world/asia/13iht-nkorea.3.7494552.html	https://news.kbs.co.kr/news/view.do?ncd=1422143
Sixth round of SPT (second phase) in Beijing	Held the second stage of the sixth Six-Party Talks (Beijing)—"The United States has endorsed a plan for dismantling North Korea's nuclear facilities by the end of the year, Bush administration officials said Tuesday. Negotiators reached agreement on a draft in Beijing on Sunday after four days of six-nation talks, but said at the time that they needed final approval from their superiors in Moscow, Washington, Seoul, Tokyo, Beijing and Pyongyang. The draft sets out a timetable for North Korea to disclose all its nuclear programs and disable all facilities in return for 950,000 metric tons of fuel oil or its equivalent in economic aid."	1	5	https://www.nytimes.com/2007/10/03/washington/03diplo.html	https://news.kbs.co.kr/news/view.do?ncd=1432044

(continued)

EventNum	StYear	StMon	StDay	EndYear	EndMon	EndDay	Duration	Type_event
81	2007	10	3	2007	10	3	1	4
90	2007	11	5	2007	11	5	1	3

Note: All events are coded in Korean Standard Time (KST).

EventDetail	EventDetail2	Type_participant	Indicator	Source1	Source2
Oct. 3 Joint Statement to implement Feb 13 agreement	On October 3, 2007, the Six Parties—the United States, China, Japan, Russia, the DPRK, and the ROK—agreed on "Second-Phase Actions for Implementation of the Joint Statement.The United States welcomes the October 3 agreement, which outlines a roadmap for a declaration of the DPRK's nuclear programs and disablement of its core nuclear facilities at Yongbyon by the end of the year. The Second-Phase actions will effectively end the DPRK's production of plutonium—a major step towards the goal of achieving the verifiable denuclearization of the Korean Peninsula.We intend to work closely with the other parties to implement Second-Phase actions as expeditiously and effectively as possible."	1	5	https://2001-2009.state.gov/r/pa/prs/ps/2007/oct/93223.htm	https://www.nytimes.com/2007/10/04/world/asia/04diplo.html
U.S. experts arrived in North Korea to begin disablement of Yongbyon facilities	"Disabling the reactor at Yongbyon, north of Pyongyang, would mark a further breakthrough in efforts to convince North Korea to scale back its nuclear program. The country conducted its first-ever nuclear test in October 2006.'By Monday morning, they will begin their work,' U.S. Assistant Secretary of State Christopher Hill said in Tokyo on Saturday, referring to the U.S. team that arrived in Pyongyang last week. South Korean nuclear envoy Chun Yung Woo said Monday that the U.S. team will determine which specific disablement measures it will take first after considering technical issues and safety concerns. Chun said he had not confirmed that the U.S. team started the disabling work as scheduled."	1	5	https://www.nytimes.com/2007/11/05/world/asia/05iht-korea.1.8190356.html	https://www.dailynk.com/%EB%B6%88%EB%8A%A5%ED%99%94%ED%8C%80-%EA%B3%A7-%EC%98%81%EB%B3%80%EC%9B%90%EC%9E%90%EB%A1%9C-%ED%8F%90%EC%97%B0%EB%A3%8C%EB%B4%89-%EC%9D%B8/

APPENDIX 2

List of U.S.-ROK Joint Military Exercises, 2005–2015

	Spring exercise		Fall exercise	
	Name	Dates	Name	Dates
2005	RSOI* Foal Eagle (FE)	March 19–25	Ulchi-Focus Lens (UFL)	August 22–September 2
2006		March 24–31		August 21–September 1
2007		March 25–31		August 20–31
2008	Key Resolve Foal Eagle (KR/FE)	March 2–7		August 18–22
2009		March 9–20	Ulchi Freedom Guardian (UFG)	August 17–28
2010		March 8–18		August 16–26
2011		February 28–April 30		August 16–26
2012		February 27–April 30		August 13–30
2013		March 1–April 30		August 19–30
2014		February 24–April 18		August 18–29
2015		March 2–April 24		August 17–28

*RSOI (Reception, Staging, Onward Movement, Integration) became known as Key Resolve starting in 2008.

APPENDIX 3

Microsurveys of DPRK Citizens and Sample Answer Sheets

2016 SURVEY

SURVEY QUESTIONS

Age: ____
Sex: M / F
Occupation: _____
Region: _____

1. What percentage of your household income is derived from the jangmadang? (W)[1]
    a. Almost all
    b. More than 75%
    c. About 50%–75%
    d. About 25%–50%
    e. About 10%–25%
    f. Less than 10%
    g. none
2. Does the public distribution system provide you with what you want for a good life?
    a. Yes
    b. No

3. Do your family, friends, or neighbors complain or make jokes about the government in private?
   a. Yes
   b. No
4. Do you ever watch or listen to foreign media, including radio, TV, dramas, movies, USBs, etc.?
   a. Yes
   b. No
4.1. If yes, how often?
   a. Once a year
   b. Once a month
   c. Once a week
   d. Everyday
   e. Other ( )
5. Do you think unification is necessary? (W)
   a. Yes
   b. No
6. If yes to Q5, what is the main reason that unification should occur? (A)[2]
   a. Shared ethnicity (North and South are "one race")
   b. Increase economic growth
   c. Increase international influence
   d. Reduce costs related to division of peninsula
   e. Defend against outside threats
   f. Resolve issue of separated families
7. Will unification happen in your lifetime?
   a. Yes
   b. No
   c. Don't know
8. Do you feel that information about the outside world is useful to you?
   a. Yes
   b. No
9. Which has a larger impact on your life?
   a. North Korean government decisions
   b. Influence from the outside world (like goods and information)

Qualitative questions

10. Which event causes you to feel greatest animosity toward the regime?
11. Would you rather receive aid from China, South Korea, or the United States? Why?

* * *

설문조사

나이: ____
성: 남 / 여
직업: _____
거주: _____

1. 월 총수익 중 장마당 경영이 차지하는 비율이 어떻게 됩니까?* (W)
    a. 거의 전부
    b. 75% 이상
    c. 약 50%–75%
    d. 약 25%–50%
    e. 약 10%–25%
    f. 10% 이하
    g. 없음
2. 배급제는 본인에게 필요한 물품을 적당히 제공합니까?
    a. 네
    b. 아니오
3. 이웃, 친구, 가족이 개인적으로 예전보다 삶에 대해 불평 및 비난을 합니까?
    a. 네
    b. 아니오
4. 라디오, 텔레비존, 드라마, 영화, USB 등을 통해 외부 정보에 접해본 적 있습니까?
    a. 네
    b. 아니오
4.1. 접해본 적이 있다면 얼마나 자주 접했습니까?
    일년에 한번
    한달에 한번
    일주일에 한번

매일

기타 (   )

5. 통일이 꼭 필요하다고 생각하십니까?* (W)
   a. 네
   b. 아니오
6. 5번의 질문에 '네'라고 답하셨으면 주된 이유가 무엇입니까?* (A)
   a. 동일한 민족이기 때문에 (North and South are "one race")
   b. 경제 성장을 위해서
   c. 국제적인 영향력 강화를 위해
   d. 한반도 분단 상태로 인한 비용 절감을 위해
   e. 외부의 위협을 막기 위해
   f. 이산가족 문제를 해결하기 위해
7. 평생 살아가는 동안 통일이 실현될 수 있다고 생각합니까?
   a. 네
   b. 아니오
   c. 모르겠음
8. 정보가 본인에게 유익하다고 생각합니까?
   a. 네
   b. 아니오
9. 다음 중 무엇이 본인 생활에 영향을 가장 끼칩니까?
   a. 행정부 및 당국 정책
   b. 외부로부터의 지원 및 영향 (외구제 물품 및 정보)

Qualitative questions

10. 국가나 사회에 대해 불평, 불말을 하게 된 가장 큰 원인이 무엇입니까?
11. 중국과 한국, 미국 중 어느 국가의 지원을 받기를 선호하십니까? 이유가 무엇입니까?

* * *

SAMPLE ANSWER SHEET FROM 2016 SURVEY RESULTS

5. 통일이 꼭 필요하다고 생각하십니까?* (W)
   a. 네
   b. 아니오
6. 5번의 질문에 '네'라고 답하셨으면 주된 이유가 무엇입니까?* (A)
   a. 동일한 민족이기 때문에
   b. 경제 성장을 위해서

c. 국제적인 영향력 강화를 위해
   d. 한반도 분단 상태로 인한 비용 절감을 위해
   e. 외부의 위협을 막기 위해
   f. 이산가족 문제를 해결하기 위해
7. 평생 살아가는 동안 통일이 실현될 수 있다고 생각합니까?
   a. 네
   b. 아니오
   c. 모르겠음
8. 정보가 본인에게 유익하다고 생각합니까?
   a. 네
   b. 아니오
9. 다음 중 무엇이 본인 생활에 영향을 가장 끼칩니까?
   a. 행정부 및 당국 정책
   b. 외부로부터의 지원 및 영향 (외구제 물품 및 정보)

Qualitative questions

12. 국가나 사회에 대해 불평, 불만을 하게 된 가장 큰 원인이 무엇입니까?
    강압적인 노력 동원, 세외부담, 노임미달
13. 중국과 한국, 미국 중 어느 국가의 지원을 받기를 선호하십니까? 이유가 무엇입니까?
    한국산 제품, 질이 좋고 같은 민족으로서 기호가 맞기 때문

***

2017 SURVEYS

SURVEY FOR GROUP A

Questions for Survey #2, GROUP A
설문조사 #2, A 그룹

There should be two groups of respondents. Both groups should have the same number of respondent in each. The first group is asked the questions from the Group A survey. The second group should be asked the questions from the Group B survey. (Questions that differ between the two surveys are questions #3, #5, #10, #14, #15, and #16.)
본 설문조사는 A와 B 두 개의 답변 그룹을 대상으로 진행되며, 각 그룹은 동일한 수의 답변자를 포함해야 합니다. 첫번째 그룹을 대상으로는 "Group A" 설문지를 사용하고 두번째 그룹을 대상으로는 "Group B" 설문지를 사용해주십시

오. 3번, 5번, 10번, 14번, 15번, 16번 질문은 A와 B 설문지 간 질문 내용이 다른 점을 유의하여 주십시오.

1. [U.S.] Do you see the United States as North Korea's enemy?
   a. Yes
   b. No
1. [미국] 귀하는 미국을 북한의 적이라고 생각하십니까?
   a. 그렇다
   b. 아니다

2. [U.S.] Are you aware that North Korea has received economic/humanitarian assistance from the United States?
   a. Yes
   b. No
2. [미국] 귀하는 북한이 미국으로부터 경제적, 인도적 지원을 받은 사실을 알고 계십니까?
   a. 알고있다
   b. 모른다

3. [UNIFICATION] [GROUP A] Do you agree with this statement? Unification will make your life better.
   a. Yes
   b. No
3. [통일] [A 그룹] 귀하는 다음 내용에 동의하십니까? 통일은 당신이 더 나은 삶을 살 수 있게 할 것이다.
   a. 그렇다
   b. 아니다

4. [UNIFICATION-QUALITATIVE] In what way will your life be better with unification?
4. [통일—질적 분석] 통일이 된다면 어떤 점에서 귀하의 삶이 나아질 것이라고 생각하십니까?

Special instructions for question #5: It is very important to explicitly emphasize to respondents not to tell the enumerators which statements they agree with, but rather how many. Often by default people will say yes, I agree with a and b but not c, for example. The enumerator should stop them if they start doing this.

5번 질문에 대한 유의사항: 본 문항에 대해 질문할 시 조사원은 답변자가 a, b, c 중 어느 항목에 동의하는지의 여부보다는 몇 개의 항목에 동의하는지 대답할 수 있도록 명확히 강조해주는 것이 매우 중요합니다. 예를 들면 답변자는 일반적으로 "저는 a와b 항목은 동의하지만 c항목에는 동의하지 않습니다" 라고 대답하는 경우가 많습니다. 조사원은 답변자가 위와 같은 방식으로 대답할 경우 설문을 멈추고 답변자가 몇 개의 항목에 동의하는지 다시 한번 질문해야 합니다.

5. [UNIFICATION] [Group A] **How many** of these statements do you agree with?
   a. Unification will be expensive
   b. Unification will unite the Korean people
   c. Koreans are a pure race

5. [통일] [A 그룹] 귀하는 다음 내용들 중 몇가지나 동의하십니까?
   a. 통일은 많은 비용을 필요로 할 것이다.
   b. 통일은 북한과 남한의 주민들을 단결시킬 것이다.
   c. 남북주민은 한민족이다.

6. [REGION] Do you think China wants or does not want unification?
   a. Wants
   b. Does not want

6. [주변국에 대한 인식] 귀하는 중국이 한반도 통일을 원한다고 생각하십니까?
   a. 원한다
   b. 원하지 않는다

7. [REGION] Do you think the United States wants or does not want unification?
   a. United States wants unification
   b. United States does not want unification

7. [주변국에 대한 인식] 귀하는 미국이 한반도 통일을 원한다고 생각하십니까?
   a. 원한다
   b. 원하지 않는다

8. [REGION] Which country's help do you think is the most necessary for unification?
   a. China
   b. South Korea
   c. Russia
   d. Japan
   e. United States
   f. We do not need any help from other countries.

8. [주변국에 대한 인식] 귀하는 한반도 통일을 위해 어느 나라의 도움이 가장 필요하다고 생각하십니까?
   a. 중국
   b. 남한
   c. 러시아
   d. 일본
   e. 미국
   f. 어느 나라의 도움도 필요 없다.

9. [NUCLEAR] Do you think North Korea's nuclear program is the source of national pride?
   a. Yes
   b. No

9. [북핵] 귀하는 북한의 핵무기가 국가적 자부심의 근원이라고 생각하십니까?
   a. 그렇다
   b. 아니다

10. [NUCLEAR] [GROUP A] Some say nuclear weapons make us a prosperous nation. Do you agree?
    a. Yes
    b. No

10. [북핵][A 그룹] 어떤이는 핵무기가 북한을 더욱 부강하게 한다고 주장합니다. 이에 동의하십니까?
    a. 동의한다
    b. 동의하지 않는다

11. [NUCLEAR] Please state your attitude toward North Korea's nuclear weapons program.
    a. Positive
    b. Neutral
    c. Negative
    d. Don't care

11. [북핵] 북한의 핵무기에 대한 귀하의 의견을 다음 중에서 선택해주십시오.
    a. 긍정적
    b. 중립적
    c. 부정적
    d. 관심 없음

12. [NUCLEAR-Qualitative] What do you think of North Korea's nuclear program?

APPENDIX 3. MICROSURVEYS 235

12. [북핵—질적 분석] 귀하는 북한의 핵무기 개발에 대해 어떻게 생각하십니까?

13. [NUCLEAR] Which would you rather have, more nuclear weapons or more goods in the markets?
    a. More nuclear weapons
    b. More goods in the markets

13. [북핵] 귀하는 다음 중 어느 쪽을 선택하시겠습니까?
    a. 더 많은 핵무기 보유
    b. 더 많은 장마당 판매 품목

Special instructions for question #14: It is very important to explicitly emphasize to the respondents not to tell the enumerators which statements they agree with, but rather how many. Often by default people will say yes, I agree with a and b but not c, for example. The enumerator should stop them if they start doing this.

14번 질문에 대한 유의사항: 본 문항에 대해 질문할 시 조사원은 답변자가 a, b, c 중 어느 항목에 동의하는지의 여부보다는 몇 개의 항목에 동의하는지 대답할 수 있도록 명확히 강조해주는 것이 매우 중요합니다. 예를 들면 답변자는 일반적으로 "저는 a와b 항목은 동의하지만 c항목에는 동의하지 않습니다" 라고 대답하는 경우가 많습니다. 조사원은 답변자가 위와 같은 방식으로 대답할 경우 설문을 멈추고 답변자가 몇 개의 항목에 동의하는지 다시 한번 질문해야 합니다.

14. [GROUP A] **How many** of these do you agree with?
    a. Markets should stay open longer
    b. The roads need repair
    c. This winter will be cold

14. [A 그룹] 귀하는 다음 내용들 중 몇가지나 동의하십니까?
    a. 장마당이 더 오래 열려있어야 한다.
    b. 도로 수리가 필요하다.
    c. 올 겨울은 추울 것이다.

15. [GROUP A] Some say nuclear weapons keep us safe. Do you agree?
    a. Yes
    b. No

15. [A 그룹] 어떤이는 핵무기가 북한 주민들을 지켜줄 것이라고 주장합니다. 이에 동의하십니까?
    a. 동의한다
    b. 동의하지 않는다

16. [GROUP A] Do you agree with this: Some people say that international sanctions do not hurt our economy. Do you agree?
    a. Yes
    b. No
16. [A 그룹] 어떤이는 국제적 대북제재가 북한 경제에 영향을 미치지 못한다고 주장합니다. 이에 동의하십니까?
    a. 동의한다
    b. 동의하지 않는다

2017 SURVEY FOR GROUP B

Questions for Survey #2, GROUP B
설문조사 #2, B 그룹

There should be two groups of respondents. Both groups should have the same number of respondents. The first group is asked the questions from the Group A survey. The second group should be asked the questions from the Group B survey. (Questions that differ between the two surveys are questions #3, #5, #10, #14, #15, and #16.)
본 설문조사는 A와 B 두 개의 답변 그룹을 대상으로 진행되며, 각 그룹은 동일한 수의 답변자를 포함해야 합니다. 첫번째 그룹을 대상으로는 "Group A" 설문지를 사용하고 두번째 그룹을 대상으로는 "Group B" 설문지를 사용해주십시오. 3번, 5번, 10번, 14번, 15번, 16번 질문은 A와 B 설문지 간 질문 내용이 다른 점을 유의하여 주십시오.

1. [U.S.] Do you see the United States as North Korea's enemy?
    a. Yes
    b. No
1. [미국] 귀하는 미국을 북한의 적이라고 생각하십니까?
    a. 그렇다
    b. 아니다

2. [U.S.] Are you aware that North Korea has received economic/humanitarian assistance from the United States?
    a. Yes
    b. No
2. [미국] 귀하는 북한이 미국으로부터 경제적, 인도적 지원을 받은 사실을 알고 계십니까?

a. 알고있다
b. 모른다

3. [UNIFICATION] [GROUP B] Do you agree with this statement? Unification under Kim Jong-un will make your life better.
   a. Yes
   b. No
3. [통일] [B 그룹] 귀하는 다음 내용에 동의하십니까? 김정은 통치하에서의 통일은 당신이 더 나은 삶을 살 수 있게 할 것이다.
   a. 그렇다
   b. 아니다

4. [UNIFICATION-QUALITATIVE] In what way will your life be better with unification?
4. [통일—질적 분석] 통일이 된다면 어떤 점에서 귀하의 삶이 나아질 것이라고 생각하십니까?

Special instructions for question #5: It is very important to explicitly emphasize to the respondents not to tell the enumerators which statements they agree with, but rather how many. Often by default people will say yes, I agree with a and b but not c, for example. The enumerator should stop them if they start doing this.

5번 질문에 대한 유의사항: 본 문항에 대해 질문할 시 조사원은 답변자가 a, b, c 중 어느 항목에 동의하는지의 여부보다는 몇 개의 항목에 동의하는지 대답할 수 있도록 명확히 강조해주는 것이 매우 중요합니다. 예를 들면 답변자는 일반적으로 "저는 a와b 항목은 동의하지만 c항목에는 동의하지 않습니다" 라고 대답하는 경우가 많습니다. 조사원은 답변자가 위와 같은 방식으로 대답할 경우 설문을 멈추고 답변자가 몇 개의 항목에 동의하는지 다시 한번 질문해야 합니다.

5. [UNIFICATION] [Group B] **How many** of these statements do you agree with?
   a. Unification will be expensive
   b. Unification will unite the Korean people
   c. Koreans are a pure race
   d. Our nuclear weapons do not help unification
5. [통일] [B 그룹] 귀하는 다음 내용들 중 몇가지나 동의하십니까?
   a. 통일은 많은 비용을 필요로 할 것이다.
   b. 통일은 북한과 남한의 주민들을 단결시킬 것이다.

c. 남북주민은 한민족이다.
   d. 북한의 핵무기는 통일에 도움이 되지 않는다.

6. [REGION] Do you think China wants or does not want unification?
   a. Wants
   b. Does not want
6. [주변국에 대한 인식] 귀하는 중국이 한반도 통일을 원한다고 생각하십니까?
   a. 원한다
   b. 원하지 않는다

7. [REGION] Do you think the United States wants or does not want unification?
   a. United States wants unification
   b. United States does not want unification
7. [주변국에 대한 인식] 귀하는 미국이 한반도 통일을 원한다고 생각하십니까?
   a. 원한다
   b. 원하지 않는다

8. [REGION] Which country's help do you think is the most necessary for unification?
   a. China
   b. South Korea
   c. Russia
   d. Japan
   e. United States
   f. We do not need any help from other countries
8. [주변국에 대한 인식] 귀하는 한반도 통일을 위해 어느 나라의 도움이 가장 필요하다고 생각하십니까?
   a. 중국
   b. 남한
   c. 러시아
   d. 일본
   e. 미국
   f. 어느 나라의 도움도 필요 없다

9. [NUCLEAR] Do you think North Korea's nuclear program is the source of national pride?
   a. Yes
   b. No

9. [북핵] 귀하는 북한의 핵무기가 국가적 자부심의 근원이라고 생각하십니까?
   a. 그렇다
   b. 아니다

10. [NUCLEAR] [GROUP B] Kim Jong-un says nuclear weapons make us a more prosperous nation. Do you agree?
    a. Yes
    b. No

10. [북핵] [B 그룹] 김정은은 핵무기가 북한을 더욱 부강하게 한다고 주장합니다. 이에 동의하십니까?
    a. 동의한다
    b. 동의하지 않는다

11. [NUCLEAR] Please state your attitude toward North Korea's nuclear weapons program.
    a. Positive
    b. Neutral
    c. Negative
    d. Don't care

11. [북핵] 북한의 핵무기에 대한 귀하의 의견을 다음 중에서 선택해주십시오.
    a. 긍정적
    b. 중립적
    c. 부정적
    d. 관심 없음

12. [NUCLEAR-Qualitative] What do you think of North Korea's nuclear program?

12. [북핵—질적 분석] 귀하는 북한의 핵무기 개발에 대해 어떻게 생각하십니까?

13. [NUCLEAR] Which would you rather have, more nuclear weapons or more goods in the markets?
    a. More nuclear weapons
    b. More goods in the markets

13. [북핵] 귀하는 다음 중 어느 쪽을 선택하시겠습니까?
    a. 더 많은 핵무기 보유
    b. 더 많은 장마당 판매 품목

Special instructions for question #14: It is very important to explicitly emphasize to the respondents not to tell the enumerators which statements they agree with, but rather how many. Often by default people will say yes, I agree with a and b but not c, for example. The enumerator should stop them if they start doing this.

14번 질문에 대한 유의사항: 본 문항에 대해 질문할 시 조사원은 답변자가 a, b, c 중 어느 항목에 동의하는지의 여부보다는 몇 개의 항목에 동의하는지 대답할 수 있도록 명확히 강조해주는 것이 매우 중요합니다. 예를 들면 답변자는 일반적으로 "저는 a와b 항목은 동의하지만 c항목에는 동의하지 않습니다" 라고 대답하는 경우가 많습니다. 조사원은 답변자가 위와 같은 방식으로 대답할 경우 설문을 멈추고 답변자가 몇 개의 항목에 동의하는지 다시 한번 질문해야 합니다.

14. [Group B] **How many** do you agree with?
    a. Markets should stay open longer
    b. The roads need repair
    c. This winter will be cold
    d. Sanctions do not affect what is in the markets
14. [B 그룹] 귀하는 다음 내용들 중 몇가지나 동의하십니까?
    a. 장마당이 더 오래 열려있어야 한다.
    b. 도로 수리가 필요하다.
    c. 올 겨울은 추울 것이다.
    f. 대북제재는 장마당에서 팔리는 물품의 가지수에 별 영향을 미치지 않는다.

15. [GROUP B] Kim Jong-un says nuclear weapons keep us safe. Do you agree with this?
    a. Yes
    b. No
15. [B 그룹] 김정은은 핵무기가 북한 주민들을 지켜줄 것이라고 주장합니다. 이에 동의하십니까?
    a. 동의한다
    b. 동의하지 않는다

16. [GROUP B] Do you agree with this: Kim Jong-un says that international sanctions do not hurt our economy. Do you agree?
    a. Yes
    b. No
16. [B 그룹] 김정은은 국제적 대북제재가 북한 경제에 영향을 미치지 못한다고 주장합니다. 이에 동의하십니까?
    a. 동의한다
    b. 동의하지 않는다

NOTES

1. THE BLACK BOX

1. "North Korean Enigma; Kim Il Sung," *New York Times*, July 12, 1961, sec. Archives, https://www.nytimes.com/1961/07/12/archives/north-korean-enigma-kim-il-sung.html.
2. Economist [@TheEconomist], "The Economist Featured Kim Jong Il on Its Covers a Few Times, Including 'Greetings, Earthlings' in June 2000," Twitter, December 19, 2011, https://twitter.com/TheEconomist/status/148727410928521217.
3. "Lil' Kim," *TIME Magazine*, cover, February 27, 2012, https://content.time.com/time/covers/0,16641,20120227,00.html.
4. See cover image in Françoise Mouly and Mina Kaneko, "Cover Story: Kim Jong-Un's Big Announcement," *New Yorker*, January 8, 2016, https://www.newyorker.com/culture/culture-desk/cover-story-anita-kunz-2016-01-18.
5. Sang-Hun Choe, "Meet Kim Jong-Un, a Moody Young Man with a Nuclear Arsenal," *New York Times*, August 10, 2017, sec. World, https://www.nytimes.com/2017/08/10/world/asia/kim-jong-un-north-korea-nuclear.html.
6. The term "Hermit Kingdom" was first used in William Elliot Griffis's book *Corea: The Hermit Nation* (1882), to describe Korea in the age of the Joseon dynasty when it pursued a policy of restricting contacts with the outside world.
7. Patrick McEachern, *Inside the Red Box: North Korea's Post-Totalitarian Politics* (New York: Columbia University Press, 2010).
8. Jenny Jun, Scott LaFoy, and Ethan Sohn, *North Korea's Cyber Operations: Strategy and Responses* (Washington, DC: Center for Strategic & International Studies and Rowman & Littlefield, 2015), 3.

9. Amy Zegart, "Kim Jong Un: The Hardest Intelligence Target," *Atlantic*, July 9, 2017, sec. Global, https://www.theatlantic.com/international/archive/2017/07/north-korea-kim-jong-un/533034/.
10. Peter Walker, "Dennis Rodman Gives Away Name of Kim Jong-Un's Daughter," *Guardian*, September 9, 2013, sec. World news, https://www.theguardian.com/world/2013/sep/09/dennis-rodman-north-korea-baby-name.
11. Ken Dilanian and Courtney Kube, "Why It's So Hard for U.S. Spies to Figure Out North Korea," *NBC News*, September 3, 2017, https://www.nbcnews.com/news/north-korea/why-it-s-so-hard-u-s-spies-figure-out-n797171; and Armed Services Committee, United States Senate, "Statement for the Record, Worldwide Threat Assessment," March 6, 2018, https://www.armed-services.senate.gov/imo/media/doc/Ashley_03-06-18.pdf. Other examples of the challenges of intelligence collection on North Korea include Jacqueline Klimas, "Why North Korea Is a Black Hole for American Spies," *Politico*, September 8, 2017, https://www.politico.com/story/2017/09/08/why-north-korea-is-a-black-hole-for-spies-242473; Ken Dilanian, "North Korea Is a Tough Target for U.S. Intelligence Agencies," *Los Angeles Times*, December 24, 2011, sec. World & Nation, https://www.latimes.com/nation/la-xpm-2011-dec-24-la-fg-korea-intel-20111225-story.html; David E. Sanger and William J. Broad, "How U.S. Intelligence Agencies Underestimated North Korea," *New York Times*, January 6, 2018, sec. World, https://www.nytimes.com/2018/01/06/world/asia/north-korea-nuclear-missile-intelligence.html; Mike Chinoy, "Why North Korean Intelligence Is so Hard to Read," CNN, April 12, 2013, https://www.cnn.com/2013/04/12/world/asia/north-korea-nuclear-capabilities/index.html.
12. Chung Min Lee and Kathryn Botto, "Reconceptualizing U.S.-ROK Cooperation in Korean Unification: A Stabilization Framework," *Unification Blue Book 2019* (Washington, DC: Carnegie Endowment for International Peace, 2019), 26.
13. Evans J. R. Revere, "Korean Reunification and U.S. Interests: Preparing for One Korea," Brookings, January 20, 2015, https://www.brookings.edu/articles/korean-reunification-and-u-s-interests-preparing-for-one-korea/; National Bureau of Asian Research, "The Fourth U.S.-ROK Dialogue on Unification and Regional Security: Assessing North Korean Stability and Preparing for Unification," n.d., https://www.nbr.org/wp-content/uploads/pdfs/programs/assessing_north_korean_stability_and_preparing_for_unification.pdf.
14. Lee and Botto, "Reconceptualizing U.S.-ROK Cooperation," 26.
15. Bruce W. Bennett, "Alternative Paths to Korean Unification" (Washington, DC: RAND Corporation, October 31, 2018), https://www.rand.org/pubs/research_reports/RR2808.html.
16. Ji-Young Lee, "Is Reunification Possible for North and South Korea?," *Conversation*, January 24, 2018, https://theconversation.com/is-a-unified-korea-possible-90071.
17. Revere, "Korean Reunification and U.S. Interests."
18. Lee and Botto, "Reconceptualizing U.S.-ROK Cooperation," 26.

19. Julian Ryall, "South Korea Looks to Germany as a Model of Reunification," *DW*, October 3, 2021, https://www.dw.com/en/south-korea-looks-to-germany-for-reunification-pointers/a-59374733.
20. Lee and Botto, "Reconceptualizing U.S.-ROK Cooperation," 32.
21. Ji-Young Lee, "Is Reunification Possible?"
22. McEachern, *Inside the Red Box*, 4.
23. Beyond Parallel, "Database: North Korean Provocations," December 20, 2019, https://beyondparallel.csis.org/database-north-korean-provocations/. For press coverage on the March 2017 tests, see Paula Hancocks and Ben Westcott, "North Korea Fires Four Ballistic Missiles Into Sea of Japan," CNN, March 5, 2017, https://www.cnn.com/2017/03/05/asia/north-korea-projectile/index.html; and Taehoon Lee and Ben Westcott, "Failed North Korean Missile Exploded 'Within Seconds,' US Says," CNN, March 22, 2017, https://www.cnn.com/2017/03/21/asia/north-korea-missile-test/. For the April 2017 tests, see Ju-min Park and Jack Kim, "North Korea Test-Fires Missile Into Sea Ahead of Trump-Xi Summit," Reuters, April 4, 2017, sec. Aerospace and Defense, https://www.reuters.com/article/us-northkorea-missiles-idUSKBN1762XX; Paula Hancocks and Barbara Starr, "North Korean Missile Test Fails, US and South Korea Say," CNN, April 15, 2017, https://www.cnn.com/2017/04/15/asia/north-korea-missile-test/index.html; and Ryan Browne and Steve Almasy, "North Korea's Missile Test Fails, US Military Says," CNN, April 28, 2017, https://www.cnn.com/2017/04/28/world/north-korea-missile-launch/index.html. For the May 2017 tests, see Sang-Hun Choe, "North Korea Says Missile It Tested Can Carry Nuclear Warhead," *New York Times*, May 15, 2017, sec. World, https://www.nytimes.com/2017/05/14/world/asia/north-korea-missile-nuclear.html; Ju-min Park, "North Korea Tests Another Missile; Seoul Says Dashes Hopes for Peace," Reuters, May 21, 2017, sec. Aerospace and Defense, https://www.reuters.com/article/us-northkorea-missiles-idUSKBN18H0A6; Sang-Hun Choe, "North Korea Fires Missile That Lands in Sea Between Korea and Japan," *New York Times*, May 28, 2017, sec. World, https://www.nytimes.com/2017/05/28/world/asia/north-korea-missile-test.html. For the June 2017 test, see Ben Westcott and Steve Almasy, "North Korea Launches 4 Anti-Ship Missiles, Fourth Test in a Month," CNN, June 7, 2017, https://www.cnn.com/2017/06/07/asia/north-korea-missiles-launch/index.html. For August 2017 tests, see Will Ripley, Jamie Crawford, and Ralph Ellis, "North Korea Launches Trio of Missiles Amidst US-South Korea Military Drills," CNN, August 25, 2017, https://www.cnn.com/2017/08/25/asia/north-korea-fires-projectile/index.html; and Joshua Berlinger, Yoko Wakatsuki, and Will Ripley, "Trump Says 'All Options on Table' After North Korea Fires Missile Over Japan," CNN, August 28, 2017, https://www.cnn.com/2017/08/28/politics/north-korea-launch-unidentified-projectile/index.html. For the September 2017 test, see Ankit Panda, "North Korea Overflies Japan with Another Intermediate-Range Ballistic Missile: Early Analysis," *Diplomat*, September 15, 2017, https://thediplomat.com/2017/09/north-korea-overflies-japan-with-another-intermediate-range-ballistic-missile-early-analysis/.

24. For details, see "Database: North Korean Provocations." For press coverage, David E. Sanger, Sang-Hun Choe, and William J. Broad, "North Korea Tests a Ballistic Missile That Experts Say Could Hit California," *New York Times*, July 28, 2017, sec. World, https://www.nytimes.com/2017/07/28/world/asia/north-korea-ballistic-missile.html and Zachary Cohen et al., "New Missile Test Shows North Korea Capable of Hitting All of US Mainland," CNN, November 28, 2017, https://www.cnn.com/2017/11/28/politics/north-korea-missile-launch/index.html.
25. For press coverage, see David E. Sanger and Sang-Hun Choe, "North Korean Nuclear Test Draws U.S. Warning of 'Massive Military Response,'" *New York Times*, September 3, 2017, sec. World, https://www.nytimes.com/2017/09/03/world/asia/north-korea-tremor-possible-6th-nuclear-test.html; Michelle Ye Hee Lee, "North Korea's Latest Nuclear Test Was so Powerful It Reshaped the Mountain Above It," *Washington Post*, December 1, 2021, https://www.washingtonpost.com/news/worldviews/wp/2017/09/14/orth-koreas-latest-nuclear-test-was-so-powerful-it-reshaped-the-mountain-above-it/.
26. In response to a question on reports about North Korea's nuclear capabilities, Trump said "North Korea best not make any more threats to the United States. They will be met with fire and fury like the world has never seen. He has been very threatening beyond a normal state. And as I said, they will be met with fire, fury, and, frankly, power, the likes of which this world has never seen before," in White House Archives, "Remarks by President Trump Before a Briefing on the Opioid Crisis," August 8, 2017, https://trumpwhitehouse.archives.gov/briefings-statements/remarks-president-trump-briefing-opioid-crisis/.
27. Alex Horton, "Why North Korea Threatened Guam, the Tiny U.S. Territory with Big Military Power," *Washington Post*, December 1, 2021, https://www.washingtonpost.com/news/worldviews/wp/2017/08/09/why-north-korea-threatened-guam-the-tiny-u-s-territory-with-big-military-power/.
28. On August 11, 2017, Trump tweeted: "Military solutions are now fully in place, locked and loaded, should North Korea act unwisely. Hopefully Kim Jong Un will find another path!" The original tweet is no longer available because Trump's Twitter account was permanently suspended in January 2021. See Peter Baker, "Trump Says Military Is 'Locked and Loaded' and North Korea Will 'Regret' Threats," *New York Times*, August 11, 2017, sec. World, https://www.nytimes.com/2017/08/11/world/asia/trump-north-korea-locked-and-loaded.html.
29. For Kim Jong-un's review of Guam strike plans, see KCNA Watch, "Kim Jong Un Inspects KPA Strategic Force Command," August 15, 2017, https://kcnawatch.org/newstream/; for North Korea's sixth nuclear test and Kim Jong-un's inspection of the nuclear device in September 2017, see Brad Lendon and Taehoon Lee, "North Korea Says It Can Make New Bomb in Volume," CNN, September 2, 2017, https://www.cnn.com/2017/09/02/asia/north-korea-kim-jong-un-nuke-lab-visit/index.html.
30. White House Archives, "Remarks by President Trump to the 72nd Session of the United Nations General Assembly," September 19, 2017, https://trump

whitehouse.archives.gov/briefings-statements/remarks-president-trump-72nd-session-united-nations-general-assembly/.

31. "Full Text of Kim Jong-Un's Response to President Trump," *New York Times*, September 22, 2017, sec. World, https://www.nytimes.com/2017/09/22/world/asia/kim-jong-un-trump.html.

32. Carol Morello, "North Korea's Top Diplomat Says Strike Against U.S. Mainland Is 'Inevitable,'" *Washington Post*, April 8, 2023, https://www.washingtonpost.com/world/national-security/north-koreas-top-diplomat-says-strike-against-us-mainland-is-inevitable/2017/09/23/c3bcb108-dd8f-4761-b55f-92044348f179_story.html.

33. For the U.S. Department of Defense statement on B1-B bomber mission off the North Korean coast, see "U.S. Flies B1-B Bomber Mission off of North Korean Coast," U.S. Department of Defense, September 23, 2017; President Trump's full tweet was "Just heard Foreign Minister of North Korea speak at U.N. If he echoes thoughts of Little Rocket Man, they won't be around much longer!" See "Trump Tweets Threats Against N. Korea After UN Speech," Reuters, September 24, 2017, sec. Industrials, https://www.reuters.com/article/northkorea-missiles-trump-un-idUKS9N19U045.

34. Matthew Nussbaum, Bryan Bender, and Brent D. Griffiths, "Mattis Warns of 'Massive Military Response' If North Korea Threatens Attack," *Politico*, September 3, 2017, https://www.politico.com/story/2017/09/03/trump-north-korea-nuclear-242289; Ben Riley-Smith, "Exclusive: US Making Plans for 'Bloody Nose' Military Attack on North Korea," *Telegraph*, December 20, 2017, https://www.telegraph.co.uk/news/2017/12/20/exclusive-us-making-plans-bloody-nose-military-attack-north/; Yochi Dreazen, "Here's What War with North Korea Would Look like," *Vox*, February 7, 2018, https://www.vox.com/world/2018/2/7/16974772/north-korea-war-trump-kim-nuclear-weapon.

35. Victor Cha, "Giving North Korea a 'Bloody Nose' Carries a Huge Risk to Americans," *Washington Post*, January 31, 2018, https://www.washingtonpost.com/opinions/victor-cha-giving-north-korea-a-bloody-nose-carries-a-huge-risk-to-americans/2018/01/30/43981c94-05f7-11e8-8777-2a059f168dd2_story.html.

36. Bob Woodward, *Fear: Trump in the White House* (New York: Simon & Schuster, 2018), 301.

37. Elise Labott, Kevin Liptak, and Nicole Gaouette, "Ambassador Candidate Dropped Over Stark Warning on North Korea," CNN, January 30, 2018, https://www.cnn.com/2018/01/30/politics/victor-cha-ambassador-to-south-korea/index.html; Peter Baker and Susan Glasser, *The Divider: Trump in the White House, 2017–2022* (New York: Anchor, 2023).

2. THE UNITED STATES–REPUBLIC OF KOREA ALLIANCE

1. David C. Kang, "Preventive War and North Korea," *Security Studies* 4, no. 2 (June 30, 1994): 330–64.

2. The United States and its allies conduct a multitude of military exercises around the world. Large-scale joint military exercises between the United States and the ROK began in the late 1970s along with the creation of the Combined Forces Command (CFC). "Team Spirit" started in 1976 as a large military maneuver exercise that practiced flowing forces to the peninsula to defend South Korea against a second North Korean invasion. Team Spirit eventually grew in size to involve over 200,000 forces. "Ulchi Focus Lens" also started in 1976 as a computer simulation exercise to test South Korean readiness in a military contingency; it was renamed Ulchi-Freedom Guardian in 2008. Team Spirit was replaced in 1994 with command post exercise "Reception, Staging, Onward Movement, and Integration" (RSO&I), which in turn was replaced in 2008 with "Key Resolve." Since 2001, RSO&I or Key Resolve has been combined with Foal Eagle, a combined field training exercise (FTX). These exercises are smaller in scale than Team Spirit, though they remain focused on force flow to the peninsula. See Robert Collins, "A Brief History of the US-ROK Combined Military Exercises," 38 North, February 26, 2014, https://www.38north.org/2014/02/rcollins022714/.
3. White House Archives, "Press Conference by President Trump," June 12, 2018, https://trumpwhitehouse.archives.gov/briefings-statements/press-conference-president-trump/.
4. James Kim, "'Team Spirit' Joint U.S.-South Korea Exercise Called Off," UPI, January 7, 1992, https://www.upi.com/Archives/1992/01/07/Team-Spirit-joint-US-South-Korea-exercise-called-off/5381694760400/.
5. For the latest work on the relationship between the U.S.-ROK joint military exercises and North Korean provocations, see Jordan Bernhardt and Lauren Sukin, "Joint Military Exercises and Crisis Dynamics on the Korean Peninsula," *Journal of Conflict Resolution* 65, no. 5 (May 1, 2021): 855–88.
6. Vito D'Orazio, "War Games: North Korea's Reaction to US and South Korean Military Exercises," *Journal of East Asian Studies* 12, no. 2 (May 2012): 275–94; Robert Daniel Wallace, "North Korea and Diversion: A Quantitative Analysis (1997–2011)," *Communist and Post-Communist Studies* 47, no. 2 (June 1, 2014): 147–58; and Bernhardt and Sukin, "Joint Military Exercises."
7. D'Orazio, "War Games," 278.
8. Wallace, "North Korea and Diversion," 152.
9. U.S. Department of State Archive, "Six Parties October 3, 2007 Agreement on 'Second-Phase Actions for the Implementation of the Joint Statement'" (Department of State, Office of Electronic Information, Bureau of Public Affairs, October 3, 2007), https://2001-2009.state.gov/r/pa/prs/ps/2007/oct/93223.htm.
10. Timothy W. Martin, "Kim Jong Un's Sister Blasts U.S.'s 'Dangerous War Exercises,' Threatens to Bolster Military," *Wall Street Journal*, August 10, 2021, sec. World, https://www.wsj.com/articles/kim-jong-uns-sister-vows-to-boost-deterrence-after-being-ignored-by-u-s-11628579896; Simon Denyer, "North Korea Complains About 'Stink' of U.S.-South Korea Military Exercises," *Washington Post*, March 16, 2021, https://www.washingtonpost.com/world/north-korea-complains-about

2. THE UNITED STATES–REPUBLIC OF KOREA ALLIANCE 247

-stink-of-us-south-korea-military-exercises/2021/03/15/415ba17c-85fa-11eb-8a67-f314e5fcf88d_story.html; Nick Cumming-Bruce, "North Korea Accuses U.S. and South of 'Inciting Military Tension,'" *New York Times*, August 6, 2019, sec. World, https://www.nytimes.com/2019/08/06/world/asia/north-korea-military.html; Simon Denyer, "North Korea Denounces Scaled-Back U.S.-South Korea Military Exercises," *Washington Post*, March 14, 2019, https://www.washingtonpost.com/world/asia_pacific/north-korea-denounces-scaled-back-us-south-korea-military-exercises/2019/03/07/b90e7508-40d5-11e9-85ad-779ef05fd9d8_story.html.

11. Cited in Barbara Starr and Ryan Browne, "US Cancels Major Military Exercise with South Korea," CNN, October 19, 2018, https://www.cnn.com/2018/10/19/politics/us-south-korea-suspend-exercise/index.html.

12. Collins, "Brief History of the US-ROK Combined Exercises." For more on the effect of U.S.-ROK military exercises on relationship with DPRK, see "Factsheet: US-ROK Military Exercises," Ploughshares Fund, June 15, 2018, https://ploughshares.org/issues-analysis/article/factsheet-us-rok-military-exercises; Youcheer Kim, "The Strategic Background Behind the ROK-US Joint Military Exercises and Their Impact on Inter-Korean Relations," Online Series CO 20–19 (Korea Institute for National Unification, August 18, 2020), https://repo.kinu.or.kr/bitstream/2015.oak/11761/1/CO20-19%28e%29.pdf; Mats Engman, "U.S.-South Korea Military Exercises: Provocation or Possibility?," Institute for Security and Development Policy, March 2018, https://isdp.eu/publication/u-s-rok-military-exercises-provocation-possibility/.

13. In a press conference with President Roh Tae-woo of South Korea in Seoul, President George H. W. Bush said, "If North Korea fulfills its obligation and takes steps to implement the inspection agreements, then President Roh and I are prepared to forgo the Team Spirit exercise for this year." "The President's News Conference with President Roh Tae Woo of South Korea in Seoul," George H. W. Bush Presidential Library & Museum, January 6, 1992, https://bush41library.tamu.edu/archives/public-papers/3819.

14. James Siebens and Mackenzie Mandile, "Concession . . . or Common Sense? Trading Drills for Dialogue," *Defense One*, June 14, 2018, https://www.defenseone.com/ideas/2018/06/trading-drills-dialogue-oft-successful-tactic/148995/.

15. Abraham M. Denmark and Lindsey W. Ford, "America's Military Exercises in Korea Aren't a Game," *Foreign Policy*, June 21, 2018, https://foreignpolicy.com/2018/06/21/americas-military-exercises-in-korea-arent-a-game; James Stravidis, "I Was a Navy Admiral. Here's Why Ending 'War Games' with South Korea Would Be a Grave Mistake," *Time*, June 12, 2018, https://time.com/5310534/donald-trump-north-korea-war-games-military-exercises/; James Dobbins, "Joint Military Exercise Can Be a Bargaining Chip with North Korea," *Hill*, February 23, 2018, https://thehill.com/opinion/national-security/375252-joint-military-exercise-can-be-a-bargaining-chip-with-north-korea/; Engman, "US-ROK Military Exercises"; Steve Miller, "Will Canceling Joint Exercises Move N. Korea Closer

toward Denuclearization?," *VOA*, October 24, 2018, https://www.voanews.com/a/ending-joint-military-exercises/4626923.html; Kyle Ferrier, "Who's Right About the New US-South Korea Joint Military Exercise? Making Sense of the New Dong Maeng Drills," *Diplomat*, March 8, 2019, https://thediplomat.com/2019/03/whos-right-about-the-new-us-south-korea-joint-military-exercise/; Steve Miller, "With Military Exercises Canceled in S. Korea, Experts Express Concern About Impact," *VOA*, March 4, 2019, https://www.voanews.com/a/us-south-korean-military/4812091.html; Lara Seligman, "Experts Question Wisdom of Canceling U.S. Exercises with South Korea, as Mattis Makes It Official," *Foreign Policy*, June 26, 2018, https://foreignpolicy.com/2018/06/26/experts-question-wisdom-of-canceling-u-s-exercises-with-south-korea-as-mattis-makes-it-official/; Henry Olsen, "Opinion | Trump Has Given North Korea a Valuable Bargaining Chip for Free," *Washington Post*, March 5, 2019, https://www.washingtonpost.com/opinions/2019/03/05/trump-has-given-north-korea-valuable-bargaining-chip-free/; John Grady, "Former U.S. Forces in Korea CO: Cancelling More Military Exercises Weakens Ability to Deter North Korea," *USNI News* (blog), July 24, 2018, https://news.usni.org/2018/07/24/former-u-s-forces-korea-co-cancelling-military-exercises-weakens-ability-deter-north-korea.

16. World Trade Organization, "Map of Disputes Between WTO Members," n.d., https://www.wto.org/english/tratop_e/dispu_e/dispu_maps_e.htm?country_selected=CAN&sense=e.
17. See Bernhardt and Sukin, "Joint Military Exercises."
18. For an introductory work on the use of time series analysis on social science inquiries, see Janet M. Box-Steffensmeier et al., *Time Series Analysis for the Social Sciences* (Cambridge: Cambridge University Press, 2014), https://doi.org/10.1017/CBO9781139025287.
19. "N. Korea Test-Fires Short-Range Missiles," *Chosun Ilbo*, March 30, 2012, https://english.chosun.com/site/data/html_dir/2012/03/30/2012033001081.html; Sang-Hun Choe and Rick Gladstone, "North Korean Rocket Fails Moments After Liftoff," *New York Times*, April 12, 2012, sec. World, https://www.nytimes.com/2012/04/13/world/asia/north-korea-launches-rocket-defying-world-warnings.html.
20. Steven Lee Myers and Sang-Hun Choe, "North Koreans Agree to Freeze Nuclear Work; U.S. to Give Aid," *New York Times*, February 29, 2012, sec. World, https://www.nytimes.com/2012/03/01/world/asia/us-says-north-korea-agrees-to-curb-nuclear-work.html.
21. Sang-Hun Choe, "As Rocket Launching Nears, North Korea Continues Shift to New 'Supreme Leader,' " *New York Times*, April 11, 2012, sec. World, https://www.nytimes.com/2012/04/12/world/asia/young-north-korean-leader-kim-jong-un-chosen-as-head-of-ruling-party.html.
22. Sang-Hun Choe, "North Korean Leader Stresses Need for Strong Military," *New York Times*, April 15, 2012, sec. World, https://www.nytimes.com/2012/04/16

/world/asia/kim-jong-un-north-korean-leader-talks-of-military-superiority-in-first-public-speech.html.
23. Box-Steffensmeier et al., *Time Series Analysis for the Social Sciences*, 30.
24. Here we use AIC to compare model fit. But using Schwartz Bayesian criteria (BIC) will yield the same result, as BIC almost always favors the more parsimonious models with less parameters.
25. Jessica L. Weeks, "Autocratic Audience Costs: Regime Type and Signaling Resolve," *International Organization* 62, no.1 (Winter 2008): 35-64.
26. For some of the key works demonstrating the need for autocratic leaders to depend on the support of domestic groups for survival, see Bruce Bueno de Mesquita et al., "An Institutional Explanation of the Democratic Peace," *American Political Science Review* 93, no. 4 (1999): 791–807; Stephen Haber, "Authoritarian Government," in *The Oxford Handbook of Political Economy* (New York: Oxford University Press, 2006).
27. Jongseok Woo, "Kim Jong-Il's Military-First Politics and Beyond: Military Control Mechanisms and the Problem of Power Succession," *Communist and Post-Communist Studies* 47, no. 2 (June 1, 2014): 117–25.

3. TECHNOLOGY AND CYBERSECURITY

1. Jenny Jun, Scott LaFoy, and Ethan Sohn, *North Korea's Cyber Operations: Strategy and Responses* (Washington, DC: Center for Strategic & International Studies and Rowman & Littlefield, 2015); and Richard Stengel, "The Untold Story of the Sony Hack: How North Korea's Battle with Seth Rogen and George Clooney Foreshadowed Russian Election Meddling in 2016," *Vanity Fair*, October 6, 2019, https://www.vanityfair.com/news/2019/10/the-untold-story-of-the-sony-hack.
2. This chapter follows on from an earlier open-source CSIS study that was received positively within U.S. intelligence and policy circles. The chapter is a collaborative effort involving the primary author and researchers from Georgetown and Stanford Universities.
3. Jun, LaFoy, and Sohn, *North Korea's Cyber Operations*, 26–27.
4. Jun, LaFoy, and Sohn, 5.
5. Joseph S. Bermudez Jr., *North Korean Special Forces* (Newport, RI: Naval Institute Press, 1997); Mirko Tasic, "Exploring North Korea's Asymmetric Military Strategy," *Naval War College Review* 72, no. 4 (October 2, 2019), https://digital-commons.usnwc.edu/nwc-review/vol72/iss4/6; Sico van der Meer, "Provoking to Avoid War: North Korea's Hybrid Security Strategies," E-International Relations, May 22, 2021, https://www.e-ir.info/2021/05/22/provoking-to-avoid-war-north-koreas-hybrid-security-strategies/; Donghui Park, "North Korea Cyber Attacks: A New Asymmetrical Military Strategy," Henry M. Jackson School of International Studies, June 28, 2016, https://jsis.washington.edu/news/north-korea-cyber-attacks-new-asymmetrical-military-strategy/.

6. Victor D. Cha, "Hawk Engagement and Preventive Defense on the Korean Peninsula," *International Security* 27, no. 1 (2002): 40–78.
7. Matthew Ha and David Maxwell, "Kim Jong Un's 'All-Purpose Sword': North Korean Cyber-Enabled Economic Warfare," Foundation for Defense of Democracies, October 3, 2018, https://www.fdd.org/analysis/2018/10/03/kim-jong-uns-all-purpose-sword/, 8.
8. Ha and Maxwell.
9. Department of Health and Human Services, Office of Information Security, "North Korean Cyber Activity," March 25, 2021, https://www.hhs.gov/sites/default/files/dprk-cyber-espionage.pdf.
10. Jun, LaFoy, and Sohn, *North Korea's Cyber Operations*, 26.
11. Park, "North Korea Cyber Attacks."
12. Kyeong-su Shin and Jin Shin, "사이버 위협의 확장과 국가안보적 대응북한 사이버 공격을 중심으로" [Scaling cyber threats and responding to national security: A focus on North Korea's cyberattacks]," 전략연구 [Journal of strategic studies] 25, no. 3 (November 2011): 61.
13. Ed Caesar, "The Incredible Rise of North Korea's Hacking Army," *New Yorker*, April 19, 2021, https://www.newyorker.com/magazine/2021/04/26/the-incredible-rise-of-north-koreas-hacking-army.
14. Park, "North Korea Cyber Attacks."
15. Jun, LaFoy, and Sohn, *North Korea's Cyber Operations*, 6; Bruce Klingner, "North Korean Cyberattacks: A Dangerous and Evolving Threat," Heritage Foundation, https://www.heritage.org/asia/report/north-korean-cyberattacks-dangerous-and-evolving-threat; Stephanie Kleine-Ahlbrandt, "North Korea's Illicit Cyber Operations: What Can Be Done?," 38 North, February 28, 2020, https://www.38north.org/2020/02/skleineahlbrandt022820/.
16. "Special Report: APT38: Un-Usual Suspects" (Milpitas, CA: FireEye, 2018), 13.
17. Vyacheslav Kopeytsev and Seongsu Park, "Lazarus Targets Defense Industry with ThreatNeedle," Secure List by Kaspersky, February 25, 2021, https://securelist.com/lazarus-threatneedle/100803/.
18. Department of Health and Human Services, "North Korean Cyber Activity."
19. Department of Health and Human Services.
20. Edith M. Lederer, "UN Report: North Korea Cyber Experts Raised up to $2 Billion," *AP News*, August 6, 2019, https://apnews.com/article/2895639125bd49da9f215f2feb0b58a3.
21. Vitali Kremez, Joshua Platt, and Jason Reaves, "Anchor Project | The Deadly Planeswalker: How the TrickBot Group United High-Tech Crimeware & APT," SentinelLABS, December 10, 2019, https://www.sentinelone.com/labs/anchor-project-the-deadly-planeswalker-how-the-trickbot-group-united-high-tech-crimeware-apt/.
22. Ben Buchanan, "How North Korean Hackers Rob Banks Around the World," *Wired*, January 28, 2020, www.wired.com/story/how-north-korea-robs-banks-around-world/.
23. Department of Health and Human Services, "North Korea Cyber Activity."

24. United Nations Security Council, "Report of the Panel of Experts Established Pursuant to Resolution 1874 (2009)," August 30, 2019, https://undocs.org/S/2019/691, 109; U.S. Department of Justice, "Press Release: Three North Korean Military Hackers Indicted in Wide-Ranging Scheme to Commit Cyberattacks and Financial Crimes Across the Globe," February 17, 2021, https://www.justice.gov/opa/pr/three-north-korean-military-hackers-indicted-wide-ranging-scheme-commit-cyberattacks-and.
25. Cybersecurity & Infrastructure Security Agency, "Alert (AA20–239A): FASTCash 2.0: North Korea's BeagleBoyz Robbing Banks," August 26, 2020, https://us-cert.cisa.gov/ncas/alerts/aa20-239a.
26. Department of Health and Human Services, "North Korea Cyber Activity."
27. Nalani Fraser et al., "APT38: Details on New North Korean Regime-Backed Threat Group," *Mandiant*, May 16, 2022, https://www.mandiant.com/resources/blog/apt38-details-on-new-north-korean-regime-backed-threat-group.
28. Stilgherrian, "North Korea Is the Most Destructive Cyber Threat Right Now: FireEye," *ZDNet*, October 4, 2018, https://www.zdnet.com/article/north-korea-is-the-most-destructive-cyber-threat-right-now-fireeye/.
29. Sansec, "North Korean Hackers Are Skimming US and European Shoppers," July 6, 2020, https://sansec.io/research/north-korea-magecart.
30. Insikt Group, "Crypto Country: North Korea's Targeting of Cryptocurrency," *Recorded Future*, November 30, 2023, https://www.recordedfuture.com/crypto-country-north-koreas-targeting-cryptocurrency.
31. United Nations Security Council, "Final Report of the Panel of Experts Established Pursuant to Resolution 1874 (2009)," August 30, 2019, https://undocs.org/S/2019/691, 109.
32. The reported figures for value of the currency stolen by hackers reflect value at the time of the heist, not current cryptocurrency prices. For example, Youbit lost 3,618 Bitcoin after its second attack, which at the time was worth approximately $4.8 million. In 2021, as of the writing of this report, the price of Bitcoin was over $60,000 per coin; this raises the value of the Youbit heist alone to approximately $217 million in 2021.
33. China Analysis Team, "The KuCoin Hack: What We Know So Far and How the Hackers Are Using DeFi Protocols to Launder Stolen Funds," *Chainalysis* (blog), September 29, 2020, https://blog.chainalysis.com/reports/kucoin-hack-2020-defi-uniswap/.
34. Reuters, "South Korean Intelligence Says N. Korean Hackers Possibly Behind Coincheck Heist—Sources," February 5, 2018, sec. Foreign Exchange Analysis, https://www.reuters.com/article/uk-southkorea-northkorea-cryptocurrency-idUSKBN1FP2XX; Min-seok Kim, "북, 암호화폐 해킹 . . . 국내 거래소서 수백억대 탈취" [North Korea hacks cryptocurrency . . . seizes several hundred billions from domestic exchange], *JoongAng Ilbo*, February 6, 2018.
35. Cybersecurity & Infrastructure Security Agency, "Alert (AA21–048A): AppleJeus: Analysis of North Korea's Cryptocurrency Malware," April 15, 2021, https://www.cisa.gov/news-events/cybersecurity-advisories/aa21-048a.

36. Daniel Van Boom, "North Korea's Crypto Hackers Are Paving the Road to Nuclear Armageddon," CNET, October 9, 2022, https://www.cnet.com/culture/features/north-koreas-crypto-hackers-are-paving-the-road-to-nuclear-armageddon/.
37. Catalin Cimpanu, "North Korean Hackers Infiltrate Chile's ATM Network After Skype Job Interview," *ZDNET*, January 15, 2019, https://www.zdnet.com/article/north-korean-hackers-infiltrate-chiles-atm-network-after-skype-job-interview/.
38. Ronin Network, "Back to Building: Ronin Security Breach Postmortem," *Ronin's Newsletter*, April 27, 2022, https://blog.roninchain.com/p/back-to-building-ronin-security-breach; Ryan Weeks, "How a Fake Job Offer Took Down the World's Most Popular Crypto Game," *Block*, July 6, 2022, https://www.theblock.co/post/156038/how-a-fake-job-offer-took-down-the-worlds-most-popular-crypto-game.
39. Stilgherrian, "North Korea Is the Most Destructive."
40. Sang-Hun Choe and David Yaffe-Bellany, "How North Korea Used Crypto to Hack Its Way Through the Pandemic," *New York Times*, June 30, 2022, sec. Business, https://www.nytimes.com/2022/06/30/business/north-korea-crypto-hack.html.
41. U.S. Department of Justice, "Press Release: U.S. Citizen Who Conspired to Assist North Korea in Evading Sanctions Sentenced to Over Five Years and Fined $100,000," April 12, 2022, https://www.justice.gov/opa/pr/us-citizen-who-conspired-assist-north-korea-evading-sanctions-sentenced-over-five-years-and.
42. Quote by China ambassador to UN Zhang Jin cited in Michelle Nichols, "U.S. Pushes U.N. to Cut N.Korea Oil Imports, Ban Tobacco, Blacklist Lazarus Hackers," Reuters, April 13, 2022, sec. World, https://www.reuters.com/world/us-pushes-un-cut-nkorea-oil-imports-ban-tobacco-blacklist-lazarus-hackers-2022-04-13/.
43. U.S. Department of the Treasury, "U.S. Treasury Issues First-Ever Sanctions on a Virtual Currency Mixer, Targets DPRK Cyber Threats," May 6, 2022, https://home.treasury.gov/news/press-releases/jy0768; U.S. Department of the Treasury, "Press Release: U.S. Treasury Sanctions Notorious Virtual Currency Mixer Tornado Cash," August 8, 2022, https://home.treasury.gov/news/press-releases/jy0916.
44. Ines Kagubare, "North Korea's Increasing Use of Crypto Heists to Fund Nukes Worries US," *Hill*, August 9, 2022, https://thehill.com/policy/technology/3590126-north-koreas-increasing-use-of-crypto-heists-to-fund-nukes-worries-us/.
45. Van Boom, "North Korea's Crypto Hackers."
46. Choe and Yaffe-Bellany, "How North Korea Used Crypto."
47. Christian Nwobodo, "North Korean Lazarus Group Targets Japanese Crypto Firms," *CryptoSlate* (blog), October 17, 2022, https://cryptoslate.com/north-korean-lazarus-group-targets-japanese-crypto-firms/.
48. Felix Ng, " 'Nobody Is Holding Them Back'—North Korean Cyber-Attack Threat Rises," *Cointelegraph*, July 12, 2022, https://cointelegraph.com/news/nobody-is-holding-them-back-north-korean-cyber-attack-threat-rises.

49. Van Boom, "North Korea's Crypto Hackers."
50. Cristina Rotaru, "The Curious Case of Marine Chain: The DPRK Cyberscam Behind a Blockchain-Powered Maritime Investment Marketplace," *Vertic* (blog), April 24, 2019, https://www.vertic.org/2019/04/the-curious-case-of-marine-chain-the-dprk-cyberscam-behind-a-blockchain-powered-maritime-investment-marketplace/.
51. Insikt Group, "Shifting Patterns in Internet Use Reveal Adaptable and Innovative North Korean Ruling Elite," *Recorded Future*, October 25, 2018, https://www.recordedfuture.com/north-korea-internet-usage.
52. U.S. Department of Justice, "Press Release: Three North Korean Military Hackers": "The U.S. Attorney's Office in Los Angeles charged Abbas in a separate case alleging that he conspired to launder hundreds of millions of dollars from BEC frauds and other scams." He was arrested in July 2020 in Dubai and turned over to the FBI, "charged as the ringleader of a lucrative international conspiracy that involved money laundering, hacking websites, identity theft and bank fraud."
53. Kaspersky, "What Is WannaCry Ransomware?," July 6, 2023, https://usa.kaspersky.com/resource-center/threats/ransomware-wannacry.
54. "North Korea Cyber Activity."
55. Jonathan Berr, "'WannaCry' Ransomware Attack Losses Could Reach $4 Billion," *CBS News*, May 16, 2017, https://www.cbsnews.com/news/wannacry-ransomware-attacks-wannacry-virus-losses/.
56. Michelle Nichols, "North Korea Says Linking Cyber-Attacks to Pyongyang Is 'Ridiculous,'" Reuters, May 19, 2017, https://www.reuters.com/article/us-cyber-attack-northkorea-idUSKCN18F1X3.
57. Zack Whittaker, "Two Years After WannaCry, a Million Computers Remain at Risk," *TechCrunch* (blog), May 12, 2019, https://techcrunch.com/2019/05/12/wannacry-two-years-on/.
58. Tara Seals, "Lazarus Group Brings APT Tactics to Ransomware," *Threatpost*, July 28, 2020, https://threatpost.com/lazarus-group-apt-tactics-ransomware/157815/.
59. Catalin Cimpanu, "Kaspersky: North Korean Hackers Are Behind the VHD Ransomware," *ZDNET*, July 28, 2020, https://www.zdnet.com/article/kaspersky-north-korean-hackers-are-behind-the-vhd-ransomware/.
60. Amitai Ben Shushan et al., "Lazarus Group's Mata Framework Leveraged to Deploy TFlower Ransomware," *Syngia* (blog), August 1, 2021, https://blog.sygnia.co/lazarus-groups-mata-framework-leveraged-to-deploy-tflower-ransomware.
61. Jack Stubbs, "Exclusive: Suspected North Korean Hackers Targeted COVID Vaccine Maker AstraZeneca—Sources," Reuters, November 27, 2020, https://www.reuters.com/article/us-healthcare-coronavirus-astrazeneca-no/exclusive-suspected-north-korean-hackers-targeted-covid-vaccine-maker-astrazeneca-sources-idUSKBN2871A2.
62. Tom Burt, "Cyberattacks Targeting Health Care Must Stop," *Microsoft on the Issues* (blog), November 13, 2020, https://blogs.microsoft.com/on-the-issues/2020/11/13/health-care-cyberattacks-covid-19-paris-peace-forum/.

63. Mike Miliard, "North Korea Tried to Hack Pfizer Vaccine Data, Reports Say," *Healthcare IT News*, February 16, 2021, https://www.healthcareitnews.com/news/asia/north-korea-tried-hack-pfizer-vaccine-data-reports-say.
64. Sangmi Cha and Hyonhee Shin, "North Korean Hackers Tried to Steal Pfizer Vaccine Know-how, Lawmaker Says," Reuters, February 16, 2021, https://www.reuters.com/article/us-northkorea-cybercrime-pfizer/north-korean-hackers-tried-to-steal-pfizer-vaccine-know-how-lawmaker-says-idUSKBN2AG0NI.
65. Michael Barnhart et al., "Not So Lazarus: Mapping DPRK Cyber Threat Groups to Government Organizations," *Mandiant* (blog), March 23, 2022, https://www.mandiant.com/resources/blog/mapping-dprk-groups-to-government.
66. "North Korea Cyber Activity."
67. Alex Weidermann, "New Campaign Targeting Security Researchers," *Google Threat Analysis Group* (blog), January 25, 2021.
68. Elizabeth Montalbano, "North Korea Targets Security Researchers in Elaborate 0-Day Campaign," *Threatpost*, January 26, 2021, https://threatpost.com/north-korea-security-researchers-0-day/163333/.
69. Gordon Corera, "UK TV Drama About North Korea Hit by Cyber-Attack," *BBC News*, October 16, 2017, sec. Technology, https://www.bbc.com/news/technology-41640976.
70. Ju-min Park and Meeyoung Cho, "South Korea Blames North Korea for December Hack on Nuclear Operator," Reuters, March 17, 2015, https://www.reuters.com/article/us-nuclear-southkorea-northkorea/south-korea-blames-north-korea-for-december-hack-on-nuclear-operator-idUSKBN0MD0GR20150317.
71. Hui-Chul Moon, "北, 원자력연구원 해킹? 해커 흔적서 나온 '문정인 E메일' 단서" [North Korea hacks Atomic Energy Research Institute? "Moon Jung-In e-mail" clue left from traces of the hacker], *JoongAng Ilbo*, June 18, 2021.
72. Si-soo Park, "North Korea-Linked Hackers Accessed South's Rocket Developer: Spy Agency," *SpaceNews*, July 9, 2021, https://spacenews.com/north-korea-linked-hackers-accessed-souths-rocket-developer-spy-agency/.
73. Tae-Kyu Kim, "軍기밀 털린 곳은 국방데이터센터 . . . 육·해·공군 정보의 '심장'" [Defense Data Center is where military secrets were stolen . . . the 'heart' of army, navy, and air force information], *JoongAng Ilbo*, December 7, 2016.
74. Kwang-seong Cheong, "北 해킹에 속수무책인 정부. . . 청와대까지 사이버 공격" [The government is helpless against North Korea's hacking . . . cyberattacks even on the Blue House], *Chosun Ilbo*, January 2020, http://monthly.chosun.com/client/news/viw.asp?nNewsNumb=202001100013.
75. Chaewon Chung, "North Korean Refugees Are at the Center of Massive Data Leak," *Coda Story* (blog), December 12, 2019, https://www.codastory.com/authoritarian-tech/surveillance/north-korea-refugees-hack/.
76. "North Korea Defector Hack: Personal Data of Almost 1,000 Leaked," *BBC News*, December 28, 2018, sec. Asia, https://www.bbc.com/news/world-asia-46698646.
77. U.S. Department of Justice, "Press Release: Three North Korean Military Hackers."

78. U.S. Department of Justice.
79. Catalin Cimpanu, "North Korea Has Tried to Hack 11 Officials of the UN Security Council," *ZDNET*, September 30, 2020, https://www.zdnet.com/article/north-korea-has-tried-to-hack-11-officials-of-the-un-security-council/.
80. United Nations Security Council, "Notes by the President of the Security Council," August 28, 2020, https://undocs.org/S/2020/840.
81. Jason Bartlett and Francis Shin, "Sanctions by the Numbers: Spotlight on North Korea," Center for a New American Security, February 8, 2021, https://www.cnas.org/publications/reports/sanctions-by-the-numbers-north-korea, 2.
82. Eun DuBois, "Building Resilience to the North Korean Cyber Threat: Experts Discuss," Brookings, December 23, 2020, https://www.brookings.edu/articles/building-resilience-to-the-north-korean-cyber-threat-experts-discuss/.
83. Leekyung Ko, "North Korea as a Geopolitical and Cyber Actor: A Timeline of Events," *New America* (blog), June 6, 2018, http://newamerica.org/cybersecurity-initiative/c2b/c2b-log/north-korea-geopolitical-cyber-incidents-timeline/.
84. David E. Sanger, David D. Kirkpatrick, and Nicole Perlroth, "The World Once Laughed at North Korean Cyberpower. No More," *New York Times*, October 15, 2017, https://www.nytimes.com/2017/10/15/world/asia/north-korea-hacking-cyber-sony.html.
85. Ko, "North Korea as a Geopolitical and Cyber Actor."
86. DuBois, "Building Resilience."
87. Shin and Shin, "Scaling Cyber Threats," 61.
88. Caesar, "The Incredible Rise of North Korea's Hacking Army."
89. Caesar; Morten Soendergaard Larsen, "While North Korean Missiles Sit in Storage, Their Hackers Go Rampant," *Foreign Policy*, March 15, 2021, https://foreignpolicy.com/2021/03/15/north-korea-missiles-cyberattack-hacker-armies-crime/.
90. Caesar, "The Incredible Rise of North Korea's Hacking Army."
91. Shin and Shin, "Scaling Cyber Threats," 63.
92. Victor Cha, "Covid Helped Isolate North Korea in a Way Sanctions Never Could. What Now?," *NBC News*, February 10, 2021, https://www.nbcnews.com/think/opinion/covid-helped-isolate-north-korea-way-sanctions-never-could-so-ncna1257143.
93. Jeongmin Kim, "COVAX Offers 4.7 Million More COVID-19 Vaccine Doses to North Korea," *NK News*, November 30, 2021, https://www.nknews.org/2021/11/covax-offers-4-7-million-more-covid-19-vaccine-doses-to-north-korea/.
94. Hyung-Jin Kim and Tong-Hyung Kim, "S. Korea Spy Agency: N. Korea Hackers Targeted Vaccine Tech," *AP News*, February 16, 2021, https://apnews.com/article/south-korea-north-korea-coronavirus-pandemic-coronavirus-vaccine-fbf9b24356946833661a8018e0524b7b.
95. Beyond Parallel, "U.S.-DPRK Negotiations and North Korean Provocations," October 2, 2017, https://beyondparallel.csis.org/dprk-provocations-and-us-negotiations/.

96. Caesar, "The Incredible Rise of North Korea's Hacking Army."
97. Won-Gi Jung, "U.S. Should Address North Korea's 'Legitimate Concerns,' Chinese FM Says," *NK News*, July 5, 2021, https://www.nknews.org/2021/07/u-s-should-address-north-koreas-legitimate-concerns-chinese-fm-says/.
98. Jun, LaFoy, and Sohn, *North Korea's Cyber Operations*, 26.
99. Min-seok Kim, "The State of the North Korean Military—Korea Net Assessment 2020: Politicized Security and Unchanging Strategic Realities," Carnegie Endowment for International Peace, March 18, 2020, https://carnegieendowment.org/2020/03/18/state-of-north-korean-military-pub-81232.
100. U.S. Department of Defense, Department of the Army, "North Korean Tactics," July 2020, https://irp.fas.org/doddir/army/atp7-100-2.pdf, 26.
101. U.S. Department of Defense, 26–27.
102. Jun, LaFoy, and Sohn, *North Korea's Cyber Operations*, 28.
103. Jun, LaFoy, and Sohn, 29.
104. Joseph S. Bermudez Jr., "North Korea's Strategic Culture," Defense Threat Reduction Agency Advanced Systems and Concepts Office, 2006, https://irp.fas.org/agency/dod/dtra/dprk.pdf.
105. Cha, "Hawk Engagement and Preventive Defense."
106. Madeline Carr, "Public-Private Partnerships in National Cyber-Security Strategies," *International Affairs* 92 (January 8, 2016): 43–62.
107. Carr, "Public-Private Partnerships," 55.
108. Amitai Etzioni, "Cybersecurity in the Private Sector," *Issues in Science and Technology* 28, no. 1 (2011), 59.
109. National Infrastructure Advisory Council (NIAC), "Securing Cyber Assets: Addressing Urgent Cyber Threats to Critical Infrastructure," September 2017.
110. NIAC, 8.
111. NIAC, 13.
112. Nicole Ogrysko, "OPM Details Core Values Behind Coming Security Clearance Reforms with New Policy Doctrine," *Federal News Network*, January 13, 2021, https://federalnewsnetwork.com/workforce/2021/01/opm-details-core-values-behind-coming-security-clearance-reforms-with-new-policy-doctrine/.
113. NIAC, "Securing Cyber Assets," 11.
114. U.S. Department of Defense, OSD A&S Industrial Policy, "Fiscal Year 2020: Industrial Capabilities Report to Congress," January 2021, https://media.defense.gov/2021/Jan/14/2002565311/-1/-1/0/FY20-INDUSTRIAL-CAPABILITIES-REPORT.PDF, 8, 104.
115. Alan Zilberman and Lindsey Ice, "Why Computer Occupations Are Behind Strong STEM Employment Growth in the 2019–29 Decade," U.S. Bureau of Labor Statistics, January 2021, https://www.bls.gov/opub/btn/volume-10/why-computer-occupations-are-behind-strong-stem-employment-growth.htm.
116. U.S. Department of Defense, OSD A&S Industrial Policy, "Fiscal Year 2020," 62.
117. National Infrastructure Advisory Council, "Actionable Cyber Intelligence: An Executive-Led Collaborative Model," December 2020, https://www.cisa.gov/sites

118. United Nations Office on Drugs and Crime, "Who Conducts Cybercrime Investigations?," n.d., https://www.unodc.org.
119. Caesar, "The Incredible Rise of North Korea's Hacking Army."
120. David Jones, "Biden Administration's FY 2023 Budget Includes 11% Increase for Cyber," Cybersecurity Dive, March 30, 2022, https://www.cybersecuritydive.com/news/biden-2023-budget-cybersecurity/621264/.
121. Cybersecurity & Infrastructure Security Agency, "Alert (AA20–133A) Top 10 Routinely Exploited Vulnerabilities," May 12, 2020, https://www.cisa.gov/news-events/cybersecurity-advisories/aa20-133a.
122. Choe and Yaffe-Bellany, "How North Korea Used Crypto."

4. MARKETS AND CIVIL SOCIETY

1. See Bradley K. Martin, *Under the Loving Care of the Fatherly Leader: North Korea and the Kim Dynasty* (New York: Thomas Dunne Books, 2004).
2. Kongdan Oh and Ralph C. Hassig, *North Korea Through the Looking Glass* (Washington, DC: Brookings Institution Press, 2000); Joseph Kim, *Under the Same Sky: From Starvation in North Korea to Salvation in America* (New York: Mariner Books, 2015); Blaine Harden, *Escape from Camp 14: One Man's Remarkable Odyssey from North Korea to Freedom in the West* (New York: Penguin Books, 2012); Chol-hwan Kang and Pierre Rigoulot, *The Aquariums of Pyongyang: Ten Years in the North Korean Gulag* (New York: Basic Books, 2001); Hyeonseo Lee, *The Girl with Seven Names: Escape from North Korea* (London: William Collins, 2016); Hyun-wook Song, "북한주민의 대남인식과 외부정보통제 변화 추이 : 북한이탈주민 면접조사를 통한 추론" [Trends in changes in North Koreans' perception of South Korea and external information control: Inference through interview survey of North Korean defectors], Ministry of Unification, 2011, https://unibook.unikorea.go.kr/board/view?boardId=20&categoryId=&page=&id=201458190&field=searchAll&searchInput=; Hyun-sil Choi, "탈북여성들의 트라우마와 정착지원 방향 연구" [A study on North Korean female defectors' trauma and the direction of settlement support], Ministry of Unification, 2010, https://unibook.unikorea.go.kr/board/view?boardId=20&categoryId=&page=&id=201458202&field=searchAll&searchInput=.
3. Reg Baker et al., "Evaluating Survey Quality in Today's Complex Environment," American Association of Public Opinion Research, May 12, 2016, https://aapor.org/wp-content/uploads/2023/01/AAPOR_Reassessing_Survey_Methods_Report_Final.pdf.
4. Myong-Hyun Go, "The Merits of Conducting Surveys Inside North Korea," Beyond Parallel, November 2, 2016, https://beyondparallel.csis.org/the-merits-of-conducting-surveys-inside-north-korea/.

5. Karl Friedhoff, "Considerations of Risk and Methodology for North Korean Surveys," Beyond Parallel, November 2, 2016, https://beyondparallel.csis.org/considerations-of-risk-and-methodology-for-north-korean-surveys/.
6. Ministry of Unification, "Number of North Korean Defectors Entering South Korea," n.d., https://www.unikorea.go.kr/eng_unikorea/relations/statistics/defectors/.
7. Soo-Am Kim et al., "Study on North Korean Defectors' Perception About Democracy and the Market Economy" (Seoul: Korea Institute for National Unification, August 2017), https://www.kinu.or.kr/pyxis-api/1/digital-files/86b3557f-afe6-4715-8b2e-44e91da83386. The UN COI held public hearings (with more than eighty witnesses/experts) and confidential interviews (over 240) with North Korean victims and witnesses; findings are reported at United Nations Human Rights Council, "Report of the Detailed Findings of the Commission of Inquiry on Human Rights in the Democratic People's Republic of Korea," February 7, 2014, https://www.ohchr.org/Documents/HRBodies/HRCouncil/CoIDPRK/Report/A.HRC.25.63.doc. For transcripts of the public hearings, see United Nations Human Rights Council, "Public Hearings (Programs, Videos, Transcripts)," n.d., https://www.ohchr.org/en/hr-bodies/hrc/co-idprk/public-hearings; Il Lim and Adam Zulawnik, *Interviews with North Korean Defectors: From Kim Shin-Jo to Thae Yong-Ho* (London: Routledge, 2021); Daniel Tudor, *Ask A North Korean: Defectors Talk About Their Lives Inside the World's Most Secretive Nation* (Rutland, VT: Tuttle, 2018).
8. Go, "The Merits of Conducting Surveys."
9. Based on 2021 numbers from the Ministry of Unification, 25,817 out of 33,721 North Korean defectors came from these two provinces (Ryanggang at 5,992 and North Hamgyong at 19,825), or about 76 percent of total defectors.
10. Jane Pong, Wen Foo, Simon Scarr and James Pearson, "North Korea Defectors," *Reuters Graphics*, May 21, 2015, http://graphics.thomsonreuters.com/15/defectors/index.html.
11. There is a vast and growing scholarly literature on markets in North Korea, including Stephan Haggard and Marcus Noland, *Famine in North Korea: Markets, Aid, and Reform* (New York: Columbia University Press, 2007); Justin V. Hastings, *A Most Enterprising Country: North Korea in the Global Economy* (Ithaca, NY: Cornell University Press, 2016); Hyung-min Joo, "Visualizing the Invisible Hands: The Shadow Economy in North Korea," *Economy and Society* 39, no. 1 (February 1, 2010): 110–45, https://doi.org/10.1080/03085140903424618; Byung-Yeon Kim, *Unveiling the North Korean Economy: Collapse and Transition* (Cambridge: Cambridge University Press, 2017); Suk-Jin Kim and Moon-Soo Yang, *The Growth of the Informal Economy in North Korea* (Seoul: Korea Institute for National Unification, 2015); Hazel Smith, *North Korea: Markets and Military Rule* (Cambridge: Cambridge University Press, 2015); and Andrew Yeo, *State, Society and Markets in North Korea* (Cambridge: Cambridge University Press, 2021).

12. Haggard and Noland, *Famine in North Korea*.
13. The numbers vary. A KINU study in 2016 counted over 400 markets; a 2017 *Daily NK* study put these at 387; a 2018 CSIS study estimated 436; and a 2019 news report estimated 500. See In Ho Park, "The Creation of the North Korean Market System" (Seoul: Daily NK, 2017); Victor Cha and Lisa Collins, "The Markets: Private Economy and Capitalism in North Korea?," Beyond Parallel, August 26, 2018, https://beyondparallel.csis.org/markets-private-economy-capitalism-north-korea/; and Je-hun Lee, "[News Analysis] North Korea's 'Marketized Economy' Already at an Irreversible Stage," *Hankyoreh*, February 5, 2019, https://english.hani.co.kr/arti/english_edition/e_northkorea/881048.html.
14. Justin Hastings, Daniel Wertz, and Andrew Yeo, "Market Activities and the Building Blocks of Civil Society in North Korea," National Committee on North Korea, February 2021, https://www.ncnk.org/sites/default/files/issue-briefs/Market_Activities_and_Civil_Society_Building_Blocks_in_North_Korea.pdf; Lee, "North Korea's 'Marketized Economy.'"
15. See appendix 3 for survey questions.
16. Only one of the thirty-six people surveyed indicated that the PDS, at one point in the past, did provide enough in the 1990s, but that it currently did not.
17. Marcus Noland, "Currency Reform Unsettles North Korea," *BBC News*, February 5, 2010, http://news.bbc.co.uk/2/hi/8500017.stm.
18. "North Korea 'Panic' After Surprise Currency Revaluation," *Guardian*, December 3, 2009, sec. World news, https://www.theguardian.com/world/2009/dec/03/north-korea-won-currency-revaluation.
19. United Nations Human Rights Council, "Report of the Detailed Findings of the Commission of Inquiry on Human Rights in the Democratic People's Republic of Korea," 6.
20. United Nations Human Rights Council, 7, 210.
21. Kyu-chang Lee et al., "White Paper on Human Rights in North Korea 2020" (Seoul: Korea Institute for National Unification, September 2020), https://www.kinu.or.kr/www/jsp/prg/api/dlVE.jsp?menuIdx=648&category=74&thisPage=1&searchField=&searchText=&biblioId=153844.
22. United Nations Human Rights Council, "Report of the Detailed Findings," 64.
23. Kyung-ok Do et al., "White Paper on Human Rights in North Korea 2015" (Seoul: Korea Institute for National Unification, September 2015), https://www.kinu.or.kr/pyxis-api/1/digital-files/3b2eeb32-d7c6-4137-b9a6-767a3e0ceaa6. See also United Nations Human Rights Council, "Report of the Detailed Findings," 11, 72–73.
24. Sangmi Han, "North Korea: Rare Footage Shows Teens Sentence to Hard Labour Over K-Drama," BBC, January 18, 2024, https://www.bbc.com/news/world-asia-68015652.
25. United Nations Human Rights Council, "Report of the Detailed Findings," 366.
26. See Nat Kretchun and Jane Kim, "A Quiet Opening: North Koreans in a Changing Media Environment," InterMedia, May 2012, https://www.gwern

.net/docs/technology/2012-kretchun.pdf; Jieun Baek, *North Korea's Hidden Revolution: How the Information Underground Is Transforming a Closed Society* (New Haven, CT: Yale University Press, 2016); Center for Strategic and International Studies, "North Korea Policy, One Year After Hanoi," February 25, 2020, https://www.foreign.senate.gov/imo/media/doc/022520_King_Testimony.pdf.

27. The Broadcasting Board of Governors survey of 350 North Korean defectors in 2015 is summarized in Nat Kretchun, Catherine Lee, and Seamus Tuohy, "Compromising Connectivity: Information Dynamics Between the State and Society in a Digitizing North Korea," InterMedia, February 1, 2017, https://seamustuohy.com/files/Compromising-Connectivity-Final-Report.pdf; also see Yonho Kim, "Cell Phones in North Korea: Has North Korea Entered the Telecommunications Revolution?," U.S. Korea Institute at SAIS, 2014, https://38north.org/wp-content/uploads/2014/03/Kim-Yonho-Cell-Phones-in-North-Korea.pdf; Daniel Tudor and James Pearson, *North Korea Confidential: Private Markets, Fashion Trends, Prison Camps, Dissenters and Defectors* (Rutland, VT: Tuttle, 2015); Amnesty International, "North Korea: Connection Denied: Restrictions on Mobile Phones and Outside Information in North Korea," March 9, 2016, https://www.amnesty.org/en/documents/asa24/3373/2016/en/; Martyn Williams, "Digital Trenches: North Korea's Information Counter-Offensive," Committee for Human Rights in North Korea, 2019, https://www.hrnk.org/uploads/pdfs/Williams_Digital_Trenches_Web_FINAL.pdf.

28. Byeong-ro Kim et al., "북한주민 통일의식 2016" [North Korean public perception on unification 2016] (Seoul: Institute for Peace and Unification Studies, Seoul National University, March 15, 2017), https://ipus.snu.ac.kr/wp-content/uploads/2020/05/2016-%EB%B6%81%ED%95%9C%EC%A3%BC%EB%AF%BC%ED%86%B5%EC%9D%BC%EC%9D%98%EC%8B%9D-%EB%82%B4%EC%A7%80%EC%B5%9C%EC%A2%85.pdf.

29. Kretchun and Kim, "A Quiet Opening."
30. Kretchun and Kim.
31. Kyung-ok Do et al., "White Paper on Human Rights in North Korea 2015," 325–26.
32. Kyung-ok Do et al., 327–30.
33. Sung Kyung Kim, "North Korean Women as New Economic Agents," Institute for Security & Development Policy, October 21, 2020, https://isdp.eu/content/uploads/2020/10/North-Korean-Women-as-New-Economic-Agents-IB-21.10.20.pdf.
34. Maximilian Ernst and Roman Jurowetzki, "Satellite Data, Women Defectors and Black Markets in North Korea: A Quantitative Study of the North Korean Informal Sector Using Night-Time Lights Satellite Imagery," *North Korean Review* 12, no. 2 (2016): 64–83.
35. Stephan Haggard and Marcus Noland, "Gender in Transition: The Case of North Korea," *World Development* 41 (January 1, 2013): 51–66.

36. Kim, "North Korean Women as New Economic Agents."
37. Sea Young Kim and Leif-Eric Easley, "The Neglected North Korean Crisis: Women's Rights," *Ethics & International Affairs* 35, no. 1 (January 2021): 19–29; Janice Lee and Benjamin Katzeff Silberstein, "North Korean Women: Markets and Power," 38 North, March 18, 2011, https://www.38north.org/2011/03/north-korean-women/; and Kyung-Ae Park, "Economic Crisis, Women's Changing Economic Roles, and Their Implications for Women's Status in North Korea," *Pacific Review* 24, no. 2 (May 1, 2011): 159–77.
38. Hastings, Wertz, and Yeo, "Market Activity and Civil Society," 3.
39. Jiyoon Kim et al., "South Korean Attitudes Toward North Korea and Reunification" (Seoul: Asan Institute for Policy Studies, February 2015), https://en.asaninst.org/contents/south-korean-attitudes-toward-north-korea-and-reunification/.
40. Timothy S. Rich and Madelynn Einhorn, "South Koreans Rarely Think About North Korea—and Why It Matters," 38 North, November 13, 2020, https://www.38north.org/2020/11/trichmeinhorn111320/.
41. Sang Sin Lee et al., "KINU Unification Survey 2021" (Seoul: Korea Institute for National Unification, July 2021), https://www.kinu.or.kr/pyxis-api/1/digital-files/87cb5812-a81a-4fdc-824c-8d359544e8f7.
42. While 25.4 percent preferred unification, 56.5 percent preferred peaceful coexistence. Lee et al., "KINU Unification Survey 2021," 7.
43. Lee et al., 8, 15.
44. Madelynn Einhorn and Timothy S. Rich, "The Ties That Bond? Attitudinal Factors Influencing South Korean Support for Unification and Peaceful Coexistence," *North Korean Review* 17, no. 2 (2021): 18–33.
45. Ju-hwa Park, "평화적 분단과 통일: 2017 통일에 대한 국민 인식 조사 결과와 함의" [Peaceful coexistence and unification: South Koreans' perception of unification 2017], Online Series CO 17-18 (Seoul: Korea Institute for National Unification, June 23, 2017), http://lib.kinu.or.kr/wonmun/008/0001484788.pdf.
46. Hak-jae Kim et al., "2019 통일의식조사" [2019 Unification Awareness Survey] (Seoul: Institute for Peace and Unification Studies, 2019), https://ipus.snu.ac.kr/wp-content/uploads/2020/04/2019-%ED%86%B5%EC%9D%BC%EC%9D%98%EC%8B%9D%EC%A1%B0%EC%82%AC_%EC%B5%9C%EC%A2%85%EC%9B%B9%EC%9A%A9.pdf, 38.
47. Quote of North Korean interviewee cited in Josh Smith, "'Cuddled in Kim Jong Un's Arms': North Koreans Envisage Unification Ahead of Summit," Reuters, September 17, 2018, sec. APAC, https://www.reuters.com/article/us-northkorea-southkorea-unification-idUSKCN1LX0F0.
48. For example, see Wan-kyu Choi, "North Korea's New Unification Strategy," *Asian Perspective* 25, no. 2 (2001): 99–122.
49. Institute for Peace and Unification Studies, Seoul National University, "북한이탈주민 조사사업 10년 분석 결과발표회" [10-year analysis result presentation of North Korean Defectors Investigation Project], May 3, 2022, https://ipus.snu.ac.kr/blog/archives/conference/6178.

50. The SNU surveys draw upon a pool of North Korean defectors who have arrived in South Korea during the previous year. Institute for Peace and Unification Studies, Seoul National University, "북한주민 통일의식" [North Korean public perception on unification], 2008–2016.
51. Kim et al., "South Korean Attitudes."
52. Lee et al., "KINU Unification Survey 2021," 9.
53. Institute for Peace and Unification Studies, Seoul National University, "SNU 2022 Unification Awareness Survey," September 29, 2022, https://ipus.snu.ac.kr/blog/archives/conference/6744.
54. Beyond Parallel, "Database: North Korean Provocations," December 20, 2019, https://beyondparallel.csis.org/database-north-korean-provocations/.
55. White House Archives, "Remarks by President Trump Before a Briefing on the Opioid Crisis," August 8, 2017, https://trumpwhitehouse.archives.gov/briefings-statements/remarks-president-trump-briefing-opioid-crisis/.
56. Eric Talmadge, "North Korea Outlines Plan to Launch Missiles toward Guam," *AP News*, August 10, 2017, https://apnews.com/article/931769550f3b433ca64f6c5e633da23b.
57. David E. Sanger and Sang-Hun Choe, "North Korean Nuclear Test Draws U.S. Warning of 'Massive Military Response,'" *New York Times*, September 3, 2017, sec. World, https://www.nytimes.com/2017/09/03/world/asia/north-korea-tremor-possible-6th-nuclear-test.html.
58. White House Archives, "Remarks by President Trump to the 72nd Session of the United Nations General Assembly," September 19, 2017, https://trumpwhitehouse.archives.gov/briefings-statements/remarks-president-trump-72nd-session-united-nations-general-assembly/.
59. Michael D. Shear and David E. Sanger, "Trump Returns North Korea to List of State Sponsors of Terrorism," *New York Times*, November 20, 2017, sec. U.S., https://www.nytimes.com/2017/11/20/us/politics/north-korea-trump-terror.html.
60. Mark Osborne, "Trump Warns North Korea 'Won't Be Around Much Longer' If Threats Continue to Escalate," *ABC News*, September 24, 2017, https://abcnews.go.com/International/trump-warns-north-korea-wont-longer-threats-continue/story?id=50053390.
61. KCNA, "Army-People Celebration Rallies Held in Cities, Counties," December 9, 2017, https://kcnawatch.org/newstream/.
62. Ye-rang Hwang, "Younger N. Korean Defectors View Nuclear Weapons as 'Source of Pride' as Well as Culprit Behind Sanctions," *Hankyoreh*, February 27, 2019, https://english.hani.co.kr/arti/english_edition/e_northkorea/883832.html; and Je Son Lee, "Ask a North Korean: What Do You Think About Nuclear Weapons?," *Guardian*, October 23, 2015, sec. World news, https://www.theguardian.com/world/2015/oct/23/ask-a-north-korean-nuclear-weapons.
63. Je Son Lee, "Ask a North Korean: Do You Hate Americans?," *Guardian*, November 4, 2015, sec. World news, https://www.theguardian.com/world/2015/nov/04/ask-a-north-korean-do-you-hate-americans.

64. Victor D. Cha, *The Impossible State: North Korea, Past and Future* (New York: Harper Collins, 2012), 7.

5. UNIFICATION THEORIES

1. Sang Sin Lee et al., "KINU Unification Survey 2021" (Seoul: Korea Institute for National Unification), July 20210, https://www.kinu.or.kr/pyxis-api/1/digital-files/87cb5812-a81a-4fdc-824c-8d359544e8f76.
2. World Bank, "GDP (current US$)—Korea, Rep." https://data.worldbank.org/indicator/NY.GDP.MKTP.CD?locations=KR.
3. Statista, "Gross National Income (GNI) per Capita of South Korea from 1980 to 2021," August 2022, https://www.statista.com/statistics/756638/south-korea-gni-per-capita/.
4. OECD, "OECD Development Assistance Committee (DAC) Welcomes Korean Membership," November 25, 2009, https://www.oecd.org/dac/oecddevelopmentassistancecommitteedacwelcomeskoreanmembership.htm.
5. According to the ICT Development Index (IDI) ranking—a benchmark measure to monitor and compare developments in ICT—compiled by the International Telecommunication Union (UN specialized agency for ICTs), the ROK was ranked second in 2017 and first in 2016. International Telecommunication Union, "Measuring the Information Society Report 2017: Volume 1," 2017, https://www.itu.int/en/ITU-D/Statistics/Documents/publications/misr2017/MISR2017_Volume1.pdf, 31.
6. According to one study, South Korea has the highest-quality democracy of all Asian countries, ranked at number 20 globally. See Democracy Matrix Research Project, University of Würzburg, "Ranking of Countries by Quality of Democracy," n.d., https://www.democracymatrix.com/ranking.
7. Ministry of Foreign Affairs, Republic of Korea, "ROK-UN Relations," n.d., https://www.mofa.go.kr/eng/wpge/m_5460/contents.do.
8. The ROK was the first country to make a national green growth strategy when President Lee Myung-bak adopted it in August 2008 with his "Low Carbon, Green Growth" plan. In July 2020 the Moon Jae-in government launched the Green New Deal (73.2 trillion won) as part of the Korean New Deal to move toward a net-zero society. See Deok Soon Yim and Jaewon Lee, "UNESCO Science Report: Towards 2030" (UNESCO, 2015), https://en.unesco.org/sites/default/files/usr15_republic_of_korea.pdf, 663. The term "green growth" was first officially used in the Fifth Ministerial Conference on Environment and Development in Asia and the Pacific (MCED 2005), held in Seoul, and the participants adopted the Seoul Initiative on Environmentally Sustainable Economic Growth (Green Growth). See International Institute for Sustainable Development, "Summary of the Fifth Ministerial Conference on Environment and Development in Asia and the Pacific: 23–29 March 2005," *MCED 2005 Bulletin* 106, no. 1 (April 1, 2005), http://enb.iisd.org/download/pdf/sd/sdvol106num1e

.pdf; Ministry of Economy and Finance, Republic of Korea, "The Korean New Deal: National Strategy for a Great Transformation," July 2020, https://english.moef.go.kr/skin/doc.html?fn=Korean%20New%20Deal.pdf&rs=/result/upload/mini/2020/07/, 25.

9. United Nations, *Statistical Yearbook 1948* (New York: United Nations, 1949), https://unstats.un.org/unsd/publications/statistical-yearbook/files/SYB1.pdf, 24.

10. Dean Rusk, *As I Saw It* (New York: Norton, 1990).

11. While the U.S. occupation of the South has been the subject of critical historical review, there is far less written about the brutal nature of the Soviet Union's occupation of North Korea. For the U.S. occupation, see Bonnie B. C. Oh, *Korea Under the American Military Government, 1945–1948* (Westport, CT: Praeger, 2002); William Stueck and Boram Yi, " 'An Alliance Forged in Blood': The American Occupation of Korea, the Korean War, and the US-South Korean Alliance," *Journal of Strategic Studies* 33, no. 2 (April 1, 2010): 177–209, https://doi.org/10.1080/01402391003590200; Hakjoon Kim, "The American Military Government in South Korea, 1945–1948: Its Formation, Policies, and Legacies," *Asian Perspective* 12, no. 1 (1988): 51–83, https://www.jstor.org/stable/42703907. For the Soviet occupation, see Adam Cathcart and Charles Kraus, "Peripheral Influence: The Sinŭiju Student Incident of 1945 and the Impact of Soviet Occupation in North Korea," *Journal of Korean Studies* 13, no. 1 (2008): 1–27; and this Soviet report on their first few months of occupation: Archives of the General Staff of the Armed Forces of the Russian Federation op. 480, 29, st. 5, p. 2, pa. 21, k. 35, "Untitled Memorandum on the Political and Morale Situation of Soviet Troops in North Korea and the Economic Situation in Korea," trans. Gary Goldberg, Wilson Center Digital Archive, January 11, 1946, https://digitalarchive.wilsoncenter.org/document/untitled-memorandum-political-and-morale-situation-soviet-troops-north-korea-and-economic.

12. Samuel, S. Kim, "Korea's Segyehwa Drive," in *Korea's Globalization*, ed. Samuel S. Kim (Cambridge: Cambridge University Press, 2000), 277.

13. According to the Bank of Korea, in 2021 the ROK's GDP was 2,071,658 (billion Korean won), and the DPRK's GDP (estimate) was 35,890.80 (billion Korean won) See Bank of Korea, "Main Annual Indicators: Gross Domestic Product (Nominal, Korean Won)," n.d., https://kosis.kr/statHtml/statHtml.do?orgId=301&tblId=DT_200Y013&conn_path=I2; and Bank of Korea, "Gross Domestic Product Estimates for North Korea in 2021," July 27, 2022, https://www.bok.or.kr/eng/bbs/E0000634/view.do?nttId=10071884&menuNo=400069.

14. This is otherwise known as the security dilemma. See Robert Jervis, "Cooperation Under the Security Dilemma," *World Politics* 30, no. 2 (1978): 167–214.

15. For comparisons to German unification, see Marcus Noland, *Avoiding the Apocalypse: The Future of the Two Koreas* (New York: Columbia University Press, 2000); Kang Suk Rhee, "Korea's Unification: The Applicability of the German Experience," *Asian Survey* 33, no. 4 (1993): 367–68, https://doi.org/10.2307/2645103;

Jin-Wook Shin, "Lessons from German Reunification for Inter-Korean Relations: An Analysis of South Korean Public Spheres, 1990–2010," *Asian Perspective* 38, no. 1 (2014): 61–88; Cae-One Kim, "A Proposal for Inter-Korean Economic Integration and Reunification: With Special Reference to the German Case," *Journal of East Asian Affairs* 5, no. 2 (1991): 350–72. For estimates of Korean unification, see Aidan Foster-Carter, *Korea's Coming Reunification: Another East Asian Superpower?*, Special Report no. M212 (London: Economist Intelligence Unit, 1992); Goohoon Kwon, "Experiences with Monetary Integration and Lessons for Korean Unification," IMF Working Papers 65 (International Monetary Fund, May 1997), https://www.imf.org/en/Publications/WP/Issues/2016/12/30/Experiences-with-Monetary-Integration-and-Lessons-for-Korean-Unification-2228; Marcus Noland, Sherman Robinson, and Li-gang Liu, "The Costs and Benefits of Korean Unification: Alternate Scenarios," *Asian Survey* 38, no. 8 (1998): 801–14, https://doi.org/10.2307/2645584; and Li-gang Liu, Marcus Noland, and Sherman Robinson, "The Costs and Benefits of Korean Unification," Working Papers 98-1, Peterson Institute for International Economics, January 1998, https://www.piie.com/publications/working-papers/costs-and-benefits-korean-unification.

16. This is not to deny that there has been frequent and consistent polling among South Korean citizens about their views on unification, but such polling is usually based on reified assumptions or scenarios about unification without a thorough investigation of those assumptions. See Sang Sin Lee et al., "KINU Unification Survey 2021"; Bum-soo Kim et al., "2020 통일의식조사" [2020 Unification awareness survey] (Siheung, South Korea: Institute for Peace and Unification Studies, Seoul National University, February 28, 2021), https://ipus.snu.ac.kr/wp-content/uploads/2021/08/2020_%ED%86%B5%EC%9D%BC%EC%9D%98%EC%8B%9D%EC%A1%B0%EC%82%AC_pdf.pdf; Norman D. Levin and Yong-Sup Han, "The Shape of Korea's Future: South Korean Attitudes Toward Unification and Long-Term Security Issues" (RAND Corporation, January 1, 1999), https://www.rand.org/pubs/monograph_reports/MR1092.html; J. James Kim, Chung-gu Kang, and Geonhui Ham, "한국인의 외교안보 인식: 2010~2020년 아산연례조사 결과" [South Koreans' perception of foreign policy and security: Results of aAsan surveys, 2010–2020]," Asan Institute for Policy Studies, September 13, 2021, http://www.asaninst.org/contents/%ED%95%9C%EA%B5%AD%EC%9D%B8%EC%9D%98-%EC%99%B8%EA%B5%90%EC%95%88%EB%B3%B4-%EC%9D%B8%EC%8B%9D-20102020%EB%85%84-%EC%95%84%EC%82%B0%EC%97%B0%EB%A1%80%EC%A1%B0%EC%82%AC-%EA%B2%B0%EA%B3%BC/; KBS 남북교류협력단KBS [Organization for South-North Exchange and Cooperation], "2020년 국민 통일의식 조사" [Survey of South Korean people's perception of national unification 2020] (Seoul: KBS, October 28, 2020), https://office.kbs.co.kr/tongil/wp-content/uploads/sites/11/2020/11/%EC%9B%B9%EC%9A%A92020-%EA%B5%AD%EB%AF%BC-%ED%86%B5%EC%9D%BC%EC%9D%98%EC%8B%9D-%EC%A1%B0%EC%82%AC.pdf;

Jae Hyun Lee and Wook Kim, "University Students' Perception on Unification and the Implications for Unification Education in Korean Universities," *Korean Unification Studies* 24, no. 1 (2015). The Peaceful Unification Advisory Council has been conducting quarterly surveys since 2014; for the latest, see Hyung-joong Park et al., "2022년 4분기 통일 여론 동향" [2022 Q4 peaceful unification: Public opinion and trends], Peaceful Unification Advisory Council, December 2022.

17. Victor Cha and David Kang, "Approaching Korean Unification What We Learn from Other Cases," USC Korean Studies Institute and Center for Strategic & International Studies, December 2010, https://csis-website-prod.s3.amazonaws.com/s3fs-public/legacy_files/files/publication/101217_Cha_Approaching Unification_WEB.pdf; Nicholas Eberstadt and Richard J. Ellings, eds., *Korea's Future and the Great Powers* (Seattle: University of Washington Press, 2001); Korea Institute for National Unification, "Korean Unification and a New East Asian Order," Seoul, December 2012, https://repo.kinu.or.kr/bitstream/2015.oak/2121/1/0001453732.pdf; Jinwook Choi and Jin-Ha Kim, "North Korean Reconstruction in the Process of Korean Unification," Korea Institute for National Unification, 2011; Selig S. Harrison, *Korean Endgame: A Strategy for Reunification and U.S. Disengagement* (Princeton, NJ: Princeton University Press, 2002); Gyu-ryun Kim et al., "통일 비용 편익 연구의 새로운 접근 포괄적 연구 요소의 도입과 대안의 모색" [A new approach to research on cost and benefit of unification: Introduction of comprehensive research elements and search for alternatives] (Seoul: Korea Institute for National Unification, December 2011), https://www.kinu.or.kr/pyxis-api/1/digital-files/f666280e-d67c-4266-87b2-c9e13a8d89e5; Jong-chul Park et al., "통일대비를 위한 국내과제" [Domestic tasks in preparation for unification] (Seoul: Korea Institute for National Unification, December 30, 2011), https://repo.kinu.or.kr/bitstream/2015.oak/1806/1/0001440975.pdf; Bruce W. Bennett, "Alternative Paths to Korean Unification" (Washington, DC: RAND Corporation, October 31, 2018), https://www.rand.org/pubs/research_reports/RR2808.html; Jonathan D. Pollack and Chung Min Lee, "Preparing for Korean Unification: Scenarios and Implications," RAND Corporation, January 1, 1999, https://www.rand.org/pubs/monograph_reports/MR1040.html; Sung-yoon Lee, "North Korea's Revolutionary Unification Policy," *International Journal of Korean Studies* 18, no. 2 (Fall 2014): 121–37; Foster-Carter, "Korea's Coming Reunification"; Han-Bum Cho et al., "The Costs and Benefits of Unification on the Korean Peninsula: In the Political, Social, and Economic Areas" (Seoul: Korea Institute for National Unification, August 2016), https://www.kinu.or.kr/pyxis-api/1/digital-files/7948488c-5019-4733-bd4f-97bf7a38490e; Bruce Cumings, *Korea's Place in the Sun: A Modern History* (New York: Norton, 1997); Sung Chul Yang, *The North And South Korean Political Systems: A Comparative Analysis* (Boulder, CO: Westview Press, 1994).

18. Hak-Joon Kim, *The Unification Policy of South and North Korea: A Comparative Study* (Seoul National University Press, 1992), 64–70, 133–36, 168–70; Yang, *North*

and South Korean Political Systems, 192–94; William Stueck, *The Korean War: An International History* (Princeton, NJ: Princeton University Press, 1995), 41; Yong-Pyo Hong, *State Security and Regime Security: President Syngman Rhee and the Insecurity Dilemma in South Korea, 1953–60* (New York: St. Martin's Press, 2000), 71–73; Victor D. Cha, "Anti-Americanism and the U.S. Role in Inter-Korean Relations," in *Korean Attitudes Towards the United States: Changing Dynamics*, ed. David I. Steinberg (Armonk, NY: M. E. Sharpe, 2005), 120; Byung Chul Koh, *Foreign Policy Systems of North and South Korea* (Berkeley: University of California Press, 1984).

19. Byung-Yeon Kim, *Unveiling the North Korean Economy: Collapse and Transition* (Cambridge: Cambridge University Press, 2017), 81.
20. Beyond Parallel, "Database: North Korean Provocations," December 20, 2019, https://beyondparallel.csis.org/database-north-korean-provocations/.
21. See Samuel S. Kim, "North Korea and the United Nations," *International Journal of Korean Studies* 1, no. 1 (Spring 1997), 79–80; Samuel S. Kim, "North Korea in 2000: Surviving Through High Hopes of Summit Diplomacy," *Asian Survey* 41, no. 1 (2001), https://www.jstor.org/stable/10.1525/as.2001.41.1.12, 12; Samuel S. Kim, *The Two Koreas and the Great Powers* (Cambridge: Cambridge University Press, 2006), 28; Samuel S. Kim, "North Korean Foreign Relations in the Post–Cold War World," Strategic Studies Institute, April 2007, 9, 73–74, 80.
22. For authoritative accounts of this fight for legitimacy, see Sheila Miyoshi Jager, *Brothers at War: The Unending Conflict in Korea* (New York: Norton, 2013); also Richard Grinker, *Korea and Its Futures: Unification and the Unfinished War* (New York: St. Martin's, 1998); and Don Oberdorfer and Robert Carlin, *The Two Koreas: A Contemporary History*, 3rd ed. (New York: Basic Books, 2014).
23. For information about South Korea's economic growth during the Park Chung-hee period, see Byung-Kook Kim and Ezra F. Vogel, *The Park Chung Hee Era: The Transformation of South Korea* (Cambridge, MA: Harvard University Press, 2011); Hyung-A. Kim and Clark W. Sorensen, eds., *Reassessing the Park Chung Hee Era, 1961–1979: Development, Political Thought, Democracy, and Cultural Influence* (Seattle: Center for Korea Studies Publications, 2011). See also Jung-en Woo, *Race to the Swift* (New York: Columbia University Press, 1991); Alice H. Amsden, *Asia's Next Giant: South Korea and Late Industrialization* (London: Oxford University Press, 1991); and David C. Kang, *Crony Capitalism: Corruption and Development in South Korea and the Philippines* (Cambridge: Cambridge University Press, 2002).
24. National Archives of Korea, "7.4 남북공동성명전문" [Full text of the July 4 North-South Joint Communiqué], n.d., https://theme.archives.go.kr/next/unikorea/seven/seven04.do. For more about the 1972 Joint Communiqué, see B. C. Koh, "North Korea: A Breakthrough in the Quest for Unity," *Asian Survey* 13, no. 1 (1973): 83–93, https://doi.org/10.2307/2642994; Chae-Jin Lee, "South Korea: The Politics of Domestic-Foreign Linkage," *Asian Survey* 13, no. 1 (1973): 94–101, https://doi.org/10.2307/2642995; Koon Woo Nam, "North-South Korean Relations: From

Dialogue to Confrontation," *Pacific Affairs* 48, no. 4 (1975): 477–99, https://www.jstor.org/stable/2756448.

25. National Unification Board, "A White Paper on South-North Dialogue in Korea" (Seoul, December 31, 1988), 35–54, 76–104. See Victor D. Cha, "Korean Unification: The Zero-Sum Past and the Precarious Future," *Asian Perspective* 21, no. 3 (Winter 1997): 63–92, https://www.jstor.org/stable/42704145.

26. North Korea suspended dialogue after it accused the South of kidnapping Kim Dae-Jung from Japan. It also unilaterally cut the hotline with South Korea in 1976. See Cha, "Korean Unification," 88.

27. For more on the Rangoon bombing in 1983, see Clyde Haberman, "Bomb Kills 19, Including 6 Key Koreans," *New York Times*, October 10, 1983, https://www.nytimes.com/1983/10/10/world/bomb-kills-19-including-6-key-koreans.html; William Chapman, "Korean Leader Lost Aides Who Made Policies Work," *Washington Post*, October 11, 1983, https://www.washingtonpost.com/archive/politics/1983/10/11/korean-leader-lost-aides-who-made-policies-work/bbe16281-a0e6-4a6a-8fae-9cc506dce79f/; William Chapman, "South Korea Buries Bomb Blast Victims, Denounces the North," *Washington Post*, October 14, 1983, https://www.washingtonpost.com/archive/politics/1983/10/14/south-korea-buries-bomb-blast-victims-denounces-the-north/2d5cfbd0-5bac-4779-b255-30e2970853d7/. For more on the KAL Flight 858 bombing, see Susan Chira, "Korean Plane, 115 Aboard, Crashes in Southeast Asia," *New York Times*, November 30, 1987, https://www.nytimes.com/1987/11/30/world/korean-plane-115-aboard-crashes-in-southeast-asia.html; Fred Hiatt, "Seoul Links N. Korea to Crash of Airliner," *Washington Post*, December 3, 1987, https://www.washingtonpost.com/archive/politics/1987/12/03/seoul-links-n-korea-to-crash-of-airliner/72a7fa53-6e5c-4749-b921-240f35ad24bd/; Peter Maass, "S. Korea Accuses North After Agent's Confession," *Washington Post*, January 16, 1988, https://www.washingtonpost.com/archive/politics/1988/01/16/s-korea-accuses-north-after-agents-confession/6ce8cf57-38b0-49a8-a585-c9a087985fb9/.

28. Dae-jung Kim, *Kim Dae-Jung's Three-Stage Approach to Korean Reunification: Focusing on the South-North Confederal Stage*, trans. T. C. Rhee (Los Angeles: Center for Multiethnic and Transnational Studies, 1997).

29. See Hak-soon Kim and Choong-sik Song, "脫정치·脫 이념·脫 패권의 統一모델 만들자" [Let's make a model for unification that is not politicized, idealized, or hegemonic], *Kyunghyang Shinmun*, August 1, 1990, https://newslibrary.naver.com/viewer/index.nhn?articleId=1990080100329226001&editNo=3&printCount=1&publishDate=1990-08 01&officeId=00032&pageNo=26&printNo=13800&publishType=00020; "내년 選擧日程 조정검토" [Review of next year's election schedule adjustment], *Kyunghyang Shinmun*, October 11, 1991, https://newslibrary.naver.com/viewer/index.nhn?articleId=1991101100329101001&editNo=15&printCount=1&publishDate=1991-10-11&officeId=00032&pageNo=1&printNo=14195&publishType=00010; "집권땐 北 흡수통일" [If I become

leader of the government, North Korea will be unified by absorption], *Chosun Ilbo*, July 5, 1992, https://newslibrary.naver.com/viewer/index.nhn?articleId =1992070500239104002&editNo=1&printCount=1&publishDate=1992-07 05&offi ceId=00023&pageNo=4&printNo=22040&publishType=00010; "北韓 흡수통일해 야" [North Korea should be unified by absorption], *Maeil Business Newspaper*, July 17, 1992, https://newslibrary.naver.com/viewer/index.nhn?articleId=199207 1700099202004&editNo=2&printCount=1&publishDate=1992-07-17&officeId =00009&pageNo=2&printNo=8159&publishType=00020; "金鍾泌 (김종필) 자민련 총재 국회연설 (요지)" [Kim Jong-pil, president of United Liberal Democrats, speech to the National Assembly (summary)], *Dong-A Ilbo*, October 25, 1996, https:// newslibrary.naver.com/viewer/index.nhn?articleId=1996102500209104006 &editNo=45&printCount=1&publishDate=1996-10-25&officeId=00020&pageNo =4&printNo=23348&publishType=00010.

30. See Pollack and Lee, *Preparing for Korean Unification*; and Sung-Hee Jwa, Chung-in Moon and Jeong-Ho Roh, eds., *Constitutional Handbook on Korean Unification, Volume 1* (Seoul: Korea Economic Research Institute, 2002).

31. See Charles Wolf Jr. and Kamiljon T. Akramov, "North Korean Paradoxes: Circumstances, Costs, and Consequences of Korean Unification" (Santa Monica: RAND Corporation, May 3, 2005), https://www.rand.org/pubs/monographs /MG333.html; David S. Maxwell, "Should the United States Support Korean Unification and If So, How?," *International Journal of Korean Studies* 18, no. 1 (2014): 139–56; Marcus Noland, "Why North Korea Will Muddle Through," *Foreign Affairs*, August 1997, https://www.foreignaffairs.com/articles/asia/1997-07-01/why -north-korea-will-muddle-through.

32. Byung-joon Ahn, "The Man Who Would Be Kim," *Foreign Affairs* 73, no. 6 (December 1994): 94–108, https://doi.org/10.2307/20046931; Nicholas Eberstadt, "Hastening Korean Unification," *Foreign Affairs* 76, no. 2 (1997): 77–92, https://doi .org/10.2307/20047938; Michael Green, "North Korean Regime Crisis: US Perspectives and Responses," *Korean Journal of Defense Analysis* 9, no. 2 (December 1, 1997): 7–25; Robert Collins, "Patterns of Collapse in North Korea," *Combined Forces Command C5 Civil Affairs Newsletter*, January 1996.

33. Selig S. Harrison, "Promoting a Soft Landing in Korea," *Foreign Policy*, no. 106 (Spring 1997): 56–75, https://doi.org/10.2307/1149174; Jae Bong Lee et al., *Korean Reunification: Alternative Pathways*, ed. Michael Haas (New York: Praeger, 1989); Tae-Hwan Kwak and Seung-Ho Joo, "The Future of the Korean Peninsula: Unification and Security Options for the 21st century," *Asian Perspective* 23, no. 2 (1999): 163–96, https://www.jstor.org/stable/42704212; Robert A. Scalapino, *North Korea at a Crossroads*, Hoover Essays in Public Policy, no. 73 (Stanford, CA: Hoover Institution Press, 1997); Keun Lee, "The Road to the Market in North Korea: Projects, Problems and Prospects," WIDER Working Paper Series, No. 139 United Nations University World Institute for Development Economics Research, August 1997, https://www.wider.unu.edu/sites/default/files/WP139.pdf.

34. See-Won Byun and Scott Snyder, "North Korean Contingency Planning and U.S.-ROK Cooperation," Center for U.S.-Korea Policy, Asia Foundation, September 2009, 4–6; Robert D. Kaplan, "When North Korea Falls," *Atlantic Monthly*, October 2006, http://www.theatlantic.com/magazine/archive/2006/10/when-north-korea-falls/305228/.
35. Victor D. Cha, *The Impossible State: North Korea, Past and Future* (New York: HarperCollins, 2012), 122.
36. Nicholas D. Kristof, "Chinese and South Koreans Formally Establish Relations," *New York Times*, August 24, 1992, https://www.nytimes.com/1992/08/24/world/chinese-and-south-koreans-formally-establish-relations.html.
37. Andrew S. Natsios, *The Great North Korean Famine* (Washington, DC: United States Institute of Peace Press, 2001); Stephan Haggard and Marcus Noland, *Famine in North Korea: Markets, Aid, and Reform* (New York: Columbia University Press, 2007).
38. Nicholas Eberstadt, *The End of North Korea* (Washington, DC: AEI Press, 1999); Robert A. Manning, "The Asian Paradox: Toward a New Architecture," *World Policy Journal* 10, no. 3 (1993): 55–64, https://www.jstor.org/stable/40209319; Leif R. Rosenberger, "Unifying Korea: Beyond Hopes and Fears," *Contemporary Southeast Asia* 16, no. 3 (1994): 295–316, https://www.jstor.org/stable/25798252; National Security Archive, George Washington University, "Exploring the Implications of Alternative North Korean Endgames: Results for a Discussion Panel on Continuing Coexistence Between North and South Korea," January 21, 1998, https://nsarchive.gwu.edu/document/18238-national-security-archive-doc-19-cia; Kongdan Oh and Ralph Hassig, "North Korea Between Collapse and Reform," *Asian Survey* 39, no. 2 (1999): 287–309, https://doi.org/10.2307/2645456; Kyung-Won Kim, "No Way Out: North Korea's Impending Collapse," *Harvard International Review* 18, no. 2 (March 22, 1996): 22–25, https://www.jstor.org/stable/42765252; Dong-Bok Lee, "Kim Jong Il's North Korea: Its Limitations and Prospects," *Korea and World Affairs* 18, no. 3 (Fall 1994): 421–42; and Choong-Nam Kim, "The Uncertain Future of North Korea: Soft Landing or Crash Landing?," *Korea and World Affairs* 20, no. 4 (Winter 1996): 623–36.
39. On South Korea as one of the Asian Tigers, see Woo, *Race to the Swift*; Amsden, *Asia's Next Giant*; Kang, *Crony Capitalism*; Barry Eichengreen, Dwight H. Perkins, and Kwanho Shin, eds., *From Miracle to Maturity: The Growth of the Korean Economy*, vol. 350 (Cambridge, MA: Harvard University Asia Center, 2012), https://doi.org/10.2307/j.ctt1x07vt4; Seung-hun Chun, *The Economic Development of South Korea: From Poverty to a Modern Industrial State* (New York: Routledge, 2018); Ha-Joon Chang, "The Political Economy of Industrial Policy in Korea," *Cambridge Journal of Economics* 17, no. 2 (1993): 131–57, https://www.jstor.org/stable/23599704; Sung Yeung Kwack, ed., *The Korean Economy at a Cross-road: Development Prospects, Liberalization, and South-North Economic Integration*

(Westport, CT: Praeger, 1994); Sakong Il and Youngsun Koh, eds., *The Korean Economy: Six Decades of Growth and Development* (Seoul: Korea Development Institute, 2010).

40. Victor D. Cha, *Beyond the Final Score: The Politics of Sport in Asia* (New York: Columbia University Press, 2008).
41. Kim Gyu-ryun et al., "통일 비용 • 편익 연구의 새로운 접근 포괄적 연구 요소의 도입과 대안의 모색" [A new approach to research on cost and benefit of unification: Introduction of comprehensive research elements and search for alternatives] (Seoul: Korea Institute for National Unification, December 2011), https://www.kinu.or.kr/pyxis-api/1/digital-files/f666280e-d67c-4266-87b2-c9e13a8d89e5; Korea Development Institute, "A Gradual Approach Toward North and South Korean Economic Integration," KDI Working Paper No. 9311, 1993, https://www.kdi.re.kr/eng/research/reportView?pub_no=921; and Kwon, "Experiences with Monetary Integration and Lessons for Korean Unification."
42. Victor D. Cha, "Politics and Democracy Under the Kim Young Sam Government: Something Old, Something New," *Asian Survey* 33, no. 9 (1993): 849–63, https://doi.org/10.2307/2645233.
43. For a good account of this time period, see Patrick McEachern, *Inside the Red Box: North Korea's Post-Totalitarian Politics* (New York: Columbia University Press, 2010), 67–75.
44. Dan Sanford, "ROK's Nordpolitik Revisited," *Journal of East Asian Affairs* 7, no. 1 (Winter/Spring 1993): 1–31, https://www.jstor.org/stable/23254205; Tae Dong Chung, "Korea's Nordpolitik: Achievements & Prospects," *Asian Perspective* 15, no. 2 (1991): 149–78; Ming Lee, "Seoul's Searching for 'Nordpolitik': Evolution and Perspective," *Asian Perspective* 13, no. 2 (1989): 141–78.
45. For text of the 1991 agreement, see United Nations Peacemaker, "Agreement on Reconciliation, Non-Aggression, and Exchanges and Cooperation between South and North Korea," December 13, 1991, https://peacemaker.un.org/korea-reconciliation-nonaggression91; for text of the 1992 joint declaration, see Republic of Korea Ministry of Foreign Affairs, "Joint Declaration on The Denuclearization of the Korean Peninsula," January 20, 1992, https://www.mofa.go.kr/eng/brd/m_5476/view.do?seq=305870&srchFr=&srchTo=&srchWord=&srchTp=&multi_itm_seq=0&itm_seq_1=0&itm_seq_2=0&company_cd=&company_nm=&page=6&titleNm=.
46. The subcommittees established by the Basic Agreement were the South-North Political Committee, South-North Military Committee, and Joint South-North Economic Exchanges and Cooperation Commission. See full text of agreement, "Agreement on Reconciliation, Non-Aggression, and Exchanges and Cooperation Between South and North Korea."
47. See Jager, *Brothers at War*; also Jae Ho Chung, *Between Ally and Partner: Korea-China Relations and the United States* (New York: Columbia University Press, 2007), 67–74.

48. United Nations Peacemaker, "Agreed Framework Between the United States of America and the Democratic People's Republic of Korea," October 21, 1994, https://peacemaker.un.org/node/1129.
49. Charles L. Pritchard, *Failed Diplomacy: How North Korea Got the Bomb* (Washington, DC: Brookings Institution, 2007); Mike Chinoy, *Meltdown: The Inside Story of the North Korean Nuclear Crisis* (New York: St. Martin's Press, 2008).
50. For an in-depth look at the policies and the rationale behind them, see Chung-in Moon, *The Sunshine Policy: In Defense of Engagement as a Path to Peace in Korea* (Seoul: Yonsei University Press, 2012). See also Victor D. Cha and David C. Kang, *Nuclear North Korea: A Debate on Engagement Strategies* (New York: Columbia University Press, 2003).
51. Ministry of Unification, Republic of Korea, "화해협력정책" [Sunshine policy], n.d., https://nkinfo.unikorea.go.kr/nkp/term/viewKnwldgDicary.do?pageIndex=1&dicaryId=233&koreanChrctr=.
52. Soon-young Hong, "Thawing Korea's Cold War: The Path to Peace on the Korean Peninsula," *Foreign Affairs* 78, no. 3 (1999): 8–12, https://doi.org/10.2307/20049275; Chung-in Moon and David I. Steinberg, eds., *Kim Dae-Jung Government and Sunshine Policy: Promises and Challenges* (Seoul: Yonsei University Press, 1999).
53. Ramon Pacheco Pardo, *Shrimp to Whale: South Korea from the Forgotten War to K-Pop* (London: Oxford University Press, 2022), chap. 4.
54. ROK president Kim Dae-jung and DPRK leader Kim Jong-il held the first inter-Korean summit in 2000. The second inter-Korean summit was held in 2007 with Kim Jong-il and ROK president Roh Moo-hyun.
55. Sang-Hun Choe, "The Lure of North Korea's Magic Mountain," *New York Times*, October 30, 2006, sec. World, https://www.nytimes.com/2006/10/30/world/asia/30iht-mount.3329914.html; James Brooke, "Tentatively, North Korea Solicits Foreign Investment and Tourism," *New York Times*, February 19, 2002, https://www.nytimes.com/2002/02/19/business/tentatively-north-korea-solicits-foreign-investment-and-tourism.html; Calvin Sims, "North Korea as the Next Tourist Spot; Hyundai Has Approval for Deepwater Docks, Spa and a 45-Hole Golf Course," *New York Times*, March 7, 2000, https://www.nytimes.com/2000/03/07/business/north-korea-next-tourist-spot-hyundai-has-approval-for-deepwater-docks-spa-45.html; Norimitsu Onishi, "South Brings Capitalism, Well Isolated, to North Korea," *New York Times*, July 18, 2006, https://www.nytimes.com/2006/07/18/world/asia/18korea.html.
56. For more on *minjung* ideology, see Gi-Wook Shin, *Ethnic Nationalism in Korea: Genealogy, Politics, and Legacy* (Stanford, CA: Stanford University Press, 2006); Soon-ok Shin, "Engagement? Containment? The Role of Identity in the Formation of South Korea's Policy Toward Pyongyang," *North Korean Review* 9, no. 1 (2013): 83–99, https://www.jstor.org/stable/43908908; and Pardo, *Shrimp to Whale*.
57. Evans J. R. Revere, "Facing the Facts: Towards a New U.S. North Korea Policy," Brookings Institution, 2013, https://www.brookings.edu/research/facing-the-facts-towards-a-new-u-s-north-korea-policy/, 6.

58. Revere.
59. Moon Jae-in, "Address at the Korber Foundation in Berlin, Germany," July 6, 2017.
60. For the best dataset on North Korean provocations, see "Database: North Korean Provocations."
61. Paul B. Stares and Joel S. Wit, "Preparing for Sudden Change in North Korea," Council on Foreign Relations, January 2009, https://www.cfr.org/report/preparing-sudden-change-north-korea; Bruce W. Bennett and Jennifer Lind, "The Collapse of North Korea: Military Missions and Requirements," *International Security* 36, no. 2 (2011): 84–119; Andrei Lankov, "North Korea's Choice: Collapse or Reform," *Foreign Affairs*, December 19, 2011, https://www.foreignaffairs.com/articles/asia/2011-12-19/north-koreas-choice-collapse-or-reform; Jack Pritchard, "My New Year's Predictions for North Korea," *Korea Economic Institute of America* (blog), December 21, 2011, https://keia.org/the-peninsula/my-new-years-predictions-for-north-korea/; and Victor Cha, "China's Newest Province?," *New York Times*, December 20, 2011, sec. Opinion, https://www.nytimes.com/2011/12/20/opinion/will-north-korea-become-chinas-newest-province.html.
62. Bruce E. Bechtol Jr., "The Implications of the Cheonan Sinking: A Security Studies Perspective," *International Journal of Korean Unification Studies* 19, no. 2 (2010): 1–40.
63. Nan Kim, "Korea on the Brink: Reading the Yŏnp'yŏng Shelling and its Aftermath," *Journal of Asian Studies* 70, no. 2 (May 2011): 337–56, https://www.jstor.org/stable/41302309.
64. See Bruce W. Bennett, "Preparing for the Possibility of a North Korean Collapse" (Santa Monica, CA: RAND Corporation, September 19, 2013), https://www.rand.org/pubs/research_reports/RR331.html.
65. For a study on this Vision 3000 plan, see Jae Jean Suh, "The Lee Myung-Bak Government's North Korea Policy" (Seoul: Korea Institute for National Unification, May 2009).
66. Colin Powell spoke in Seoul in November 2008; see Ashley Rowland, "Powell Calls Obama a 'Transformational Figure,'" *Stars and Stripes*, November 9, 2008, https://www.stripes.com/news/powell-calls-obama-a-transformational-figure-1.85019. Richard Haas spoke in Seoul in May 2010; see Young-jin Kim, "NK Leadership Succession Should Be Used for Policy Change," *Korea Times*, May 14, 2010, sec. National, https://www.koreatimes.co.kr/www/nation/2023/08/113_65914.html.
67. Victor D. Cha and David C. Kang, "Challenges for Korean Unification Planning: Justice, Markets, Health, Refugees, and Civil-Military Transitions" (Washington DC: Center for Strategic and International Studies, December 21, 2011), https://www.csis.org/analysis/challenges-korean-unification-planning.
68. "Unification May Be Jackpot: Park," *Korea JoongAng Daily*, January 6, 2014, https://koreajoongangdaily.joins.com/2014/01/06/politics/Unification-may-be-jackpot-Park/2983129.html.

69. Embassy of the Republic of Korea to Denmark, "Speech by President Geun-Hye Park, 'An Initiative for Peaceful Unification on the Korean Peninsula' at Dresden University of Technology," March 28, 2014, https://overseas.mofa.go.kr/dk-en/brd/m_7038/view.do?seq=716122&srchFr=&amp%3BsrchTo=&amp%3BsrchWord=&amp%3BsrchTp=&amp%3Bmulti_itm_seq=0&amp%3Bitm_seq_1=0&amp%3Bitm_seq_2=0&amp%3Bcompany_cd=&amp%3Bcompany_nm=.
70. See Seong-ho Sheen, "Dilemma of South Korea's Trust Diplomacy and Unification Policy," *International Journal of Korean Unification Studies* 23, no. 2 (2014): 97–122; also Evans J. R. Revere, "Korean Reunification and U.S. Interests: Preparing for One Korea," Brookings Institution, January 20, 2015. https://www.brookings.edu/on-the-record/korean-reunification-and-u-s-interests-preparing-for-one-korea/.
71. National Assembly Budget Office, "Economic Effects of Korean Unification," Seoul, 2014, 3.
72. Jiyoon Kim et al., "South Korean Attitudes Toward North Korea and Reunification" (Seoul: Asan Institute, 2014), http://en.asaninst.org/contents/south-korean-attitudes-toward-north-korea-and-reunification/, 18.
73. Ministry of Unification, Republic of Korea, "2014 White Paper on Korean Unification," Seoul, 2014, https://www.unikorea.go.kr/eng_unikorea/news/Publications/whitepaper/.
74. See the Presidential Committee for Unification Preparation at http://www.pcup.go.kr/main.do.
75. Blue House, "100 Policy Tasks: Five-Year Plan of the Moon Jae-in Administration," Seoul, July 19, 2017.
76. Moon Jae-in, "Address at the Korber Foundation in Berlin, Germany."
77. Moon Jae-in, "Address by President Moon Jae-in at May Day Stadium in Pyeongyang, North Korea," September 20, 2018.
78. Ministry of Foreign Affairs, Republic of Korea, "Audacious Initiative," August 15, 2022, https://www.mofa.go.kr/eng/wpge/m_25501/contents.do.

6. UNIFICATION DATA

1. A total of 110 responses were returned for the initial pilot study conducted in spring 2016. The survey respondents were pulled from a sample of U.S. experts, officials, scholars, and opinion leaders in the fields of Korea and East Asia.
2. The standard deviation for U.S. responses is 0.38, and the sample variance is 0.14. The mean is 5.19.
3. UN Human Rights Council, "Report of the Detailed Findings of the Commission of Inquiry on Human Rights in the Democratic People's Republic of Korea,"

February 7, 2014, https://www.ohchr.org/Documents/HRBodies/HRCouncil/CoIDPRK/Report/A.HRC.25.63.doc.
4. Victor Cha and Robert L. Gallucci, "Toward a New Policy for North Korea," George W. Bush Institute, November 2016, https://gwbcenter.imgix.net/Resources/gwbi-toward-a-new-policy-for-north-korea.pdf.
5. A total of 108 responses were returned for the initial pilot study conducted in spring 2016. The survey respondents were pulled from a sample of South Korean experts, officials, scholars, and opinion leaders in the fields of Korea and East Asia.
6. The mean for the South Korea sample is 5.07. The standard deviation is 0.26, and the sample variance is .07.
7. An earlier version of this data was presented in Marie DuMond, "Comparing South Korea and U.S. Perceptions of Korean Unification," Beyond Parallel, November 13, 2017, https://beyondparallel.csis.org/comparing-south-korea-u-s-perceptions-korean-unification/.

7. THE HARDEST OF HARD TARGETS

1. Jung H. Pak, *Becoming Kim Jong Un: A Former CIA Officer's Insights Into North Korea's Enigmatic Young Dictator* (New York: Ballantine Books, 2020), 3.
2. Patrick McEachern, *Inside the Red Box: North Korea's Post-Totalitarian Politics* (New York: Columbia University Press, 2010), 11.
3. Pak, *Becoming Kim Jong Un*, 3.
4. Matthew Ha and David Maxwell, "Kim Jong Un's 'All-Purpose Sword': North Korean Cyber-Enabled Economic Warfare," Foundation for Defense of Democracies, October 3, 2018, https://www.fdd.org/analysis/2018/10/03/kim-jong-uns-all-purpose-sword/.
5. David E. Sanger, *The Perfect Weapon: War, Sabotage, and Fear in the Cyber Age* (New York: Crown, 2018).
6. Justin Hastings, Daniel Wertz, and Andrew Yeo, "Market Activities and the Building Blocks of Civil Society in North Korea," National Committee on North Korea, February 2021, 3.
7. Thomas Byrne, "The Coronavirus Has Pushed North Korea's Economy to the Edge," *Foreign Policy*, April 27, 2020, https://foreignpolicy.com/2020/04/27/coronavirus-north-korea-economy-bonds-crisis/.
8. Kevin Gray and Jong-Woon Lee, *North Korea and the Geopolitics of Development* (Cambridge: Cambridge University Press, 2021); Andrei Lankov et al., "North Korea's New Capitalists and Their Workers: Business Practice and Labor Relations," *Communist and Post-Communist Studies* 50, no. 3 (2017): 157–67; and Hastings, Wertz, and Yeo, "Market Activities and Building Blocks."

9. Andrei Lankov and SeokHyang Kim, "Useless Men, Entrepreneurial Women, and North Korea's Post-Socialism: Transformation of Gender Roles Since the Early 1990s," *Asian Journal of Women's Studies* 20, no. 2 (January 1, 2014): 68–96, https://doi.org/10.1080/12259276.2014.11666182.
10. Hastings, Wertz, and Yeo, "Market Activities and Building Blocks," 5, citing Ralph Hassig and Kongdan Oh, *The Hidden People of North Korea: Everyday Life in the Hermit Kingdom* (Lanham, MD: Rowman and Littlefield, 2015), 47.
11. Je-hun Lee, "[News Analysis] North Korea's 'Marketized Economy' Already at an Irreversible Stage," *Hankyoreh*, February 5, 2019, https://english.hani.co.kr/arti/english_edition/e_northkorea/881048.html.
12. Cited in chapter 5.
13. Jieun Baek, *North Korea's Hidden Revolution: How the Information Underground is Transforming a Closed Society* (New Haven, CT: Yale University Press, 2016); Nat Kretchun and Jane Kim, "A Quiet Opening: North Koreans in a Changing Media Environment," InterMedia, May 2012, https://www.gwern.net/docs/technology/2012-kretchun.pdf; Nat Kretchun, Catherine Lee, and Seamus Tuohy, "Compromising Connectivity: Information Dynamics Between the State and Society in a Digitizing North Korea," InterMedia, February 1, 2017, https://seamustuohy.com/files/Compromising-Connectivity-Final-Report.pdf; and Martyn Williams, "Digital Trenches: North Korea's Information Counter-Offensive," Committee for Human Rights in North Korea, 2019, https://www.hrnk.org/uploads/pdfs/Williams_Digital_Trenches_Web_FINAL.pdf.
14. HON imagery collection is taken at angles to the target rather than from directly overhead (e.g., 49 degrees rather than 0 degrees off nadir), allowing for imagery collections showing the sides and relative heights of objects on the ground. Thermal imagery analysis measures relative heat signatures emanating from the ground surface areas. For example, see Joseph S. Bermudez Jr. et al., "Thermal Imagery Analysis of Yongbyon," Beyond Parallel, December 8, 2021, https://beyondparallel.csis.org/thermal-imagery-analysis-of-yongbyon/; and Joseph S. Bermudez Jr. and Victor Cha, "Sharp Focus: A Unique View of North Korea's Sinpo South Shipyard," Beyond Parallel, June 17, 2021, https://beyondparallel.csis.org/sharp-focus-a-unique-view-of-north-koreas-sinpo-south-shipyard/.
15. "North Korea Appears to Lift COVID Mask Mandate, Reports Say," Reuters, July 4, 2023, sec. Asia Pacific, https://www.reuters.com/world/asia-pacific/north-korea-appears-lift-covid-mask-mandate-reports-say-2023-07-04/; Josh Smith, "North Korea Locks Down Capital City over 'Respiratory Illness,'" Reuters, January 25, 2023 https://www.reuters.com/business/healthcare-pharmaceuticals/north-korea-locks-down-capital-city-over-respiratory-illness-report-2023-01-25/.
16. Frank Smith, "Coronavirus: How the Pandemic Is Hitting North Korea Hard," dw.com, April 12, 2021, https://www.dw.com/en/coronavirus-how-the-pandemic

-is-hitting-north-korea-hard/a-57168554; "The Latest: N Korea Says It Still Has No Coronavirus Cases," *AP News*, April 6, 2021, https://apnews.com/article/biden-cabinet-europe-global-trade-south-korea-coronavirus-pandemic-089215a25b49bc9c57388d2db638f71d; and Seulkee Jang, "North Korea Has 24 COVID-19 Quarantine Facilities for the Military," *Daily NK,* December 4, 2020, https://www.dailynk.com/english/north-korea-24-covid-19-quarantine-facilities-military/.

17. Victor Cha, Katrin Fraser Katz, and J. Stephen Morrison, "North Korea's Covid-19 Lockdown: Current Status and Road Ahead," Center for Strategic and International Studies, March 9, 2022, https://www.csis.org/analysis/north-koreas-covid-19-lockdown-current-status-and-road-ahead.

18. Hyonhee Shin, "N. Korea's Trade with China Plunges 80% as COVID-19 Lockdown Bites," Reuters, January 19, 2021, sec. China, https://www.reuters.com/world/china/nkoreas-trade-with-china-plunges-80-covid-19-lockdown-bites-2021-01-19/; Joori Roh, "N. Korea's Economy Shrank Most in 23 Years Amid COVID-19, Sanctions—S. Korea C.Bank," Reuters, July 30, 2021, https://www.reuters.com/world/asia-pacific/nkoreas-economy-shrank-most-23-years-amid-covid-19-sanctions-skorea-cbank-2021-07-30/; Sang-Hun Choe, "North Korea, Fighting to Hold Back Virus and Floods, Says No Thanks to Outside Aid," *New York Times*, August 14, 2020, sec. World, https://www.nytimes.com/2020/08/14/world/asia/north-korea-floods-coronavirus.html.

19. "North Korea Accused of Hacking Pfizer for Covid-19 Vaccine Data," *BBC News*, February 16, 2021, sec. Technology, https://www.bbc.com/news/technology-56084575.

20. "North Korea Rejects Offer of Almost Three Million Covid-19 Jabs," *BBC News*, September 1, 2021, sec. Asia, https://www.bbc.com/news/world-asia-58408913; Bryan Betts, "North Korea Warns Daily of Omicron Dangers, Still Reports Zero Covid Cases," *NK News*, December 6, 2021, https://www.nknews.org/2021/12/north-korea-warns-daily-of-omicron-dangers-still-reports-zero-covid-cases/; and "Kim Jong-Un: North Korea to Focus on Economy in 2022," *BBC News*, January 1, 2022, https://www.bbc.com/news/world-asia-59845636.

21. "North Korea's Kim Sacks Top Officials Over Handling of Covid-19 Outbreak," *France 24*, June 30, 2021, https://www.france24.com/en/asia-pacific/20210630-north-korea-s-kim-sacks-top-officials-over-handling-of-covid-19-outbreak; and "North Korea 'Killed and Burned South Korean Official,'" *BBC News*, September 24, 2020, sec. Asia, https://www.bbc.com/news/world-asia-54275649.

22. Joseph S. Bermudez Jr., Victor Cha, and Jennifer Jun, "North Korea Attempting to Reverse COVID-19 Border Shutdown with Import Disinfection Facilities," Beyond Parallel, November 15, 2021, https://beyondparallel.csis.org/north-korea-attempting-to-reverse-covid-19-border-shutdown-with-import-disinfection-facilities/.

23. Bermudez, Cha, and Jun.
24. This paragraph borrows from Cha, Katz, and Morrison, "North Korea's Covid-19 Lockdown."
25. Myoung-don Oh et al., "Middle East Respiratory Syndrome What We Learned from the 2015 Outbreak in the Republic of Korea," *Korean Journal of Internal Medicine* 33 no. 2 (March 2018): 233–46, https://doi.org/10.3904/kjim.2018.031; Myoung-don Oh, "The Korean Middle East Respiratory Syndrome Coronavirus Outbreak and Our Responsibility to the Global Scientific Community," *Infection and Chemotherapy* 48 no. 2 (June 1, 2016): 145–46, https://dx.doi.org/10.3947/ic.2016.48.2.145; "South Korea Declares 'de Facto End' to Mers Virus," *BBC News*, July 28, 2015, sec. Asia, https://www.bbc.com/news/world-asia-33684981.
26. Korea Central News Agency, "Congratulatory Speech from Russian President to Meeting Celebrating V-Day," July 28, 2023, http://www.kcna.kp/en/article/q/2706c1b69e571dd66bd3219ad079aceb.kcmsf.
27. Victor Cha, *The Impossible State: North Korea, Past and Future* (New York: Harper Collins, 2012), chap. 8.
28. White House, "Press Briefing by Press Secretary Karine Jean-Pierre and NSC Coordinator for Strategic Communications John Kirby," January 20, 2023, https://www.whitehouse.gov/briefing-room/press-briefings/2023/01/20/press-briefing-by-press-secretary-karine-jean-pierre-and-nsc-coordinator-for-strategic-communications-john-kirby-8/.
29. Joseph Bermudez Jr., Victor Cha, and Jennifer Jun, "Arms for Energy: War Brings Together Russia and North Korea," Beyond Parallel, February 17, 2023, https://beyondparallel.csis.org/arms-oil-and-coal-the-tumangang-khasan-railroad-crossing/.
30. See Joseph Bermudez Jr., Victor Cha, and Jennifer Jun, "Activity at Najin Points to Continued DPRK-Russia Arms Transfers," Beyond Parallel, December 8, 2023, https://beyondparallel.csis.org/activity-at-najin-points-to-continued-dprk-russia-arms-transfers/; Bermudez, Cha, and Jun, "Ongoing Arms Transfer Activity at Najin Port," Beyond Parallel, October 17, 2023, https://beyondparallel.csis.org/ongoing-arms-transfer-activity-at-najin-port/.
31. Andy Lim and Victor Cha, "Dataset: China-North Korea High Level Visits Since 1953," Beyond Parallel, March 17, 2017, https://beyondparallel.csis.org/china-dprk-high-level-visits-since-1953/.
32. Jake Sullivan, "A Statement of U.S. Policy on North Korea," Center for Strategic and International Studies, December 1, 2022, https://www.csis.org/analysis/statement-us-policy-north-korea.
33. Jeffrey Lewis, "Opinion | It's Time to Accept That North Korea Has Nuclear Weapons," *New York Times*, October 13, 2022, sec. Opinion, https://www.nytimes.com/2022/10/13/opinion/international-world/north-korea-us-nuclear.html.

APPENDIX 3: MICROSURVEYS OF DPRK CITIZENS AND SAMPLE ANSWER SHEETS

1. (W) = Question modeled after survey from Noland and Haggard's "Witness to Transformation."
2. (A) = Question modeled after 2015 survey from Asan Institute on South Korean views of unification.

BIBLIOGRAPHY

Ahn, Byung-joon. "The Man Who Would Be Kim." *Foreign Affairs* 73, no. 6 (December 1994): 94–108.

Amnesty International. "North Korea: Connection Denied: Restrictions on Mobile Phones and Outside Information in North Korea." March 9, 2016. https://www.amnesty.org/en/documents/asa24/3373/2016/en/.

Amsden, Alice H. *Asia's Next Giant: South Korea and Late Industrialization*. London: Oxford University Press, 1991.

AP News. "The Latest: N Korea Says It Still Has No Coronavirus Cases." April 6, 2021. https://apnews.com/article/biden-cabinet-europe-global-trade-south-korea-coronavirus-pandemic-089215a25b49bc9c57388d2db638f71d.

Archives of the General Staff of the Armed Forces of the Russian Federation op. 480, 29, st. 5, p. 2, pa. 21, k. 35. "Untitled Memorandum on the Political and Morale Situation of Soviet Troops in North Korea and the Economic Situation in Korea," trans. Gary Goldberg. Wilson Center Digital Archive, January 11, 1946. https://digitalarchive.wilsoncenter.org/document/untitled-memorandum-political-and-morale-situation-soviet-troops-north-korea-and-economic.

Baek, Jieun. *North Korea's Hidden Revolution: How the Information Underground Is Transforming a Closed Society*. New Haven, CT: Yale University Press, 2016.

Baker, Peter. "Trump Says Military Is 'Locked and Loaded' and North Korea Will 'Regret' Threats." *New York Times*, August 11, 2017, sec. World. https://www.nytimes.com/2017/08/11/world/asia/trump-north-korea-locked-and-loaded.html.

Baker, Reg, Mike Brick, Scott Keeter, Paul Biemer, Courtney Kennedy, Frauke Kreuter, Andrew Mercer, and George Terhanian. "Evaluating Survey Quality in Today's Complex Environment." American Association of Public Opinion Research,

May 12, 2016. https://aapor.org/wp-content/uploads/2023/01/AAPOR_Reassessing_Survey_Methods_Report_Final.pdf.

Bank of Korea. "Gross Domestic Product Estimates for North Korea in 2021." July 27, 2022. https://www.bok.or.kr/eng/bbs/E0000634/view.do?nttId=10071884&menuNo=400069.

———. "Main Annual Indicators: Gross Domestic Product (Nominal, Korean Won)." n.d. https://kosis.kr/statHtml/statHtml.do?orgId=301&tblId=DT_200Y013&conn_path=I2.

Barnhart, Michael, Michelle Cantos, Jeffrey Johnson, Elias Fox, Gary Freas, and Dan Scott. "Not So Lazarus: Mapping DPRK Cyber Threat Groups to Government Organizations." *Mandiant* (blog), March 23, 2022. https://www.mandiant.com/resources/blog/mapping-dprk-groups-to-government.

Bartlett, Jason, and Francis Shin. "Sanctions by the Numbers: Spotlight on North Korea." Center for a New American Security, February 8, 2021. https://www.cnas.org/publications/reports/sanctions-by-the-numbers-north-korea.

BBC News. "Kim Jong-Un: North Korea to Focus on Economy in 2022." January 1, 2022, sec. Asia. https://www.bbc.com/news/world-asia-59845636.

———. "North Korea Accused of Hacking Pfizer for Covid-19 Vaccine Data." February 16, 2021, sec. Technology. https://www.bbc.com/news/technology-56084575.

———. "North Korea Defector Hack: Personal Data of Almost 1,000 Leaked." December 28, 2018, sec. Asia. https://www.bbc.com/news/world-asia-46698646.

———. "North Korea 'Killed and Burned South Korean Official.'" September 24, 2020, sec. Asia. https://www.bbc.com/news/world-asia-54275649.

———. "North Korea Rejects Offer of Almost Three Million Covid-19 Jabs." September 1, 2021, sec. Asia. https://www.bbc.com/news/world-asia-58408913.

———. "South Korea Declares 'de Facto End' to Mers Virus." July 28, 2015, sec. Asia. https://www.bbc.com/news/world-asia-33684981.

Bechtol Jr., Bruce E. "The Implications of the Cheonan Sinking: A Security Studies Perspective." *International Journal of Korean Unification Studies* 19, no. 2 (2010): 1–40.

Bennett, Bruce W. "Alternative Paths to Korean Unification." Washington, DC: RAND Corporation, October 31, 2018. https://www.rand.org/pubs/research_reports/RR2808.html.

———. "Preparing for the Possibility of a North Korean Collapse." Santa Monica, CA: RAND Corporation, September 19, 2013. https://www.rand.org/pubs/research_reports/RR331.html.

Bennett, Bruce W., and Jennifer Lind. "The Collapse of North Korea: Military Missions and Requirements." *International Security* 36, no. 2 (2011): 84–119.

Berlinger, Joshua, Yoko Wakatsuki, and Will Ripley. "Trump Says 'All Options on Table' After North Korea Fires Missile Over Japan | CNN Politics." CNN, August 28, 2017. https://www.cnn.com/2017/08/28/politics/north-korea-launch-unidentified-projectile/index.html.

Bermudez Jr., Joseph S. *North Korean Special Forces*. Newport, RI: Naval Institute Press, 1997.

——. "North Korea's Strategic Culture." Defense Threat Reduction Agency Advanced Systems and Concepts Office, 2006. https://irp.fas.org/agency/dod/dtra/dprk.pdf.

Bermudez Jr., Joseph S., and Victor Cha. "Sharp Focus: A Unique View of North Korea's Sinpo South Shipyard." Beyond Parallel, June 17, 2021. https://beyondparallel.csis.org/sharp-focus-a-unique-view-of-north-koreas-sinpo-south-shipyard/.

Bermudez Jr., Joseph S., Victor Cha, Andy Dinville, and Jennifer Jun. "Thermal Imagery Analysis of Yongbyon." Beyond Parallel, December 8, 2021. https://beyondparallel.csis.org/thermal-imagery-analysis-of-yongbyon/.

Bermudez Jr., Joseph S., Victor Cha, and Jennifer Jun. "North Korea Attempting to Reverse COVID-19 Border Shutdown with Import Disinfection Facilities." Beyond Parallel, November 15, 2021. https://beyondparallel.csis.org/north-korea-attempting-to-reverse-covid-19-border-shutdown-with-import-disinfection-facilities/.

Bernhardt, Jordan, and Lauren Sukin. "Joint Military Exercises and Crisis Dynamics on the Korean Peninsula." *Journal of Conflict Resolution* 65, no. 5 (May 1, 2021): 855–88. https://journals.sagepub.com/doi/10.1177/0022002720972180.

Berr, Jonathan. "'WannaCry' Ransomware Attack Losses Could Reach $4 Billion." *CBS News*, May 16, 2017. https://www.cbsnews.com/news/wannacry-ransomware-attacks-wannacry-virus-losses/.

Betts, Bryan. "North Korea Warns Daily of Omicron Dangers, Still Reports Zero COVID Cases." *NK News*, December 6, 2021. https://www.nknews.org/2021/12/north-korea-warns-daily-of-omicron-dangers-still-reports-zero-covid-cases/.

Beyond Parallel. "Database: North Korean Provocations." December 20, 2019. https://beyondparallel.csis.org/database-north-korean-provocations/.

——. "U.S.-DPRK Negotiations and North Korean Provocations." October 2, 2017. https://beyondparallel.csis.org/dprk-provocations-and-us-negotiations/.

Blue House. "100 Policy Tasks: Five-Year Plan of the Moon Jae-in Administration." Seoul, July 19, 2017.

Box-Steffensmeier, Janet M., John R. Freeman, Matthew P. Hitt, and Jon C. W. Pevehouse. *Time Series Analysis for the Social Sciences*. Cambridge: Cambridge University Press, 2014. https://doi.org/10.1017/CBO9781139025287.

Brooke, James. "Tentatively, North Korea Solicits Foreign Investment and Tourism." *New York Times*, February 19, 2002, sec. Business. https://www.nytimes.com/2002/02/19/business/tentatively-north-korea-solicits-foreign-investment-and-tourism.html.

Browne, Ryan, and Steve Almasy. "North Korea's Missile Test Fails, US Military Says." CNN, April 28, 2017. https://www.cnn.com/2017/04/28/world/north-korea-missile-launch/index.html.

Buchanan, Ben. "How North Korean Hackers Rob Banks Around the World." *Wired*, February 28, 2020. https://www.wired.com/story/how-north-korea-robs-banks-around-world/.

Burt, Tom. "Cyberattacks Targeting Health Care Must Stop." *Microsoft on the Issues* (blog), November 13, 2020. https://blogs.microsoft.com/on-the-issues/2020/11/13/health-care-cyberattacks-covid-19-paris-peace-forum/.

Byrne, Thomas. "The Coronavirus Has Pushed North Korea's Economy to the Edge." *Foreign Policy*, April 27, 2020. https://foreignpolicy.com/2020/04/27/coronavirus-north-korea-economy-bonds-crisis/.

Byun, See-Won, and Scott Snyder. "North Korean Contingency Planning and U.S.-ROK Cooperation." Center for U.S.-Korea Policy, Asia Foundation, September 2009.

Caesar, Ed. "The Incredible Rise of North Korea's Hacking Army." *New Yorker*, April 19, 2021. https://www.newyorker.com/magazine/2021/04/26/the-incredible-rise-of-north-koreas-hacking-army.

Carr, Madeline. "Public-Private Partnerships in National Cyber-Security Strategies." *International Affairs* 92 (January 8, 2016): 43–62.

Cathcart, Adam, and Charles Kraus. "Peripheral Influence: The Sinŭiju Student Incident of 1945 and the Impact of Soviet Occupation in North Korea." *Journal of Korean Studies* 13, no. 1 (2008): 1–27.

Center for Strategic and International Studies, "North Korea Policy, One Year After Hanoi." February 25, 2020. https://www.foreign.senate.gov/imo/media/doc/022520_King_Testimony.pdf.

Cha, Sangmi, and Hyonhee Shin. "North Korean Hackers Tried to Steal Pfizer Vaccine Know-How, Lawmaker Says." Reuters, February 16, 2021, sec. Healthcare & Pharmaceuticals. https://www.reuters.com/article/us-northkorea-cybercrime-pfizer-idUSKBN2AG0NI.

Cha, Victor. "Anti-Americanism and the U.S. Role in Inter-Korean Relations." In *Korean Attitudes Towards the United States: Changing Dynamics*. Armonk, NY: M. E. Sharpe, 2005.

———. "China's Newest Province?" *New York Times*, December 20, 2011, sec. Opinion. https://www.nytimes.com/2011/12/20/opinion/will-north-korea-become-chinas-newest-province.html.

———. "Covid Helped Isolate North Korea in a Way Sanctions Never Could. What Now?" *NBC News*, February 10, 2021. https://www.nbcnews.com/think/opinion/covid-helped-isolate-north-korea-way-sanctions-never-could-so-ncna1257143.

———. "Giving North Korea a 'Bloody Nose' Carries a Huge Risk to Americans." *Washington Post*, January 31, 2018. https://www.washingtonpost.com/opinions/victor-cha-giving-north-korea-a-bloody-nose-carries-a-huge-risk-to-americans/2018/01/30/43981c94-05f7-11e8-8777-2a059f168dd2_story.html.

———. "Splendid Isolation: North Korea and COVID-19." Center for Strategic and International Studies, April 30, 2020. https://www.csis.org/analysis/splendid-isolation-north-korea-and-covid-19.

Cha, Victor D. *Beyond the Final Score: The Politics of Sport in Asia*. New York: Columbia University Press, 2008.

———. "Hawk Engagement and Preventive Defense on the Korean Peninsula." *International Security* 27, no. 1 (2002): 40–78.

———. "Korean Unification: The Zero-Sum Past and the Precarious Future." *Asian Perspective* 21, no. 3 (Winter 1997): 63–92.

———. "Politics and Democracy Under the Kim Young Sam Government: Something Old, Something New." *Asian Survey* 33, no. 9 (1993): 849–63.

———. *The Impossible State: North Korea, Past and Future*. New York: Harper Collins, 2012.

Cha, Victor, and Lisa Collins. "The Markets: Private Economy and Capitalism in North Korea?" Beyond Parallel, August 26, 2018. https://beyondparallel.csis.org/markets-private-economy-capitalism-north-korea/.

Cha, Victor, and Robert L. Gallucci. "Toward a New Policy for North Korea." George W. Bush Institute, November 2016. https://gwbcenter.imgix.net/Resources/gwbi-toward-a-new-policy-for-north-korea.pdf.

Cha, Victor, and David Kang. "Approaching Korean Unification What We Learn from Other Cases." USC Korean Studies Institute and Center for Strategic & International Studies, December 2010. https://csis-website-prod.s3.amazonaws.com/s3fs-public/legacy_files/files/publication/101217_Cha_ApproachingUnification_WEB.pdf.

———. "Challenges for Korean Unification Planning: Justice, Markets, Health, Refugees, and Civil-Military Transitions." Washington DC: Center for Strategic and International Studies, December 21, 2011. https://www.csis.org/analysis/challenges-korean-unification-planning.

———. *Nuclear North Korea: A Debate on Engagement Strategies*. New York: Columbia University Press, 2003.

Cha, Victor, Katrin Fraser Katz, and J. Stephen Morrison. "North Korea's Covid-19 Lockdown: Current Status and Road Ahead." Center for Strategic and International Studies, March 9, 2022. https://www.csis.org/analysis/north-koreas-covid-19-lockdown-current-status-and-road-ahead.

Chang, Ha-Joon. "The Political Economy of Industrial Policy in Korea." *Cambridge Journal of Economics* 17, no. 2 (1993): 131–57.

Chapman, William. "Korean Leader Lost Aides Who Made Policies Work." *Washington Post*, October 11, 1983. https://www.washingtonpost.com/archive/politics/1983/10/11/korean-leader-lost-aides-who-made-policies-work/bbe16281-a0e6-4a6a-8fae-9cc506dce79f/.

———. "South Korea Buries Bomb Blast Victims, Denounces the North." *Washington Post*, October 14, 1983. https://www.washingtonpost.com/archive/politics/1983/10/14/south-korea-buries-bomb-blast-victims-denounces-the-north/2d5cfbd0-5bac-4779-b255-30e2970853d7/.

Cheong, Kwang-seong. "北 해킹에 속수무책인 정부... 청와대까지 사이버 공격" [The Government Is Helpless Against North Korea's Hacking... Cyberattacks Even on the Blue House]. *Chosun Ilbo*, January 2020. http://monthly.chosun.com/client/news/viw.asp?nNewsNumb=202001100013.

China Analysis Team. "The KuCoin Hack: What We Know So Far and How the Hackers Are Using DeFi Protocols to Launder Stolen Funds." *Chainalysis* (blog), September 29, 2020. https://blog.chainalysis.com/reports/kucoin-hack-2020-defi-uniswap/.

Chinoy, Mike. *Meltdown: The Inside Story of the North Korean Nuclear Crisis*. New York: St. Martin's Press, 2008.

———. "Why North Korean Intelligence Is so Hard to Read." CNN, April 12, 2013. https://www.cnn.com/2013/04/12/world/asia/north-korea-nuclear-capabilities/index.html.

Chira, Susan. "Korean Plane, 115 Aboard, Crashes in Southeast Asia." *New York Times*, November 30, 1987, sec. World. https://www.nytimes.com/1987/11/30/world/korean-plane-115-aboard-crashes-in-southeast-asia.html.

Cho, Han-Bum, Weh-Sol Moon, Young Hoon Song, and Sun-Jae Hwang. "The Costs and Benefits of Unification on the Korean Peninsula: In the Political, Social, and Economic Areas." Seoul: Korea Institute for National Unification, August 2016. https://www.kinu.or.kr/pyxis-api/1/digital-files/7948488c-5019-4733-bd4f-97bf7a38490e.

Choe, Sang-Hun. "As Rocket Launching Nears, North Korea Continues Shift to New 'Supreme Leader.'" *New York Times*, April 11, 2012, sec. World. https://www.nytimes.com/2012/04/12/world/asia/young-north-korean-leader-kim-jong-un-chosen-as-head-of-ruling-party.html.

———. "The Lure of North Korea's Magic Mountain." *New York Times*, October 30, 2006, sec. World. https://www.nytimes.com/2006/10/30/world/asia/30iht-mount.3329914.html.

———. "Meet Kim Jong-Un, a Moody Young Man with a Nuclear Arsenal." *New York Times*, August 10, 2017, sec. World. https://www.nytimes.com/2017/08/10/world/asia/kim-jong-un-north-korea-nuclear.html.

———. "North Korea, Fighting to Hold Back Virus and Floods, Says No Thanks to Outside Aid." *New York Times*, August 14, 2020, sec. World. https://www.nytimes.com/2020/08/14/world/asia/north-korea-floods-coronavirus.html.

———. "North Korea Fires Missile That Lands in Sea Between Korea and Japan." *New York Times*, May 28, 2017, sec. World. https://www.nytimes.com/2017/05/28/world/asia/north-korea-missile-test.html.

———. "North Korea Says Missile It Tested Can Carry Nuclear Warhead." *New York Times*, May 15, 2017, sec. World. https://www.nytimes.com/2017/05/14/world/asia/north-korea-missile-nuclear.html.

———. "North Korean Leader Stresses Need for Strong Military." *New York Times*, April 15, 2012, sec. World. https://www.nytimes.com/2012/04/16/world/asia/kim-jong-un-north-korean-leader-talks-of-military-superiority-in-first-public-speech.html.

Choe, Sang-Hun, and Rick Gladstone. "North Korean Rocket Fails Moments After Liftoff." *New York Times*, April 12, 2012, sec. World. https://www.nytimes.com

/2012/04/13/world/asia/north-korea-launches-rocket-defying-world-warnings.html.

Choe, Sang-Hun, and David Yaffe-Bellany. "How North Korea Used Crypto to Hack Its Way Through the Pandemic." *New York Times*, June 30, 2022, sec. Business. https://www.nytimes.com/2022/06/30/business/north-korea-crypto-hack.html.

Choi, Hyun-sil. "탈북여성들의 트라우마와 정착지원 방향 연구" [A Study on North Korean female defectors' trauma and the direction of settlement support]. Ministry of Unification, 2010. https://unibook.unikorea.go.kr/board/view?boardId=20&categoryId=&page=&id=201458202&field=searchAll&searchInput=.

Choi, Jinwook, and Jin-Ha Kim. "North Korean Reconstruction in the Process of Korean Unification." Korea Institute for National Unification, 2011.

Choi, Wan-kyu. "North Korea's New Unification Strategy." *Asian Perspective* 25, no. 2 (2001): 99–122.

Chosun Ilbo. "집권땐 北 흡수통일" [If I become leader of the government, North Korea will ne unified by absorption]. July 5, 1992. https://newslibrary.naver.com/viewer/index.nhn?articleId=1992070500239104002&editNo=1&printCount=1&publishDate=1992-07 05&officeId=00023&pageNo=4&printNo=22040&publishType=00010.

———. "N. Korea Test-Fires Short-Range Missiles." March 30, 2012. //english.chosun.com/site/data/html_dir/2012/03/30/2012033001081.html.

Chun, Seung-hun. *The Economic Development of South Korea: From Poverty to a Modern Industrial State*. London: Routledge, 2018.

Chung, Chaewon. "North Korean Refugees Are at the Center of Massive Data Leak." *Coda Story* (blog), December 12, 2019. https://www.codastory.com/authoritarian-tech/surveillance/north-korea-refugees-hack/.

Chung, Jae Ho. *Between Ally and Partner: Korea-China Relations and the United States*. New York: Columbia University Press, 2007.

Chung, Tae Dong. "Korea's Nordpolitik: Achievements & Prospects." *Asian Perspective* 15, no. 2 (1991): 149–78.

Cimpanu, Catalin. "Kaspersky: North Korean Hackers Are behind the VHD Ransomware." ZDNET, July 28, 2020. https://www.zdnet.com/article/kaspersky-north-korean-hackers-are-behind-the-vhd-ransomware/.

———. "North Korea Has Tried to Hack 11 Officials of the UN Security Council." ZDNET, September 30, 2020. https://www.zdnet.com/article/north-korea-has-tried-to-hack-11-officials-of-the-un-security-council/.

———. "North Korean Hackers Infiltrate Chile's ATM Network After Skype Job Interview." ZDNET, January 15, 2019. https://www.zdnet.com/article/north-korean-hackers-infiltrate-chiles-atm-network-after-skype-job-interview/.

Cohen, Zachary, Ryan Browne, Nicole Gaouette, and Taehoon Lee. "New Missile Test Shows North Korea Capable of Hitting All of US Mainland." CNN, November 28, 2017. https://www.cnn.com/2017/11/28/politics/north-korea-missile-launch/index.html.

Collins, Robert. "A Brief History of the US-ROK Combined Military Exercises." 38 North, February 26, 2014. https://www.38north.org/2014/02/rcollins022714/.

———. "Patterns of Collapse in North Korea." *Combined Forces Command C5 Civil Affairs Newsletter*, January 1996.

Corera, Gordon. "UK TV Drama about North Korea Hit by Cyber-Attack." *BBC News*, October 16, 2017, sec. Technology. https://www.bbc.com/news/technology-41640976.

Cumings, Bruce. *Korea's Place in the Sun: A Modern History*. New York: Norton, 1997.

Cumming-Bruce, Nick. "North Korea Accuses U.S. and South of 'Inciting Military Tension.'" *New York Times*, August 6, 2019, sec. World. https://www.nytimes.com/2019/08/06/world/asia/north-korea-military.html.

Cybersecurity & Infrastructure Security Agency. "Alert (AA20–133A) Top 10 Routinely Exploited Vulnerabilities." May 12, 2020. https://www.cisa.gov/news-events/cybersecurity-advisories/aa20-133a.

———. "Alert (AA20–239A): FASTCash 2.0: North Korea's BeagleBoyz Robbing Banks." August 26, 2020. https://www.cisa.gov/news-events/cybersecurity-advisories/aa20-239a.

———. "Alert (AA21–048A): AppleJeus: Analysis of North Korea's Cryptocurrency Malware." April 15, 2021. https://www.cisa.gov/news-events/cybersecurity-advisories/aa21-048a.

Democracy Matrix Research Project, University of Würzburg. "Ranking of Countries by Quality of Democracy," n.d. https://www.democracymatrix.com/ranking.

Denmark, Abraham M., and Lindsey W. Ford. "America's Military Exercises in Korea Aren't a Game." *Foreign Policy*, June 21, 2018. https://foreignpolicy.com/2018/06/21/americas-military-exercises-in-korea-arent-a-game/.

Denyer, Simon. "North Korea Complains About 'Stink' of U.S.-South Korea Military Exercises." *Washington Post*, March 16, 2021. https://www.washingtonpost.com/world/north-korea-complains-about-stink-of-us-south-korea-military-exercises/2021/03/15/415ba17c-85fa-11eb-8a67-f314e5fcf88d_story.html.

———. "North Korea Denounces Scaled-Back U.S.-South Korea Military Exercises." *Washington Post*, March 14, 2019. https://www.washingtonpost.com/world/asia_pacific/north-korea-denounces-scaled-back-us-south-korea-military-exercises/2019/03/07/b90e7508-40d5-11e9-85ad-779ef05fd9d8_story.html.

Dilanian, Ken. "North Korea Is a Tough Target for U.S. Intelligence Agencies." *Los Angeles Times*, December 24, 2011, sec. World & Nation. https://www.latimes.com/nation/la-xpm-2011-dec-24-la-fg-korea-intel-20111225-story.html.

Dilanian, Ken, and Courtney Kube. "Why It's So Hard for U.S. Spies to Figure Out North Korea." *NBC News*, September 3, 2017. https://www.nbcnews.com/news/north-korea/why-it-s-so-hard-u-s-spies-figure-out-n797171.

Do, Kyung-ok, Soo-Am Kim, Dong-ho Han, Keum-Soon Lee, and Min Hong. "White Paper on Human Rights in North Korea 2015." Seoul: Korea Institute for National Unification, September 2015. https://www.kinu.or.kr/pyxis-api/1/digital-files/3b2eeb32-d7c6-4137-b9a6-767a3e0ceaa6.

Dobbins, James. "Joint Military Exercise Can Be a Bargaining Chip with North Korea." *Hill*, February 23, 2018. https://thehill.com/opinion/national-security/375252-joint-military-exercise-can-be-a-bargaining-chip-with-north-korea/.

Dong-A Ilbo. "金鍾泌 (김종필) 자민련 총재 국회연설 (요지)" [Kim Jong-Pil, president of United Liberal Democrats, speech to the National Assembly (summary)]. October 25, 1996. https://newslibrary.naver.com/viewer/index.nhn?articleId=1996102500209104006&editNo=45&printCount=1&publishDate=1996-10-25&officeId=00020&pageNo=4&printNo=23348&publishType=00010.

D'Orazio, Vito. "War Games: North Korea's Reaction to US and South Korean Military Exercises." *Journal of East Asian Studies* 12, no. 2 (May 2012): 275–94.

Dreazen, Yochi. "Here's What War with North Korea Would Look like." *Vox*, February 7, 2018. https://www.vox.com/world/2018/2/7/16974772/north-korea-war-trump-kim-nuclear-weapon.

DuBois, Eun. "Building Resilience to the North Korean Cyber Threat: Experts Discuss." Brookings, December 23, 2020. https://www.brookings.edu/articles/building-resilience-to-the-north-korean-cyber-threat-experts-discuss/.

DuMond, Marie. "Comparing South Korea and U.S. Perceptions of Korean Unification." Beyond Parallel, November 13, 2017. https://beyondparallel.csis.org/comparing-south-korea-u-s-perceptions-korean-unification/.

Eberstadt, Nicholas. *The End of North Korea*. Washington, DC: AEI Press, 1999.

——. "Hastening Korean Reunification." *Foreign Affairs* 76, no. 2 (1997): 77–92.

Eberstadt, Nicholas, and Richard J. Ellings, eds. *Korea's Future and the Great Powers*. Seattle: University of Washington Press, 2001.

Eichengreen, Barry, Dwight H. Perkins, and Kwanho Shin, eds. *From Miracle to Maturity: The Growth of the Korean Economy*. Vol. 350. Cambridge, MA: Harvard University Asia Center, 2012. https://doi.org/10.2307/j.ctt1x07vt4.

Einhorn, Madelynn, and Timothy S. Rich. "The Ties That Bond? Attitudinal Factors Influencing South Korean Support for Unification and Peaceful Coexistence." *North Korean Review* 17, no. 2 (2021): 18–33.

Embassy of the Republic of Korea to Denmark. "Speech by President Geun-Hye Park, 'An Initiative for Peaceful Unification on the Korean Peninsula' at Dresden University of Technology," March 28, 2014. https://overseas.mofa.go.kr/dk-en/brd/m_7038/view.do?seq=716122&srchFr=&amp%3BsrchTo=&amp%3BsrchWord=&amp%3BsrchTp=&amp%3Bmulti_itm_seq=0&amp%3Bitm_seq_1=0&amp%3Bitm_seq_2=0&amp%3Bcompany_cd=&amp%3Bcompany_nm=.

Engman, Mats. "U.S.–South Korea Military Exercises: Provocation or Possibility?" Institute for Security and Development Policy, March 2018. https://isdp.eu/publication/u-s-rok-military-exercises-provocation-possibility/.

Ernst, Maximilian, and Roman Jurowetzki. "Satellite Data, Women Defectors and Black Markets in North Korea: A Quantitative Study of the North Korean Informal Sector Using Night-Time Lights Satellite Imagery." *North Korean Review* 12, no. 2 (2016): 64–83.

Etzioni, Amitai. "Cybersecurity in the Private Sector." *Issues in Science and Technology* 28, no. 1 (2011): 58–62.
Ferrier, Kyle. "Who's Right About the New US-South Korea Joint Military Exercise? Making Sense of the New Dong Maeng Drills." *Diplomat*, March 8, 2019. https://thediplomat.com/2019/03/whos-right-about-the-new-us-south-korea-joint-military-exercise/.
Foster-Carter, Aidan. *Korea's Coming Reunification: Another East Asian Superpower?* Special Report no. M212. London: Economist Intelligence Unit, 1992.
France 24. "North Korea's Kim Sacks Top Officials Over Handling of Covid-19 Outbreak," June 30, 2021. https://www.france24.com/en/asia-pacific/20210630-north-korea-s-kim-sacks-top-officials-over-handling-of-covid-19-outbreak.
Fraser, Nalani, Jaqueline O'Leary, Vincent Cannon, and Fred Plan. "APT38: Details on New North Korean Regime-Backed Threat Group." *Mandiant*, May 16, 2022. https://www.mandiant.com/resources/blog/apt38-details-on-new-north-korean-regime-backed-threat-group.
Friedhoff, Karl. "Considerations of Risk and Methodology for North Korean Surveys." Beyond Parallel, November 2, 2016. https://beyondparallel.csis.org/considerations-of-risk-and-methodology-for-north-korean-surveys/.
George H. W. Bush Presidential Library & Museum. "The President's News Conference with President Roh Tae Woo of South Korea in Seoul." January 6, 1992. https://bush41library.tamu.edu/archives/public-papers/3819.
Go, Myong-Hyun. "The Merits of Conducting Surveys Inside North Korea." Beyond Parallel, November 2, 2016. https://beyondparallel.csis.org/the-merits-of-conducting-surveys-inside-north-korea/.
Grady, John. "Former U.S. Forces in Korea CO: Cancelling More Military Exercises Weakens Ability to Deter North Korea." *USNI News* (blog), July 24, 2018. https://news.usni.org/2018/07/24/former-u-s-forces-korea-co-cancelling-military-exercises-weakens-ability-deter-north-korea.
Gray, Kevin, and Jong-Woon Lee. *North Korea and the Geopolitics of Development*. Cambridge: Cambridge University Press, 2021.
Green, Michael. "North Korean Regime Crisis: US Perspectives and Responses." *Korean Journal of Defense Analysis* 9, no. 2 (December 1, 1997): 7–25.
Grinker, Richard. *Korea and Its Futures: Unification and the Unfinished War*. New York: St Martin's, 1998.
Guardian. "North Korea 'Panic' After Surprise Currency Revaluation." December 3, 2009, sec. World news. https://www.theguardian.com/world/2009/dec/03/north-korea-won-currency-revaluation.
Ha, Matthew, and David Maxwell. "Kim Jong Un's 'All-Purpose Sword:' North Korean Cyber-Enabled Economic Warfare." Foundation for Defense of Democracies, October 3, 2018. https://www.fdd.org/analysis/2018/10/03/kim-jong-uns-all-purpose-sword/.
Haber, Stephen. "Authoritarian Government." In *The Oxford Handbook of Political Economy*. New York: Oxford University Press, 2006.

Haberman, Clyde. "Bomb Kills 19, Including 6 Key Koreans." *New York Times*, October 10, 1983, sec. World. https://www.nytimes.com/1983/10/10/world/bomb-kills-19-including-6-key-koreans.html.
Haggard, Stephan, and Marcus Noland. *Famine in North Korea: Markets, Aid, and Reform*. New York: Columbia University Press, 2007.
———. "Gender in Transition: The Case of North Korea." *World Development* 41 (January 1, 2013): 51–66.
Han, Sangim, and Yoonyoung Kim. "북한의 금융기관 사이버테러 실태 대응 개선방안 연구" [A Study on Improvement Measures to Protect the Korean Financial Network against Cyber Terrorism by North Korea]. 치안정책연구 [Police Science Institute], 2020.
Hancocks, Paula, and Barbara Starr. "North Korean Missile Test Fails, US and South Korea Say." *CNN*, April 15, 2017. https://www.cnn.com/2017/04/15/asia/north-korea-missile-test/index.html.
Hancocks, Paula, and Ben Westcott. "North Korea Fires Four Ballistic Missiles into Sea of Japan." *CNN*, March 5, 2017. https://www.cnn.com/2017/03/05/asia/north-korea-projectile/index.html.
Harden, Blaine. *Escape from Camp 14: One Man's Remarkable Odyssey from North Korea to Freedom in the West*. New York: Penguin Books, 2012.
Harrison, Selig S. *Korean Endgame: A Strategy for Reunification and U.S. Disengagement*. Princeton, NJ: Princeton University Press, 2003. https://press.princeton.edu/books/paperback/9780691116266/korean-endgame.
———. "Promoting a Soft Landing in Korea." *Foreign Policy*, no. 196 (Spring 1997). https://doi.org/10.2307/1149174.
Hassig, Ralph, and Kongdan Oh. *The Hidden People of North Korea: Everyday Life in the Hermit Kingdom*. Lanham, MD: Rowman & Littlefield, 2015.
Hastings, Justin V. *A Most Enterprising Country: North Korea in the Global Economy*. Ithaca, New York: Cornell University Press, 2016.
Hastings, Justin, Daniel Wertz, and Andrew Yeo. "Market Activities and the Building Blocks of Civil Society in North Korea." National Committee on North Korea, February 2021. https://www.ncnk.org/sites/default/files/issue-briefs/Market_Activities_and_Civil_Society_Building_Blocks_in_North_Korea.pdf.
Hiatt, Fred. "Seoul Links N.Korea to Crash of Airliner." *Washington Post*, December 3, 1987. https://www.washingtonpost.com/archive/politics/1987/12/03/seoul-links-n-korea-to-crash-of-airliner/72a7fa53-6e5c-4749-b921-240f35ad24bd/.
Hong, Soon-young. "Thawing Korea's Cold War: The Path to Peace on the Korean Peninsula." *Foreign Affairs* 78, no. 3 (1999): 8–12.
Hong, Yong-Pyo. *State Security and Regime Security: President Syngman Rhee and the Insecurity Dilemma in South Korea, 1953–60*. New York: St. Martin's Press, 2000.
Horton, Alex. "Why North Korea Threatened Guam, the Tiny U.S. Territory with Big Military Power." *Washington Post*, December 1, 2021. https://www.washingtonpost.com/news/worldviews/wp/2017/08/09/why-north-korea-threatened-guam-the-tiny-u-s-territory-with-big-military-power/.

Hwang, Ye-rang. "Younger N. Korean Defectors View Nuclear Weapons as 'Source of Pride' as Well as Culprit behind Sanctions." *Hankyoreh*, February 27, 2019. https://english.hani.co.kr/arti/english_edition/e_northkorea/883832.html.

Il, Sakong, and Youngsun Koh, eds. *The Korean Economy: Six Decades of Growth and Development*. Seoul: Korea Development Institute, 2010.

Insikt Group. "Crypto Country: North Korea's Targeting of Cryptocurrency." *Recorded Future*, November 30, 2023. https://www.recordedfuture.com/crypto-country-north-koreas-targeting-cryptocurrency.

———. "Shifting Patterns in Internet Use Reveal Adaptable and Innovative North Korean Ruling Elite." *Recorded Future*, October 25, 2018. https://www.recordedfuture.com/north-korea-internet-usage.

Institute for Peace and Unification Studies, Seoul National University. "North Korean Public Perception on Unification 2015."

———. "SNU 2022 Unification Awareness Survey," September 29, 2022. https://ipus.snu.ac.kr/blog/archives/conference/6744.

———. "북한이탈주민 조사사업 10년 분석 결과발표회" [Ten-year analysis result presentation of North Korean Defectors Investigation Project], May 3, 2022. https://ipus.snu.ac.kr/blog/archives/conference/6178.

International Institute for Sustainable Development. "Summary of the Fifth Ministerial Conference on Environment and Development in Asia and the Pacific: 23–29 March 2005." *MCED 2005 Bulletin* 106, no. 1 (April 1, 2005). http://enb.iisd.org/download/pdf/sd/sdvol106num1e.pdf.

International Telecommunication Union. "Measuring the Information Society Report 2017: Volume 1." 2017. https://www.itu.int/en/ITU-D/Statistics/Documents/publications/misr2017/MISR2017_Volume1.pdf.

Jager, Sheila Miyoshi. *Brothers at War: The Unending Conflict in Korea*. New York: Norton, 2013.

Jang, Seulkee. "North Korea Has 24 COVID-19 Quarantine Facilities for the Military." *Daily NK*, December 4, 2020. https://www.dailynk.com/english/north-korea-24-covid-19-quarantine-facilities-military/.

Jervis, Robert. "Cooperation Under the Security Dilemma." *World Politics* 30, no. 2 (1978): 167–214.

Jones, David. "Biden Administration's FY 2023 Budget Includes 11% Increase for Cyber." Cybersecurity Dive, March 30, 2022. https://www.cybersecuritydive.com/news/biden-2023-budget-cybersecurity/621264/.

Joo, Hyung-min. "Visualizing the Invisible Hands: The Shadow Economy in North Korea." *Economy and Society* 39, no. 1 (February 1, 2010): 110–45.

Jun, Jenny, Scott LaFoy, and Ethan Sohn. *North Korea's Cyber Operations: Strategy and Responses*. Washington, DC: Center for Strategic & International Studies and Rowman & Littlefield, 2015.

Jung, Won-Gi. "U.S. Should Address North Korea's 'Legitimate Concerns,' Chinese FM Says." *NK News*, July 5, 2021. https://www.nknews.org/2021/07/u-s-should-address-north-koreas-legitimate-concerns-chinese-fm-says/.

Jwa, Sung-Hee, Chung-in Moon, and Jeong-Ho Roh, eds. *Constitutional Handbook on Korean Unification*. Vol. 1. Seoul: Korea Economic Research Institute, 2002.

Kagubare, Ines. "North Korea's Increasing Use of Crypto Heists to Fund Nukes Worries US." *Hill*, August 9, 2022. https://thehill.com/policy/technology/3590126-north-koreas-increasing-use-of-crypto-heists-to-fund-nukes-worries-us/.

Kang, Chol-hwan, and Pierre Rigoulot. *The Aquariums of Pyongyang: Ten Years in the North Korean Gulag*. New York: Basic Books, 2001.

Kang, David C. *Crony Capitalism: Corruption and Development in South Korea and the Philippines*. Cambridge: Cambridge University Press, 2002.

———. "Preventive War and North Korea." *Security Studies* 4, no. 2 (June 30, 1994): 330–64.

Kaonga, Gerrard. "Late Night Hosts Turn on Joe Biden, Relentlessly Mock President." *Newsweek*, July 28, 2022. https://www.newsweek.com/joe-biden-mocked-president-late-night-host-jimmy-fallon-stephen-colbert-blunder-1728670.

Kaplan, Robert D. "When North Korea Falls." *Atlantic Monthly*, October 2006. http://www.theatlantic.com/magazine/archive/2006/10/when-north-korea-falls/305228/.

Kaspersky. "What Is WannaCry Ransomware?" July 6, 2023. https://usa.kaspersky.com/resource-center/threats/ransomware-wannacry.

KBS 남북교류협력단KBS [Organization for South-North Exchange and Cooperation]. "2020년 국민 통일의식 조사" [Survey of South Korean people's perception of national unification 2020]. Seoul: KBS, October 28, 2020. https://office.kbs.co.kr/tongil/wp-content/uploads/sites/11/2020/11/%EC%9B%B9%EC%9A%A92020-%EA%B5%AD%EB%AF%BC-%ED%86%B5%EC%9D%BC%EC%9D%98%EC%8B%9D-%EC%A1%B0%EC%82%AC.pdf.

KCNA. "Army-People Celebration Rallies Held in Cities, Counties." December 9, 2017. https://kcnawatch.org/newstream/.

KCNA Watch. "Kim Jong Un Inspects KPA Strategic Force Command." August 15, 2017. https://kcnawatch.org/newstream/.

Kim, Bum-soo, Byung-ro Kim, Hak-jae Kim, Hee-jung Kim, Won-ho Park, Jong-min Lee, Gyu-bin Choi, Kyung-hoon Lim, and Hyun-jung Choi. "2020 통일의식조사" [2020 Unification Awareness Survey]. Siheung, South Korea: Institute for Peace and Unification Studies, Seoul National University, February 28, 2021. https://ipus.snu.ac.kr/wp-content/uploads/2021/08/2020_%ED%86%B5%EC%9D%BC%EC%9D%98%EC%8B%9D%EC%A1%B0%EC%82%AC_pdf.pdf.

Kim, Byeong-ro, Dong-joon Jung, Geun-sik Jung, Kyung-hyo Chun, Gyu-bin Choi, and Chang-hyun Hwang. "북한주민 통일의식 2016" [North Korean public perception on unification 2016]. Seoul: Institute for Peace and Unification Studies, Seoul National University, March 15, 2017. https://ipus.snu.ac.kr/wp-content/uploads/2020/05/2016-%EB%B6%81%ED%95%9C%EC%A3%BC%EB%AF%BC%ED%86%B5%EC%9D%BC%EC%9D%98%EC%8B%9D-%EB%82%B4%EC%A7%80%EC%B5%9C%EC%A2%85.pdf.

Kim, Byung-Kook, and Ezra F. Vogel, eds. *The Park Chung Hee Era: The Transformation of South Korea*. Cambridge, MA: Harvard University Press, 2011.

Kim, Byung-Yeon. *Unveiling the North Korean Economy: Collapse and Transition*. Cambridge: Cambridge University Press, 2017.

Kim, Cae-One. "A Proposal for Inter-Korean Economic Integration and Reunification: With Special Reference to the German Case." *Journal of East Asian Affairs* 5, no. 2 (1991): 350–72.

Kim, Choong-Nam. "The Uncertain Future of North Korea: Soft Landing or Crash Landing?" *Korea and World Affairs* 20, no. 4 (Winter 1996).

Kim, Dae-jung. *Kim Dae-Jung's Three-Stage Approach to Korean Reunification: Focusing on the South-North Confederal Stage*, trans. T. C. Rhee. Los Angeles: Center for Multiethnic and Transnational Studies, 1997.

Kim, Gyu-ryun, Byung-duk Hwang, Kyung-suk Kim, In-whi Park, Byung-in Bae, Donghui Lee, Sang-jun Lee, Hye-won Jeon, Woo-jae Ju, and Sun-jik Hong. "통일 비용 편익 연구의 새로운 접근 포괄적 연구 요소의 도입과 대안의 모색" [A new approach to research on cost and benefit of unification: Introduction of comprehensive research elements and search for alternatives]. Seoul: Korea Institute for National Unification, December 2011. https://www.kinu.or.kr/pyxis-api/1/digital-files/f666280e-d67c-4266-87b2-c9e13a8d89e5.

Kim, Hak-jae, Chae-yeon Kang, Bum-soo Kim, Byung-ro Kim, Hee-jung Kim, Sungwoo Lee, Gyu-bin Choi, Kyung-hoon Lim, and Yong-shin Cho. "2019 통일의식조사" [2019 Unification Awareness Survey]. Seoul: Institute for Peace and Unification Studies, 2019. https://ipus.snu.ac.kr/wp-content/uploads/2020/04/2019-%ED%86%B5%EC%9D%BC%EC%9D%98%EC%8B%9D%EC%A1%B0%EC%82%AC_%EC%B5%9C%EC%A2%85%EC%9B%B9%EC%9A%A9.pdf.

Kim, Hakjoon. "The American Military Government in South Korea, 1945–1948: Its Formation, Policies, and Legacies." *Asian Perspective* 12, no. 1 (1988): 51–83.

———. *The Unification Policy of South and North Korea: A Comparative Study*. Seoul: Seoul National University Press, 1992.

Kim, Hak-soon, and Choong-sik Song. "脫정치·脫 이념·脫 패권의 統一모델 만들자" [Let's make a model for unification that is not politicized, idealized, or hegemonic]. *Kyunghyang Shinmun*, August 1, 1990. https://newslibrary.naver.com/viewer/index.nhn?articleId=1990080100329226001&editNo=3&printCount=1&publishDate=1990-08-01&officeId=00032&pageNo=26&printNo=13800&publishType=00020.

Kim, Hyung-A., and Clark W. Sorensen, eds. *Reassessing the Park Chung Hee Era, 1961–1979: Development, Political Thought, Democracy, and Cultural Influence*. Seattle: Center for Korea Studies Publications, 2011.

Kim, Hyung-Jin, and Tong-Hyung Kim. "S. Korea Spy Agency: N. Korea Hackers Targeted Vaccine Tech." *AP News*, February 16, 2021. https://apnews.com/article/south-korea-north-korea-coronavirus-pandemic-coronavirus-vaccine-fbf9b24356946833661a8018e0524b7b.

Kim, J. James, Chung-gu Kang, and Geonhui Ham. "한국인의 외교안보 인식: 2010~2020년 아산연례조사 결과" [South Koreans' perception of foreign policy and security: Results of annual Asan surveys, 2010–2020]. Asan Institute for Policy Studies, September 13, 2021. http://www.asaninst.org/contents/%ED%95%9C%EA%B5%AD%EC%9D%B8

%EC%9D%98-%EC%99%B8%EA%B5%90%EC%95%88%EB%B3%B4
-%EC%9D%B8%EC%8B%9D-20102020%EB%85%84-%EC%95%84%EC%82%B0%
EC%97%B0%EB%A1%80%EC%A1%B0%EC%82%AC-%EA%B2%B0%EA%B3%BC/.

Kim, James. "Team Spirit' Joint U.S.-South Korea Exercise Called Off." UPI, January 7, 1992. https://www.upi.com/Archives/1992/01/07/Team-Spirit-joint-US-South-Korea-exercise-called-off/5381694760400/.

Kim, Jeongmin. "COVAX Offers 4.7 Million More COVID-19 Vaccine Doses to North Korea." *NK News*, November 30, 2021. https://www.nknews.org/2021/11/covax-offers-4-7-million-more-covid-19-vaccine-doses-to-north-korea/.

Kim, Jiyoon, Karl Friedhoff, Chungku Kang, and Euicheol Lee. "South Korean Attitudes Toward North Korea and Reunification." Seoul: Asan Institute, 2014. http://en.asaninst.org/contents/south-korean-attitudes-toward-north-korea-and-reunification/.

———. "South Korean Attitudes Toward North Korea and Reunification." Seoul: Asan Institute for Policy Studies, February 2015. https://en.asaninst.org/contents/south-korean-attitudes-toward-north-korea-and-reunification/.

"Kim Jong Il's North Korea: Its Limitations and Prospects." *Korea and World Affairs* 18, no. 3 (Fall 1994): 421–42.

Kim, Joseph. *Under The Same Sky: From Starvation in North Korea to Salvation in America*. New York: Mariner Books, 2015.

Kim, Kyung-Won. "No Way out: North Korea's Impending Collapse." *Harvard International Review* 18, no. 2 (March 22, 1996). https://go.gale.com/ps/i.do?p=AONE&sw=w&issn=07391854&v=2.1&it=r&id=GALE%7CA30006339&sid=googleScholar&linkaccess=abs.

Kim, Min-seok. "The State of the North Korean Military—Korea Net Assessment 2020: Politicized Security and Unchanging Strategic Realities." Carnegie Endowment for International Peace, March 18, 2020. https://carnegieendowment.org/2020/03/18/state-of-north-korean-military-pub-81232.

———. "북, 암호화폐 해킹 . . . 국내 거래소서 수백억대 탈취" [North Korea hacks cryptocurrency . . . seizes several hundred billions from domestic exchange]. *JoongAng Ilbo*, February 6, 2018.

Kim, Nan. "Korea on the Brink: Reading the Yŏnp'yŏng Shelling and Its Aftermath." *Journal of Asian Studies* 70, no. 2 (May 2011): 337–56.

Kim, Samuel S. "Korea's Segyehwa Drive." In *Korea's Globalization*, ed. Samuel S. Kim. Cambridge: Cambridge University Press, 2000.

———. "North Korea and the United Nations." *International Journal of Korean Studies* 1, no. 1 (Spring 1997).

———. "North Korea in 2000: Surviving Through High Hopes of Summit Diplomacy." *Asian Survey* 41, no. 1 (2001): 12–29.

———. "North Korean Foreign Relations in the Post-Cold War World." Strategic Studies Institute, April 2007.

———. *The Two Koreas and the Great Powers*. Cambridge: Cambridge University Press, 2006. https://doi.org/10.1017/CBO9780511510496.

Kim, Sea Young, and Leif-Eric Easley. "The Neglected North Korean Crisis: Women's Rights." *Ethics & International Affairs* 35, no. 1 (January 2021): 19–29.

Kim, Soo-Am, Wha Soon Kim, Tae Eun Min, and Junhwa Park. "Study on North Korean Defectors' Perception About Democracy and the Market Economy." Seoul: Korea Institute for National Unification, August 2017. https://www.kinu.or.kr/pyxis-api/1/digital-files/86b3557f-afe6-4715-8b2e-44e91da83386.

Kim, Suk-Jin, and Moon-Soo Yang. *The Growth of the Informal Economy in North Korea*. Seoul: Korea Institute for National Unification, 2015.

Kim, Sung Kyung. "North Korean Women as New Economic Agents." Institute for Security & Development Policy, October 21, 2020. https://isdp.eu/content/uploads/2020/10/North-Korean-Women-as-New-Economic-Agents-IB-21.10.20.pdf.

Kim, Tae-Kyu. "軍기밀 털린 곳은 국방데이터센터 . . . 육·해·공군 정보의 '심장'" [Defense Data Center is where military secrets were stolen . . . the 'heart' of army, navy, and air force information]. *JoongAng Ilbo*, December 7, 2016.

Kim, Yonho. "Cell Phones in North Korea: Has North Korea Entered the Telecommunications Revolution?" U.S. Korea Institute at SAIS, 2014. https://38north.org/wp-content/uploads/2014/03/Kim-Yonho-Cell-Phones-in-North-Korea.pdf.

Kim, Youcheer. "The Strategic Background Behind the ROK-US Joint Military Exercises and Their Impact on Inter-Korean Relations." Online Series CO 20–19. Korea Institute for National Unification, August 18, 2020. https://repo.kinu.or.kr/bitstream/2015.oak/11761/1/CO20-19%28e%29.pdf.

Kim, Young-jin. "NK Leadership Succession Should Be Used for Policy Change." *Korea Times*, May 14, 2010, sec. National. https://www.koreatimes.co.kr/www/nation/2023/08/113_65914.html.

Kleine-Ahlbrandt, Stephanie. "North Korea's Illicit Cyber Operations: What Can Be Done?" 38 North, February 28, 2020. https://www.38north.org/2020/02/skleineahlbrandt022820/.

Klimas, Jacqueline. "Why North Korea Is a Black Hole for American Spies." *Politico*, September 8, 2017. https://www.politico.com/story/2017/09/08/why-north-korea-is-a-black-hole-for-spies-242473.

Klingner, Bruce. "North Korean Cyberattacks: A Dangerous and Evolving Threat." Heritage Foundation, n.d. https://www.heritage.org/asia/report/north-korean-cyberattacks-dangerous-and-evolving-threat.

Ko, Leekyung. "North Korea as a Geopolitical and Cyber Actor: A Timeline of Events." *New America* (blog), June 6, 2018. http://newamerica.org/cybersecurity-initiative/c2b/c2b-log/north-korea-geopolitical-cyber-incidents-timeline/.

Koh, Byung Chul. *Foreign Policy Systems of North and South Korea*. Berkeley: University of California Press, 1984.

——. "North Korea: A Breakthrough in the Quest for Unity." *Asian Survey* 13, no. 1 (1973): 83–93.

Kopeytsev, Vyacheslav, and Seongsu Park. "Lazarus Targets Defense Industry with ThreatNeedle." Secure List by Kaspersky, February 25, 2021. https://securelist.com/lazarus-threatneedle/100803/.

Korea Development Institute. "A Gradual Approach Toward North and South Korean Economic Integration." KDI Working Paper No. 9311. Korea Development Institute, 1993. https://www.kdi.re.kr/eng/research/reportView?pub_no=921.

Korea Institute for National Unification. "Korean Unification and a New East Asian Order." Seoul, December 2012. https://repo.kinu.or.kr/bitstream/2015.oak/2121/1/0001453732.pdf.

Korea JoongAng Daily. "Unification May Be Jackpot: Park." January 6, 2014. https://koreajoongangdaily.joins.com/2014/01/06/politics/Unification-may-be-jackpot-Park/2983129.html.

KOSIS. "Gross Domestic Product (Nominal, in Dollars, USD)." https://kosis.kr/statHtml/statHtml.do?orgId=&tblId=DT_111Y002&conn_path=I3

Kremez, Vitali, Joshua Platt, and Jason Reaves. "Anchor Project | The Deadly Planeswalker: How the TrickBot Group United High-Tech Crimeware & APT." SentinelLABS, December 10, 2019. https://www.sentinelone.com/labs/anchor-project-the-deadly-planeswalker-how-the-trickbot-group-united-high-tech-crimeware-apt/.

Kretchun, Nat, and Jane Kim. "A Quiet Opening: North Koreans in a Changing Media Environment." *InterMedia*, May 2012. https://www.gwern.net/docs/technology/2012-kretchun.pdf.

Kretchun, Nat, Catherine Lee, and Seamus Tuohy. "Compromising Connectivity: Information Dynamics Between the State and Society in a Digitizing North Korea." *InterMedia*, February 1, 2017. https://seamustuohy.com/files/Compromising-Connectivity-Final-Report.pdf.

Kristof, Nicholas D. "Chinese and South Koreans Formally Establish Relations." *New York Times*, August 24, 1992, sec. World. https://www.nytimes.com/1992/08/24/world/chinese-and-south-koreans-formally-establish-relations.html.

Kwack, Sung Yeung, ed. *The Korean Economy at a Crossroad: Development Prospects, Liberalization, and South-North Economic Integration*. Westport, CT: Praeger, 1994.

Kwak, Tae-Hwan, and Seung-Ho Joo. "The Future of the Korean Peninsula: Unification and Security Options for the 21st Century." *Asian Perspective* 23, no. 2 (1999): 163–96.

Kwon, Goohoon. "Experiences with Monetary Integration and Lessons for Korean Unification." IMF Working Papers 65. International Monetary Fund, May 1997. https://www.imf.org/en/Publications/WP/Issues/2016/12/30/Experiences-with-Monetary-Integration-and-Lessons-for-Korean-Unification-2228.

Kyunghyang Shinmun. "내년 選擧日程 조정검토" [Review of next year's election schedule adjustment]. October 11, 1991. https://newslibrary.naver.com/viewer/index.nhn?articleId=1991101100329101001&editNo=15&printCount=1&publishDate=1991-10-11&officeId=00032&pageNo=1&printNo=14195&publishType=00010.

Lankov, Andrei. "North Korea's Choice: Collapse or Reform." *Foreign Affairs*, December 19, 2011. https://www.foreignaffairs.com/articles/asia/2011-12-19/north-koreas-choice-collapse-or-reform.

Lankov, Andrei, and SeokHyang Kim. "Useless Men, Entrepreneurial Women, and North Korea's Post-Socialism: Transformation of Gender Roles Since the Early 1990s." *Asian Journal of Women's Studies* 20, no. 2 (January 1, 2014): 68–96.

Lankov, Andrei, Peter Ward, Ho-yeol Yoo, and Ji-young Kim. "North Korea's New Capitalists and Their Workers: Business Practice and Labor Relations." *Communist and Post-Communist Studies* 50, no. 3 (2017): 157–67.

Larsen, Morten Soendergaard. "While North Korean Missiles Sit in Storage, Their Hackers Go Rampant." *Foreign Policy*, March 15, 2021. https://foreignpolicy.com/2021/03/15/north-korea-missiles-cyberattack-hacker-armies-crime/.

Lederer, Edith M. "UN Report: North Korea Cyber Experts Raised up to $2 Billion." *AP News*, August 6, 2019. https://apnews.com/article/2895639125bd49da9f215f2feb0b58a3.

Lee, Chae-Jin. "South Korea: The Politics of Domestic-Foreign Linkage." *Asian Survey* 13, no. 1 (1973): 94–101.

Lee, Chung Min, and Kathryn Botto. "Reconceptualizing U.S.-ROK Cooperation in Korean Unification: A Stabilization Framework." *Unification Blue Book 2019*. Washington, DC: Carnegie Endowment for International Peace, 2019. https://carnegieendowment.org/2019/04/30/reconceptualizing-u.s.-rok-cooperation-in-korean-unification-stabilization-framework-pub-78737.

Lee, Hyeonseo. *The Girl with Seven Names: Escape from North Korea*. London: William Collins, 2016.

Lee, Jae Bong, Theodore L. Becker, Johan Galtung, Glenn D. Paige, Dae Sook Suh, and Oran R. Young. *Korean Reunification: Alternative Pathways*, ed. Michael Haas. New York: Praeger, 1989.

Lee, Jae Hyun, and Wook Kim. "University Students' Perception on Unification and the Implications for Unification Education in Korean Universities." *Korean Unification Studies* 24, no. 1 (2015).

Lee, Janice, and Benjamin Katzeff Silberstein. "North Korean Women: Markets and Power." 38 North, March 18, 2011. https://www.38north.org/2011/03/north-korean-women/.

Lee, Je Son. "Ask a North Korean: Do You Hate Americans?" *Guardian*, November 4, 2015, sec. World news. https://www.theguardian.com/world/2015/nov/04/ask-a-north-korean-do-you-hate-americans.

———. "Ask a North Korean: What Do You Think About Nuclear Weapons?" *Guardian*, October 23, 2015, sec. World news. https://www.theguardian.com/world/2015/oct/23/ask-a-north-korean-nuclear-weapons.

Lee, Je-hun. "[News Analysis] North Korea's 'Marketized Economy' Already at an Irreversible Stage." *Hankyoreh*, February 5, 2019. https://english.hani.co.kr/arti/english_edition/e_northkorea/881048.html.

Lee, Ji-Young. "Is Reunification Possible for North and South Korea?" *Conversation*, January 24, 2018. https://theconversation.com/is-a-unified-korea-possible-90071.

Lee, Keun. "The Road to the Market in North Korea: Projects, Problems and Prospects." WIDER Working Paper Series, No. 139. United Nations University World

Institute for Development Economics Research, August 1997. https://www.wider.unu.edu/sites/default/files/WP139.pdf.

Lee, Kyu-chang, Sookyung Kim, Ji Sun Yee, Eun Mee Jeong, and Yejoon Rim. "White Paper on Human Rights in North Korea 2020." Seoul: Korea Institute for National Unification, September 2020. https://www.kinu.or.kr/www/jsp/prg/api/dlVE.jsp?menuIdx=648&category=74&thisPage=1&searchField=&searchText=&biblioId=153844.

Lee, Michelle Ye Hee. "North Korea's Latest Nuclear Test Was So Powerful It Reshaped the Mountain Above It." *Washington Post*, December 1, 2021. https://www.washingtonpost.com/news/worldviews/wp/2017/09/14/orth-koreas-latest-nuclear-test-was-so-powerful-it-reshaped-the-mountain-above-it/.

Lee, Ming. "Seoul's Searching for 'Nordpolitik:' Evolution and Perspective." *Asian Perspective* 13, no. 2 (1989): 141–78.

Lee, Sang Sin, Tae-eun Min, Kwang-il Yoon, and Bon-sang Koo. "KINU Unification Survey 2021." Seoul: Korea Institute for National Unification, July 2021. https://www.kinu.or.kr/pyxis-api/1/digital-files/87cb5812-a81a-4fdc-824c-8d359544e8f7.

Lee, Sang-sin, Tae-eun Min, Gwang-il Yun, and Pon-sang Ku. "통일·북한 인식의 새로운 접근" [KINU Unification Perception Survey 2021: A new approach to the perception of unification and North Korea]. Seoul: Korea Institute for National Unification, December 30, 2021. https://www.kinu.or.kr/pyxis-api/1/digital-files/886042b7-4f1c-4d5e-b7f6-71a4005a39a1.

Lee, Sung-yoon. "North Korea's Revolutionary Unification Policy." *International Journal of Korean Studies* 18, no. 2 (Fall 2014): 121–37.

Lee, Taehoon, and Ben Westcott. "Failed North Korean Missile Exploded 'Within Seconds,' US Says." CNN, March 22, 2017. https://www.cnn.com/2017/03/21/asia/north-korea-missile-test/.

Lendon, Brad, and Taehoon Lee. "North Korea Says It Can Make New Bomb in Volume." CNN, September 2, 2017. https://www.cnn.com/2017/09/02/asia/north-korea-kim-jong-un-nuke-lab-visit/index.html.

Levin, Norman D., and Yong-Sup Han. "The Shape of Korea's Future: South Korean Attitudes Toward Unification and Long-Term Security Issues." RAND Corporation, January 1, 1999. https://www.rand.org/pubs/monograph_reports/MR1092.html.

Lewis, Jeffrey. "Opinion | It's Time to Accept That North Korea Has Nuclear Weapons." *New York Times*, October 13, 2022, sec. Opinion. https://www.nytimes.com/2022/10/13/opinion/international-world/north-korea-us-nuclear.html.

Lim, Andy, and Victor Cha. "Dataset: China-North Korea High Level Visits Since 1953." Beyond Parallel, March 17, 2017. https://beyondparallel.csis.org/china-dprk-high-level-visits-since-1953/.

Lim, Il, and Adam Zulawnik. *Interviews with North Korean Defectors: From Kim Shin-Jo to Thae Yong-Ho*. London: Routledge, 2021.

Liu, Li-gang, Marcus Noland, and Sherman Robinson. "The Costs and Benefits of Korean Unification." Working Papers 98-1. Peterson Institute for International

Economics, January 1998. https://www.piie.com/publications/working-papers/costs-and-benefits-korean-unification.

Maass, Peter. "S. Korea Accuses North after Agent's Confession." *Washington Post*, January 16, 1988. https://www.washingtonpost.com/archive/politics/1988/01/16/s-korea-accuses-north-after-agents-confession/6ce8cf57-38b0-49a8-a585-c9a087985fb9/.

Maeil Business Newspaper. "北韓 흡수통일해야" [North Korea should be unified by absorption]. July 17, 1992. https://newslibrary.naver.com/viewer/index.nhn?articleId=1992071700099202004&editNo=2&printCount=1&publishDate=1992-07-17&officeId=00009&pageNo=2&printNo=8159&publishType=00020.

Manning, Robert A. "The Asian Paradox: Toward a New Architecture." *World Policy Journal* 10, no. 3 (1993): 55–64.

Martin, Bradley K. *Under the Loving Care of the Fatherly Leader: North Korea and the Kim Dynasty*. New York: Thomas Dunne Books, 2004.

Martin, Timothy W. "Kim Jong Un's Sister Blasts U.S.'s 'Dangerous War Exercises,' Threatens to Bolster Military." *Wall Street Journal*, August 10, 2021, sec. World. https://www.wsj.com/articles/kim-jong-uns-sister-vows-to-boost-deterrence-after-being-ignored-by-u-s-11628579896.

Maxwell, David. "Should The United States Support Korean Unification And If So, How?" *International Journal of Korean Studies* 18, no. 1 (2014): 139–56.

McEachern, Patrick. *Inside the Red Box: North Korea's Post-Totalitarian Politics*. New York: Columbia University Press, 2010.

Meer, Sico van der. "Provoking to Avoid War: North Korea's Hybrid Security Strategies." E-International Relations, May 22, 2021. https://www.e-ir.info/2021/05/22/provoking-to-avoid-war-north-koreas-hybrid-security-strategies/.

Mesquita, Bruce Bueno de, James D. Morrow, Randolph M. Siverson, and Alastair Smith. "An Institutional Explanation of the Democratic Peace." *American Political Science Review* 93, no. 4 (1999): 791–807.

Miliard, Mike. "North Korea Tried to Hack Pfizer Vaccine Data, Reports Say." *Healthcare IT News*, February 16, 2021. https://www.healthcareitnews.com/news/asia/north-korea-tried-hack-pfizer-vaccine-data-reports-say.

Miller, Steve. "Will Canceling Joint Exercises Move N. Korea Closer toward Denuclearization?" *VOA*, October 24, 2018. https://www.voanews.com/a/ending-joint-military-exercises/4626923.html.

———. "With Military Exercises Canceled in S. Korea, Experts Express Concern About Impact." *VOA*, March 4, 2019. https://www.voanews.com/a/us-south-korean-military/4812091.html.

Ministry of Economy and Finance, Republic of Korea. "The Korean New Deal: National Strategy for a Great Transformation." July 2020. https://english.moef.go.kr/skin/doc.html?fn=Korean%20New%20Deal.pdf&rs=/result/upload/mini/2020/07/.

Ministry of Foreign Affairs, Republic of Korea. "Audacious Initiative," August 15, 2022. https://www.mofa.go.kr/eng/wpge/m_25501/contents.do.

———. "Joint Declaration on the Denuclearization of the Korean Peninsula." January 20, 1992. https://www.mofa.go.kr/eng/brd/m_5476/view.do?seq=305870&srchFr=&srchTo=&srchWord=&srchTp=&multi_itm_seq=0&itm_seq_1=0&itm_seq_2=0&company_cd=&company_nm=&page=6&titleNm=.

———. "ROK-UN Relations," n.d. https://www.mofa.go.kr/eng/wpge/m_5460/contents.do.

Ministry of Unification, Republic of Korea. "Number of North Korean Defectors Entering South Korea," n.d. https://www.unikorea.go.kr/eng_unikorea/relations/statistics/defectors/.

———. "화해협력정책" [Sunshine policy], n.d. https://nkinfo.unikorea.go.kr/nkp/term/viewKnwldgDicary.do?pageIndex=1&dicaryId=233&koreanChrctr=.

———. "2014 White Paper on Korean Unification." Seoul: Ministry of Unification of the Republic of Korea, 2014. https://www.unikorea.go.kr/eng_unikorea/news/Publications/whitepaper/.

Montalbano, Elizabeth. "North Korea Targets Security Researchers in Elaborate 0-Day Campaign." Threatpost, January 26, 2021. https://threatpost.com/north-korea-security-researchers-0-day/163333/.

Moon, Chung-in. *The Sunshine Policy: In Defense of Engagement as a Path to Peace in Korea*. Seoul: Yonsei University Press, 2012.

Moon, Chung-in, and David I. Steinberg, eds. *Kim Dae-Jung Government and Sunshine Policy: Promises and Challenges*. Seoul: Yonsei University Press, 1999.

Moon, Hui-Chul. "北, 원자력연구원 해킹? 해커 흔적서 나온 '문정인 E메일' 단서" [North Korea hacks Atomic Energy Research Institute? "Moon Jung-In e-mail" clue left from traces of the hacker]. *JoongAng Ilbo*, June 18, 2021.

Moon, Jae-in. "Address at the Korber Foundation in Berlin, Germany." July 6, 2017.

———. "Address by President Moon Jae-in at May Day Stadium in Pyeongyang, North Korea." September 20, 2018.

Morello, Carol. "North Korea's Top Diplomat Says Strike Against U.S. Mainland Is 'Inevitable.'" *Washington Post*, April 8, 2023. https://www.washingtonpost.com/world/national-security/north-koreas-top-diplomat-says-strike-against-us-mainland-is-inevitable/2017/09/23/c3bcb108-dd8f-4761-b55f-92044348f179_story.html.

Mouly, Françoise, and Mina Kaneko. "Cover Story: Kim Jong-Un's Big Announcement." *New Yorker*, January 8, 2016. https://www.newyorker.com/culture/culture-desk/cover-story-anita-kunz-2016-01-18.

Myers, Steven Lee, and Sang-Hun Choe. "North Koreans Agree to Freeze Nuclear Work; U.S. to Give Aid." *New York Times*, February 29, 2012, sec. World. https://www.nytimes.com/2012/03/01/world/asia/us-says-north-korea-agrees-to-curb-nuclear-work.html.

Nam, Koon Woo. "North-South Korean Relations: From Dialogue to Confrontation." *Pacific Affairs* 48, no. 4 (1975): 477–99.

National Archives of Korea. "7.4 남북공동성명전문" [Full text of the July 4 North-South Joint Communiqué], n.d. https://theme.archives.go.kr/next/unikorea/seven/seven04.do.

National Assembly Budget Office. "Economic Effects of Korean Unification." Seoul: National Assembly Budget Office, 2014.

National Bureau of Asian Research. "The Fourth U.S.-ROK Dialogue on Unification and Regional Security: Assessing North Korean Stability and Preparing for Unification," n.d. https://www.nbr.org/wp-content/uploads/pdfs/programs/assessing_north_korean_stability_and_preparing_for_unification.pdf.

National Infrastructure Advisory Council. "Actionable Cyber Intelligence: An Executive-Led Collaborative Model." December 2020. https://www.cisa.gov/sites/default/files/publications/NIAC%20Actionable%20Cyber%20Intelligence_FINAL_508_0.pdf.

———. "Securing Cyber Assets: Addressing Urgent Cyber Threats to Critical Infrastructure." September 2017.

National Security Archive, George Washington University. "Exploring the Implications of Alternative North Korean Endgames: Results for a Discussion Panel on Continuing Coexistence Between North and South Korea." January 21, 1998. https://nsarchive.gwu.edu/document/18238-national-security-archive-doc-19-cia.

National Unification Board. "A White Paper on South-North Dialogue in Korea." Seoul: National Unification Board, December 31, 1988.

Natsios, Andrew S. *The Great North Korean Famine*. Washington, DC: United States Institute of Peace Press, 2001.

New York Times. "Full Text of Kim Jong-Un's Response to President Trump." September 22, 2017, sec. World. https://www.nytimes.com/2017/09/22/world/asia/kim-jong-un-trump.html.

———. "North Korean Enigma; Kim Il Sung." July 12, 1961, sec. Archives. https://www.nytimes.com/1961/07/12/archives/north-korean-enigma-kim-il-sung.html.

Ng, Felix. " 'Nobody Is Holding Them Back'—North Korean Cyber-Attack Threat Rises." *Cointelegraph*, July 12, 2022. https://cointelegraph.com/news/nobody-is-holding-them-back-north-korean-cyber-attack-threat-rises.

Nichols, Michelle. "North Korea Says Linking Cyber Attacks to Pyongyang Is 'Ridiculous.' " Reuters, May 19, 2017, sec. Technology News. https://www.reuters.com/article/us-cyber-attack-northkorea-idUSKCN18F1X3.

———. "U.S. Pushes U.N. to Cut N.Korea Oil Imports, Ban Tobacco, Blacklist Lazarus Hackers." Reuters, April 13, 2022, sec. World. https://www.reuters.com/world/us-pushes-un-cut-nkorea-oil-imports-ban-tobacco-blacklist-lazarus-hackers-2022-04-13/.

NK PRO. "Coronavirus in North Korea: COVID-19 Tracker." n.d. https://www.nknews.org/pro/coronavirus-in-north-korea-tracker/.

Noland, Marcus. *Avoiding the Apocalypse: The Future of the Two Koreas*. New York: Columbia University Press, 2000.

———. "Currency Reform Unsettles North Korea." *BBC News*, February 5, 2010. http://news.bbc.co.uk/2/hi/8500017.stm.

———. "Why North Korea Will Muddle Through." *Foreign Affairs*, August 1997. https://www.foreignaffairs.com/articles/asia/1997-07-01/why-north-korea-will-muddle-through.

Noland, Marcus, Sherman Robinson, and Li-gang Liu. "The Costs and Benefits of Korean Unification: Alternate Scenarios." *Asian Survey* 38, no. 8 (1998): 801–14.

Nussbaum, Matthew, Bryan Bender, and Brent D. Griffiths. "Mattis Warns of 'Massive Military Response' If North Korea Threatens Attack." *Politico*, September 3, 2017. https://www.politico.com/story/2017/09/03/trump-north-korea-nuclear-242289.

Nwobodo, Christian. "North Korean Lazarus Group Targets Japanese Crypto Firms." *CryptoSlate* (blog), October 17, 2022. https://cryptoslate.com/north-korean-lazarus-group-targets-japanese-crypto-firms/.

Oberdorfer, Don, and Robert Carlin. *The Two Koreas: A Contemporary History*. 3rd ed. New York: Basic Books, 2014.

OECD. "OECD Development Assistance Committee (DAC) Welcomes Korean Membership." November 25, 2009. https://www.oecd.org/dac/oecddevelopmentassistancecommitteedacwelcomeskoreanmembership.htm.

Ogrysko, Nicole. "OPM Details Core Values Behind Coming Security Clearance Reforms with New Policy Doctrine." *Federal News Network*, January 13, 2021. https://federalnewsnetwork.com/workforce/2021/01/opm-details-core-values-behind-coming-security-clearance-reforms-with-new-policy-doctrine/.

Oh, Bonnie B.C. *Korea Under the American Military Government, 1945–1948*. Westport, CT: Praeger, 2002.

Oh, Kongdan, and Ralph Hassig. "North Korea Between Collapse and Reform." *Asian Survey* 39, no. 2 (1999): 287–309.

———. *North Korea Through the Looking Glass*. Washington, DC: Brookings Institution Press, 2000.

Oh, Myoung-don. "The Korean Middle East Respiratory Syndrome Coronavirus Outbreak and Our Responsibility to the Global Scientific Community." *Infection & Chemotherapy* 48, no. 2 (June 1, 2016): 145–46.

Oh, Myoung-don, Wan Beom Park, Sang-Won Park, Pyoeng Gyun Choe, Ji Hwan Bang, Kyoung-Ho Song, Eu Suk Kim, Hong Bin Kim, and Nam Joong Kim. "Middle East Respiratory Syndrome: What We Learned from the 2015 Outbreak in the Republic of Korea." *Korean Journal of Internal Medicine* 33, no. 2 (March 2018): 233–46.

Olsen, Henry. "Opinion | Trump Has Given North Korea a Valuable Bargaining Chip for Free." *Washington Post*, March 5, 2019. https://www.washingtonpost.com/opinions/2019/03/05/trump-has-given-north-korea-valuable-bargaining-chip-free/.

Onishi, Norimitsu. "South Brings Capitalism, Well Isolated, to North Korea." *New York Times*, July 18, 2006, sec. World. https://www.nytimes.com/2006/07/18/world/asia/18korea.html.

Osborne, Mark. "Trump Warns North Korea 'Won't Be Around Much Longer' If Threats Continue to Escalate." *ABC News*, September 24, 2017. https://abcnews.go.com/International/trump-warns-north-korea-wont-longer-threats-continue/story?id=50053390.

Pak, Jung H. *Becoming Kim Jong Un: A Former CIA Officer's Insights into North Korea's Enigmatic Young Dictator*. New York: Ballantine Books, 2020.

Panda, Ankit. "North Korea Overflies Japan with Another Intermediate-Range Ballistic Missile: Early Analysis." *Diplomat*, September 15, 2017. https://thediplomat.com/2017/09/north-korea-overflies-japan-with-another-intermediate-range-ballistic-missile-early-analysis/.

Pardo, Ramon Pacheco. *Shrimp to Whale: South Korea from the Forgotten War to K-Pop*. London: Oxford University Press, 2022.

Park, Donghui. "North Korea Cyber Attacks: A New Asymmetrical Military Strategy." Henry M. Jackson School of International Studies, June 28, 2016. https://jsis.washington.edu/news/north-korea-cyber-attacks-new-asymmetrical-military-strategy/.

Park, Hyung-joong, Jin-a Kim, Won-gon Park, joo-hwa Park, Soo-suk Lee, Eun-joo Choi, and Soo-hwan Hwang. "2022년 4분기 통일 여론 동향" [2022 Q4 peaceful unification: public opinion and trends]. Peaceful Unification Advisory Council, December 2022.

Park, In Ho. "The Creation of the North Korean Market System." Seoul: Daily NK, 2017.

Park, Jong-chul, Moon-young Huh, Il-kyu Kang, Hak-sung Kim, Hyun-mo Yang, Sun-won Jung, Eun-mi Jung, and Eun-suk Choi. "통일대비를 위한 국내과제" [Domestic tasks in preparation for unification]. Seoul: Korea Institute for National Unification, December 30, 2011. https://repo.kinu.or.kr/bitstream/2015.oak/1806/1/0001440975.pdf.

Park, Ju-hwa. "평화적 분단과 통일: 2017 통일에 대한 국민 인식 조사 결과와 함의" [Peaceful coexistence and unification: South Koreans' perception of unification 2017]. Online Series CO 17–18. Seoul: Korea Institute for National Unification, June 23, 2017. http://lib.kinu.or.kr//wonmun/008/0001484788.pdf.

Park, Ju-min. "North Korea Tests Another Missile; Seoul Says Dashes Hopes for Peace." Reuters, May 21, 2017, sec. Aerospace and Defense. https://www.reuters.com/article/us-northkorea-missiles-idUSKBN18H0A6.

Park, Ju-min, and Meeyoung Cho. "South Korea Blames North Korea for December Hack on Nuclear Operator." Reuters, March 17, 2015, sec. Internet News. https://www.reuters.com/article/us-nuclear-southkorea-northkorea-idUSKBN0MD0GR20150317.

Park, Ju-min, and Jack Kim. "North Korea Test-Fires Missile into Sea Ahead of Trump-Xi Summit." Reuters, April 4, 2017, sec. Aerospace and Defense. https://www.reuters.com/article/us-northkorea-missiles-idUSKBN1762XX.

Park, Kyung-Ae. "Economic Crisis, Women's Changing Economic Roles, and Their Implications for Women's Status in North Korea." *Pacific Review* 24, no. 2 (May 1, 2011): 159–77.

Park, Si-soo. "North Korea–Linked Hackers Accessed South's Rocket Developer: Spy Agency." *SpaceNews*, July 9, 2021. https://spacenews.com/north-korea-linked-hackers-accessed-souths-rocket-developer-spy-agency/.

Ploughshares Fund. "Factsheet: US-ROK Military Exercises." June 15, 2018. https://ploughshares.org/issues-analysis/article/factsheet-us-rok-military-exercises.

Pollack, Jonathan D., and Chung Min Lee. "Preparing for Korean Unification: Scenarios and Implications." RAND Corporation, January 1, 1999. https://www.rand.org/pubs/monograph_reports/MR1040.html.

Pong, Jane, Wen Foo, Simon Scarr, and James Pearson. "North Korea Defectors." Reuters Graphics, May 21, 2015. http://graphics.thomsonreuters.com/15/defectors/index.html.

Pritchard, Charles L. *Failed Diplomacy: The Tragic Story of How North Korea Got the Bomb*. Washington DC: Brookings Institution Press, 2007.

Pritchard, Jack. "My New Year's Predictions for North Korea." *Korea Economic Institute of America* (blog), December 21, 2011. https://keia.org/the-peninsula/my-new-years-predictions-for-north-korea/.

Reuters. "North Korea Appears to Lift COVID Mask Mandate, Reports Say." July 4, 2023, sec. Asia Pacific. https://www.reuters.com/world/asia-pacific/north-korea-appears-lift-covid-mask-mandate-reports-say-2023-07-04/.

———. "South Korean Intelligence Says N. Korean Hackers Possibly Behind Coincheck Heist—Sources." February 5, 2018, sec. Foreign Exchange Analysis. https://www.reuters.com/article/uk-southkorea-northkorea-cryptocurrency-idUSKBN1FP2XX.

———. "Trump Tweets Threats Against N.Korea After UN Speech." September 24, 2017, sec. Industrials. https://www.reuters.com/article/northkorea-missiles-trump-un-idUKS9N19U045.

Revere, Evans J. R. "Facing the Facts: Towards a New U.S. North Korea Policy." Brookings, 2013. https://www.brookings.edu/articles/facing-the-facts-towards-a-new-u-s-north-korea-policy/.

———. "Korean Reunification and U.S. Interests: Preparing for One Korea." Brookings, January 20, 2015. https://www.brookings.edu/articles/korean-reunification-and-u-s-interests-preparing-for-one-korea/.

Rhee, Kang Suk. "Korea's Unification: The Applicability of the German Experience." *Asian Survey* 33, no. 4 (1993): 360–75.

Rich, Timothy S., and Madelynn Einhorn. "South Koreans Rarely Think About North Korea—and Why It Matters—38 North: Informed Analysis of North Korea." 38 North, November 13, 2020. https://www.38north.org/2020/11/trichmeinhorn111320/.

Riley-Smith, Ben. "Exclusive: US Making Plans for 'Bloody Nose' Military Attack on North Korea." *Telegraph*, December 20, 2017. https://www.telegraph.co.uk/news/2017/12/20/exclusive-us-making-plans-bloody-nose-military-attack-north/.

Ripley, Will, Jamie Crawford, and Ralph Ellis. "North Korea Launches Trio of Missiles Amidst US-South Korea Military Drills." CNN, August 25, 2017. https://www.cnn.com/2017/08/25/asia/north-korea-fires-projectile/index.html.

Roh, Joori. "N.Korea's Economy Shrank Most in 23 Years Amid COVID-19, Sanctions—S.Korea c.Bank." Reuters, July 30, 2021, sec. Asia Pacific. https://www.reuters.com/world/asia-pacific/nkoreas-economy-shrank-most-23-years-amid-covid-19-sanctions-skorea-cbank-2021-07-30/.

Ronin Network. "Back to Building: Ronin Security Breach Postmortem." *Ronin's Newsletter*, April 27, 2022. https://blog.roninchain.com/p/back-to-building-ronin-security-breach.

Rosenberger, Leif R. "Unifying Korea: Beyond Hopes and Fears." *Contemporary Southeast Asia* 16, no. 3 (1994): 295–316.

Rotaru, Cristina. "The Curious Case of Marine Chain: The DPRK Cyberscam Behind a Blockchain-Powered Maritime Investment Marketplace." *Vertic* (blog), April 24, 2019. https://www.vertic.org/2019/04/the-curious-case-of-marine-chain-the-dprk-cyberscam-behind-a-blockchain-powered-maritime-investment-marketplace/.

Rowland, Ashley. "Powell Calls Obama a 'Transformational Figure.'" *Stars and Stripes*, November 9, 2008. https://www.stripes.com/news/powell-calls-obama-a-transformational-figure-1.85019.

Rusk, Dean. *As I Saw It*. New York: Norton, 1990.

Ryall, Julian. "South Korea Looks to Germany as a Model of Reunification." *DW*, October 3, 2021. https://www.dw.com/en/south-korea-looks-to-germany-for-reunification-pointers/a-59374733.

Sanford, Dan C. "ROK's Nordpolitik: Revisited." *Journal of East Asian Affairs* 7, no. 1 (Winter/Spring 1993): 1–31.

Sanger, David E. *The Perfect Weapon: War, Sabotage, and Fear in the Cyber Age*. New York: Crown, 2018.

Sanger, David E., and William J. Broad. "How U.S. Intelligence Agencies Underestimated North Korea." *New York Times*, January 6, 2018, sec. World. https://www.nytimes.com/2018/01/06/world/asia/north-korea-nuclear-missile-intelligence.html.

Sanger, David E., and Sang-Hun Choe. "North Korean Nuclear Test Draws U.S. Warning of 'Massive Military Response.'" *New York Times*, September 3, 2017, sec. World. https://www.nytimes.com/2017/09/03/world/asia/north-korea-tremor-possible-6th-nuclear-test.html.

Sanger, David E., Sang-Hun Choe, and William J. Broad. "North Korea Tests a Ballistic Missile That Experts Say Could Hit California." *New York Times*, July 28, 2017, sec. World. https://www.nytimes.com/2017/07/28/world/asia/north-korea-ballistic-missile.html.

Sanger, David E., David D. Kirkpatrick, and Nicole Perlroth. "The World Once Laughed at North Korean Cyberpower. No More." *New York Times*, October 15, 2017, sec. World. https://www.nytimes.com/2017/10/15/world/asia/north-korea-hacking-cyber-sony.html.

Sansec. "North Korean Hackers Are Skimming US and European Shoppers," July 6, 2020. https://sansec.io/research/north-korea-magecart.

Scalapino, Robert A. *North Korea at a Crossroads*. Hoover Essays in Public Policy, no. 73. Stanford, CA: Hoover Institution Press, 1997.

Seals, Tara. "Lazarus Group Brings APT Tactics to Ransomware." Threatpost, July 28, 2020. https://threatpost.com/lazarus-group-apt-tactics-ransomware/157815/.

Seligman, Lara. "Experts Question Wisdom of Canceling U.S. Exercises with South Korea, As Mattis Makes It Official." *Foreign Policy*, June 26, 2018. https://foreignpolicy.com/2018/06/26/experts-question-wisdom-of-canceling-u-s-exercises-with-south-korea-as-mattis-makes-it-official/.

Shear, Michael D., and David E. Sanger. "Trump Returns North Korea to List of State Sponsors of Terrorism." *New York Times*, November 20, 2017, sec. U.S. https://www.nytimes.com/2017/11/20/us/politics/north-korea-trump-terror.html.

Sheen, Seong-ho. "Dilemma of South Korea's Trust Diplomacy and Unification Policy." *International Journal of Korean Unification Studies* 23, no. 2 (2014): 97–122.

Shin, Gi-Wook. *Ethnic Nationalism in Korea: Genealogy, Politics, and Legacy*. Stanford, CA: Stanford University Press, 2006.

Shin, Hyonhee. "N.Korea's Trade with China Plunges 80% as COVID-19 Lockdown Bites." Reuters, January 19, 2021, sec. China. https://www.reuters.com/world/china/nkoreas-trade-with-china-plunges-80-covid-19-lockdown-bites-2021-01-19/.

Shin, Jin-Wook. "Lessons from German Reunification for Inter-Korean Relations: An Analysis of South Korean Public Spheres, 1990–2010." *Asian Perspective* 38, no. 1 (2014): 61–88.

Shin, Kyeong-su, and Jin Shin. "사이버 위협의 확장과 국가안보적 대응북한 사이버 공격을 중심으로" [Scaling cyber threats and responding to national security: A focus on North Korea's cyberattacks]. 전략연구 [Journal of strategic studies] 25, no. 3 (November 2011).

Shin, Soon-ok. "Engagement? Containment? The Role of Identity in the Formation of South Korea's Policy Toward Pyongyang." *North Korean Review* 9, no. 1 (2013): 83–99.

Shushan, Amitai Ben, Noam Lifshitz, Amnon Kushnir, Martin Korman, and Boaz Wasserman. "Lazarus Group's Mata Framework Leveraged to Deploy TFlower Ransomware." *Syngia* (blog), August 1, 2021. https://blog.sygnia.co/lazarus-groups-mata-framework-leveraged-to-deploy-tflower-ransomware.

Siebens, James, and Mackenzie Mandile. "Concession . . . or Common Sense? Trading Drills for Dialogue." *Defense One*, June 14, 2018. https://www.defenseone.com/ideas/2018/06/trading-drills-dialogue-oft-successful-tactic/148995/.

Sims, Calvin. "North Korea as the Next Tourist Spot; Hyundai Has Approval for Deepwater Docks, Spa and a 45-Hole Golf Course." *New York Times*, March 7, 2000, sec. Business. https://www.nytimes.com/2000/03/07/business/north-korea-next-tourist-spot-hyundai-has-approval-for-deepwater-docks-spa-45.html.

Smith, Frank. "Coronavirus: How the Pandemic Is Hitting North Korea Hard." *DW.com*, April 12, 2021. https://www.dw.com/en/coronavirus-how-the-pandemic-is-hitting-north-korea-hard/a-57168554.

Smith, Hazel. *North Korea: Markets and Military Rule*. Cambridge: Cambridge University Press, 2015.

Smith, Josh. " 'Cuddled in Kim Jong Un's Arms:' North Koreans Envisage Unification Ahead of Summit." Reuters, September 17, 2018, sec. APAC. https://www.reuters.com/article/us-northkorea-southkorea-unification-idUSKCN1LX0F0.

———. "North Korea Locks down Capital City over 'Respiratory Illness.'" *Reuters*, January 25, 2023, sec. Healthcare & Pharmaceuticals. https://www.reuters.com/business/healthcare-pharmaceuticals/north-korea-locks-down-capital-city-over-respiratory-illness-report-2023-01-25/.

Song, Hyun-wook. "북한주민의 대남인식과 외부정보통제 변화 추이 : 북한이탈주민 면접조사를 통한 추론" [Trends in changes in North Koreans' perception of South Korea and external information control: Inference through interview survey of North Korean defectors]. Ministry of Unification, 2011. https://unibook.unikorea.go.kr/board/view?boardId=20&categoryId=&page=&id=201458190&field=searchAll&searchInput=.

"Special Report: APT38: Un-Usual Suspects." Milpitas, CA: FireEye, 2018.

Stares, Paul B., and Joel S. Wit. "Preparing for Sudden Change in North Korea." Council on Foreign Relations, January 2009. https://www.cfr.org/report/preparing-sudden-change-north-korea.

Starr, Barbara, and Ryan Browne. "US Cancels Major Military Exercise with South Korea." CNN, October 19, 2018. https://www.cnn.com/2018/10/19/politics/us-south-korea-suspend-exercise/index.html.

Statista. "Gross National Income (GNI) per Capita of South Korea from 1980 to 2021," August 2022. https://www.statista.com/statistics/756638/south-korea-gni-per-capita/.

Stengel, Richard. "The Untold Story of the Sony Hack: How North Korea's Battle with Seth Rogen and George Clooney Foreshadowed Russian Election Meddling in 2016." *Vanity Fair*, October 6, 2019. https://www.vanityfair.com/news/2019/10/the-untold-story-of-the-sony-hack.

Stilgherrian. "North Korea Is the Most Destructive Cyber Threat Right Now: FireEye." *ZDNet*, October 4, 2018. https://www.zdnet.com/article/north-korea-is-the-most-destructive-cyber-threat-right-now-fireeye/.

Stravidis, James. "I Was a Navy Admiral. Here's Why Ending 'War Games' with South Korea Would Be a Grave Mistake." *Time*, June 12, 2018. https://time.com/5310534/donald-trump-north-korea-war-games-military-exercises/.

Stubbs, Jack. "Exclusive: Suspected North Korean Hackers Targeted COVID Vaccine Maker AstraZeneca—Sources." Reuters, November 27, 2020, sec. Technology News. https://www.reuters.com/article/us-healthcare-coronavirus-astrazeneca-no-idUSKBN2871A2.

Stueck, William. *The Korean War: An International History*. Princeton, NJ: Princeton University Press, 1995.

Stueck, William, and Boram Yi. "'An Alliance Forged in Blood': The American Occupation of Korea, the Korean War, and the US–South Korean Alliance." *Journal of Strategic Studies* 33, no. 2 (April 1, 2010): 177–209.

Suh, Jae Jean. "The Lee Myung-Bak Government's North Korea Policy." Seoul: Korea Institute for National Unification, May 2009.

Sullivan, Jake. "A Statement of U.S. Policy on North Korea." Center for Strategic and International Studies, December 1, 2022. https://www.csis.org/analysis/statement-us-policy-north-korea.

Talmadge, Eric. "North Korea Outlines Plan to Launch Missiles toward Guam." *AP News*, August 10, 2017. https://apnews.com/article/931769550f3b433ca64f6c5e633da23b.

Tasic, Mirko. "Exploring North Korea's Asymmetric Military Strategy." *Naval War College Review* 72, no. 4 (October 2, 2019). https://digital-commons.usnwc.edu/nwc-review/vol72/iss4/6.

TIME Magazine. "Lil' Kim." Cover, February 27, 2012. https://content.time.com/time/covers/0,16641,20120227,00.html.

Trading Economics. "North Korea GDP Annual Growth Rate." 2022. https://tradingeconomics.com/north-korea/gdp-annual-growth-rate.

Tudor, Daniel. *Ask a North Korean: Defectors Talk About Their Lives Inside the World's Most Secretive Nation*. Rutland, VT: Tuttle, 2018.

Tudor, Daniel, and James Pearson. *North Korea Confidential: Private Markets, Fashion Trends, Prison Camps, Dissenters and Defectors*. Rutland, VT: Tuttle, 2015.

United Nations. *Statistical Yearbook 1948*. New York: United Nations, 1949. https://unstats.un.org/unsd/publications/statistical-yearbook/files/SYB1.pdf.

United Nations Human Rights Council. "Public Hearings (Programs, Videos, Transcripts)," n.d. https://www.ohchr.org/en/hr-bodies/hrc/co-idprk/public-hearings.

———. "Report of the Detailed Findings of the Commission of Inquiry on Human Rights in the Democratic People's Republic of Korea." February 7, 2014. https://www.ohchr.org/Documents/HRBodies/HRCouncil/CoIDPRK/Report/A.HRC.25.63.doc.

United Nations Office on Drugs and Crime. "Who Conducts Cybercrime Investigations?" n.d. https://www.unodc.org.

United Nations Peacemaker. "Agreed Framework Between the United States of America and the Democratic People's Republic of Korea." October 21, 1994. https://peacemaker.un.org/node/1129.

———. "Agreement on Reconciliation, Non-Aggression, and Exchanges and Cooperation Between South and North Korea." December 13, 1991. https://peacemaker.un.org/korea-reconciliation-nonaggression91.

United Nations Security Council. "Final Report of the Panel of Experts Established Pursuant to Resolution 1874 (2009)." November 5, 2010. https://www.undocs.org/S/2010/571.

———. "Notes by the President of the Security Council." August 28, 2020. https://undocs.org/S/2020/840.

———. "Report of the Panel of Experts Established Pursuant to Resolution 1874 (2009)." August 30, 2019. https://undocs.org/S/2019/691.

U.S. Department of Defense. "U.S. Flies B1-B Bomber Mission off of North Korean Coast." September 23, 2017. https://www.defense.gov/News/Releases/Release/Article/1322213/us-flies-b1-b-bomber-mission-off-of-north-korean-coast/https%3A%2F%2Fwww.defense.gov%2FNews%2FReleases%2FRelease%2FArticle%2F1322213%2Fus-flies-b1-b-bomber-mission-off-of-north-korean-coast%2F.

U.S. Department of Defense, Department of the Army. "North Korean Tactics." July 2020. https://irp.fas.org/doddir/army/atp7-100-2.pdf.

U.S. Department of Defense, OSD A&S Industrial Policy. "Fiscal Year 2020: Industrial Capabilities Report to Congress." January 2021. https://media.defense.gov/2021/Jan/14/2002565311/-1/-1/0/FY20-INDUSTRIAL-CAPABILITIES-REPORT.PDF.

U.S. Department of Health and Human Services, Office of Information Security. "North Korean Cyber Activity." March 25, 2021. https://www.hhs.gov/sites/default/files/dprk-cyber-espionage.pdf.

U.S. Department of Justice. "Press Release: Three North Korean Military Hackers Indicted in Wide-Ranging Scheme to Commit Cyberattacks and Financial Crimes Across the Globe." February 17, 2021. https://www.justice.gov/opa/pr/three-north-korean-military-hackers-indicted-wide-ranging-scheme-commit-cyberattacks-and.

———. "Press Release: U.S. Citizen Who Conspired to Assist North Korea in Evading Sanctions Sentenced to Over Five Years and Fined $100,000." April 12, 2022. https://www.justice.gov/opa/pr/us-citizen-who-conspired-assist-north-korea-evading-sanctions-sentenced-over-five-years-and.

U.S. Department of State Archive. "Six Parties October 3, 2007 Agreement on 'Second-Phase Actions for the Implementation of the Joint Statement.'" Department of State, Office of Electronic Information, Bureau of Public Affairs, October 3, 2007. https://2001-2009.state.gov/r/pa/prs/ps/2007/oct/93223.htm.

U.S. Department of the Treasury. "Press Release: U.S. Treasury Sanctions Notorious Virtual Currency Mixer Tornado Cash." August 8, 2022. https://home.treasury.gov/news/press-releases/jy0916.

———. "U.S. Treasury Issues First-Ever Sanctions on a Virtual Currency Mixer, Targets DPRK Cyber Threats." May 6, 2022. https://home.treasury.gov/news/press-releases/jy0768.

U.S. Senate, Armed Services Committee. "Statement for the Record, Worldwide Threat Assessment." March 6, 2018. https://www.armed-services.senate.gov/imo/media/doc/Ashley_03-06-18.pdf.

Van Boom, Daniel. "Crypto Hackers Are Secretly Funding North Korea's Nuclear Weapons." CNET, October 9, 2022. https://www.cnet.com/culture/features/north-koreas-crypto-hackers-are-paving-the-road-to-nuclear-armageddon/.

———. "North Korea's Crypto Hackers Are Paving the Road to Nuclear Armageddon." CNET, October 9, 2022. https://www.cnet.com/culture/features/north-koreas-crypto-hackers-are-paving-the-road-to-nuclear-armageddon/.

Walker, Peter. "Dennis Rodman Gives Away Name of Kim Jong-Un's Daughter." *Guardian*, September 9, 2013, sec. World news. https://www.theguardian.com/world/2013/sep/09/dennis-rodman-north-korea-baby-name.

Wallace, Robert Daniel. "North Korea and Diversion: A Quantitative Analysis (1997–2011)." *Communist and Post-Communist Studies* 47, no. 2 (June 1, 2014): 147–58.

Weeks, Jessica L. "Autocratic Audience Costs: Regime Type and Signaling Resolve." *International Organization* 62, no.1 (Winter 2008): 35-64

Weeks, Ryan. "How a Fake Job Offer Took Down the World's Most Popular Crypto Game." *Block*, July 6, 2022. https://www.theblock.co/post/156038/how-a-fake-job-offer-took-down-the-worlds-most-popular-crypto-game.
Weidermann, Alex. "New Campaign Targeting Security Researchers." *Google Threat Analysis Group* (blog), January 25, 2021.
Westcott, Ben, and Steve Almasy. "North Korea Launches 4 Anti-Ship Missiles, Fourth Test in a Month." CNN, June 7, 2017. https://www.cnn.com/2017/06/07/asia/north-korea-missiles-launch/index.html.
White House Archives. "Press Conference by President Trump." June 12, 2018. https://trumpwhitehouse.archives.gov/briefings-statements/press-conference-president-trump/.
——. "Remarks by President Trump Before a Briefing on the Opioid Crisis." August 8, 2017. https://trumpwhitehouse.archives.gov/briefings-statements/remarks-president-trump-briefing-opioid-crisis/.
——. "Remarks by President Trump to the 72nd Session of the United Nations General Assembly." September 19, 2017. https://trumpwhitehouse.archives.gov/briefings-statements/remarks-president-trump-72nd-session-united-nations-general-assembly/.
Whittaker, Zack. "Two Years after WannaCry, a Million Computers Remain at Risk." *TechCrunch* (blog), May 12, 2019. https://techcrunch.com/2019/05/12/wannacry-two-years-on/.
Williams, Martyn. "Digital Trenches: North Korea's Information Counter-Offensive." Committee for Human Rights in North Korea, 2019. https://www.hrnk.org/uploads/pdfs/Williams_Digital_Trenches_Web_FINAL.pdf.
Wolf, Charles, Jr., and Kamiljon T. Akramov. "North Korean Paradoxes: Circumstances, Costs, and Consequences of Korean Unification." Santa Monica, CA: RAND Corporation, May 3, 2005. https://www.rand.org/pubs/monographs/MG333.html.
Woo, Jongseok. "Kim Jong-Il's Military-First Politics and Beyond: Military Control Mechanisms and the Problem of Power Succession." *Communist and Post-Communist Studies* 47, no. 2 (June 1, 2014): 117–25.
Woo, Jung-en. *Race to the Swift*. New York: Columbia University Press, 1991.
Woodward, Bob. *Fear: Trump in the White House*. 2nd ed. New York: Simon & Schuster, 2018.
World Trade Organization. "Map of Disputes Between WTO Members," n.d. https://www.wto.org/english/tratop_e/dispu_e/dispu_maps_e.htm?country_selected=CAN&sense=e.
Yang, Sung Chul. *The North and South Korean Political Systems: A Comparative Analysis*. Boulder, CO: Westview Press, 1994.
Yeo, Andrew. *State, Society and Markets in North Korea*. Cambridge: Cambridge University Press, 2021.
Yim, Deok Soon, and Jaewon Lee. "UNESCO Science Report: Towards 2030." UNESCO, 2015. https://en.unesco.org/sites/default/files/usr15_republic_of_korea.pdf.

Zegart, Amy. "Kim Jong Un: The Hardest Intelligence Target." *Atlantic*, July 9, 2017, sec. Global. https://www.theatlantic.com/international/archive/2017/07/north-korea-kim-jong-un/533034/.

Zemler, Emily. " 'He's Like a Racist Jason Bourne': Late-Night Hosts React to FBI Raid of Trump's Mar-a-Lago." *Rolling Stone* (blog), August 16, 2022. https://www.rollingstone.com/tv-movies/tv-movie-news/trump-fbi-raid-late-night-tv-1397459/.

Zilberman, Alan, and Lindsey Ice. "Why Computer Occupations Are Behind Strong STEM Employment Growth in the 2019–29 Decade." U.S. Bureau of Labor Statistics, January 2021. https://www.bls.gov/opub/btn/volume-10/why-computer-occupations-are-behind-strong-stem-employment-growth.htm.

CONTRIBUTORS

Victor D. Cha is Distinguished University Professor, D. S. Song-KF chairholder, and professor of government in the Department of Government and School of Foreign Service at Georgetown University. He is also senior vice president for Asia and Korea Chair at the Center for Strategic and International Studies in Washington, DC.

Marie DuMond is in the Office of the Vice Provost for Research and Innovation at American University.

Julian W. Fox received his M.S. degree in foreign service from Georgetown University.

Seiyeon Ji is associate fellow in the Korea Chair at the Center for Strategic and International Studies in Washington, DC.

Na Young Lee is a doctoral candidate in political science at the University of Southern California.

Andy Lim is associate fellow in the Korea Chair at the Center for Strategic and International Studies in Washington, DC.

Katelyn N. Radack is an instructor at the Department of Social Sciences at the United States Military Academy at West Point.

Jae Seung Shim received his M.S. degree in foreign service from Georgetown University.

Rebecca Spencer is a graduate student at the Doerr School of Sustainability at Stanford University.

INDEX

Page numbers in *italics* indicate figures; those followed by a *t* indicate tables.

Abbas, Ramon Olorunwa, 52
action metrics, 176
Adobe Flash vulnerabilities, 75
Advanced Persistent Threat
 (APT) groups, 41–43, 46–47,
 54, 72
Agreed Framework (1994), 130
AIC statistical test, 249n24
Alaumary, Ghaleb, 52
"Anchor Project," 43
Andarial hacking group, 41
antimarket activities, 85–87,
 86t
AppleJeus malware, 48
APT groups. *See* Advanced Persistent
 Threat groups
"Arduous March," 84
Ashley, Robert, 4
"Asian Tigers," 129
AstraZeneca, 55, 63
ATM cyberattacks, 46, 49–50, 59
"audience cost," 35
autocorrelation, 29–31
autoregressive (AR) model, 28–29,
 32–33, 33t
Axie Infinity crypto heist, 50, 51

B-1B bombers, 12, 105
Baek, Jieun, 177
ballistic missiles, 11–12, 51, 67, 105–6,
 173, 178, 194
Bangladesh, 46, 48
BankIslami Pakistan, 46, 59
bartering, 83–85, 85t
Basic Agreement on Reconciliation,
 Non-aggression, and Exchanges and
 Cooperation (1991), 130, 271n46
Beagle Boyz (hacking group), 43, 46
Belarus, 41, 76
Bermudez, Joseph, 67
Bernhardt, Jordan, 22, 23
BIC statistical test, 249n24
Biden, Joseph, 87; cybersecurity policies
 of, 71–74; on DPRK's cybercrimes, 51;
 Kim Jong-un and, 14, 194, 195, 197
Bitcoin. *See* digital currencies
black market, 85, 94; *jangmadang*
 market and, 83–84, 97; shadow
 market and, 174–75, 179. *See also*
 market economy
"bloody nose" strike plan, 12–14
Bluenoroff Group (hacking group),
 41, 46

Bolton, John, 195
Bonesteel, Charles "Tic," 115
brinksmanship tactics, 41, 178
Brookings Institution, 6
Bureau 121 cyberattacks, 41
Bureau 325 cyberattacks, 55, 56
Bush, George H. W., 20, 24, 247n13
Bush, George W., 37, 109; JMEs and, 20; Six-Party Talks of, 189, 196
byungjin strategy, 174

Caesar, Ed, 62
Canada, 26, 55
Carnegie Endowment for International Peace, 7
Center for Future Unified Korean Peninsula, 140
Center for Strategic and International Studies (CSIS), 15, 41, 42, 66
Cerium (hacking group), 55, 56
Chainanalysis (blockchain analysis firm), 51
Charman, Matt, 57
Cheonan sinking (2010), 135
China, 110, 111t, 192–93t; Cultural Revolution in, 186; cyberattacks by, 41–42, 46, 75; DPRK hackers and, 41, 62, 64; DPRK summits with, 189–91, 190t; DPRK trade with, 179, *180*, 181t, 183; Korean unification and, 6–7, 16, 118, 146t, 149–54, 151t, 155t, 159, 161t, *168*; Olympic Games (2022) in, 181; refoulement policy of, 82; Russia-DPRK relations and, 186–87; Tiananmen Square massacre in, 131; Winter Olympics in, 181
Chosun Expo Joint Venture, 53
Christianity, 92
Chun Doo-hwan, 126
civil society, 14, 78, 98, 174
Clapper, James, 1, 3
Clinton, Bill, 24
Coats, Daniel, 4
Cochrane-Orcutt Estimation (COE), 28, 29
codebook for U.S.-DPRK event data, 205–7, 208–23t
Cold War, 6, 115, 124, 126
Combined Forces Command (CFC), 246n2
"competitive delegitimation," 116, 125

Confucianism, 189
corporate espionage, 55–56, 60, 62–63, 66
Covid-19 pandemic, 14, 177–84, 185t; China-DPRK trade during, 179, *180*, 181t, 183; lockdown during, 49, 63, 83, 112, 178–79, 183–84
Covid-19 vaccines, 55–56, 63, 179, 183
criticism of government, 87–91, 90t, 111
cryptocurrencies, 59, 60, 172–73; hacking of, 43, 47–52, 172–73; security measures for, 75
CSIS (Center for Strategic and International Studies), 15, 41, 42, 66
currency redenomination, 84–87
cyberattacks, 40–43, 52–54, 172–73; defensive/offensive, 65–68; electronic warfare and, 40–43, 66, 67; evolution of, 40–43; on financial institutions, 43–47, *44–45*, 63–66; goals of, 60–68; Kim Jong-un on, 61, 67, 172–73; malware for, 43, 46–50; money laundering and, 51–52; prevention of, 72, 73–77; ransomware for, 50, 52–53, 75–76; retaliatory, 77; on Sony, 15, 39, 42, 49, 57, 59; types of, 43, *44–45*; U.S. responses to, 72–73
cybercrime, 43, 66, 73–76, 172–73, 196
cybersecurity, 15, 39–40, 47; diplomacy efforts for, 68, 76–77; improvements to, 74–75; job growth in, 70, 73; public-private partnerships for, 69–70; research on, 56
Cybersecurity and Infrastructure Security Agency (CISA), 71
Cybersecurity State Coordinator Act (2020), 71
cyberterrorism, 43, 51, 68, 172–73
cyber warfare, 39, 61, 63–68, 72

data collection, 8–9; on JMEs, 21; methodologies of, 14–15; for policy making, 9–14; problems with, 3–4
defectors, 81–83, 109–10, 111t, 182; outside media exposure of, 91–94, 93t, 174; on unification, 102, 103t. *See also* refugees
Defense Industrial Base (DIB) report, 70, 71
Demers, John, 62

Demilitarized Zone (DMZ), 10, 116; Panmunjom Summit at, 13
Democratic People's Republic of Korea (DPRK), 36; Chinese summits with, 189–91, 190t; Chinese trade with, 179, *180*, 181t, 183; creation of, 4–6; criticism of, 87–91, 90t; establishment of, 116; famine of mid-1990s in, 5, 84, 96, 110, 128, 174, 179, 183; first nuclear test by, 37; GDP growth in, 65t; market growth in, 15–16; missile program of, 11–12, 51, 67, 105–6, 173, 194; oil imports of, 128; public health system of, 63; Russia and, 186–89, *187*, *188*; sanctions against, 13, 60–61, 72–73; telecommunication systems of, 177; UN sanctions on, 43; U.S. event data of, 205–7, 208–23t; warfighting doctrine of, 40–41, 65–68. *See also* nuclear weapons
Deng Xiaoping, 190t
denuclearization, 12, 21, 36–37, 194–98; China on, 64; cybersecurity policies and, 76–77; U.S. on, 149. *See also* Six-Party Talks
digital currencies. *See* cryptocurrencies
disaster risk reduction (DRR) issues, 158–59
distributed denial-of-service (DDoS) attacks, 42, 43
donju (merchant class), 173–74
D'Orazio, Vito, 22–23
DPRK. *See* Democratic People's Republic of Korea

Ebola, 184, 185t
echo chamber effect, 3
electronic warfare, 40–43, 66, 67. *See also* cyberattacks
entrepreneurship, 85, 94–95, 95t, 173; women and, 96–98, 97t
environmentalism, 121t, 139, 146t, 158, 263n8
Exclusive Economic Zone (EEZ), 11

famine in DPRK, 5, 128, 174, 179, 183; foreign aid during, 110; unofficial markets during, 84, 96
field training exercise (FTX), 246n2

Germany, 116; reunification of, 7, 127, 199
Go, Myong-Hyun, 80–81
Google's Threat Analysis Group, 56
GPS jamming, 42
"green growth," 263n8
Griffis, William Elliot, 241n6
Griffith, Virgil, 50
Guam, 105
Guardians of Peace (hacker group), 42

Haass, Richard, 137, 273n66
Hanoi Summit (2019), 13
healthcare cyberattacks, 53, 55–56. *See also* Covid-19 vaccines
Hidden Cobra (hacking group), 43
Hu Jintao, 190t
human rights, 82, 88, 121t, 146t, 147–48
human trafficking, 82
Hussein, Saddam, 131
Hutchins, Marcus, 53
Hwasong-12 missiles, 11
Hwasong-15 missiles, 11, 105

IBM's cybersecurity team, 55
ICT Development Index (IDI), 263n5
India, 41, 114
inflation, 86
information control, 91–94, 93t
Integrated Crisis Early Warning System (ICEWS), 22
intellectual property (IP) theft, 62–64
intercontinental ballistic missiles (ICBMs), 11, 105–6. *See also* ballistic missiles
internally displaced persons (IDPs), 121t, 155. *See also* refugees
International Atomic Energy Agency (IAEA), 23
internet: availability of, 61, 177; influencers on, 52
Interview, The (film), 2, 42
Iranian cyberattacks, 41–42

jangmadang (unofficial) markets, 83–84, 97
Japan, 110, 111t; cyberattacks on, 48; Korean unification and, 6, 16, 117–18, 146t, 149, 152t, 155t, 159, 162t; Olympic Games (2020) in, 181
Jervis, Robert, 198

Jiang Zemin, 190t
Johnson & Johnson, 55
Joint Declaration on Denuclearization of the Korean Peninsula (1992), 130
joint military exercises (JMEs), 15, 19–20, 27, 171–72, 225t; analysis of, 29–38, 30, 31t, 33t, 37; cancellation of, 20, 24–25, 172; data-set on, 21; effects of, 20–21, 25–26, 34; Foal Eagle, 23, 246n2; history of, 246n2; previous studies on, 22–25; research design for, 25–29; Team Spirit, 20, 172, 246n2, 247n13; Vigilant Ace, 24
Jon Chang Hyok, 59
Joseon dynasty, 241n6

Kaesong Industrial Complex, 132, 184
KAL Flight 858 bombing, 126
kangson taeguk ("strong and prosperous nation"), 106
Kaspersky (cybersecurity firm), 53, 54
Keong, Jonathan Foong Kah, 52
Kim Dae-jung, 5, 36, 268n26, 272n54; Sunshine Policy of, 131–32; on unification, 127
Kim Il-sung, 59, 79, 115, 124; centennial of, 32; China visits by, 190t, 192t; death of, 128; legacy of, 175; Russian policies of, 186–87; U.S. media coverage of, 1; World War II documentary on, 91
Kim, Jane, 93, 177
Kim Jong-il, 35, 272n54; China visits by, 190t, 192–93t; death of, 5, 135; legacy of, 175; at Singapore Summit, 19–21; U.S. media coverage of, 1, 2
Kim Jong-un: Biden and, 14, 194, 195, 197; China visits by, 190–93t; on cyber warfare, 61, 67, 172–73; family of, 4; legacy of, 175; Putin and, 186; titles of, 32; Trump and, 11–14, 191, 195; U.S. media coverage of, 1–2
Kim Ju-ae, 4
Kim, Samuel, 116
Kim Young-sam, 130
Kim Chaek University of Technology, 62
Kim Il-sung University, 62
Kimsuky (hacking group), 56, 58, 60
Korea Aerospace Industries (KAI), 58
Korea Central News Agency (KCNA), 106, 185t

Korea Development Institute (KDI), 129
Korea Hydro and Nuclear Power Co., 57
Korea Institute for National Unification (KINU), 86–89, 95, 129, 259n13; surveys of, 99–100, 102, 113
Korea Institute of Fusion Energy, 58
Korean Romanization, vii
Korean War, 115–16, 124, 189
Kretchun, Nat, 93, 177
Kumgang (Diamond) Mountain, 133
Kwanliso prison camp, 88

"Language Reactionary" (*mal bandong*), 89
Lazarus, 41–43, 46, 49, 173; Covid-19 vaccine hacking by, 55; ransomware of, 53–54, 59–60; sanctions on, 50–51, 73
Leap Day Agreement (2012), 31
Lee Myung-bak, 135–37, 141, 142, 263n8
Libya model, 195, 197–98

Malaysia, 41
malware, 43, 46–50. *See also* cyberattacks
Mandiant (cybersecurity firm), 56
Mao Zedong, 190t
Marine Chain platform, 51–52
market economy, 83–85, 85t, 174–75; Covid-19's effect on, 179; household income from, 94–96, 95t, 96t; political reforms of, 173–75; surveys of, 259n13; unification and, 15–16, 146t; women in, 96–98, 97t. *See also* black market
Marshall, George C., 115
MATA framework, 54
McEachern, Patrick, 3
medical facilities. *See* healthcare cyberattacks
methodology, 80–81, 82t, 111, 120–22, 121t
Microsoft Office vulnerabilities, 75
Middle East respiratory syndrome (MERS), 184, 185t
Military Demarcation Line, 13
minjung ideology, 133, 139, 141, 142, 272n56
missile program, 11–12, 51, 67, 105–6, 173, 194
money laundering, 51–52, 76
"money masters" (*donju*), 96–97

Moon Jae-in, 1, 36, 132, 134, 141–42, 263n8
moving average (MA) model, 32, 33t

National Health Service (NHS), 53
National Infrastructure Advisory Council (NIAC), 69–72, 74
natural time unit, 27–28
Neighborhood Watch groups (*inminban*), 89–90
Neuberger, Anne, 51
Non-Proliferation Treaty (NPT), 130
Nordpolitik (Northern Diplomacy), 130
North Korea. *See* Democratic People's Republic of Korea (DPRK)
North-South Coordinating Committee (NSCC), 126
North-South joint communiqué, 5, 6, 126
Novavax Inc., 55
nuclear power plants, 57–58
nuclear weapons, 11, 104–8, 105t, 107t; cyber warfare and, 39, 63, 72; as unification issue, 118, 121t, 145–46, 146t, 149, 156–59
"null effect," 171–72

Obama, Barack, 11, 109; strategic patience policy of, 195
Office 91 cyber operations, 41
Olympic Games: Beijing, 181; Seoul, 1, 116, 129; Tokyo, 181
Opposite Number (TV series), 57
ordinary least squares (OLS) method, 29–31
Organization for Economic Cooperation and Development (OECD), 114

Panmunjom Summit (2019), 13
Park Chung-hee, 124, 139
Park Geun-hye, 138–41
Park Jin Hyok, 53
Peace Corps (Korean), 114
Persian Gulf War (1991), 131
Pfizer, 55, 183
Powell, Colin, 137, 273n66
public distribution system (PDS), 83–87, 85t, 259n16
Putin, Vladimir, 186, 189

questionnaires. *See* surveys
"quick war, quick end" strategy, 40

RAND study on unification, 7, 265n16
ransomware, 50, 52–54, 75–76. *See also* cyberattacks
Reconnaissance General Bureau (RGB), 41, 46, 59, 61–62, 66
refugees, 82–83; outside media exposure of, 91–94, 93t, 174; as unification issue, 103t, 121t, 146t, 149, 154–59. *See also* defectors
Republic of Korea (ROK), 7; creation of, 4–6; cyberattacks on, 42, 48, 57–59; democratization of, 114, 263n6; economy of, 113–14, 116, 127, 129; establishment of, 116; GDP of, 113–14; GNI of, 114; history of, 114–15; JMEs of, 15, 18–38; joint cybersecurity with, 76; MERS outbreak in, 184; as threat to peace, 110, 111t; Unification Ministry of, 6, 58–59, 129; unification views of, 99–104, 116–17, 155–69, 155t, 157t, 160–63t, *165*, *168*; U.S. alliance with, 15, 18–19
reunification. *See* unification
Rhee, Syngman, 124
Ri Sol-Ju, 4
Rodman, Dennis, 2, 4
Roh Moo-hyun, 36, 132
Roh Tae-woo, 130, 247n13
ROK. *See* Republic of Korea (ROK)
ROKS *Cheonan*, 135
Romanization of Korean, vii
Rusk, Dean, 115
Russia: cyberattacks by, 41–42, 75; DPRK hackers and, 62; Korean unification and, 6, 16, 146t, 153t, 154, 155t, 159–64, 163t, *168*; PDRK alliance with, 186–89, *187*, *188*; PDRK hackers and, 41; as threat to peace, 110, 111t; Ukraine invasion by, 186, 195

Sansec (cybersecurity firm), 47
satellite surveillance, 4, 170, 177–78, 186
Schelling, Thomas, 3
security clearance process, 73–74
security dilemma theory, 19
self-reliance (*juche*), 62–63
Seoul National University (SNU), 84, 90, 110; Peace and Unification Studies of, 99–100, 102, 103t
Seoul Olympic Games (1988), 1, 116, 129
Shadow Brokers (hacking group), 54

shadow economy, 174-75, 179. *See also* black market
Shoigu, Sergei, 186
Singapore Summit (2018), 13, 19-21
Six-Party Talks, 21, 23, 76, 189, 196
Slovenia, 48
songbun caste system, 174
Sony cyberattack, 15, 39, 42, 49, 57, 59
South Korea. *See* Republic of Korea (ROK)
special operations forces, 40, 66
Stardust Chollima (hacking group), 46
strategic patience policy, 195
submarine-launched ballistic missile (SLBM), 11, 178
Sukin, Lauren, 22, 23
sunshine policy, 131-35, 139, 141, 142
surveys, 176, 227-40; demographics of, 82t; on household incomes, 95; on markets, 259n13; sampling methods of, 80-81, 82t, 111, 275nn5-6; on unification, 99-102, 113, 120-22, 144-69, 265n16
SWIFT banking network, 46
Sygnia (cybersecurity firm), 54

technology workers, 73-74
telecommunications, 177
terrorism, 18, 126, 126t; cyber, 43, 51, 68, 172-73; state sponsor of, 105
TFlower ransomware, 54
Trickbot (crimeware), 43, 54
Trump, Donald, 105, 109, 141; DPRK sanctions of, 13; JME cancellation by, 24, 172; Kim Jong-un and, 11-14, 191, 195; secret documents case against, 87; at Singapore Summit, 19-21
"trustpolitik," 139

Uiju cargo disinfection facility, *182*, *183*
Ukraine, Russian invasion of, 186, 195
unification, 4-8, 112, 120-22, 144-69, 170-77, 193-94; absence of data on, 118-19, 122; Chinese views of, 6-7, 16, 118, 146t, 149-54, 155t, 159, 161t, *168*; cost of, 129, 138, 140, 146t; defectors and, 102, 103t; by force, 125; "hard/soft" predictions of, 5, 118, 128; issues of, 121t, *146*; Japanese views of, 6, 16, 117-18, 146t, 149, 152t, 155t, 159, 162t, *168*; Kim Dae-jung on, 127; military forces after, 121t; Moon Jae-in on, 1, 132, 134, 141-42; mystery of, 117-19; North Korean views of, 100-104, 101t, 103t, 104t, 116-17; nuclear weapons and, 118, 121t, 145-46, 146t, 149, 156-59; Park Geun-hye on, 138-39; questionnaires on, 176-77, 227-40; refugees and, 103t, 121t, 146t, 149, 154, 156-59; Russian views of, 6, 16, 146t, 153t, 154, 155t, 159-64, 163t, *168*; South Korean Ministry of, 6, 58-59, 129; South Korean views of, 99-104, 116-17, 155-64, 155t, 157t, 160-63t; transparency indices of, 146t, *165*, *168*; U.S. views of, 6, 16, 118, 144-54, 146t, 148-53t, 160t
unification theories, 113-17, 123-41; jackpot, 138-41; pragmatism, 135-38; sunshine policy, 131-35, 139, 141, 142; too difficult, too dangerous, 127-31; winner take all, 124-27
United Nations: Commission of Inquiry on Human Rights in DPRK, 82, 88-89, 92, 258; Office on Drugs and Crime, 76; Security Council, 72-73; World Food Programme, 110
United States: cyberattacks against, 59-60; cyberattacks from, 50, 52; Cyber Command of, 41; DPRK event data of, 205-7, 208-23; DPRK policies of, 18-20, 27, 37, 68-72, 108-9; Korean unification and, 6, 16, 118, 144-54, 146t, 148-53t, 155t, 164-69, *165*, *168*; ROK alliance with, 15, 18-38; as threat to peace, 110, 111t
USS *Pueblo*, 36

Velvet Chollima. *See* Kimsuky
VHD ransomware, 54
video games, 62
Visual Studio Project, 56

Wagner Group, 187
Wallace, Robert, 22
Wang Yi, 64
WannaCry 2.0 ransomware, 52-54, 59
weapons of mass destruction (WMD), 51, 67, 72
Williams, Martyn, 177

Workers' Party Central Military Commission, 32
World Friends Korea, 114
World Health Organization (WHO), 55, 63
World Trade Organization (WTO), 26
World War II, 115, 125

X-force (IBM's cybersecurity team), 55
Xi Jinping, 83, 190t, 191

Yongbyon nuclear facilities, 23, 31, 196
Yoon Suk Yeol, 142–43

Zaif Crypto Exchange, 51

GPSR Authorized Representative: Easy Access System Europe, Mustamäe tee 50, 10621 Tallinn, Estonia, gpsr.requests@easproject.com